A Guide to Alcohol and Drug Dependence

J. S. MADDEN
MB, FRCP (Ed), FRC Psych
Consultant-in-Charge
Mersey Regional Alcohol and Drug Dependence Unit
Consultant Psychiatrist, West Cheshire Hospital
Clinical Lecturer in Psychiatry at the University of Liverpool

With a Foreword by
GRIFFITH EDWARDS

Second Edition

WRIGHT
BRISTOL
1984

Published by:
John Wright & Sons Ltd, 823–825 Bath Road, Bristol BS4 5NU, England.

First edition, 1979
Second edition, 1984

British Library Cataloguing in Publication Data
Madden, J. S.
  A guide to alcohol and drug dependence.—2nd ed.
  1. Alcoholism   2. Drug abuses
  I. Title
  362.2'9   HV5035

ISBN 0 7236 0755 9

Library of Congress Catalog Card Number: 84–50392

Typeset by Severntype Repro Services Ltd.

Printed in Great Britain by
John Wright & Sons (Printing) Ltd.
at the Stonebridge Press, Bristol BS4 5NU

PREFACE TO THE SECOND EDITION

During the interval since the first edition of this book alterations have taken place in the prevalence of alcohol and drug misuse and in relevant professional attitudes. The rising frequency of alcohol problems has halted in many countries, or shown a downturn, following a similar trend in alcohol consumption. This intriguing development may reflect an economic recession, and therefore prove temporary; more hopefully the change might form an initial pointer to a cyclical decrease of the kind observed in previous eras. By contrast, the availability and usage of heroin has expanded to a degree that calls for a clearer and more widespread appreciation of drug dependence. Changing perspectives emphasize the detection and early treatment of alcohol misuse, its distinctive features among special groups, the detoxification of drug users followed by drug-free counselling, and preventive measures.

Fortunately the timing of the second edition allows consideration of the developments. New information has been introduced on the recognition of alcohol misuse, on alcohol dependence among the elderly and among doctors, and on outpatient withdrawal from opioids. Attention is drawn to fresh ideas on behavioural and physical aspects of dependence, and on levels of drinking that may be least likely to entail harm. All other sections have been revised carefully and when necessary modified.

Since organic causes and sequelae are closely intertwined with dependence, its themes have a distinctive medical element. The reader who does not possess a background allied with medicine can be encouraged by the reflection that many aspects of the subject (and therefore of this book) are not biological. The contents acknowledge the important contributions to our understanding that have been provided alike by distinguished nonmedical and medical investigators.

PREFACE TO THE FIRST EDITION

Remarkable changes have taken place during the past twenty years with regard to alcohol and drug dependence. Most parts of the world have witnessed a growth in the extent of alcohol problems. In the 1960s there was a rapid thrust of illicit drug consumption; its results remain with us in the form of increased psychoactive drug use, especially among young people. A process of international dispersal has meant that patterns of social and excessive alcohol usage, and of drug consumption, are losing any distinctive regional flavours that they may have possessed. Altered attitudes and mores have led to the more liberal intake of alcohol by females and youngsters, thereby enhancing the number of females and young adults who develop medical and social disabilities from their drinking. Drugs that are currently causing concern include heroin and other morphine-like substances, barbiturates, amphetamines and hallucinogens.

The responses of governmental, professional and lay organizations have been numerous and varied. Recent studies of prophylactic methods have furthered an understanding of measures which should prove effective, and would lead to the conclusion that a lack of will, but not of methods, explains the limited successes in prevention.

Therapy for persons with alcohol and drug problems, and the facilities for providing therapy, have developed extensively. Yet here also there remains a reluctance, prejudice or uneasiness in the minds of some professional therapists when they are required to treat an alcoholic or a drug user. An awareness of contemporary views about the processes that induce alcohol and drug dependence, and knowledge of the treatment prospects, can dispel such inhibitions.

It is therefore time for a book which attempts to deal, in a comprehensive way, with the theme of chemical dependence. In this volume the sections describe the basic issues and lead the reader towards an appreciation of more subtle or controversial matters. The references offer opportunities for further study both from basic research sources and from key reviews. Inevitably the approach concentrates on some aspects more than on others, but it is not intended that the perspective would exclude important topics or detract from the richness and complexity of the subject.

The volume recognizes that a wide range of professional interests now focuses on alcohol and drug problems. Recognition is given to the increasing awareness of the importance of social factors in the origin, development and prevention of harmful patterns of substance consumption. The care of individual alcoholics and drug users is not the preserve of a few specialists, or indeed only of doctors. The contents of the book should therefore interest persons involved in social work and the probation service as well as psychiatrists and other medical readers.

The proliferation of ideas, investigations and publications about alcohol and drug use has led to some confusion in the employment of words and concepts. There are, for instance, over one hundred definitions of the term 'alcoholism'. Yet the importance of clear and acceptable terminology is paramount. One of the foundations of Chinese society was the advice of Confucius: 'Rectify words'. This volume attempts to follow this precept by defining terms as necessary, by applying them in a simple and consistent manner, and by avoiding controversies that are semantic. Fortunately, the delimitation of the syndrome of alcohol dependence has opened a clear way from the jungle of alcohol terminology; its implications set an example for the area of drug dependence.

Many persons have stimulated and led the author by their encouragement, breadth of vision and initiative. They are too numerous to list, although I wish to express special thanks to Professor John Copeland for his generosity with time and advice. The failings of the book are not attributable to contemporaries or to the heritage left by forerunners, but are my responsibility.

Acknowledgements for permission to employ and adapt material are given to Dr Griffith Edwards, to Mr Derek Rutherford of the National Council on Alcoholism, and to Mrs Joy Moser of the World Health Organization.

Mrs J. M. Roberts afforded valuable assistance with the provision of books and journals. Mrs Hazel Moon coped tirelessly with the drafts and alterations of the manuscript. Mr Roy Baker of John Wright & Sons provided advice and constant support throughout the writing of the text.

I am grateful in two other respects: first to my patients, whose tolerance and good humour refreshed and sustained the author, and secondly to my wife, without whose prompting and patience I would neither have started nor finished this book.

J. S. M.

CONTENTS

FOREWORD

By Griffith Edwards

Addiction Research Unit,
Institute of Psychiatry, London

Professional interest in alcohol and drug problems has greatly increased in Britain over the last 25 years. This has been not so much a discovery but a re-discovery of interest: alcohol problems and the misuse of opium were taken seriously by the medical profession during large parts of the nineteenth century. But there can be no doubt that during many of the earlier years of the present century only a few isolated enthusiasts spoke out against this neglect.

The fact that such a textbook as the present one can today be written bears witness to the renaissance. British work on alcohol and drugs has been much influenced by activities in other countries, and this is an area where the internationalism of medicine and science has been particularly important, but one of the stories which each chapter of this book implicitly tells is that over the last quarter century or so there has been a resurgence of British interest in the treatment and prevention of these problems, and there have been contributions from many centres to wide aspects of related research.

There has been a new awareness of the need for inter-disciplinary work, and the nature of the problems which are set by substance use may have contributed to a revision of some of the rather fusty attitudes of the medical profession towards the social sciences. The treatment problems that are encountered are similarly and nicely designed to overthrow oldfashioned notions of medical dominance: the interests of social work, nursing, occupational therapy and clinical psychology in treatment of alcohol and drug problems have been vital to the emergence of present concepts of care.

There has been a burgeoning of voluntary projects, and the establishment of Alcoholics Anonymous in this country has been of profound importance. Government committees have issued a number of major reports, which both for alcohol and drugs have sometimes constituted very worthwhile and influential contributions to thinking— Government departments which once seemed remarkably laggard in their interests now in many respects give an effective leadership. Relevant professional education is much better organized. The field has its debates and divisions, but what is more generally remarkable is the sense of co-operation and shared enthusiasm.

If this book, by its combination of astonishing range and thoroughness and wise selectivity, offers a text which bears witness to the energies and progress of recent years, its publication has significance also for the further forward march. The advance of any subject can sometimes at a particular moment be much helped by the arrival of the right textbook. This is such a book. By its stature as a work of scholarship, enlivened by keen determination to turn scholarship towards the most practical problems, this book is certain significantly to enhance an awareness of the seriousness of the matters of which it treats, and by its own stature it contributes to the stature of its subject. It is a book that will win wide admiration.

Chapter 1

TERMINOLOGY, PREVALENCE, CAUSATION

Substances that change mental processes have been known throughout recorded history over all parts of the world. Many of the substances have been used in ways that are not necessarily harmful. The careful medical use of morphine, the occasional consumption of small amounts of alcohol to promote relaxation among participants at social gatherings, the inducement of slight mental stimulation by caffeine preparations are forms of drug usage that have been sanctioned by many cultures and are generally practised without adverse effects. But the consumption of morphine or alcohol can be damaging; many other drugs with the ability to affect the mind can also produce mental, physical and social disabilities for the consumer and adverse effects on society. Harm results in some instances from the single or infrequent use of a psychoactive agent, while unfortunate consequences are common during repeated usage if the individual is showing at least some of the features of dependence.

TERMINOLOGY

The Expert Committee on Drug Dependence of the World Health Organisation reaffirmed in 1974 several of its previous definitions and descriptions. In order to avoid the unnecessary use of alternative concepts the succeeding account follows in certain respects the WHO outline (World Health Organisation, 1974).

Drug dependence is a state, psychic and sometimes also physical, characterized by a compulsion to take the drug on a continuous or periodic basis in order to experience its mental effects, and sometimes to avoid the discomfort of its absence. Tolerance may or may not occur. A person can develop dependence to more than one drug; multiple dependencies can occur at the same time, or succeed or alternate with each other.

Psychological (psychic) dependence is a condition in which the drug promotes a feeling of satisfaction and a drive to repeat the consumption of the drug in order to induce pleasure or avoid discomfort.

Physical dependence is a state that shows itself by physical

1

disturbances when the amount of drug in the body is markedly reduced. The disturbances form a withdrawal or abstinence syndrome composed of somatic and mental symptoms and signs which are characteristic for each drug type.

Several types of dependence-producing drugs have been listed in the WHO account:

1. Alcohol-barbiturate type—for example, ethyl alcohol, barbiturates, benzodiazepines, chloral hydrate and other general sedatives.
2. Amphetamine type—including amphetamine itself, dexamphetamine, methylamphetamine, phenmetrazine.
3. Cannabis type—products of *Cannabis sativa.*
4. Cocaine type—coca leaves and their active ingredient cocaine.
5. Hallucinogen type—for instance, lysergic acid diethylamide (LSD), mescaline.
6. Khat type—preparations of *Catha edulis.*
7. Morphine type— substances naturally occurring in opium or their chemical derivatives (e.g. morphine, codeine, heroin), together with synthetic drugs that have morphine-like effects (such as methadone and pethidine).
8. Inhalants and volatile solvents—for example, carbon tetrachloride and toluene.

Withdrawal syndromes have been conclusively established only with drugs of the alcohol-barbiturate, amphetamine, cannabis and morphine types.

Although tobacco produces dependence and physical damage to the user, its effects on cerebral and mental function are slight. The WHO Committee therefore considered that it should give tobacco little attention compared with the other dependence-producing drugs.

There are also special psychological and social aspects of alcohol usage which justify, in some respects, the separate consideration of alcohol. Like tobacco, alcohol is socially and legally permitted by many nations. Legislation to prohibit its use was introduced in this century in Finland, Norway, Iceland and the United States, but was later repealed. In countries where alcohol is currently allowed, legal measures to enforce prohibition are unlikely to succeed unless the large majority of inhabitants come to desire this measure. Such a profound change of attitude is not likely in the foreseeable future. Measures to minimize alcohol disabilities should concentrate on promoting both the restrained use of alcohol and abstinence as acceptable means of prevention; the choice of means is personal and rests with the individual. Because of the wide degree of cultural and legal acceptability of alcohol its connotations differ from other drugs, while alcoholics as a group tend to resemble the rest of the population more closely in mental and social characteristics than do persons dependent on alternative substances. It is appropriate therefore to give alcohol more special consideration and, while continuing to view it as a drug, to refer to it in a separate category from other psychoactive substances.

It is logically feasible to suggest certain alternatives to the WHO types of dependence-producing drugs. Employing pharmacological concepts, cocaine differs mainly from amphetamine in the occurrence of doubts whether tolerance develops to the former. The potent ingredients of khat are allied to amphetamine in pharmacological action and chemical structure. Cocaine, khat, the amphetamines, and certain sympathomimetic drugs like ephedrine, could be linked together as stimulants of the central nervous system. The distinction between amphetamines and some hallucinogens is artificial; certain hallucinogens are similar in structure to amphetamine, while the amphetamines themselves produce hallucinations.

The list of drugs of dependence should undoubtedly be extended to cover certain simple analgesics, i.e. pain-relieving substances not of the morphine kind. Drugs that resemble atropine and have anticholinergic actions also possess psychotropic activity and should receive consideration.

The alcohol-barbiturate type of drugs and the morphine-like type are central nervous system (CNS) depressants; each of these two categories produces a strong abstinence syndrome with its own distinctive pattern on cessation of the repeated, excessive consumption of a drug from the category. CNS stimulants of the amphetamine type, and cannabis, induce withdrawal effects which are detectable but mild.

'Drug addiction' and 'drug habituation' were terms which used to engender a good deal of semantic argument about their differentiation. WHO in 1964 boldly resolved the predicament by proposing the abolition of both terms; it recommended that they should be discontinued and replaced by the title 'drug dependence' (World Health Organisation 1964). People remain addicted to verbal habits, so the phrases 'drug addiction' and 'drug addict' are still sometimes used—or misused.

Misuse and *abuse* are employed to denote the nonmedical use of drugs or, in the case of alcohol, its excessive use. Both words imply value judgements that vary between societies and are difficult to validate. Additionally, 'abuse' is an unfortunate choice as it is especially pejorative and abusive to drug and alcohol misusers. The terms, however, retain employment to cover consumption patterns that may fall short of dependence. A further report from the World Health Organisation has proposed a series of concepts that are both objective and detailed (WHO Memorandum, 1981; Commentaries, 1982).

Unsanctioned use denotes alcohol or drug usage that is socially disapproved. The phrase simply reports the disapproval and does not necessarily defend its grounds.

Hazardous use describes consumption which may lead to harm for the user (e.g. cigarette smoking).

Dysfunctional use indicates that impairment of psychological or social function has developed (for example, difficulties at work or in marriage).

Harmful use intimates that organic damage or mental illness have been produced in the user.

Dysfunction and harm may arise from hazardous use among individuals who have not developed dependence.

The phrase 'physical dependence' gives rise to confusion, since it is not always accompanied by further alcohol or drug consumption or even by the desire to take the substances. For instance, the postoperative use of morphine-like compounds to relieve pain may induce abstinence symptoms in patients who do not wish to continue the drugs; they could hardly be considered to possess dependence since they do not show drug-seeking behaviour or experience the drive to take drugs. For this reason, and because physical dependence and tolerance often develop in parallel, the 1981 WHO Memorandum proposed the term *neuro-adaptation*. The name denotes the adaptive nerve changes which underlie both tolerance and the withdrawal features of physical dependence.

The Memorandum noted that dependence is a syndrome which shows a range of intensity and which involves the following features:
— subjective experience of a compulsion to use a drug, usually during endeavours to reduce or cease drug intake.
— the desire to stop drug intake although consumption continues.
— a relatively stereotyped and inflexible pattern of drug consumption.
— neuroadaptation (shown by tolerance and withdrawal features).
— salience of drug-seeking behaviour over other activities.
— rapid renewal of the syndrome after an interval of abstinence.

A separate WHO publication has focused on alcohol dependence; the report has noted the difficulties that have arisen in reaching an acceptable definition of alcoholism and proposed that the term is replaced by the phrase 'alcohol dependence syndrome' (Edwards et al., 1977). A similar approach is adopted by the ninth revision of the International Classification of Diseases (ICD); from January 1979 the preferred ICD title has been 'alcohol dependence syndrome', with 'alcoholism' listed under the title as an inclusion term.

Practical assessment of a patient or client who possesses an alcohol or drug difficulty should note:
— the pattern of intake of alcohol, drug or drugs.
— degree of dependence, if present.
— nonmedical and medical disabilities induced by alcohol or drug consumption.
— results of past and present periods of care and treatment.
— drawbacks and assets in the individual and environment that can promote or curb the alcohol or drug intake.

PREVALENCE

The correct answer to queries concerning the exact prevalence of alcohol and drug misuse, dependence and consequent disabilities is to reply that their prevalence is unknown. Because of social and legal stigma the conditions are often concealed. There are merely approximate estimates of their incidence, based on case findings surveys and on indirect indices that point to their frequency or to variations in their frequency.

Relevant case finding should involve two distinct and complementary research activities. The first comprises tactfully worded enquiries among a representative sample of the population about the extent of personal alcohol or drug consumption and attendant harm. The second approach obtains data from the numerous agencies, official and voluntary, that are likely to encounter people who have alcohol or drug disabilities. A full range of agencies, and both methods of approach, are necessary. For example, an assessment of alcoholics known to their general practitioners in England and Wales estimated an incidence of 1·1 alcoholics per thousand adult patients; this figure produced a total estimate for the two countries of about 40 000 (Parr, 1957). It is generally agreed that this assessment, although praiseworthy as a pioneer study, resulted in a considerable underestimate since general practitioners are aware of only a small proportion of the alcoholics in their practices. In the English county of Cambridgeshire, Moss and Beresford Davies (1967) obtained data from general practitioners, psychiatrists, hospitals, police, probation officers, a Salvation Army hostel, children's welfare agencies, marriage guidance counsellors and Alcoholics Anonymous. The research uncovered an incidence for the county population aged 15 and over of 6·2 alcoholics per thousand males and 1·4 per thousand females. But the study, painstaking though it was, omitted a general population survey.

Two parallel enquiries of the dual nature recommended above have been conducted in a London suburb (Edwards et al., 1973). The first enquiry, of a wide range of agencies, revealed an incidence of problem drinkers per thousand persons aged 16 or over as 8·6 for men, 1·3 for women and 4·7 overall. The other enquiry consisted of a household survey and gave a prevalence of problem drinking per thousand adults aged 18 or over as 61·3 for men, 7·7 for women and 31·3 overall. Only 13% of the excessive alcohol users identified in the house-to-house sample were reported by the agencies which were requested to notify their problem drinkers.

The difficulties of case finding are further highlighted by studies of the Washington Heights suburb of New York (Bailey et al., 1965, 1966). A household survey revealed 19 persons with alcoholism per thousand population aged 20 or over; the ratio of men to women was 3·6 to 1. The most vulnerable inhabitants were widowers, and divorced or separated persons of both sexes. There were associations between excessive drinking, race and religion; the alcoholism rates per thousand were 40 for Negro Baptists, 20 for other Protestants, 24 for Roman Catholics, and 2 for Jews. This sample survey of households uncovered 132 alcoholics, yet it is significant that a psychiatric register revealed another 7 who had been admitted to mental hospitals with alcoholism but who gave no evidence of drinking problems during interview. Also disturbing from the viewpoint of scientific precision were the results of repeat interviews in the same suburb of 99 of the alcoholics and their spouses, together with a comparison group of 343 of the previous respondents who had not been revealed as problem drinkers: 25 of the alcohol misusers did not acknowledge a drinking problem in the second survey; 29 of the comparison group were identified as alcoholics only in the second interview. The researchers suggested that under-reporting was produced by the stigma of alcoholism, by temporal modification of excessive drinking towards abstinence or moderation, and by alterations with time of controlled drinking towards excess consumption. Relevant here are the comments of Edwards (1973) on the methodological problems appertaining to the epidemiology of alcoholism. The difficulties include definition of the condition, but problems also arise from transient drinking reactions that are acted out for a period by some of the surveyed subjects. Edwards (1973) has also described the implications of case finding for treatment facilities.

There are several indirect indices of the prevalence of alcohol disabilities, including dependence. Arguments can be levelled against the validity of each, but when the majority of indices point the same way it is permissible to draw instructive conclusions about the relative prevalence of alcohol disabilities and dependence in different nations or ethnic groups, and to form judgements concerning temporal alterations of prevalence.

National consumption levels of beverage alcohol both determine and reflect the prevalence of dependence and other alcohol problems. The more alcohol that is consumed *per capita* by a community then the more persons among the community drink heavily. Personal consumption in excess of 15 cl of absolute alcohol* per day is associated with alcohol disabilities and is typically reported by alcoholic patients (de Lint, 1974). High national consumption figures raise the numbers of drinkers who exceed a daily average of 15 cl of absolute alcohol, and are correlated with an increased death rate from cirrhosis of the liver (de Lint and Schmidt, 1972; Smith, 1982). High national rates of alcohol consumption and cirrhosis deaths are found most markedly in France, but also in Austria, Portugal and Italy.

---

*15 cl (approximately 120 grams) of absolute alcohol is equivalent to 375 ml (12·7 oz) of spirits containing 40% alcohol, or 937 ml (31·6 oz) of wine containing 16% alcohol, or 3000 ml (101·4 oz) of beer possessing 5% alcohol.

Alcohol dependence is a major contributor to the *death rate from cirrhosis of the liver*. The association afforded the basis for the formula devised by the late E. M. Jellinek for estimating the incidence of alcoholism.

The equation that Jellinek originally proposed was $A = \dfrac{PD}{K}$.

A = total number of alcoholics with physical complications in a given year.

P = proportion of deaths from cirrhosis of the liver attributable to alcoholism.

D = number of reported deaths from cirrhosis of the liver.

K = proportion of alcoholics with complications to die from liver cirrhosis.

The formula was modified later to include the numerator R, which is the ratio of all alcoholics to those who have complications.

On the basis that a quarter of alcoholics have physical complications WHO employed the Jellinek formula to report in 1951 that there were about 370 000 alcoholics in England and Wales (World Health Organisation, 1951). Although Jellinek (1959) later advocated discontinuance of his formula, subsequent estimates show a consistently rising prevalence in England and Wales and suggest that the original WHO calculations were approximately correct when made.

Convictions for drunkenness and for drinking and driving bear some relation to alcohol dependence, as well as to the drinking behaviour of nonalcoholics and the activities of the police. A London study of drunkenness offenders found that 50% were physically dependent on alcohol and that another 26% possessed serious drinking problems; the majority therefore were not merely casual roisterers (Gath et al., 1968). The major age group of drinking and driving offenders in Britain comprises persons aged under 30; many of these young people (and some of their older counterparts) are not dependent on alcohol, but obviously alcoholics who drive after taking alcohol are prone to arrest for drinking and driving offences.

Hospital admissions for alcoholism, and alcoholic psychosis afford another indication of the prevalence of alcohol dependence. This remark applies even though the data for hospital admissions also reflect the willingness of problem drinkers to enter hospital and the readiness of hospitals to receive them. Many countries, including Britain and Ireland, have shown a rise since 1960 of the number of alcoholic admissions to hospital.

The reported death rate from alcohol disabilities is a relatively poor pointer to the frequency of dependent drinking or other forms of alcohol misuse. Not all the relevant deaths receive a correct assessment of their cause. In many instances (for example, of alcoholic cirrhosis deaths) when alcohol consumption is recognized by a doctor in Britain as the responsible agent it is deliberately omitted from the death certificate.

The figures for mortality produced by alcohol—as distinct from mortality, ascertained from death records, among known hazardous drinkers—are misleadingly low. A Swedish study revealed that alcohol was the commonest underlying factor in the mortalities of an unselected group of middle-aged males, yet only one-sixth of the deaths from alcohol misuse appeared as such in the official statistics (Petersson et al., 1982).

Trends of alcohol consumption and of disabilities produced by alcohol in England and Wales can be judged from *Tables* 1–4. All the indices rose during the 1960s and 1970s.

Table 1. United Kingdom consumption of alcohol; *per capita* figures in pints based on population aged 15 years and over.

Year ending 31 March	Beer	Spirits	Wine
1959–60	192·5	3·9	4·7
1964–65	207·3	5·1	7·1
1969–70	228·3	4·7	8·1
1974–75	263·1	8·7	14·9
1977–78	271·9	8·6	15·1
1978–79	270·8	10·7	17·4
1979–80	276·7	11·2	19·2
1980–81	261·3	9·9	18·0

Source: *U.K. Statistical Handbook, 1982.* London, The Brewers' Society.

Table 2. Deaths from cirrhosis of the liver in England and Wales.

	Rate per million	
Year	Male	Female
1960	31	25
1965	31	27
1970	31	26
1975	38	36
1978	43	36
1979	50	39
1980	48	42
1981	48	41

Due to changes in the International Classification of Diseases in 1979 the deaths from that year include chronic hepatitis and chronic liver disease.

Table 3. Drunkenness convictions in England and Wales.

Year	Male	Female	Total
1960	63861	4248	68109
1965	69091	3889	72980
1970	77072	5302	82374
1975	96880	7572	104452
1980	112152	10107	122259
1981	99696	8895	108591

Table 4. Admissions to mental hospitals and units in England and Wales of patients with a diagnosis connected with alcohol misuse.

Year	Male	Female	Total
1960	—	—	2479
1965	5322	1554	6876
1970	6648	2060	8708
1975	9732	3700	13432
1978	11020	4660	15680
1979	10870	4879	15749
1980	11825	5533	17358
1981	11836	5700	17536

Due to changes in the International Classification of Diseases in 1979 the figures refer to a primary or secondary diagnosis of alcoholism or alcoholic psychosis up to 1978 (under ICD 8), but to a main or underlying/associated diagnosis of alcohol dependence syndrome, alcoholic psychosis or nondependent abuse of alcohol from 1979 (under ICD 9).

For England and Wales, the Department of Health and Social Security (1976) has suggested that there are about 500000 people who possess a serious drinking problem; the estimate requires a rate of 11·9 persons per 1000 population. A projection that employed both the Jellinek method and general practitioner surveys concluded that this estimate is a rather minimum total (Donnan and Haskey, 1977); an approximate figure of 600000 persons for England and Wales is commonly accepted. The prevalences for Scotland and Ireland are relatively higher for their smaller populations. Estimates for the United States are in the order of between 8–10 million alcoholics. In the first decade of the present century there were in the United States about 15 deaths from liver cirrhosis for 100000 of the population; during Prohibition the numbers dropped to fewer than 8 per 100000, but since the repeal of Prohibition the death rate from liver cirrhosis gradually increased, to reach 16·2 per 100000 in 1972. U.S. mortality from cirrhosis has subsequently further risen (Garagliano et al., 1979).

The rising incidence of alcohol problems, including dependence, that is shown by the British, Irish and U.S. data has also taken place in many countries. It is associated with public naïveté about the hazards of alcohol, with increased permissiveness towards extensive usage of the substance, and with a decreasing cost of alcohol beverages relative to the income available for personal expenditure on commodities. Fortunately an international tendency developed in the early 1980s for the data to reach a platèau level and to remain at steady though unacceptably high amounts (Armyr et al., 1982). Worldwide economic depression probably contributed to the plateau effect.

The prevalence of drug misuse, drug dependence and their adverse consequences is even more difficult to assess than for alcohol, because the patterns of consumption of the relevant drugs are often illegal. The quantities of dependence-producing drugs that are prescribed, and the numbers of patients to whom they are medically given, constitute poor indicators of the scale of illicit consumption. The official British statistics on drug addiction (*sic*), which are based on patients attending clinics for prescriptions of morphine-like drugs, are acknowledged as underestimates. The figures take little account of multiple drug usage, of persons dependent on barbiturates or amphetamines, or of users of morphine-like drugs who attend the clinics and do not receive prescriptions, or who keep away from the clinics.

Blumberg (1975) has reported on the numerous surveys from many countries of drug use among young people. The percentage who had taken drugs illegally at least once ranged from 6% (among English school attenders) to 70% (among U.S. college students and undergraduates). The most widely used category of drug consumption involved cannabis preparations; amphetamines, barbiturates and hallucinogens were intermediate in popularity; morphine-like drugs were the least popular. A more recent and continuing study of student drug use in the United States has revealed an upsurge in consumption of phencyclidine, which among other effects can induce hallucinations (Johnston et al., 1980). A further national U.S. study has recurrently analysed drug misuse among household members (Fishburne et al., 1980).

The extent of illicit drug use among individuals has been found to correlate positively with their level of tobacco consumption, and with generally permissive attitudes and lack of religious affiliation. Drug users show more frequent use of alcohol than control subjects, though the relationship between the two activities is not clear-cut.

Prevalence and fashions of drug usage rapidly fluctuate. The rise of illicit drug consumption that developed in many countries during the 1960s was temporarily checked. It was claimed that alcohol replaced drugs in popularity, among young persons especially. Then disturbing reports appeared of a growing prevalence of heroin consumption in Western Europe, including Britain. Assessments of the number of persons dependent on heroin (mostly imported from the East) ranged in the middle 1970s from 10 thousand to 30 thousand in Holland, 15 thousand in West Germany, 5 thousand to 6 thousand in France, and 3 thousand each in Belgium and Britain (*The Times*, 1976). By 1980 there were believed to be around 20 000 persons in Britain who were dependent on drugs. In 1981 the British Customs service seized a record amount of 86 kilograms of heroin. In 1982 the Advisory Council on the Misuse of Drugs reported that there may be 40 000 people in Britain with serious drug problems, frequently involving heroin or allied preparations (Advisory Council, 1982). Western Europe also resembles other regions in retaining a substantial illicit market in CNS stimulants.

CAUSATION

The aetiology of alcohol and drug misuse and dependence is three-fold: the environment, the soil and the seed. The environment here denotes cultural influences surrounding the individual, particularly those relating to alcohol or drug usage in the community. The soil refers to the constitution of the individual; the potentials and drawbacks of physique and personality are initially laid down by heredity and are moulded, mostly in childhood, by events subsequent to conception. The seed implies the qualities inherent in alcohol and drugs which determine their liability to induce misuse or dependence.

Environmental factors

Socio-cultural aspects which affect the *acceptability* and *availability* of alcohol and drugs are the most influential features in producing harmful personal consumption. Only the fluctuations that occur in these matters could account for the wide variations between countries and races in regard to alcohol and drug problems, and explain the changes within communities that can develop in a decade for alcohol-induced and more rapidly for drug-induced disabilities. Such variations of prevalence, particularly the temporal alterations, are not accountable by differences, genetic or acquired, in the constitutional natures of people.

There are four reasons why an individual member of society can take a psychoactive substance. The first is to obtain the substance's value, real or supposed, as a medicament. Clearly many drugs affecting the mind have valuable properties in treatment, but some substances are popularly overvalued for their alleged therapeutic qualities. For example, there is a current overesteem for prescribed CNS depressants which has led to their misuse and dependence. Myths attach a curative role to some substances, notably to simple analgesics and to beverages containing alcohol. Persons self-administer simple analgesics (possessing ingredients like aspirin, codeine and paracetamol) or alcoholic drinks, and recommend them to others, in the belief that these preparations are tonics, or stimulants, or are appropriate treatments for anxiety, depression, insomnia or fatigue.

The second aim of taking a substance that affects the mind applies almost exclusively to beverage alcohol. Fluids possessing alcohol are drunk because they are considered to have nutritional value. Alcohol does in itself provide calories, and there are additional small quantities of nutriments in beer and wine, but the dietary value of alcoholic drinks is in fact minimal. Their consumption to the neglect of normal articles of food promotes nutritional deficiencies. The supposedly dietary values which are attached to alcoholic beverages overlap in their connotations with the concepts held by naïve persons concerning the medical assets of alcohol and of certain drugs.

The remaining two purposes for psychoactive substance consumption are employed by ill-informed and sophisticated people alike. The symbolic aspects of taking alcohol or a drug are manifold and important.

1. The offering and acceptance of a substance amongst persons is a gesture of friendship.
2. In a group setting joint alcohol or drug consumption symbolizes unity.
3. An individual who is taking part with others in alcohol or drug activity feels accepted by them. Acceptance is a basic human need.
4. Alcohol or drug consumption is deliberately used to confirm an agreement, to seal as it were a contract.
5. Rites of passage and initiation are often accompanied by ritualistic substance consumption.
6. Adulthood, masculinity, or membership of a social or occupational class are marked by the pattern of use, or avoidance, of certain kinds of alcoholic beverages or drugs.
7. Religions attach significance to substance use. Christianity and Judaism employ wine in small amounts for this purpose. In Islam the Koranic ban on alcohol denotes the true believer; Muslim exegetes interpret the conjunction to cover all intoxicants.
8. Rejection of conventional social values emphasizing tradition, success and status can be expressed by substance use. The Persian poet Omar Khayyám praised wine in his *Rubáiyát* partly because alcohol received official disapproval in his country. More recently one of the many reasons why some young people take drugs has been because illicit drug consumption is frowned on by their elders.
9. Deviant and delinquent subgroups are more likely to adopt unconventional patterns of alcohol or drug consumption. Non-conforming or inadequate persons can find acceptance in a social subculture by sharing its favoured alcohol or drug-using behaviour.
10. The act of taking alcohol or a drug can denote a break from work or responsibilities into a period of relaxation.
11. Unrestrained behaviour, particularly of a sexual or aggressive nature, is sometimes more socially acceptable when the individual choosing to demonstrate the behaviour has taken alcohol or drugs.

The final broad category of reason for consuming alcohol or a drug liable to misuse or to dependence is 'utilitarian'. This cold term is applied by sociologists to refer to the usefulness of a substance in the production of pleasurable effects on the mind.

It is apparent from the above account that the pharmacological action of a psychotropic substance on the brain is only one of the determinants of its employment within a community, and that there are many customs, beliefs and attitudes that influence the extent and nature of substance usage. Social controls, for instance, contribute to the lower prevalence in the Indian subcontinent of cannabis consumption among professional and managerial strata, compared with occupational groups that bear less responsibility and status. Persons of Chinese or Jewish race are not usually total abstainers from alcohol, yet possess a low incidence of alcohol problems because of their strong disapproval of drunkenness and their close-knit family structure. A contributory factor with Jews is their employment of moderate amounts of alcohol in religious ceremony; alcohol excess is viewed almost as a sacrilege and Jews learn to drink in a controlled manner through the ceremonial use of alcohol with their parents (Snyder, 1952; Glatt, 1970). The view of Keller (1970) is particularly hopeful and constructive: that the Jewish race were at one time prone to inebriety but overcame this tendency some two and a half thousand years ago. The Irish, by contrast, show a high incidence of alcohol problems, and not only in Ireland. Bales (1962) has suggested that the vulnerability of Irish males to alcohol stems from their traditions of drinking, which have been more conducive to drinking to the point of drunkenness than have the drinking practices of some other races, and which have favoured alcohol usage as a substitute for sexual activity and as a relief from female dominated homes.

An examination by the anthropologist Horton (1943) of reports on the drinking habits of 77 primitive societies led to his interpretation of the extent of drunkenness in any society as an expression of the level of anxiety in that community. Horton proposed that inebriety among males was associated with threats to their society posed by an insecure food supply and by acculturation. His conclusions have been challenged by Field (1962) who argued that societies with subsistence economies are not comparable in social structure to more sophisticated communities and that the controls exerted in primitive societies on behaviour, including drinking activity, become weakened when exposed to new cultural traits.

The protection afforded by social controls against injurious alcohol or drug consumption is dimished when a person moves from the influence of a specific community or in times of rapid sociocultural change. The former development happens, for example, to Jews who depart from orthodoxy and whose drinking behaviour increases towards that of the general population. A breakdown of traditional attitudes and conventions, including those restraining the use of intoxicants, historically took place in Persia after the Mongol invasion, in Britain and the European continent during the Industrial Revolution, and is currently occurring among the developing countries of the Third World.

Social acceptability of alcohol or drugs is an important factor determining their levels of consumption; another key role is played by their accessibility. The ready availability of heroin contributed to the high rate of intake of this drug among U.S. servicemen in Vietnam. The U.S. cities near to the border with Mexico have a considerable prevalence of heroin usage, partly because supplies of the drug are plentiful, relatively inexpensive, and of considerable purity (Greene, 1975). The south-western region of the United States possesses a greater prevalence of marijuana consumption (experimental, intermittent or regular) than the rest of the nation since the drug is easily smuggled into that area. Opium is extensively grown in the 'Golden Triangle' region, which is a hilly and mountainous district composed of adjacent parts of Burma, Laos and Thailand; as a result Thailand has 300 000–400 000 inhabitants dependent on opium or heroin out of a population of some 40 million. In Japan amphetamine and methaqualone were formerly sold legally without prescriptions; epidemics arose of amphetamine, and later methaqualone, misuse which were eventually checked by controls on the sale of the drugs. Heroin consumption and dependence increased in Britain during the 1960s in part because of the over-willingness of a few doctors to prescribe the substance. A similar phenomenon occurred in Britain with ampoules of methylamphetamine used for intravenous injection, until the supply of ampoules was severely curtailed (de Alarcón, 1972).

Availability of alcohol is determined by restrictions on its sale and by its price relative to personal disposable income. In 1916 the British Prime Minister, Lloyd George,* took several measures to reduce the extent of alcohol consumption and its consequent problems in order to make the country more efficient for war. The measures were strikingly successful (Weeks, 1938; Glatt, 1958) and Britain still benefits; the methods included shortening of the licensing hours and an increase of the tax on drink.

Nelker (1975) has summarized several related findings concerning the availability of alcohol, its level of consumption and the incidence of disabilities induced by alcohol.

1.   In Denmark during World War I high prices on alcoholic drinks reduced consumption and lowered the incidence of cirrhosis.
2.   In Sweden liberalization of the sales control system in 1955–56 led to increases in consumption, in drunkenness and in delirium. A rise of taxes reversed the increases.
3.   Also in Sweden, during 1963, a strike among employees of the state alcohol monopoly lowered the prevalence of drunkenness, drunken driving, traffic accidents and of attendance at alcoholism clinics.

---

*Unlike Asquith, his predecessor, Lloyd George was not an alcoholic, but he has been described as a 'typical Welsh drinker'; he took the pledge in his own village and drank in the next township.

4. Again in Sweden between 1965 and 1974 more liberal sales legislation on beer increased the consumption of beer without a decrease in consumption of wine or spirits; alcohol problems became more prevalent among young persons.
5. In Finland increased legal availability of alcohol led to an enhancement of consumption levels and of drunkenness arrests from 1968.
6. The age limit in Ontario for permitted drinking in bars was lowered in 1971 from 21 to 18 years, leading to an increase in the number of traffic accidents caused by young drivers.

Another study in Ontario associated changes of alcohol price (expressed as a fraction of average disposable income) with consumption of alcohol (de Lint and Schmidt, 1971); over the period 1929–1959 there was a remarkably close and inverse correlation between the two factors. In Britain a similar link between price and alcohol consumption has existed throughout the past three centuries (Spring and Buss, 1977). McGuinness (1975) has confirmed the association during a recent twenty year span and noted that during the latter period the enhanced availability of alcohol from an increased number of retail outlets also made an impact on alcohol sales. There are, in fact, data from several countries which support the association between the relative price of alcohol, *per capita* consumption, hospital admissions for alcoholism, alcoholic deaths, and social consequences (World Health Organisation, 1974; Smith, 1982).

When dealing with an individual who has an alcohol or drug disability, it is sometimes helpful to reflect that the socio-economic aspect is the most influential kind of factor in the development of personal alcohol and drug problems, including dependence, and that it is a causative aspect not within the control of the individual. It does not benefit a person with a recurrent alcohol or drug difficulty to consider him devoid of free will, but the subject should at the same time be viewed as in considerable measure a victim of cultural forces for which he is not responsible.

Constitutional factors

Heredity

It is tempting to propose that personal patterns of consumption of alcohol or drugs are, in part, genetically determined. In a broad sense there must exist a genetic element, since an established pattern of consumption by an individual involves an interaction between psychotropic substances and somatic structures, and the genes lay down the basic structures of the body. The issue whether heredity helps to explain why some people develop dependence and others do not has hardly been raised for drugs but has been widely debated for alcohol.

There is no doubt that alcohol dependence has a strong tendency to recur in families. Reports of the percentage of alcoholics who possess alcoholic fathers range between 21% and 47%, while the percentage with alcoholic mothers lies between 2% and 20%; the proportion of brothers of alcoholics who are also alcoholic falls between 12% and 40%, and of sisters between 2% and 13% (Cotton, 1979). Of course, a familial tendency does not necessarily entail a genetic disposition; patterns of excessive drinking could be communicated over the generations by means of parental example and filial modelling, while the strains of living with an alcoholic parent could promote emotional difficulties in children that later are temporarily relieved in adult life by alcohol.

Studies on twins have been conducted with the aim of eliminating, as far as possible, the effects of nonhereditary influences during upbringing. Twins are either monozygotic (MZ) and identical, or dizygotic (DZ) and nonidentical. MZ twins possess the same genetic constitutions; DZ twins are genetically no more similar than ordinary siblings. Yet twins from either category share, if reared together, almost the same environmental conditions. If MZ twins are more alike ('concordant') for a trait than DZ twins then the similarity is attributable to their genetic equalness. Kaij (1960) in Sweden classified the drinking patterns of twins in a range from abstinence to alcoholism; MZ twins were more concordant than DZ for all patterns, especially for the alcoholism category. Hubrec and Omenn (1981) studied the records of American armed forces veterans; MZ twins were more concordant for alcoholism than DZ twins. On the other hand, reports have emerged from Finland (Partanen et al., 1966) and from Sweden (Jonsson and Nilsson, 1968) that demonstrate an increased concordance among MZ twins for frequency and quantity of drinking, but not for the adverse consequences that are associated with alcoholism.

Investigations of adoptees have taken place that attempt, by a different strategy, to disentangle the influences of heredity and of upbringing. Goodwin and his coworkers (1973) compared adopted sons of alcoholics with control adoptees; alcoholism was four times more common amongst the former. The same workers (Goodwin et al., 1974) later examined sons of alcoholics; some of the sons were raised by their alcoholic parents while others were reared by surrogate parents; alcoholism in a biological parent, not the circumstances of rearing, formed the determining feature for alcoholism among the subjects. The same group of researchers (Schuckitt et al., 1972) conducted another enquiry into children of alcoholic parents; its data showed an almost identical rate of alcohol dependence irrespective of whether the children were raised by a biological parent or by a substitute parent; dependence on alcohol was predicted with greater certainty by alcoholism in a biological parent than by childhood environmental factors. Cadoreth and Gath (1978, 1980) studied subjects who were removed from their parents as babies; an increased rate of alcoholism appeared among those adoptees who possessed a biological relative who had been a heavy drinker or an alcoholic.

An early investigation by Roe (1944) looked at the progress in adulthood of children reared in foster homes; neither the children of heavy drinkers nor controls developed drinking problems in adulthood, and Roe discountenanced an hereditary influence on drinking. But the work of Roe has received adverse criticism (Goodwin et al., 1973) because of its small number of male subjects, its obscurity about the precise nature of 'heavy drinking' in the biological parents of its probands, and the high proportion of its subjects who were reared in rural areas or small towns, where excessive drinking is less common than in cities.

The studies outlined above on adoptees have concentrated on male children. An examination of female adoptees in Denmark did not reveal a genetic element to alcohol dependence (Goodwin et al., 1977a). In contrast, an enquiry based on Swedish records of adoptees has reported an hereditary influence for both sexes (Cloninger et al., 1981; Bohman et al., 1981). The latter investigators suggested two types of inherited alcohol problems among their subjects in Sweden; firstly, a form of alcohol misuse that is common to both sexes and whose frequency and severity are considerably modified by environmental factors; secondly, a type of alcoholism that is limited to males and whose manifestation is little affected by the environment.

A genetic approach that links alcohol dependence with depression was postulated in Iowa by Winokur and associates (Winokur et al., 1971a; Winokur, 1972). They noted a report from Liverpool (Hopkinson and Ley, 1969) of a lower incidence of affective illness in the relatives of patients whose depression began in later life (aged 40 years or over) compared with relatives of patients with early onset depression. The Iowa investigators proposed two forms of depression; the first exhibited as a prototype a female with early onset depression who showed a high frequency of depression in her female first-degree relatives and of alcoholism and sociopathy in her male first-degree relatives; the second type was characterized by a male with late onset depression who showed less depression in his relatives and no family history of alcoholism or sociopathy. The first form of depression was considered to represent a spectrum of depressive disease; the second kind was labelled as pure depressive illness. Alcoholism and sociopathy were viewed as equivalents, in males, of the former type of depression. In the view of Winokur and his colleagues further proof is afforded by their study of alcoholics and their relatives (Winokur et al., 1971b). Among the male relatives who developed a psychiatric illness the diagnosis of the majority was alcoholism (viewed for this purpose as a psychiatric

disorder); most of the female relatives with psychiatric illnesses were diagnosed as depressives.

A differing conclusion on a genetic link between alcohol dependence and depression has been reached by Goodwin and colleagues (1977b). They examined daughters, both adopted and non-adopted, of alcoholics and found that daughters who were reared by their alcoholic parents portrayed a considerably higher incidence of depression than daughters raised by nonalcoholic surrogate parents. The findings suggested that the stress of living with an alcoholic parent produced a susceptibility to depression.

Another line of enquiry (Kaij and Dock, 1975) has investigated grandsons of alcoholics, primarily to consider whether the X chromosome might be influential in determining the higher incidence of alcohol dependence amongst males than amongst females. The researchers tested the hypothesis that grandsons of an alcoholic man who carry his X chromosome (the sons of his daughters) would possess a higher rate of alcohol misuse than grandsons who carry his Y chromosome (the sons of his sons). Alcohol misuse was defined as showing the social complications of excess drinking, ranging from a single drunkenness conviction to severe social decline. The results refuted the hypothesis, but did show a threefold rise of alcohol misuse among grandsons of alcoholics compared with the general population.

In North America the Indians and Eskimos are more prone to alcohol problems than Caucasians and take longer to become sober after heavy drinking. Because of these observations Fenna and coworkers (1971) administered alcohol experimentally to volunteers with normal liver function from the three races. The levels of blood alcohol concentration fell more rapidly among Caucasians than among Indians or Eskimos. The differential rate of alcohol metabolism could not be accounted for by diet or previous alcohol consumption, and was attributed by the researchers to genetic factors. But it is not necessary to adduce racial differences in the rate of alcohol metabolism. The susceptibility of people of American Indian, or Eskimo race to the dependence-producing qualities of alcohol can be adequately explained on cultural and historical grounds related to the social and psychological difficulties of ethnic minorities.

American Indians and Eskimos belong to the Oriental group of races, yet differ from many Oriental peoples by the possession of a high incidence of alcohol problems. Orientals often develop unpleasant symptoms—flushing, headaches, palpitations—if they take alcohol; the symptoms are said to protect against the development of heavy drinking and have been attributed to the accumulation of acetaldehyde. Alcohol is converted by the enzyme alcohol dehydrogenase (ADH) to acetaldehyde, which is in turn changed by the enzyme aldehyde dehydrogenase (ALDH) to acetate. Japanese subjects possess an isoenzyme variant of ADH that quickly converts alcohol to acetaldehyde (von Wartburg, 1976; 1980). An additional finding is that about 50% of investigated Japanese lack the isoenzyme form of ALDH that is present in Occidental peoples and that rapidly oxidizes acetaldehyde (Agarwal et al., 1981; Harada et al., 1981). The proposition is that persons who possess either the ADH or the ALDH phenotypes which favour acetaldehyde accumulation would develop flushing and allied discomforts on drinking and therefore might be less likely, for genetic reasons, to develop dependence on alcohol. There has indeed been a subsequent finding amongst Japanese subjects of a decreased occurrence of the rapidly acting form of ALDH in alcoholics compared with controls (Harada et al., 1982).

The results from Japan, if confirmed, would support a genetic contribution to alcohol dependence but they also lead, perhaps paradoxically, to a further conclusion. The Japanese drink—or titrate, as it were—their way through the symptoms attributable to acetaldehyde and, by reason of their drinking traditions, possess a high prevalence of alcohol problems. Furthermore, the alcoholism prevalence in Japan, in common with many nations, has grown considerably during the second half of the present century during a time interval too short to produce significant genetic changes in populations. The position emphasizes the overriding importance of socio-cultural factors in determination of general patterns of drinking and of the overall level of alcohol consumption. However, the cardinal role exerted by social and economic features allows for their interaction with more personal elements, such as the genetic endowments of individuals.

Further lines of research have been conducted in attempts to correlate alcohol dependence with biological features that are largely determined by heredity. Colour blindness has been reported from Chile by Cruz-Coke and his colleagues to possess an increased incidence in cirrhotic patients (Cruz-Coke, 1964, 1965) and in alcoholics (Cruz-Coke and Varela, 1965, 1966; Varela et al., 1969). The Chilean workers postulated that alcoholism is part of an X-linked genetic polymorphism. In their view the biological advantage to the heterozygotes, who are female, takes the form of increased fertility.

Several repeat studies have been performed elsewhere. Swinson (1972a) has reviewed their results. The findings fall into three groups: no association between alcoholism and colour vision defects, or a temporary association which disappeared on retesting, or a consistent association. Among his own alcoholic patients Swinson noted an increased incidence of colour defective vision that appeared to be acquired rather than genetic; in his subjects the proportion with impaired colour vision was comparable between the sexes, and was not consistent with a sex-linked genetic factor. The conflicting studies on alcohol blindness among alcoholics have received criticism from Edwards

(1970) and from McCance (1970) on the grounds of inadequacy of the control samples and of incorrect interpretation of the findings.

Another genetic marker that has received investigation in alcohol dependence consists of taste sensitivity for phenylthiocarbamide (PTC). Diminished sensitivity for PTC has been reported among alcoholics, though the phenomenon probably results, not from a predisposition to alcohol dependence, but from a loss of taste sensitiveness due to age and to tobacco and alcohol consumption (Swinson, 1972b).

ABO blood groups have been examined among alcoholics, with conflicting results. The ABO groups were first studied by Achté (1958) in Finland and found to show a similar distribution in alcoholics and controls. On the other hand, Nordmo (1959) uncovered in Colorado an increase of blood group A among alcoholics. Madden (1967) noted in a sample of United Kingdom alcoholics an excess of group O and a decrease of group A; a study of a larger group of his alcoholic patients detected a statistically significant decrease of group A compared with control subjects (Swinson and Madden, 1973). But Camps and his associates, also in the United Kingdom, reported a normal distribution of ABO substances in alcoholics (Camps and Dodd, 1967; Camps and Lincoln, 1969).

An analysis has been conducted by Swinson and Madden (1973) of several of the above results on blood groups, using the statistical method of Woolf (1954). The conclusion was that the findings were significantly heterogeneous, i.e. they differed markedly from each other, but that there was no consistent trend in the results. Perhaps the issue has been settled by a later report from the United Kingdom that found no anomalies of ABO blood group distribution among alcoholics (Faizallah et al., 1982).

The importance of cultural factors in the causation of alcohol dependence makes it difficult to interpret an association between the condition and a genetic marker if the latter, like ABO blood grouping, varies with race. The association could result from cultural features determining the alcoholism rate of an ethnic group, or be due to a pleiotropic genetic mechanism, or derive from a causal relationship between the hereditary trait and alcohol consumption. The problem of ethnic stratification could be avoided if siblings of alcoholics were used as controls.

The secretion of ABO substances into the saliva has an hereditary element which does not vary as widely with race as the incidence of ABO groups in the blood. Camps and coworkers (Camps and Dodd, 1967; Camps and lincoln, 1969) found a higher proportion of nonsecretors in alcoholics, particularly in those of blood group A. The higher incidence of nonsecretors in alcoholics possessing blood group A has received independent confirmation (Swinson and Madden, 1973). If a genetic feature contributed both to alcohol dependence and to the higher rate of nonsecretion among alcoholics with blood group A there should develop an augmented number of group A alcoholics; none of the studies of secretor status detected an increased number of alcoholics in group A. Yet it remains difficult to envisage how excess alcohol intake could impair the secretion into the saliva of ABO substance in group A alcoholics and not in alcoholics with other blood groups.

In summary, the studies on heredity and alcohol dependence are suggestive but not quite conclusive. Many of the researches on drinking practices in relatives of alcoholics have been conducted on small numbers of subjects; the studies differ in their definitions of alcoholism; a few adopt a superficial approach to definition. It must be stressed that a high familial and ethnic incidence of alcohol dependence is not necessarily caused by genetic processes. In respect to somatic anomalies that may be found in problem drinkers many physical attributes which are laid down by genes are susceptible to prenatal alteration by the alcohol intake or associated life style of an alcoholic mother; after birth they can be modified by a variety of influences, including the individual's living pattern and alcohol consumption.

It is likely that genetic elements affect alcohol consumption and dependence but their nature is uncertain and their power is weak compared to sociocultural factors. The comparable formulation for drug usage is even more tentative. The difficulties in the establishment of a hereditary aspect for either alcohol or drug intake are similar, but have particularly acted to deter intensive appropriate investigations of persons with drug problems.

Personality features

Emotional problems that arise within the constitution and that stem from genetic and childhood influences play a role in the causation of harmful levels of psychoactive substance consumption. The difficulty in the useful elaboration of this concept lies in the determination of which emotional anomalies that may be found in excessive drinkers or drug users preceded, and which were produced by, their alcohol or drug intake.

A study of subjects, examined in childhood and traced into adulthood, has not been performed purely for the purpose of ascertaining the early characteristics of those who developed alcohol or drug difficulties. There have, however, been three prospective researches that were conducted for wider aims, but were able to provide data on those subjects who became alcohol misusers.

The first prospective study of this nature was initiated by the McCords on boys; the subjects were followed up with the original intention of ascertaining which childhood features were associated with subsequent criminal behaviour, but the number who became alcoholic allowed the investigation to extend to alcohol dependence (McCord and McCord,

1960). Compared with controls, the prealcoholic subjects were in childhood more self-confident outwardly, more active than passive, more aggressive, and more often held unfavourable attitudes towards their mothers. The prealcoholics tended to be reared by erratic mothers who oscillated in displays of affection and so produced strong emotional dependency needs in their sons. The prealcoholic boys also lacked a stable male adult figure to provide a model for responsible behaviour. It was considered that the aggressive masculinity of the prealcoholics concealed requirements for emotional dependency which led in adulthood to the overtly tough male behaviour of excessive drinking. It is relevant to the McCord's findings that an investigation of male alcoholics indicated that over half showed dependent attitudes towards their mothers and nearly half held a similar outlook towards their wives (Jones, 1963).

The results of the other two prospective studies were comparable in many ways to the first. A survey of subjects who had attended a child guidance clinic revealed that the prealcoholics showed predominantly antisocial difficulties rather than neurotic symptoms; their fathers also displayed antisocial behaviour and were inadequate as parents (Robins et al., 1962). A long-term survey of normal boys found that those who became alcoholic had been rebellious and impulsive in childhood (Jones, 1968).

There are many studies of the personalities of subjects who have alcohol or drug dependence. The studies are often combined with efforts to determine retrospectively the psychological and social circumstances that had influenced the subjects from an early age. But the reader will keep in mind that there is a limitation on the validity of attempts to disentangle premorbid traits from emotional developments that are consequent on alcohol or drug consumption.

An investigation of young persons with alcohol and drug dependence found that both groups were normally distributed on the extraversion-introversion continuum, that the alcoholics were neurotic, and that most of the subjects in both groups possessed premorbid personality disorders associated with family disruption and childhood antisocial behaviour (Rosenberg, 1969). A preference for alcohol was related to family patterns of excessive drinking, to a masculine facade and to neuroticism. A choice for drugs was associated with a desire for experimental pleasures in a deviant subgroup, to sexual deviation, and to inclinations to intellectual and artistic pursuits. A further study by the same researcher of 16 families of drug-dependent adolescents revealed psychiatric ill health in 21 of the parents, which usually took the form in the fathers of alcoholism and in the mothers of depressive illness (Rosenberg, 1971).

Wells and Stacey (1976) examined by questionnaire and personality inventories a sample of illicit drug users who were not necessarily dependent on drugs, and compared them with non-users of drugs. Those who employed drugs were more neurotic and anxious, were more likely to have an unhappy home and school life, were more involved with tobacco, alcohol and with sex outside marriage, and were more prone to employment problems.

Heroin-dependent females who had been remanded to a London prison were surveyed by d'Orban (1970). All but one were multiple drug users. Their lives before the onset of drug dependence showed a high incidence of broken homes, homosexuality, petty delinquency, educational failure, inability to retain jobs, unstable drifting, mood disturbance and suicidal gestures. Another London study, of male patients attending a drug dependence clinic, indicated that 48% had been convicted before the onset of drug use (Gordon, 1973).

Dependence on drugs leads to criminal offences involving illegal possession or supply of drugs as well as to crimes of theft performed to obtain drugs or the money to exchange for drugs. But other surveys than the last mentioned have confirmed that a considerable proportion of drug-dependent persons incurred minor convictions before they became implicated with drug consumption. For example, Willis (1971) performed a dual study of London and New York users of morphine-like drugs and found that the proportions with convictions before drug use comprised 54·5% of the English subjects and 48% of the American group.

The problems of reporting on the personalities of drug users are further compounded by the multiplicity of psychoactive drugs that may be misused. But despite the frequent tendency to multiple drug use displayed by persons extensively involved in illicit drug consumption, the possibility exists that specific personalities are attracted to specific drugs or to specific routes of drug administration. Gossop et al. (1975) found a higher incidence of acts of self-injury among patients who were orally dependent on drugs than among intravenous drug users; the oral users mostly took amphetamines and barbiturates, the injectors preferred morphine-like drugs. The authors suggested that personality factors as well as the pharmacological actions of the drugs explained the difference between the groups. An investigation with a dissimilar conclusion was performed by Toomey (1974); using the Minnesota Multiphase Personality Inventory (MMPI) he reported that although subjects who took hallucinogenic drugs scored higher for mania than those who consumed morphine-like substances, the personality profiles of the two groups of drug user were essentially similar. A comparison of Henriques et al. (1972) has also found comparable personality features among barbiturate and heroin consumers.

The concept that specific drugs attract specific kinds of personality has not therefore received validation. A relationship between drug preference and personality traits would be difficult to show at the present time, in view of the frequency of multiple drug use among consumers of illicit drugs. Persons who are taking drugs illegally can transfer easily from one substance to another, in accordance with the availability of particular drugs and with the ever changing vogues in illicit drug usage. Transfer readily takes place between drugs of diverse pharmacological action; the same individual may, for instance, alternate phases of regular consumption of a morphine-like substance with periods of amphetamine or general sedative intake.

The MMPI has been studied both among problem drinkers and among drug users. Although the differences between individual alcoholic subjects are extensive they tend as a group to score highly on the depression and psychopathic deviate scales (Hill et al., 1962; Rae and Forbes, 1966). The elevated scores for depression and social deviancy fall during inpatient treatment (Rohan et al., 1969).

The scores given by alcoholics in five psychological tests, including the 16 Personality Factor Questionnaire (16PF), were recorded by Walton (1968). The scores indicated that, compared with normal controls, the alcoholic subjects were more affected by their feelings, more tense and diffident, and less cheerful. There were interesting personality differences associated with the two main patterns of excessive alcohol intake; subjects who drank in bouts were more afraid of their own impulses and were more hostile towards themselves than alcoholics with a continuous pattern of consumption. Hoy (1969) detected several differences in the 16PF scores between his group of alcoholics and other reported samples, including the alcoholic patients of Walton; Hoy suggested that the differences reflect patient selection factors which influence the composition of any given clinic population of alcoholics.

Although the prospective studies of male children, some of whom became alcoholic, have, as described earlier, revealed antisocial trends and an overt facade of masculine toughness among the prealcoholics, it should be noted that among established alcoholics there is not a specific 'alcoholic personality'. Dependent drinkers tend to show depression and anxiety (in part, at least, as consequences of their excess alcohol consumption) but they portray a wide range of temperaments from normal to extremely neurotic or sociopathic. A community like the French nation which possesses a high rate of alcohol dependence because its cultural and economic features determine a large *per capita* alcohol consumption will have more alcoholics with normal, or near normal, personalities than a society where levels of alcohol consumption and dependence are so small that only the more vulnerable members become alcoholics.

A similar point applies to drug use. When a substantial proportion of members of a society has consumed a drug then it could hardly be claimed that persons who took the substance are deviant, either statistically or in their personalities and attitudes. Of course, their characteristics may fall towards a particular side of the average; members who consume the drug frequently will show more marked departures from the norm in background and mores, though they will not necessarily exhibit psychiatric abnormalities.

Both drug users and alcoholics show a high incidence among their parents of alcohol misuse, separation and divorce. Youthful drug takers are not necessarily neurotic, but possess personality anomalies that are revealed in scholastic and occupational under-achievement, and in sexual and interpersonal maladjustment; young drug users frequently adhere to subcultures in which nonconformity or criminality are the norms. Older subjects who develop dependence on sedatives or stimulants that have been prescribed to them, or who misuse simple analgesics, are more likely to have emotional problems of a neurotic nature. Neither alcoholics nor drug dependent persons differ markedly as a group from the general population with respect to intelligence.

Learning reactions between the constitution and alcohol or drugs

Learning theory contributes to an understanding of the development of alcohol and drug dependence. In a classic animal experiment Masserman and colleagues (Masserman and Yum, 1944; Masserman et al., 1946) trained cats to manipulate a switch to obtain food pellets, and then induced neurosis by giving an electric shock or a puff of air on some of the occasions that the animals triggered the switch. Cats who had been rendered neurotic in this manner were then confronted with a choice between plain milk or milk with alcohol; they chose the alcoholic milk. Under the influence of alcohol the neurotic cats overcame their fears of moving the switch. The cats had learned to take alcohol to relieve stress; their reward (or 'reinforcement', to use the technical term) for so doing consisted in the diminution of emotions which in humans would be described as anxiety or fear. After recovery from neurosis there was a decrease of the desire for alcohol. The experiment had established a pattern of alcohol ingestion by means of a process of operant conditioning. The process has been analysed by Orford (1976) who noted that the reinforcements in humans for taking alcohol are both pharmacological (the euphoric and disinhibiting effects of alcohol) and social (approach to and unity with other people).

In addition to operant conditioning the process of classic or Pavlovian conditioning is also influential in the production of alcohol dependence; neutral stimuli associated with alcohol come to trigger the desire or act of drinking. The stimuli to drink are wide-ranging; they include the sight and smell of alcoholic beverages, licensed premises, and circumstances (whether pleasant or unpleasant) that have preceded alcohol intake.

A similar application of learning theory to drug dependence has been formulated by Wikler (1961). He pointed out that a person who is physically dependent on a drug learns to take the substance in order to suppress the abstinence syndrome; the relief afforded to the symptoms of withdrawal provides a reinforcement to continued drug consumption. Drug-seeking behaviour that was originally reinforced in this way becomes conditioned to secondary reinforcers, that is to stimuli regularly associated with the administration of the drug. Furthermore, some of the abstinence symptoms become conditioned to occur in response to situations where drugs are available, such as the observation of companions consuming drugs. These mechanisms help to explain how conditioning processes can provoke a relapse in a former drug user.

Further learning reactions are involved (WHO Memorandum, 1981; Commentaries, 1982). Through the process of stimulus generalization, cues in the environment that trigger the desire for alcohol or drugs become broadened in number and scope. For instance, if an individual takes alcohol or a drug in response to a particular stress then substance consumption may recur when fresh difficulties arise. So alcohol or drug intake to relieve the anxiety that is experienced during withdrawal may lead to substance consumption to reduce anxiety from other causes. Alcohol or drug consumption constitutes a strongly reinforced response to a stimulus and therefore may produce extinction of other responses; thus an individual may lose the capacity to respond to a stimulus such as anxiety by reactions other than the capture of chemical relief.

Numerous social features promote the learning of alcohol or drug intake. The alcohol consumption of parents and their attitudes to drinking are mirrored in their progeny (O'Connor, 1976); imitative alcohol and drug behaviour also develops from peer influence. Persons working in occupations that require the handling of alcohol or drugs of dependence have opportunities to consume frequently these substances and can learn to do so; dependence may then develop as an occupational hazard, even in people (like many alcoholic publicans and customs officers) who possess normal personalities. The behavioural response of reacting to unpleasant emotional stimuli by obtaining chemical relief is easily learned, particularly when the response is given the sanction of the culture or subculture with which the individual wishes to conform.

Dependence-promoting properties of alcohol and drugs

The subjective changes produced in the short term by a psychotropic substance are so attractive to some persons that they take the substance in a hazardous manner and may develop dependence or other forms of harm. The neurochemical mechanisms by which alcohol and individual drugs acutely modify cerebral function, with transient effects on mental processes and the risk of misuse or dependence, are ill understood but will receive some consideration in the later sections devoted to specific substances. Most of this section deals with possible mechanisms by which the properties of psychoactive agents may interact with the body to induce the associated phenomena of tolerance and abstinence syndromes. Throughout this section the word 'drug' also refers to alcohol, unless the text makes clear a distinction.

Tolerance and withdrawal features

An alternative term to tolerance is tachyphylaxis. Both words refer to decreased responsiveness to a drug that has been previously administered. When tolerance develops larger quantities of the substance need to be taken in order to obtain the required effects. Tolerance does not necessarily occur to all the effects of a chemical agent; for example, in man repeated doses of morphine induce tolerance to the depressant effects of the drug on the central nervous system, but not to its effects on pupil size and bowel mobility. *Cross-tolerance* denotes restricted responsiveness to one substance that follows the administration of another compound. Often cross-tolerance develops among drugs of the same pharmacological group, and is accompanied by *cross-dependence.* The latter concept implies that the substitution in adequate dose of one drug for another suppresses the withdrawal symptoms of the replaced drug and introduces physical dependence to the drug that is substituted.

Tolerance and the abstinence features of physical dependence tend to develop together. Their parallel course has been outlined for alcohol by Gross (1977), who has pointed out that although they wane with abstinence they become reinstated with progressive rapidity during successive phases of drinking. Their joint occurrence depends on neurophysiological changes which, among other results, allow the substance to be taken without its full acute effects. Since the neural changes resist the immediate effects of the intoxicant they promote homeostasis and are viewed as an adaptive response. Yet the two phenomena are not in full alliance. Tolerance develops to drugs, for example hallucinogens, that do not produce withdrawal features. Tolerance occurs in tissues outside the nervous system, whereas the underlying disturbances of withdrawal syndromes are confined to central and peripheral nervous structures. It has been argued that tolerance is associated with physical dependence merely because tolerance allows exposure of the body to drug doses that are high enough to induce dependence; according to this argument, in the absence of tolerance such doses would not be administered without immediate, unpleasant effects which in some instances might be lethal.

There are three biological processes which could promote the development of tolerance. Firstly, the quantity of drug present at its sites of action can be reduced by *altered disposition* of the drug in the body. Secondly, *homeostatic mechanisms* in physiological systems not directly affected by a substance could come into force to counteract the effects of the drug on target tissues. Thirdly, the target cells could become less responsive through the process of *cellular or functional tolerance*.

The quantity of a drug available for pharmacological activity is capable of modification at successive stages: by altering its absorption, by its inactivation at neutral sites, by its metabolism, and by excretion. It was at one time speculated that immunological reactions might inactivate morphine-like drugs, but so far as is known the most effective method of reducing the bioavailability of a drug is through enhancement of its metabolic degradation.

Alcohol, barbiturates and other preparations of the alcohol-barbiturate type induce the enzymes in the liver which transform these substances. Cannabis is also metabolized more quickly after its repeated consumption. Some studies have reported that repeated morphine intake leads to an accelerated rate of biotransformation of the drug, but not all reports confirm this finding. It is unclear whether amphetamines are more rapidly transformed in man after repetitive administration. The metabolism of hallucinogenic agents in tolerant subjects has received little investigation.

More rapid biotransformation of the active substance is reponsible for much of the tolerance noted to short-acting barbiturates. But enhancement of metabolism is not sufficient to account for the greater part of the tolerance which develops to long-acting barbiturates and to alcohol. Accelerated metabolism cannot explain the marked tolerance that is found to morphine-like drugs, and is still less able to account for the remarkable and rapid degree of tolerance that is found to stimulant compounds and hallucinogens.

Homeostatic mechanisms of tolerance are largely hypothetical. They could involve both physiological and psychological processes, the latter taking the form of learned responses which obviate the effects of a drug on the nervous system. Laboratory animals that are repeatedly given alcohol or morphine develop tolerance more readily when their substance intake takes place in unchanged surroundings; in other words, their tolerance is abetted by environmental cues (Tabakoff et al., 1982).

We are left with cellular adaptation, in neural organs directly affected by drugs, as the major route of tolerance. The neuroadaptive changes that promote tolerance are considered to be closely similar or identical to the changes that underlie physical dependence and lead to withdrawal features. The consideration arises because the symptoms and signs following cessation of the long-term use of a drug are often the opposite of those induced by its immediate actions. Thus, depression of mood follows stoppage of the repeated administration of the stimulant drug amphetamine; anxiety develops during the abstinence syndrome following discontinuance of sedatives of the barbiturate-alcohol type; morphine deprivation is accompanied by dilated pupils, tachypnoea, restlessness and insomnia. It appears that during administration of a drug which is capable of producing physical dependence, neural adjustments take place to counteract the acute effects of the substance; the adjustments are suppressed by the drug, though increasing drug doses may be needed to produce the suppression ('tolerance'). When the substance is discontinued the adaptive measures emerge in full force to produce rebound overactivity of the suppressed nerve system. In relation to drugs resembling morphine, the phenomenon of suppression of neural function during drug administration with release of excess activity on drug cessation has been termed 'latent hyperexcitability'.

Since the sites and modes of action of psychotropic drugs are not fully elucidated, it is understandable that the mechanisms of tolerance and of withdrawal features are unclear. Fortunately the relevant concepts are subject to an evolutionary process that is gaining momentum.

During the nineteenth century it was suggested that the repeated administration of a drug provoked the production in the organism of a compound of contrary effect, and that withdrawal of the drug allowed the compound to exert fully its activity. This ingenious and innovatory concept has been discarded, because no compound of the nature proposed has been detected.

A later proposal concerned morphine and postulated two sites of action of the drug. The first site constituted a locus on the cell membrane; according to the hypothesis drug interaction with this site depresses neuronal activity. The second proposed site was placed within the neuron; drug occupancy of the second site leads to excitation of the neuron. Following morphine withdrawal (or administration of a morphine antagonist such as naloxone) the morphine is cleared more rapidly from the first receptor site, leading to predominance of the second site. This hypothesis did not involve the 'latent hyperexcitability' concept of adaptation to the effect of morphine and is no longer offered in its initial formulation.

Considerable attention now focuses on the naturally occurring neurotransmitter substances in the brain that promote, inhibit or modulate the transmission of nerve impulses. Depending on its mode of action a psychotropic drug may interfere with the production of neurotransmitters, with their storage in synaptic vesicles, with their release from storage vesicles and passage across presynaptic membrane, and with their occupancy of neurotransmitter receptor sites on postsynaptic membrane. Alternatively a drug could alter the uptake of transmitter substances back into nerve terminals, or influence the catabolism of transmitters and their renewed storage before further release. Certain psychoactive drugs may affect transmission of nerve impulses along axons.

Drugs with psychoactive results could reduce the activity of selected neurotransmitters at the postsynaptic receptor sites for neural transmitters, either directly through competitive occupation of the receptors or indirectly through actions on the synthesis, storage or release of the neurotransmitters. Pharmacological denervation in peripheral tissues leads to supersensitivity of the receptor system. Reduction of receptor activity in the brain because of the actions of a psychotropic drug could lead to supersensitivity of the receptors to available amounts of the neurotransmitter (that is, to tolerance). Supersensitivity may arise either through changes in the conformation of existing receptors or through induction of new receptors. Discontinuance of the drug would induce, for a time, overreaction of the receptors to the transmitter, with the appearance of withdrawal features.

The available quantity of a neurotransmitter may become depleted by its repeated release from nerve endings. This mechanism takes place with amphetamine-like drugs in respect of depletion of noradrenaline (norepinephrine) and dopamine. The process is capable of inducing both tolerance and withdrawal phenomena.

It is likely that feedback mechanisms are involved. Alterations induced by a drug in neurotransmitter activity could, through negative or positive feedback, produce long-term changes in the enzymatic production of the relevant neurotransmitter or in its storage or release from nerve terminals.

Morphine-like drugs occupy the same receptor sites on neurons as the endogenous opioid peptides. Activation of the receptor sites by a morphine-like drug could suppress the production of endogenous opioids and so induce tolerance; drug withdrawal would lead to abstinence features until manufacture of the naturally occurring opioids returns to normal (Hughes, 1976).

Alcohol and barbiturates stabilize nerve membranes and thereby inhibit the initiation and transmission of stimuli in the nervous system. Benzodiazepines occupy loci that lie adjacent to the receptor sites for the endogenous neuroinhibitor gamma-aminobutyric acid (GABA); as an acute effect benzodiazepines enhance the actions of GABA. There is evidence that the stabilizing action of alcohol on nerve membranes includes a facilitating effect on GABA-containing synapses (Littleton et al., 1979). On the other hand, long-term, administration of benzodiazepines and possibly of alcohol counteracts their acute effects on GABA and so promotes tolerance and abstinence phenomena (Cowan and Nutt, 1982).

It has been suggested that many of the ill effects of chronic excessive alcohol consumption are produced, not by alcohol itself, but by its metabolite acetaldehyde (Korsten et al., 1975). The brain damage and heart muscle disease encountered in some alcoholics have been attributed to acetaldehyde toxicity; 'acetaldehydism' has been offered as a realistic term to replace 'alcoholism' (Raskin, 1975). Acetaldehyde has been implicated in physical dependence on alcohol beverages. It has been proposed that the substance promotes condensation products between aldehydes and phenylethylamines or indoleamines to form tetrahydroisoquinolines (e.g. tetrahydropapaveroline) or beta-carbolines, and that such condensation products induce dependence through morphine-like actions (Davis and Walsh, 1970; Badawy and Evans, 1975). Yet the early studies on acetaldehyde have been compromized by errors in the assessment of acetaldehyde levels in animals and human preparations; the laboratory methods permitted spontaneous removal of acetaldehyde or its artificial formation (von Wartburg, 1980). Furthermore, the alcohol and morphine withdrawal syndromes are dissimilar in both animals and humans (Goldstein and Judson, 1971). For these and other reasons, the role of acetaldehyde remains debatable (Eriksson, 1982).

The neurochemical theories of tolerance and withdrawal features are intriguing and exciting. Many of the offered explanations are not mutually exclusive; some may in the course of time be found to complement each other. Fuller appreciation of the neuroadaptive reactions that underlie tolerance and abstinence syndromes will foster progress in treatment and possibly in prevention. Advances in the particular field of morphine tolerance and dependence should contribute to a better comprehension of the wider but poorly understood subject of the neural mechanisms responsible for the receipt of pain. It is hoped that this survey of the relevant speculations has whetted the reader's appetite for the subject.

Assessment of the dependence liability of drugs

A WHO scientific group has surveyed the methodology of evaluation of the dependence potential of drugs (World Health Organisation, 1975); the survey gave a valuable account of the variety and scope of the relevant issues. The group of researchers pointed out the predictive value of experiments on animals to elicit drug-seeking behaviour and physical dependence; useful information has been gathered, not only from intact animals, but from *in vitro* models that employ tissue preparations. In man there are a variety of approaches to the clinical assessment of the subjective effect of drugs and of tolerance and physical dependence. The WHO scientists commented that epidemiology contributes to the study of the dependence liability of drugs, but noted a need to improve the methods of monitoring the use and misuse of psychotropic substances among communities.

It was the view of the WHO scientific group that conceptual and methodological problems added to the difficulties encountered in the prediction of the dependence potential of drugs. The operational employment of concepts is not always clearly defined; methods are not adequately validated; the behaviours or events which are measured are sometimes not sufficiently described or quantified.

A number of factors militate against comparison of studies of the dependence liability of drugs. Many studies employ different measuring methods, or use the same method in differing ways; subject samples, or the sociocultural setting and expectations in which the experiments are conducted, are often widely dissimilar.

The recommendations of the scientific group for priority action retain their interest and pertinence. Several areas received emphasis; they comprise standardization of methods, multidisciplinary research, collaborative research and training centres, refinement of techniques appropriate for transcultural expansion, and integration of results from preclinical, clinical and epidemiological studies.

Improvement, on these suggested lines, of the foundations for research will further fundamental understanding of the process underlying misuse and dependence. On the practical level more careful and rapid monitoring of drugs for their dependence potential should forestall or reduce the problems produced by their consumption.

REFERENCES

Achté K. (1958) Correlation of ABO blood groups with alcoholism. *Duodecim* **74**, 20–22.

Advisory Council on the Misuse of Drugs (1982) *Treatment and Rehabilitation.* London, HMSO.

Argarwal D. P., Harada S. and Goedde H. W. (1981) Racial differences in biological sensitivity to ethanol: the role of alcohol dehydrogenase and aldehyde dehydrogenase isozymes. *Alcoholism (NY)* **5**, 12–16.

Armyr G., Elmer A. and Herz U. (1982) *Alcohol in the World of the 80s.* Eastbourne, Ansvar Insurance Company.

Badawy A. A. and Evans M. (1974) Alcohol and tryptophan metabolism—a review. *J. Alcohol.* **9**, 97–116.

Bailey M. B., Haberman P. W. and Alksne H. (1965) The epidemiology of alcoholism in an urban residential area. *Q. J. Stud. Alcohol* **26**, 19–40.

Bailey M. B., Haberman P. W. and Sheinberg J. (1966) Identifying alcoholics in population surveys; a report on reliability. *Q. J. Stud. Alcohol* **27**, 300–315.

Bales R. F. (1962) Attitudes towards drinking in the Irish culture. In: Pittman D. J. and Snyder C. R. (ed.), *Society Culture and Drinking Patterns.* New York, Wiley, pp. 157–187.

Blumberg H. H. (1975) Surveys of drug use among young people. *Int. J. Addict.* **10**, 699–719.

Bohman M., Sigvardsson S. and Cloninger C. R. (1981) Maternal inheritance of alcohol abuse: cross-fostering analysis of adopted women. *Arch. Gen. Psychiatry* **38**, 965–969.

Cadoreth R. J. and Gath A. (1978) Inheritance of alcoholism in adoptees. *Br. J. Psychiatry* **132**, 252–258.

Cadoreth R. J., Cain C. A. and Grove W. M. (1980) Development of alcoholism in adoptees raised apart from alcoholic biologic relatives. *Arch. Gen. Psychiatry* **37**, 561–563.

Camps F. E. and Dodd B. E. (1967) Increase in the incidence of non-secretors of ABH blood group substances amongst alcoholic patients. *Br. Med. J.* **1**, 30–31.

Camps F. E. and Lincoln P. J. (1969) Frequencies of secretors and non-secretors of ABH group substances among 1000 alcoholic patients. *Br. Med. J.* **4**, 457–459.

Cloninger C. R., Bohman M. and Sigvardsson S. (1981) Inheritance of alcohol abuse: cross-fostering analysis of adopted men. *Arch. Gen. Psychiatry* **38**, 861–868.

Commentaries (1982) Nomenclature and classification of drug- and alcohol-related problems: a shortened version of a WHO memorandum. *Br. J. Addict.* **77**, 3–20.

Cotton N. S. (1979) The familial incidence of alcoholism; a review. *J. Stud. Alc.* **40**, 89–116.

Cowan P. J. and Nutt D. J. (1982) Abstinence symptoms after withdrawal of tranquillizing drugs: is there a common neurochemical mechanism? *Lancet* **ii**, 360–362.

Cruz-Coke R. (1964) Colour blindness and cirrhosis of the liver. *Lancet* **ii**, 1064–1065.

Cruz-Coke R. (1965) Colour blindness and cirrhosis of the liver. *Lancet* **ii**, 1131–1133.

Cruz-Coke R. and Varela A. (1965) Colour blindness and alcohol addiction (Letter.). *Lancet* **ii**, 1348.

Davis V. E. and Walsh M. J. (1970) Alcohol, amines and alkaloids. *Science* **167**, 1005–1007.

de Alarcón R. (1972) An epidemiological evaluation of a public health measure aimed at reducing the availability of methylamphetamine. *Psychol. Med.* **2**, 293–300.

de Lint J. (1974) The epidemiology of alcoholism. In: Kessel N., Hawker A. and Chalke H. (ed.), *Alcoholism: A Medical Profile, Proceedings of the First International Medical Conference on Alcoholism.* London, Edsell, pp. 75–108.

de Lint J. and Schmidt W. (1971) Consumption averages and alcoholism prevalence: a brief review of epidemiological investigations. *Br. J. Addict.* **66**, 97–107.

Department of Health and Social Security (1976) *Prevention and Health.* London, HMSO.

Donnan S. and Haskey J. (1977) Alcoholism and cirrhosis of the liver. In: *Population Trends 7.* London, HMSO, pp. 18–24.

d'Orban P. T. (1970) Heroin dependence and delinquency in women—a study of heroin addicts in Holloway prison. *Br. J. Addict.* **65**, 67–78.

Edwards G. (1970) The status of alcoholism as a disease. In: Phillipson R. V. (ed.), *Modern Trends in Drug Dependency and Alcoholism.* London, Butterworths, pp. 140–163.

Edwards G. (1973) Epidemiology applied to alcoholism: a review and an examination of purposes. *Q. J. Stud. Alcohol* **34**, 28–56.

Edwards G., Hawker A., Hensman C. et al. (1973) Alcoholics known or unknown to agencies: epidemiological studies in a London suburb. *Br. J. Psychiatry* **123**, 169–183.

Edwards G., Gross M. M., Keller M. et al. (1977) *Alcohol-related Disabilities.* WHO Offset Publication No. 32.

Eriksson C. J. P. (1982) The role of acetaldehyde in drinking behaviour and tissue damage. *Br. J. Alcohol Alcoholism* **17**, 57–69.

Faizallah R., Woodrow J. C., Krasner N. K. et al. (1982) Are HLA antigens important in the development of alcohol-induced liver disease? *Br. Med. J.* **285**, 533–534.

Fenna A., Mix L., Schaeffer O. et al. (1971) Ethanol metabolism in various racial groups. *Can. Med. Assoc. J.* **105**, 472–475.

Field P. B. (1962) A new cross-cultural study of drunkenness. In: Snyder C. R. and Pittman D. J. (ed.), *Society, Culture and Drinking Patterns.* New York, Wiley, pp. 48–74.

Fishburne R. M., Abelson H. I. and Cisini I. (1980) *National Survey on Drug Abuse: Main Findings: 1979.* DHSS Publication No. (ADM) 180–976. Washington, U.S. Government Printing Office.

Garagliano C. F., Lilienfeld A. M. and Mendeloff A. I. (1979) Incidence rates of liver cirrhosis and related diseases in Baltimore and selected areas of the United States. *J. Chron. Dis.* **32**, 543–544.

Gath D., Hensman C., Hawker A. et al. (1968) The drunk in court: survey of drunkenness offenders from two London courts. *Br. Med. J.* **4**, 808–811.

Glatt M. M. (1958) The English drink problem: its rise and decline through the ages. *Br. J. Addict.* **55**, 51–67.

Glatt M. M. (1970) Alcoholism and drug dependence amongst Jews. *Br. J. Addict.* **64**, 297–304.

Goldstein A. and Judson B. A. (1971) Alcohol dependence and opiate dependence: Lack of relationship in mice. *Science* **172**, 290–292.

Goodwin D. W., Schulsinger F., Hermansen L. et al. (1973) Alcohol problems in adoptees raised apart from alcoholic biological parents. *Arch. Gen. Psychiatry* **28**, 238–242.

Goodwin D. W., Schulsinger F., Møller N. et al. (1974) Drinking problems in adopted and nonadopted sons of alcoholics. *Arch. Gen. Psychiatry* **31**, 164–169.

Goodwin D. W., Schulsinger F., Knop J. et al. (1977a) Alcoholism and depression in adopted-out daughters of alcoholics. *Arch. Gen. Psychiatry.* **34**, 751–755.

Goodwin D. W., Schulsinger F., Knop J. at al. (1977b) Psychopathology in adopted and nonadopted daughters of alcoholics. *Arch. Gen. Psychiatry* **34**, 1005–1009.

Gordon A. M. (1973) Patterns of delinquency in drug addiction. *Br. J. Psychiatry* **122**, 205–210.

Gossop M. R., Cobb J. P. and Connell P. H. (1975) Self-destructive behaviour in oral and intravenous drug-dependent groups. *Br. J. Psychiatry* **126**, 266–269.

Greene H. (1975) Geographical and ethnic differences in heroin use incidence trends. In: *Proceedings of the 31st International Congress on Alcoholism and Drug Dependence.* Lausanne, International Council on Alcohol and Addictions, pp. 500–507.

Gross M. M. (1977) Psychobiological contributions to the alcohol dependence syndrome: a selective review of recent research. In: Edwards G., Gross M. M., Keller M., Moser J. and Room R. (ed.) *Alcohol-related Disabilities* WHO Offset Publication No. 32, pp. 101–131.

Harada S., Agarwal D. P., Goedde H. W. (1981) Aldehyde dehydrogenase deficiency as cause of facial flushing response in Japanese (Letter). *Lancet* **ii**, 982.

Harada S., Agarwal D. P., Goedde H. W. et al. (1982) Possible protective role against alcoholism for aldehyde dehydrogenase isozyme deficiency in Japan (Letter). *Lancet* **ii**, 827.

Henriques E., Arsenian J., Cutter H. et al. (1972) Personality characteristics and drug of choice. *Int. J. Addict.* **71**, 73–76.

Hill H. E., Haertzen C. A. and Davis H. (1962) An MMPI factor analytic study of alcoholics, narcotic addicts and criminals. *Q. J. Stud. Alcohol* **3**, 411–431.

Hopkinson G. and Ley P. (1969) A genetic study of affective disorder. *Br. J. Psychiatry* **115**, 917–922.

Horton D. (1943) The functions of alcohol in primitive societies: a cross cultural study. *Q. J. Stud. Alcohol* **4**, 199–320.

Hoy R. M. (1969) the personality of inpatient alcoholics in relation to group psychotherapy, as measured by the 16-P.F. *Q. J. Stud. Alcohol* **30**, 401–407.

Hubrec Z., and Omenn G. S. (1981) Evidence of genetic predisposition to alcoholic cirrhosis and psychosis: twin concordances for alcoholism and its biological end points by zygosity among male veterans. *Alcoholism (NY)* **5**, 207–215.

Hughes J. (1976) Enkephalins and drug dependence. *Br. J. Addict.* **71**, 199–209.

Jellinek E. M. (1959) Estimating the prevalence of alcoholism: modified values in the Jellinek formula and an alternative approach. *Q. J. Stud. Alcohol.* **20**, 261–269.

Johnston L. D., Bachman J. G. and O'Malley D. M. (1980) *Highlights from Student Drug Use in America, 1975–80.* DHSS Publication No. (ADM) 81–1066. Washington, U. S. Government Printing Office.

Jones H. (1963) *Alcoholic Addiction.* London, Tavistock Publications, p. 50.

Jones M. C. (1968) Personality correlates and antecedents of drinking patterns in adult males. *J. Consult. Clin. Psychol.* **32**, 2–12.

Jonsson E. and Nilsson T. (1968) Alcohol consumption in monzygotic and dizygotic pairs of twins. *Nordisk Hygienisk Tidskrift* **49**, 21–25.

Kaij L. (1960) *Alcoholism in Twins.* Stockholm, Almqvist and Wiksells.

Kaij L. and Dock J. (1975) Grandsons of alcoholics: a test of sex-linked transmission of alcohol abuse.

Keller M. (1970) The great Jewish drink mystery. *Br. J. Addict.* **64**, 287–296.

Korsten M. A., Matsuzaki S., Feinman L. et al. (1975) High blood acetaldehyde levels after ethanol administration; difference between alcoholic and nonalcoholic subjects. *N. Engl. J. Med.* **292**, 386–389.

Littleton J. M., John G. R., Jones P. A. et al. (1979) The rapid onset of functional tolerance to ethanol —role of different neurotransmitters and synaptosomal membrane lipids. *Acta Psychiatrica Scand.* Suppl. 286, **62**, 137–151.

McCance C. (1970) Aetiological factors in alcoholism: some areas of research. *J. Psychosom. Res.* **14**, 285–294.

McCord W. and McCord J. (1960) *Origins of Alcoholism.* Stanford, Stanford University Press.

Madden J. S. (1967) ABO blood groups and alcoholism. Unpublished.

Masserman J. H. and Yum K. S. (1946) An analysis of the influence of alcohol on experimental neurosis in cats. *Psychosom. Med.* **8**, 36–52.

Masserman J. H., Yum K. S., Nicholson M. R. et al. (1944) Neurosis and alcohol. An experimental study. *Am. J. Psychiatry* **101**, 389–395.

McGuinness T. (1979) *An Econometric analysis of total demand for alcoholic beverages in the UK, 1956–75.* Edinburgh, Scottish Health Education Unit.

Moss M. C. and Beresford Davies E. (1967) *A Survey of Alcoholism in an English County.* London, Geigy Scientific Publications.

Nelker G. (1975) Prevention of misuse of alcohol through control of the total consumption. In: *Proceedings of the 31st International Congress on Alcoholism and Drug Dependence.* Lausanne, International Council on Alcohol and Addictions, pp. 90–97.

Nordmo S. H. (1959) Blood groups in schizophrenia, alcoholism and mental deficiency. *Am. J. Psychiatry* **116**, 460–461.

O'Connor J. (1976) Social and cultural factors influencing drinking. In: Davies D. L. (ed.), *Aspects of Alcoholism.* London, Alcohol Education Centre.

Orford J. (1976) Psychological considerations. In: Davies D. K. (ed.), *Aspects of Alcoholism.* London, Alcohol Education Centre.

Parr D. (1957) Alcoholism in general practice. *Br. J. Addict.* **54**, 25–31.

Partanen J., Bruun K., and Markkanen T. (1966) *Inheritance of Drinking Behaviour. A Study on Intelligence, Personality, and Use of Alcohol of Adult Twins.* Helsinki, Finnish Foundation for Alcohol Studies.

Petersson B., Krantz P., Kristensson H. et al. (1982) Alcohol-related death: a major contribution to mortality in urban middle-aged men. *Lancet* **ii**, 1088–1090.

Rae J. B. and Forbes A. R. (1966) Clinical and psychometric characteristics of the wives of alcoholics. *Br. J. Psychiatry* **112**, 197–200.

Raskin N. H. (1975) Alcoholism or acetaldehydism? (editorial). *N. Engl. J. Med.* **292**, 422–423.

Robins L. N., Bates W. M. and O'Neal P. (1962) Adult drinking patterns of former problem children. In: Pittman D. J. and Snyder C. R. (ed.) *Society, Culture and Drinking Patterns.* New York, Wiley, pp. 395–412.

Roe A. (1944) the adult adjustment of children of alcoholic parents raised in fosterhomes. *Q. J. Stud. Alcohol* **5**, 378–393.

Rohan W. P., Tatro R. L. and Rotman S. R. (1969) MMPI changes in alcoholics during hospitalization. *Q. J. Stud. Alcohol* **30**, 389–400.

Rosenberg C. M. (1969) Determinants of psychiatric illness in young people. *Br. J. Psychiatry* **115**, 907–915.

Rosenberg C. M. (1971) The young addict and his family. *Br. J. Psychiatry* **118**, 469–470.

Schuckitt M. A., Goodwin D. A. and Winokur G. (1972) A study of alcoholism in half siblings. *Am. J. Psychiatry* **128**, 1132–1136.

Smith R. (1982) *Alcohol Problems*. London, The Publisher, British Medical Journal.

Snyder C. R. (1962) Culture and Jewish sobriety; the ingroup-outgroup factor. In: Pittman D. J. and Snyder C. R. (ed.) *Society, Culture and Drinking Patterns*. New York, Wiley, pp. 188–225.

Spring J. A. and Buss D. H. (1977) Three centuries of alcohol in the British diet. *Nature* **270**, 567–572.

Swinson R. P. (1972a) Genetic polymorphism and alcoholism. *Ann. NY Acad. Sci.* **197**, 129–133.

Swinson R. P. (1972b) Colour vision defects in alcoholism. *Br. J. Physiol. Opt.* **27**, 43–50.

Swinson R. P. and Madden J. S. (1973) ABO blood groups and ABH substance secretion in alcoholics. *Q. J. Stud. Alcohol* **34**, 64–70.

Tabakoff B., Melchior C. and Hoffman P. L. (1982) Commentary on ethanol tolerance. *Alcoholism (NY)* **6**, 252–259.

The Times (1976) Article, 1 October. London.

Toomey T. C. (1974) Personality and demographic characteristics of two sub-types of drug abusers. *Br. J. Addict.* **69**, 115–158.

Varela A., Rivera L., Mardones J. et al. (1969) Colour vision defects in non-alcoholic relatives of alcoholic patients. *Br. J. Addict.* **64**, 67–73.

Walton H. J. (1968) Personality as a determinant of the form of alcoholism. *Br. J. Psychiatry* **114**, 761–766.

von Wartburg J. P. (1976) Biological aspects of alcohol: remarks to the sessions on the biochemistry of alcohol. *Ann. NY Acad. Sci.* **273**, 146–158.

von Wartburg J. P. (1980) Acetaldehyde. In: Sandler M. (ed.) *Psychopharmacology of Alcohol.* New York, Raven Press, pp. 137–147.

Weeks C. C. (1938) *Alcohol and Human Life,* 2nd ed. London, Lewis, pp. 342–343.

Wells W. P. and Stacey B. G. (1976) Social and psychological features of young drug misusers. *Br. J. Addict.* **71**, 243–251.

Wikler A. (1961) On the nature of addiction and habituation. *Br. J. Addict.* **57**, 73–79.

Willis J. (1971) Delinquency and drug dependence in the United Kingdom and the United States. *Br. J. Addict.* **66**, 235–248.

Winokur G. (1972) Types of depressive illness. *Br. J. Psychiatry* **120**, 265–266.

Winokur G., Cadoret R., Durzab J. and Baker M. (1971a) Depressive disease: a genetic study. *Arch. Gen. Psychiatry* **24**, 135–144.

Winokur G., Rimmer J. and Reich T. (1971b) Alcoholism IV: is there more than one type of alcoholism? *Br. J. Psychiatry* **118**, 525–531.

Woolf B. (1954) On estimating the relation between blood groups and disease. *Ann. Hum. Genet.* **19**, 251–253.

World Health Organisation (1951) Expert Committee on Mental Health: Report on the First Session of the Alcoholism Subcommittee. *WHO Tech. Rep. Ser.* No. 42, Annexe 42.

World Health Organisation (1964) Expert Committees on Addiction–producing Drugs. *WHO Tech. Rep. Ser.* No. 273.

World Health Organisation (1974) Expert Committee on Drug Dependence: Twentieth Report. *WHO Tech. Rep. Ser.* No. 551.

World Health Organisation (1975) Evaluation of Dependence Liability and Dependence Potential of Drugs. Report of a WHO Scientific Group. *WHO Tech. Rep. Ser.* No. 5777.

World Health Organisation (1981) Nomenclature and classification of drug- and alcohol-related problems. *Bull. WHO* **59**, 225–242.

Chapter 2

ALCOHOL AND ALCOHOL DEPENDENCE

Who, after his wine, prates of poverty? HORACE

ALCOHOL

Ethyl alcohol (ethanol) has the formula CH_3CH_2OH. There are many other members of the chemical series of alcohols; the most widely known is methyl alcohol (methanol), which possesses the formula CH_3OH. Unless stated otherwise the term 'alcohol' will be used in the text to refer to ethyl alcohol.

The substance occurs naturally as a decomposition product of plant carbohydrates; the breakdown to alcohol is facilitated by the presence of yeast fungi which are added accidentally by nature, or deliberately by man. The intoxicating effects of alcohol have been known since ancient times; there are few races that have not consumed alcoholic beverages to induce states of altered consciousness. Fermentation with the catalytic aid of yeast permits a maximum alcohol concentration of about 10% by volume; higher concentrations are not possible from fermentation since the alcohol would kill off the yeast. More concentrated preparations, for industrial use or for drinking, are produced by using alcohol obtained from distillation. The isolation of a strong preparation of alcohol through distillation was first achieved by the Persian chemist Rhases about the year 800 A.D.; he published his findings in Arabic, the international language of his region. Scholars of that time and place came to consider that a fine invisible powder was emitted when fermented material was boiled; the Arabic phrase for 'the powder' is 'al kohl', hence the name of alcohol. Beverage spirits, containing distilled alcohol, were introduced into Europe in the late Middle Ages. It is arguable that the popularity of distilled preparations led to an increase in the medico-social problems arising from excess alcohol consumption, and that the increase persists to the present era (Diethelm, 1965).

The properties of alcoholic beverages are modified by congeners. These are substances other than ethyl alcohol; chemically many are higher alcohols. Congeners effect the aroma and taste of alcoholic drinks; they are thought to increase the intoxicating results and hangovers, but they are present in such small amounts relative to ethyl alcohol that their contribution to the misuse and dependence potential of alcoholic beverages is minimal.

Acute effects of alcohol

When alcoholic beverages are drunk their aroma and the alcohol itself reflexly stimulate the salivary and gastric secretions through excitation of nerve endings in oronasal and gastric mucosa; in addition, the psychological aspects attached to alcoholic drinks can psychically increase the same secretions. Moderate amounts of alcohol in the stomach directly induce gastric secretion through release of gastrin or histamine. Strong alcoholic beverages inhibit gastric secretion except for mucus, and produce the inflammatory changes of gastritis. Although potent alcoholic preparations were formerly used as a treatment for diarrhoea regular drinkers rarely complain of constipation, since alcohol stimulates bowel motility and impairs absorption of electrolytes and of water.

Absorption of alcohol rapidly takes place through the mucosa of the gastrointestinal tract and lungs. Inhalation of alcoholic fluids that have been vaporized by pouring on a hot surface is a rapid means of intoxication occasionally practised in Finland in sauna baths. After drinking alcohol its effects are pronounced within half an hour. The cutaneous vessels become dilated and perspiration is increased; heat loss through the skin is therefore augmented. Initially there may be quickening of respiration; heart rate and blood pressure also increase, partly because of a rise in circulating noradrenaline (norepinephrine). Depression of the vital centres in the nervous system by large quantities of alcohol produces slow breathing and a drop in blood pressure. Alcoholic beverages are hyperosmolar fluids, due to their alcohol content; therefore their ingestion leads to a rise in plasma osmolality (Gill et al., 1982). Alcohol inhibits the release from the posterior pituitary of the antidiuretic hormone (arginine vasopressin) and of oxytocin; suppression of the former contributes to the diuresis that results from drinking alcoholic beverages.

Alcohol produces release of catecholamines from the adrenal medulla. The substance also provokes stimulation of the adrenal cortex, with a rise in serum cortisol levels. Adrenocortical stimulation by alcohol was not found in experiments on animals that had undergone hypophysectomy, nor in two human subjects with pituitary lesions (Jenkins and Connolly, 1968). So the anterior pituitary gland and corticotrophin are presumably involved as mediators in the results of alcohol intake on the adrenal cortex. The anterior lobe of the pituitary is additionally implicated in the elevations of serum prolactin and growth hormone levels that follow alcohol ingestion.

The depressant actions of alcohol on the central nervous system affect first the higher cerebral functions responsible for concern about personal behaviour and for self-restraint. The resultant freedom from anxiety and inhibition produces euphoria and apparent stimulation, with vivacity of speech and action. As drinking progresses, responses to stimuli are slowed and muscle control is impaired; clumsiness, ataxia and nystagmus develop. Decrements of motor function are detectable at a blood-alcohol concentration (BAC) of 50mg/dl; they are more severe at greater concentrations and arise from impairment of many structures, including the cerebellum and cerebellar tracts. Alcohol adversely affects information processing powers, such as the abilities to solve problems or to memorize, and reduces performance in complex reactions like those needed for driving. The oculomotor nuclei are impaired, so that squint and double vision can develop. Very large amounts of alcohol, producing a BAC over 400mg/dl, sedate to the extent of coma; fatalities occur from rapid excess ingestion of alcoholic beverages. The deaths are usually accompanied by BAC levels between 400–500 mg/dl, though survivals have taken place despite remarkably high levels. One survivor possessed a BAC of 1127 mg/dl (Berild and Hasselbach, 1981); Johnson and colleagues (1982) have reported recovery of a female whose serum concentration of alcohol was 1510 mg/dl (serum concentrations of alcohol are 10–15% higher than whole blood levels).

Depression of the central nervous system is accompanied by slowing of the EEG and by an increase in the amplitude of the less rapid waves. Considerable quantities of alcohol induce slow wave spindles, marked theta and delta activity, and finally flattening of the EEG. A single amount of alcohol within the limits of normal drinking promotes, if taken at bedtime, sleep for the first half of the night; the sleep is accompanied by a decrease in those EEG patterns that are associated with rapid eye movement (REM) and dreaming. During the second half of the night rapid eye movement sleep is increased beyond the normal and sleep is broken; there is therefore no net benefit from alcohol in the quantity and quality of sleep. The repeated ingestion of large amounts of alcohol considerably reduces the quantity of time spent in REM sleep; cessation of alcohol is then followed by a marked rebound increase of REM sleep. The effect on REM sleep of regular consumption of high quantities of alcohol should receive interpretation as a feature of physical dependence (Gross et al., 1966; Greenberg and Pearlman, 1967).

Alcohol releases the sexual drive from the restraint of the cerebral cortex but inhibits conduction along the neuronal pathways responsible for sexual function. The result has been described succinctly by Shakespeare in *Macbeth:* 'It provokes the desire, but it takes away the performance'. In addition alcohol metabolism inhibits production by the testis of the male sex hormone testosterone; this is achieved directly through depression of testicular functions (by acetaldehyde or by an altered redox ratio), and indirectly through depression of the hypo- thalamic end of the hypothalamic-pituitary axis responsible for gonadotrophic luteinizing hormone (Cicero, 1982). Small amounts of alcohol are capable of producing neuronal excitation as a direct effect, and not merely through release of some nervous pathways from inhibitory control. In animals the application of alcohol to the cerebral cortex stimulates neurones at low concentrations and suppresses at high concentrations. At a blood alcohol concentration of 20–50mg/dl some aspects of animal behavioural performance are stimulated. For example, at this level of BAC, increases in the frequency and amplitude of the EEG alpha rhythm are observed that are consistent with augmented cerebral activity.

Although alcohol diffuses throughout the brain several regions of the organ are especially susceptible to the substance. They are the cerebral cortex, reticular formation and hippocampus. But a major research difficulty, in the elucidation of the differential effects of alcohol on localities within the brain, is that changes monitored in one area may reflect alterations produced elsewhere in the nervous system by alcohol. In particular there are considerable gaps in knowledge of the effects of alcohol on the cerebellum and its connecting tracts.

At cellular level it is possible that alcohol has important effects on brain function through the intermediary of neuroglial structures, but little is known of the role of neuroglia on neuronal activity, and less about the action of alcohol on glia. Research on the results of alcohol on brain cells has concentrated on neurons. Alcohol does not directly influence energy processes within neurons to an extent that inhibits nerve activity; in common with many other sedatives its significant actions are considered to take place largely in the nerve cell membrane and at the synaptic junction between cells. Alcohol acts against the initiation and con- duction of nerve impulses through a depressant effect on the rate of rise and the amplitude of the action potential; this effect is probably related to alcohol-induced decrease of ion conductance across nerve membrane. The rapid transfer of ions through neural membrane is inhibited, and so the action potential is delayed or prevented. The inhibition of ion conductance may in turn partly arise from the fluidity ('disorder') that alcohol is thought to promote in nerve membrane as an acute chemical and biophysical action (Goldstein, 1981).

Depression of transmission across synapses involves interference with neurotransmitters. Most of the research on the results of alcohol on neurotransmitter substances has been confined to the peripheral turnover of the compounds, though interest is growing that concerns the central actions of alcohol on catecholamines, on serotonin, acetyl- choline and on the inhibitory substance gamma-aminobutyric acid.

Distribution, excretion and metabolism

Alcohol is 30 times more soluble in water than in fat; after absorption it is quickly distributed in water throughout the body. Although small amounts of absorbed alcohol are excreted unchanged in the breath, perspiration and urine, most of the alcohol that enters the blood-stream is metabolized. The rate of elimination of alcohol from the blood varies between and within subjects. The average rate of fall of blood alcohol concentration is about 15mg per dl in an hour. Many factors, such as body weight, the presence of food in the stomach, speed and duration of drinking, and the proportion of alcohol in drinks, affect the blood-alcohol concentration. It is not possible, therefore, to predict accurately legal or behavioural safety to drive from the number of drinks consumed.

Females reach higher BAC levels than males after consuming equal quantities of alcohol (Jones and Jones, 1976); the explanation partly rests in the lower body weight of females, but another aspect is involved. Alcohol is especially soluble in water, while females have proportionately less of their body weight allotted to water than have males. Therefore females possess less body water in which to distribute alcohol than males of the same weight, so more alcohol remains in the female circulation.

The major pathway in the body for the initial biotransformation of alcohol involves the enzyme alcohol dehydrogenase (ADH). The enzyme is concentrated in the liver; only small quantities of it are found in other tissues, notably the brain and testis. Over 90% of absorbed alcohol is metabolized in the liver. The process affords considerable energy; 1 gram of alcohol produces 29·4 joules (7 calories).

In the liver cells the metabolism of alcohol takes place in the cytosol. The process is one of oxidative dehydrogenation; hydrogen is removed from ethyl alcohol to transform the molecule to acetaldehyde, and hydrogen further removed from acetaldehyde to produce acetate. The latter substance is either broken down further or used for the synthesis of a variety of compounds; 50–80% of the acetate derived from alcohol is dealt with outside the liver. The hydrogen ions that are taken away from alcohol and acetaldehyde are passed over to the cofactor nicotinamide adenine dinucleotide (NAD). The process is shown in *Fig.* 1.

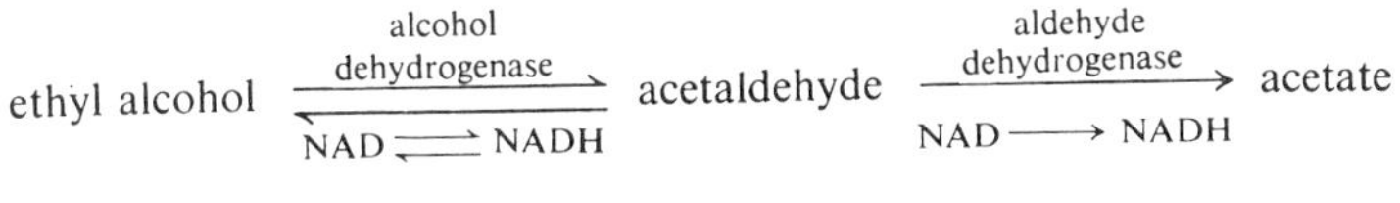

Fig. 1. Metabolism of ethyl alcohol.

The first stage of the process is capable of catalysis in either direction by ADH, but after the absorption of alcohol the initial chemical reaction in the body is always towards the production of acetaldehyde. ADH and aldehyde dehydrogenase occur in more than one allelic form; the variations differ in their potency. ADH is found in many animal species; if it were absent the accidental ingestion of fermented juices could be lethal. ADH also protects against endogenous alcohol, which is present in the blood in small but detectable amounts and is mainly formed by organisms in the gut. There is a surplus of ADH in the liver beyond possible requirements; the rate-limiting step in alcohol degradation is not the amount of the enzyme but the quantity of NAD available for hydrogen acceptance.

NAD is reformed from NADH by the passage of hydrogen from the cytosol of the liver cell onto a series of chemical substrate pairs in the mitochondria. Several coupled substrates (redox pairs) are available that each consist of a reduced and oxidized form; they include malate/oxaloacetate, lactate/pyruvate and β-hydroxybutyrate/acetoacetate. If the system of redox pairs that progressively shuttle hydrogen away from NADH is saturated with hydrogen ions, then the formation of NAD from NADH is blocked, and the metabolism of alcohol is inhibited.

There are two other enzyme systems in the liver that possess lesser roles in the oxidation of alcohol. One route involves the microsomal enzyme oxidizing system (MEOS); the cofactor process for acceptance of hydrogen here employs NADPH, which is the phosphorylated derivative of NADH. A certain amount of induction of MEOS results from repeated alcohol consumption. The remaining route of alcohol metabolism requires catalase as an enzyme and utilizes hydrogen peroxide; the significance, if any, of the catalase system for alcohol biotransformation is unclear.

Suggestions have been made that intoxicated subjects could be sobered by substances that increase the rate of metabolism of alcohol. Pyruvate, and D-glyceraldehyde formed from fructose, are able to accept hydrogen; but as one molecule of either compound is needed for oxidation of one molecule of alcohol impossibly large quantities would be required. Intravenous fructose has been given as an amethystic agent ('amethystos', Greek for 'sober'), but the possible metabolic hazards of large quantities of fructose given rapidly require close investigation before recommending its intravenous use for alcohol intoxication (Heuckenkamp and Zöllner, 1973).

Oxidative dehydrogenation of alcohol alters the ratio of the substrate redox pairs in the direction of the reduced form in each couple. This shift in the redox state of the body has considerable significance. For example, the acute ingestion of a large quantity of alcohol greatly augments the amount of lactate, which is the hydrogenated member of the lactate/pyruvate couple; the resultant hyperlacticacidaemia inhibits the active renal tubular excretion of uric acid. An attack of gouty arthritis can then follow in a patient with hyperuricaemia. This mechanism, together with the high purine content of some alcoholic beverages, has contributed to the reputation of alcohol as a culprit in the causation of gout.

The activity of ADH in the testis is essential for the production of androgen. Repeated depletion of the cofactor NAD because of chronic excessive alcohol consumption could reduce the quantity of testosterone, and help to explain why male alcoholics commonly develop sexual dysfunction (Akhtar, 1977).

In general, the alteration of redox state that is induced during alcohol biotransformation directs metabolic processes from oxidative to reductive pathways. The shift involves the metabolic pathways of monoamine neurotransmitters. Lowered activity of the monoamine neurotransmitter serotonin (5-hydroxytryptamine) is considered to play a role in the production of a depressed mood, and could contribute to the frequent finding of an affect of depression in alcoholics (van Praag, 1982). The effects of alcohol, of acetaldehyde, and of increased concentrations of NADH, on the indoleamine pathways that lead to and from serotonin are complex and await full clarification.

Alcohol metabolism inhibits the oxidation of fatty acids and favours the reductive process of fatty acid synthesis. There are several other ways in which alcohol may increase the amount of fat in the liver: augmented synthesis of triglycerides from free fatty acids, decreased transport of fatty acids out of the liver, and enhanced transport of fatty acids to the liver. The latter effect is promoted by alcohol-induced peripheral release of catecholamines, which leads to adipose tissue lipolysis and to hyperlipaemia.

Saturation with hydrogen of the redox pairs during alcohol metabolism partially blocks the oxidation in the liver of precursors of glucose. Lactate, for instance, is one of the most important substrates of glucose formation; the initial stage of the lactate contribution to gluconeogenesis consists in the transformation of lactate to pyruvate. This first step is checked by alcohol metabolism because the shift in redox state induced during the breakdown of alcohol increases the concentration of lactate at the expense of pyruvate. In addition to a restraint of gluconeogenesis the metabolism of alcohol curtails the conversion of glycogen to glucose. Hypoglycaemia can therefore follow the excess consumption of alcohol, especially in children and poorly nourished subjects.

Paradoxically, alcohol is also able to produce the opposite condition of glucose intolerance or hyperglycaemia (Dornhurst and Duyang, 1971). The effect does not depend on the caloric value of alcohol nor on impaired secretion of insulin. One possible factor is that acetate, which is released from the liver as a breakdown product of alcohol, competes with glucose, particularly in the muscles; the peripheral utilization of glucose and its uptake from the blood are thereby prevented. Another factor may result from the effect of alcohol in promoting the release of cate-cholamines from the adrenal medulla; the increase of circulating adrenaline (epinephrine) induces glycogenolysis and might thereby favour a rise of blood sugar.

Reviews of the effects of alcohol on metabolism have been provided by Badawy and Evans (1974), Forsander (1974), Lieber (1977, 1981) and by Peters (1982).

Tolerance

Some resistance to the effects of alcohol develops with repeated consumption; adaptation to alcohol is not confined to persons who consume excessive quantities but also occurs in social drinkers who take alcohol frequently in moderate amounts. Metabolic tolerance is minimal; some, though not all, studies find that the heavy use of alcohol is associated with an accelerated rate of alcohol elimination from the blood, but the increase of metabolic clearance, when present, is small. Functional tolerance in the nervous system is more evident; the result is that regular users of alcohol ingest moderately large quantities without experiencing or showing intoxication. Because of tolerance alcoholics require to drink considerable quantities before feeling the desired effects; as the rate at which alcohol leaves the blood is only marginally, if at all, enhanced they are liable to arrest, if they drive vehicles, for possessing BACs that are incompatible in nonalcoholics with any significant ability to drive. A BAC above 150mg/dl in the absence of marked intoxication is highly suspicious of alcohol dependence.

In the advanced stages of dependence on alcohol tolerance can drop. Decreased turnover of alcohol should be easy to detect in alcoholics with loss of tolerance but has not been demonstrated. Like enhancement of tolerance, erosion of tolerance is presumably due for the most part to changes in the target sites within the nervous system at which alcohol acts.

The degree of tolerance that is developed to alcohol is not so marked as to opioids; in this, as in many respects, alcohol resembles other nonopioid sedatives. The level of alcohol required for a lethal dose in an alcoholic with tolerance is not as a rule considerably higher than in a nontolerant person.

Acute tolerance to alcohol is found. After ingestion of a single quantity the signs of CNS depression are less evident when the BAC is falling than they were at comparable rising levels of blood alcohol.

Alcohol withdrawal features

Dependence on alcohol (alcoholism) has psychological and physical aspects that are intertwined in its causation. The physical features are not necessarily the most important, and are not always easy to distinguish from the psychological facets, but will be described here, so that later they may be fitted into the general picture of the alcohol dependence syndrome. The organic aspects centre on the withdrawal features of physical dependence that develop when the concentration of alcohol in the body drops below the level necessary to ward off abstinence symptoms and signs. The desire to suppress withdrawal symptoms contributes to further alcohol ingestion as a form of relief drinking.

Tremor is an early feature that commonly develops within a few hours of the last drink. At first it is only present in the fingers and hands, though it may be accompanied by a feeling of internal muscular quivering. A fine tremor can be apparent to the subject on performing a delicate motor task such as carrying a cup and saucer; a slight tremble is demonstrable to an observer if the alcoholic is asked to hold forward outstretched arms and hands. Like many forms of tremor the tremble induced by alcohol withdrawal is aggravated by scrutiny; for example, the subject may be able to write when unobserved but has difficulty in doing so in front of another person. A more marked tremor interferes with shaving and dressing. Gross tremor involves other regions than the hands; at first the tongue and finally the whole of the limbs and trunk are involved in shaking. Another distressing though infrequent neuromuscular aspect of alcohol withdrawal takes the form of spasmodic contractions of voluntary muscles.

Sweating is an acute result of alcohol intake, but is also a withdrawal feature. Alcoholics can notice that their night attire and bed sheets are soaked in perspiration. Anxiety, depression, irritability and restlessness may develop. A sensation as if the stomach were shaking, anorexia, nausea and vomiting are other features of the alcohol abstinence syndrome. Blood pressure and pulse rate are increased while taking alcohol; their elevation continues after cessation of drinking as a sign of the withdrawal phase.

Insomnia is common. When sleep occurs it is accompanied by frequent and vivid dreams. During the periods while falling asleep and waking visual and auditory hallucinations are present. The sleep phenomena are associated with a decrease of the interval between the onset of sleep and the commencement of REM sleep, and with an increase in the quantity of REM sleep; most of the time spent asleep may be accompanied by REM sleep and dreams (Greenberg and Pearlman, 1967). The dreams, and the hallucinations experienced while going to sleep or waking ('hypnagogic' and 'hypnopompic' hallucinations respectively), are heralds of the severe form of the alcohol abstinence syndrome—delirium tremens (DT).

In most cases the features of alcohol withdrawal do not progress to delirium tremens but run a benign course. The symptoms and signs are pronounced by the second day, reach a peak on the third day, and then subside, so that by the end of the first week only minor alterations remain. The majority of subjects do not develop delirium or withdrawal convulsions.

Delirium tremens

Like many descriptive titles for diseases and syndromes the term 'delirium tremens' is evocative and informative. The tremor is gross, generalized and communicated to adjacent structures, so that when the patient is lying down even the bed can shake. Consciousness is clouded; there is disorientation for time and place; attention span is shortened, so that the subject is distracted by external and internal (psychic) events, and is unable to concentrate for long on one topic. It is difficult for an interviewer to retain the patient's interest. Answers are jerky and inadequate; when left undisturbed a restless flow of spontaneous speech can develop that is often concentrated on the patient's usual occupation, which the alcoholic imagines himself to be in the midst of pursuing. Since the preferred occupation may have been drinking the 'occupational delirium' can focus on this activity; the patient in a hospital ward can invite those persons nearby to join in a drink and noisily places orders with a non-existent barman.

Illusions may be present. The illusional misinterpretations of perceived stimuli are frequently of a kind to reassure the patient that familiar surroundings and people are adjacent; so the nurse can be mistaken for a relative, the doctor mistaken for a friend.

Visual hallucinations are common. The images are occasionally of large objects; the patient may be terrified, for example, because a life-size bear is visualized in the corner of the room. In one instance the excessive drinking of a retired colonel who was living in lodgings came to light when his landlady heard a crash from his room; he had hallucinated a realistic dancing girl, reached out of bed to embrace her, and had fallen through the image to break his arm on the floor. More usually the visual hallucinations involve small images; sometimes they are also rapidly moving, and interpreted by the subject as perceptions of small animals or birds. Hence arose in common parlance the synonym of 'the rats' for DT. The images may involve objects which in actuality are large, such as persons, but that in delirium are scaled down to a size of between approximately 10–40 centimetres. Shrunken images of this nature are referred to as 'Lilliputian hallucinations'. The hallucinated images may be vague and lacking in detail, but often they are well-formed and highly coloured. The traditional 'pink elephants' are of course largely an apocryphal feature, but when perceived (presumably because of unconscious mental associations between alcohol withdrawal and their presence) the mammals are Lilliputian in size.

Hallucinations of an auditory nature are also frequent in delirium tremens. Some of the coarse sounds that are heard in DT (cracking, banging, whistling, roaring) might be produced by contractions of the middle ear muscles, tensor tympani and stapedius. The contractions could trigger impulses along the auditory nerve; in this case the noises would not be classed as hallucinations, which are defined as perceptions that develop without stimuli in the appropriate sensory organ. But complex sounds, in the form of voices or often of music, occur in DT; they arise from hallucinatory disturbances of perceptual function within the brain. If the hallucinated sounds accompany visual images then the two kinds of hallucination are commonly synchronized; for example, a group of little musicians may be seen and heard, with their actions keeping time with the music.

Delusions, when they are present, are paranoid in type; in part they can be understood as attempts by the patient to account for the delirious phenomena, in part they arise within a mood setting of fear and they aggravate the subject's terror. For instance, experiences involving flashes of light and high pitched noises are interpreted by the alcoholic as flames and the shrieks of family members that arise from a torture chamber; in the delirium it is imagined that the torturers will soon apprehend the patient.

The predominant affect is anxiety, progressing to fear. Suspicion, and anger, are often present. Interspersed with these unpleasant moods are periods of alcoholic euphoria. Marked restlessness may develop.

DT is more pronounced at night. During night time the lack of normal stimuli that is induced by restriction of human contact and by diminution of light and sound aggravates all delirious states. In treatment, therefore, circumstances that favour sensory deprivation are best avoided.

The onset of DT is usually during the second 24 hours of alcohol withdrawal, as an exaggeration of less pronounced abstinence features. Physically the condition promotes dehydration and deficiency of sodium, potassium and magnesium. In severe forms hyperthermia, cardiovascular collapse and death may ensue, especially in patients who are already in poor health, as from malnourishment, pneumonia or heart disease. Fortunately the usual course of the delirium is towards recovery within 5–7 days from cessation of alcohol. Mild degrees are common in which the patient is delirious for just 1 or 2 nights, yet by day retains clear consciousness and is quietly rational.

On rare occasions alcohol withdrawal can induce a subacute delirious state. The onset is delayed until 1–2 weeks after ceasing alcohol, when the course is rather milder and more prolonged than in the classic form of DT.

Eugen Bleuler, who has been one of the most outstanding descriptive psychiatrists of the twentieth century, considered that delirium tremens had some characteristic features that distinguished it from other deliria (Bleuler, 1916). He stressed the suggestibility of the patient, who can easily be persuaded to develop illusions, hallucinations and false ideas. The subject may, for instance, be encouraged to read from a blank sheet of paper; Bleuler cited a group of delirious alcoholic inpatients who hallucinated a fish that they imagined to slip in their grasp from one to another. The visual hallucinations, Bleuler noted, are often long and slender: they commonly take the form of flashes of light, or less transient visions of objects extended in one dimension. It is, for instance, not uncommon for a patient with DT to see lengthy hairs growing from his skin. Bleuler also taught that musical hallucinations, and the intercalation of euphoria with unpleasant moods, are frequent in delirium tremens but are rare in other forms of delirium. It would be interesting to compare a schedule of symptoms and signs among subjects who had delirium from varied causes in order to ascertain whether certain aspects are more commonly encountered in DT.

A withdrawal convulsion of the grand mal type is another sequel of the sudden cessation of excessive alcohol consumption. In severe but rare instances a series of fits can develop, progressing to status epilepticus, in which each convulsion is rapidly succeeded by another without an interval of restoration of consciousness. The most usual timing for an alcohol withdrawal fit is between 30 and 40 hours after ceasing alcohol, but a convulsion can be delayed from 5–7 days. The technique of nuclear magnetic resonance has revealed a decrease of free water in the brain during intoxication and an increase during alcohol withdrawal; the changes are found in both grey and white matter but are especially pronounced in the frontal grey matter (Besson et al., 1981). The alterations are inconsistent with the general view that the abstinence syndrome involves dehydration, but are in accord with the depressant effect of alcohol on vasopressin secretion. The hydration of the brain after alcohol cessation could contribute to withdrawal seizures.

Attempts have been made to group into categories the aspects of the alcohol abstinence syndrome. Gross and coworkers (1971, 1972) employed cluster analysis and described three groups of features. The first, which accounted for 27% of the variance, comprised tinnitus, hallucinations (tactile, auditory and visual), pruritus, paraesthesiae, muscle pains and agitation. The second category, forming 19% of the variance, consisted of sweating, tremor, anxiety and depression; it was attributed by the researchers to dysfunction in the limbic system and midbrain. The third cluster, which amounted to 20% of the variance and was considered to arise from the brain stem, involved clouding of consciousness, impaired gait and nystagmus.

Hershon (1977) proposed two categories of abstinence features. The first, and more common, consisted of affective characteristics: anxiety, restlessness, panic, guilt, depression, tiredness, and the idea that people are against the subject. The second group comprised the physical symptoms of nausea, vomiting, sweating, tremors, palpitations, tinnitus, hyperacusis, and auditory and visual hallucinations.

The plasma levels of noradrenaline (norepinephrine), and the urinary levels of noradrenaline, adrenaline (epinephrine) and their metabolites, have been noted to rise during alcohol withdrawal (Giacobini et al., 1960; Carlsson and Haggerdal, 1967; Ogata et al., 1971). The release of catecholamines is largely nonspecific and attributable to the sympathetic overactivity, anxiety and muscular work that cessation of alcohol provokes, but withdrawal may also exert a more specific effect on catecholamine production and release, both peripherally and within the central nervous system. The elevated catecholamine levels return to normal as the withdrawal syndrome subsides. Urinary excretion of magnesium is also increased, leading to hypomagnesaemia in the initial few days of alcohol withdrawal. During the first two days of alcohol cessation there is a 20% drop in cerebral blood flow (Berglund and Risberg, 1977).

The abstinence syndrome from alcohol deprivation is similar to that arising from withdrawal of the other central nervous system depressants that are not morphine-like in their actions. Cross-dependence occurs between individual members, including alcohol, of the nonopioid or general class of sedatives; that is, the administration of suitable quantities of one substance in this category suppresses the features consequent on stopping the prolonged excess consumption of another substance in the group. Cross-dependence permits the treatment of alcohol withdrawal by another sedative which is then gradually withdrawn; historically paraldehyde and barbiturates were employed for such a purpose; more recently chlormethiazole, and at present the benzodiazepines, are so favoured.

THE ALCOHOL DEPENDENCE SYNDROME (ALCOHOLISM)

Introduction

The concept of the alcohol dependence syndrome (ADS) was formulated by a WHO group of investigators (Edwards et al., 1977). They employed the term 'syndrome' to imply that a number of phenomena are found together often enough to comprise a recognizable group of features. The features of the alcohol dependence syndrome involve behavioural, subjective and psychobiological changes, with impaired control over alcohol intake as a leading aspect. The alterations in behaviour centre on the drinking activities of the individual, which become less responsive to social pressures or painful consequences and progressively more stereotyped or inflexible in repertoire. The subjective changes consist of the individual's awareness of impairment of control over drinking, together with craving for and preoccupation with alcohol. Alterations in the psychobiological sphere comprise withdrawal symptoms and signs, drinking for relief of withdrawal, and a high degree of tolerance of alcohol.

Conceptually ADS indicates the similarities between alcohol dependence and dependence on other drugs. It denotes a condition in which there are degrees of severity, which is modified by personal and cultural factors, which can be checked (by abstinence or by gaining the ability to control drinking at a moderate level), but which if unchecked is likely to produce an aggregation of alcohol-induced difficulties.

The WHO investigators used the phrase 'alcohol-related disability' to denote an impairment of the physical, mental or social functioning of an individual such that it is reasonable to deduce that alcohol played a part in its causation. The investigators pointed out that it is often difficult or valueless to attempt a precise formation of the role of drinking in the production of the disability. They added that alcohol can contribute to disabilities (e.g. accidents or suicide) in the absence of alcohol dependence; that is, some alcohol-related disabilities are not alcohol-dependence-related.

The adjectival phrase 'alcohol-related has therefore the advantage of drawing attention to a wider range of conditions than those produced by dependent drinking, but the title has a flaw. When two features are described as 'related' the term does not necessarily infer that one feature contributed to cause the other; it can also imply that both features are found together because of a common third factor. A relevant example is lung cancer, which is a disability that is related to alcohol consumption, but only because heavy smokers tend to drink heavily. People who encounter or use the phrase 'alcohol-related disability' may possibly take it to include a condition associated with alcohol because of a joint factor, unless they are aware of the causal role for alcohol that the term is intended to convey; not all persons are so aware.

The term 'acute alcoholism' is a grandiloquent title for drunkenness produced by alcohol. The label conveys the incorrect impression that intoxication and what is generally regarded as alcoholism have much in common. The phrase has justly fallen into disuse.

Because of the difficulties that have arisen over its definition the word 'alcoholism' will also come to be employed less frequently, but as its connotations retain a core of widely understood significance it is sometimes used in this book to refer to chronic alcoholism, to the syndrome of dependence on alcohol. In 1952 the World Health Organisation defined the alcoholic as follows:

'Alcoholics are those excessive drinkers whose dependence on alcohol has reached such a degree that they show a noticeable mental disturbance or an interference with their mental and bodily health, their interpersonal relations and their smooth social and economic functioning, or who show the prodromol signs of such developments.

'They therefore require treatment.' (World Health Organisation, 1952).

The final sentence was an addendum to the main body of the definition which WHO had provided in the previous year. In addition to mental and physical complications, social factors such as community attitudes to heavy drinking, play a part in determining whether an individual's alcohol intake is affecting relationships with others and is impairing occupational standing.

A comparable description, again focusing on the consequences of drinking, has been formulated by Keller (1960): 'Alcoholism is a chronic disease manifested by repeated implicative (suspicion arousing) drinking so as to cause injury to the drinker's health or to his social or economic functioning.'

One other definition should receive mention for its brevity and neatness: 'Alcoholism is the intermittent or continual ingestion of alcohol leading to dependence or harm.' (Davies, 1974.)

There has been a surfeit of definitions of alcoholism and of the alcoholic. The definition of alcoholism came under debate partly because of challenges offered to the disease concept of alcoholism. Robinson (1972) has summarized the objections to the sickness label, and particularly emphasized that its use could lead alcoholics to negate their sense of responsibility. The same author has also listed numerous nonmedical aspects of alcoholism (Robinson, 1973). Features that are not medical include sociological, legal, interpersonal and spiritual facets, each of which has been claimed as the essential feature of the condition. Hershon (1973) did not consider that a learned pattern of excess drinking constitutes a disease, even when the alcoholic has learned to drink in order to forestall the withdrawal symptoms of physical dependence (Hershon, 1974). Pattison (1969) affirmed that the disease label is applied for the purpose of attracting sympathy and caring resources towards alcoholics; this aim is not in accord with the usual canons of nosology.

An understanding of the philosophical ideas appertaining to definition can help to resolve the issues concerning the disease nature of alcohol dependence. There are two kinds of definition. The first, an essentialist definition, poses a fundamental nature or essence for the defined condition that makes the entity different in essence from all other conditions. The alternative approach employs a nominalist definition, which is simply a working label for a designated group of phenomena.

The essentialist type of definition postulates a profound statement that requires testing, yet assertions about essence are not susceptible to the scientific procedure of a hypothetico-deductive experiment. It is not feasible to assess experimentally the accuracy of a proposition about the essential nature of alcohol dependence, or of disease, or of any concept. A nominalist definition does not require testing since its only function is to provide a shorthand title for a cluster of features. The label can be altered, or applied to a different cluster, if the change is considered useful. Changes in nominalist definitions tend to arise in the course of time because of modifications in the use of words and in the ideas denoted by words. Alteration of a nominalist definition is quite acceptable, provided that the change is widely appreciated.

Using the nominalist approach to definition alcohol dependence can be defined as an illness becaue it has features in common with other conditions labelled as diseases. The shared attributes include impaired physical and mental functioning, weakened self-control over some aspects of behaviour, structural alterations to the body (in certain alcoholics), and decreased life expectancy. At the same time alcohol dependence can be grouped with nonmedical conditions with which it also has shared features. Statements should not be issued to the effect that dependence on alcohol is essentially or exclusively a disease, or not a disease (Madden, 1976). The qualities and implications of the condition range beyond the medical model.

Another difficulty in defining alcoholism as such arises through the rigours of its delimitation from 'problem drinking'. It has been proposed that the latter term should be eliminated, and problem drinking subsumed under the alcoholism label (Davies, 1974). In contrast, Hore (1974), noting that some people with alcohol problems baulked at the connotations of 'alcoholism', argued for dropping the alcoholism term. The distinctions have been largely verbal, arising from the superficial issue of which features should be denoted by which label, yet it it easy to understand why some individuals with early alcohol dependence reject the alcoholism title. Their excess drinking may be confined, for example, to weekends, and have adverse effects on their home lives but show little detriment to other areas of adjustment; it does not follow that their drinking, even if it augments, will bring them within the popular, albeit incorrect, notion of an alcoholic as a person who leads a Skid Row existence or drinks crude spirits. Yet despite the objections to both terms, 'problem drinking' and particularly 'alcoholism' are titles that will not fall out of use in the immediate future; both terms are encountered in many of the classic descriptive and research writings, and must perforce receive employment in this volume. For purposes of simplicity and clarity the two titles are here viewed as synonymous and interchangeable with each other and with alcohol dependence. 'Alcohol misuse' is employed, notwithstanding its unhappily pejorative ring, because it is a widely used term, not necessarily implying dependence, that denotes the excessive consumption of alcohol on one or more occasions.

The phrase 'alcoholic drinking' is often applied to the high alcohol consumption of alcoholics. The term has the disadvantage that it is applicable to all forms of alcohol ingestion, including the normal drinking of nonalcoholics. Among the many felicitous neologisms coined by Mark Keller is the adjective 'alcoholismic', which denotes abnormal drinking by alcoholics. 'Alcoholologist' is a cumbersome title for a person professionally interested in alcoholism; Walker (1976) has proposed 'ethanologist' as an alternative that is more euphonious and more easily pronounced.

Development and course of alcohol dependence

The early drinking of an incipient problem drinker is, in some subjects, no different from that of his or her peers. This statement is perhaps especially applicable to middle-aged females who, after a decade or two of infrequent and moderate drinking, develop the dependence syndrome in response to a single, severe psychological stress. Yet commonly the drinking of a future dependent drinker is dissimilar to the alcohol consumption of companions. Alcoholics, compared with nonalcoholics, are more likely to have their first drink at a slightly later age, and to remember it more vividly (Jones, 1963); at an early stage in their drinking career alcoholics tend to show a greater avidity for alcohol than their colleagues. As tolerance develops they drink more rapidly than their companions, sneak drinks during drinking parties, stay late at drinking sessions, and take alcohol before and after social drinking. Relief drinking occurs to counteract tension, depression or other disagreeable moods. Increased time, money and mental preoccupation are spent on alcohol. Guilt feelings develop over drinking; interpersonal relations are strained. The drinker takes more than intended on an increasing number of drinking occasions; the impaired control over alcohol intake promotes either drunkenness, or the extension of drinking over the greater part of the day without necessarily marked intoxication. Memory blackouts become common; in regard to alcoholism the term 'blackout' has a precise meaning, and refers to the subsequent inability to recall behaviour while drinking. Only traces of the past events remain in the mind (hence the title 'palimpsest' as an alternative label for the partial amnesia); yet on enquiry the excessive drinker may find that the forgotten behaviour did not suggest drunkenness to observers.

The amount of ingested alcohol is minimized to others and, by self-deceit, to the alcoholic. Excuses are made for drinking; other people, and circumstances, are blamed for the difficulties that arise from excess alcohol intake. Because of the abstinence symptoms of physical dependence the individual is compelled to drink from a progressively earlier time in the day. A 'liquid lunch' can become usual. Problem drinkers from a social background that is rarely associated with the presence of drink in the house may never take alcohol home, but have a morning drink as early as they can in licensed premises. Other subjects replace breakfast by alcohol at home; because of alcoholic gastritis they may vomit the first one or two drinks, but withdrawal symptoms compel them to continue until enough alcohol is retained and absorbed to suppress the abstinence features. Sleep may be broken by withdrawal features, so that alcohol is consumed in the middle of the night.

There is increasing friction at home, with arguments and sometimes violence. The violence does not always emanate from the excessive drinker. Sober husbands, who in other respects are peaceful and law abiding, can beat their drunken wives. Threats of separation or divorce are followed by short or lengthy periods of actual separation. Legal separation and divorce are common outcomes.

Working capacity suffers. At first the effects on work are confined to hangovers which reduce competence. Then absenteeism occurs, particularly on Monday mornings. There are failures to return from lunch, and longer periods of absence develop that may be covered by sick notes for vague respiratory, gastrointestinal or neurotic complaints. When at work the subject is temperamental, and shows changes of mood and loquacity after lunch. Work output is uneven; periods of low productivity are compensated by phases of increased activity when sober. Dismissal occurs, or the problem drinker is selected first for redundancy; commonly the individual anticipates these measures by resigning. Re-employment then takes place at a lower level of responsibility and income.

A conviction for drinking and driving may occur. Blood-alcohol concentrations over 50mg/dl are associated with significant impairment of driving skills and with an increased liability to accidents. Glatt (1964) has described how alcoholics frequently drive after heavy drinking. Another study of 100 dependent drinkers, found that the subjects had sustained 61 prosecutions for driving offences, of which 28 (45·9%) involved drunken driving; the alcoholics had incurred 4 times as many driving prosecutions and twice as many accidents as a control group of drivers (Clare and Cooney, 1973). Although legislation related to drinking and driving varies widely between countries (Nelker, 1975), the proneness of alcoholics to convictions for driving after drinking is present from an early stage in their dependence. Compared with nonalcoholics, dependent drinkers are especially liable to convictions for driving with high levels of blood level (approaching 200 mg/dl or over), or to incur repeated convictions for drinking and driving. Sometimes, but far from invariably, prosecution for this kind of offence jolts the alcoholic into effective curtailment of the alcohol intake.

Continued alcohol intake, despite adverse effects on interpersonal relationships, occupation and law involvement, points to dysfunctional drinking and to a high priority allotted to alcohol consumption over other activities. It indicates a subjective experience of compulsion to take alcohol, and a pattern of consumption that is rigidly excessive. Tolerance and withdrawal features demonstrate that neuroadaptation has taken place in response to repeated high quantities of alcohol. There is often a desire to cease alcohol intake although drinking may continue. If a phase of abstinence is interrupted by further drinking, there is usually a rapid reinstatement of the dependence syndrome. In these respects ADS exhibits the cardinal features of dependence described by a 1981 WHO report (WHO Memorandum, 1981; Commentaries, 1982).

Some alcoholics confine their beverage to beer, but frequently stronger preparations (spirits, wines or fortified wines) predominate in the drinking of alcoholic subjects. A small percentage take to crude spirits. A minority move to cheap lodging houses in decayed urban areas. These areas, known as 'Skid Row', received their title from Skid Road in Seattle, which was a thoroughfare along which logs were skidded to the river and which was lined by inexpensive apartments and bars.

Among alcoholics concomitant dependence on cigarettes is the rule. Studies of the proportion who consume drugs other than alcohol or tobacco have been reviewed by Freed (1973); he concluded that about 20% of persons dependent on alcohol or drugs abused both kinds of substance. But experience points to a lower proportion of drug usage among problem drinkers in Britain. This has been confirmed by Edwards et al. (1974), who investigated dependent drinkers in England; in their study only 3·4% of the male and 3·9% of the female subjects had misused drugs.

The toxic effects of prolonged excess ingestion of alcohol are compounded by defective nutrition. There are several elements contributory to malnutrition. Money is diverted from food to purchase alcoholic beverages; gastritis provoked by alcohol curtails appetite; absorption from the small intestine is impaired; alcohol and other carbohydrates in alcoholic drinks provide calories though not adequate amounts of necessary foodstuffs, especially vitamins.

Reduced tolerance may develop; the alcoholic becomes drunk on amounts of alcohol which formerly had little intoxicating effect. Depression of mood is frequent. Suicidal attempts occur; suicide is a not uncommon termination. Because of acts of self-harm, or because of delirium tremens or other physical or psychological disabilities, admission to hospital may be needed, sometimes repeatedly.

The age of onset of alcohol dependence, and the speed at which it develops, vary between individuals, But typically in a male, several years of heavy drinking while aged between twenty to thirty pass over gradually to definite dependence in the early thirties and to receiving treatment when between the ages of approximately 35–45. In women the classic picture has been for heavy drinking to start in early middle age and to deteriorate into dependence within 6–18 months. The frequent occurrence of alcoholism in middle-aged women has been attributed, on poor evidence, to the menopause or to menopausal depression. In recent years, because of increased drinking by young people and by females two new features have developed: a rise in the number of young problem drinkers encountered in their twenties (not in their teens though the subjects began regular drinking as adolescents), and an increased proportion of female subjects, often also aged between 20–30 years.

A full progression of ADS is not inevitable. Most alcoholics do not transfer to a Skid Row habitation. Many, although drinking abnormally in short or long phases, avoid gross social disorganization and maintain a reasonable level of affective relationships and income. Others correct their excessive consumption, usually to abstinence but in some instances to moderation, and so arrest the pathway of progression.

In the development of alcohol dependence some of the specific features are missed by individual alcoholics, although there is a definite sequence detectable across personal and cultural differences. A comparison of the age of onset and frequency of occurrence of 47 features of alcoholism was conducted on Finnish and English subjects (Park, 1962). The results showed high coefficients of correlation between the two national groups, with considerable uniformity in the subjects despite the postulated occurrence of subtypes of alcoholism. The early items of dependence were more comparable between the two groups than the later items; the Finns became alcoholic more quickly than the English. A later comparison of problem drinkers in Finland and the U.S.A. revealed that although there were some cultural disparities the significant experiences of the subjects unfolded in a similar manner in both groups (Park and Whitehead, 1973). An analysis in England of the features developed by chronic alcohol misusers has also shown a sequence of events, which was especially apparent when the symptoms and signs were assembled into three compartments; in order of temporal development the compartments were psychological dependence, physical dependence and amnesia, and alcoholic psychosis (Orford and Hawker, 1974).

In their exposition, which showed remarkable insight, of the clinical picture of alcohol dependence Edwards and Gross (1976) affirmed that mild degrees of dependence can regress, so that the subject reverts to normal drinking. The writers pointed out that an anomalous presentation may result from associated drug consumption or from an underlying affective disorder or phobic state. Their description stressed that severe alcohol dependence produces an internally consistent collection of symptoms and signs, and that if some of the expected features are missing then the history has been sketchy or the alcoholic has been less than frank.

It must be emphasized that alcohol dependence is sometimes reversible, particularly in its early stages which are not far removed from drinking practices that are socially acceptable. Complete reversal implies that drinking has become moderate; partial reversal denotes a reduction in the level or frequency of excess drinking although intake remains at times dysfunctional or harmful. There is a continuum in the population which ranges from the infrequent use of alcohol through more regular intake to repeated excessive drinking despite adverse consequences. People can move in either direction, although the more advanced stages tend, not merely to irreversibility, but if drinking continues to further progression. Therefore remission or arrest of the moderate and severe degrees of dependence requires abstinence.

Jellinek's patterns of alcoholism

Five patterns of excessive drinking were proposed by the former doyen of alcoholism studies, E. M. Jellinek, and described by him in his book *The Disease Concept of Alcoholism* (Jellinek, 1960). He employed a broad concept of alcoholism, defining it as 'any use of alcoholic beverages that causes any damage to the individual or society or both'. Jellinek utilized Greek alphabet letters as neutral titles for the patterns because the letters are devoid of connotations.

Alpha alcoholism consists of a psychological dependence on alcohol. 'Undisciplined drinking' is a phrase also used to describe the condition. An individual with alpha alcoholism can proceed to develop physical dependence and the other features of gamma alcoholism.

Beta alcoholism represents socially determined heavy drinking with physical sequelae. Jellinek considered that the phenomenon is most common in wine drinking countries. Often it is associated with malnutrition. According to Jellinek neither psychological nor physical dependence are present.

Gamma alcoholism consists of drinking to the extent of drunkenness in phases that last for days, weeks or months. Physical dependence is present, shown by withdrawal symptoms when alcohol intake is curtailed. In between bouts of excessive drinking the gamma alcoholic either abstains or drinks in a controlled manner. The condition is said to show 'loss of control' in the sense that once the subject takes a drink the craving for alcohol may be evoked and the drinking continues to intoxication. In this context Jellinek referred to the warning that is often cited by Alcoholics Anonymous: 'One drink is too many and twenty are not enough.'

Delta alcoholism is characterized by a high volume of consumption throughout each day, although there is retention of the ability to avoid frequent outright drunkenness. Neuroadaption is pronounced. There is marked functional tolerance, while the withdrawal features of physical dependence help to explain the drinker's inability to abstain, even for a day.

The final variant proposed by Jellinek is *epsilon alcoholism*. Formerly known as 'dipsomania', the pattern consists of infrequent short-lived phases of drunkenness, with lengthy periods of abstinence between recurrences. It must be distinguished from brief relapses into excessive drinking by gamma or delta alcoholics who are seeking abstinence and who are able to cut short their occasional spells of drinking.

Many ethanologists consider the Jellinek definition of alcoholism is too wide in its range of application, but it should be noted that he attached the disease concept only to the gamma and delta patterns, in which physical dependence occurs. The existence of beta alcoholism is suspect; it must be doubted if individuals could drink over a long term to the extent of physical complications if they were not both psychologically and physically dependent on alcohol. Epsilon alcoholism could be viewed as a form of gamma alcoholism; it is likely that there is a continuum between the two extremes, with the distribution in frequency and duration of drinking episodes making the distinction between epsilon and gamma alcoholism arbitrary and artificial.

The main contributions of the Jellinek classification consist in the description of undisciplined drinking (alpha alcoholism) and particularly in the delimitation of the gamma and delta patterns. The gamma type is the variety made familiar by Alcoholics Anonymous and attributed by Jellinek to spirit drinking cultures. Delta alcoholism is common in areas of viticulture, where it is usual to take wine on several occasions in a day, every day; in France the condition is known as *l'alcoolisme sans ivresse*.

Several studies from the United Kingdom have indicated that continuous drinking is not uncommon among dependent drinkers in Britain (Madden and Jones, 1972). The delta pattern is more frequent in males than in females; it is especially common among alcoholic subjects who have backgrounds, such as the licensed trade, that are associated with the regular intake of alcohol, and among males from professional or managerial occupations. Social factors can account for the differential distribution noted between British subjects for continuous and bout patterns of drinking. Female problem drinkers usually restrict their excess drinking to the home, where social pressures to avert intoxication are minimal; they are therefore more readily able than males to develop the marked drunkenness of bout drinking rather than the partial intoxication of continuous drinking. Similarly, males who occupy positions of considerable responsibility or prestige respond, if they become alcoholic, to their obligation to avoid obvious drunkenness by a tendency to develop the continuous rather than the bout pattern of excessive consumption.

Loss of control over alcohol intake or intoxication may not occur on every occasion that an alcoholic drinks; the reduced control may only manifest itself after a period of gradual progression from a controlled level of drinking, or when the stimuli that trigger excess consumption are present in sufficient strength. The stimuli can be internal (as from emotions or from a requisite level of alcohol in the body) or external from perceptual cues; several kinds of stimuli may combine to precipitate a phase of excessive drinking (Glatt, 1967, 1976; Keller, 1972, 1977).

It is therefore preferable to refer to 'impairment', rather than to 'loss', of control over drinking. Impairment indicates that the reduction in control may be intermittent and reversible. Impairment of control over alcohol intake (though not necessarily over the degree of intoxication) is by implication present in all forms of repeated drinking that involve dependence or harm.

REFERENCES

Akhtar M. J. (1977) Sexual disorders in male alcoholics. In: Madden J. S., Walker R. and Kenyon W. H. (ed.), *Alcoholism and Drug Dependence: A Multidisciplinary Approach.* New York and London, Plenum, pp. 3–13.

Badawy A. A. and Evans M. (1974) Alcohol and tryptophan metabolism—a review. *J. Alcoholism* 9, 97–116.

Berglund M. and Risberg J. (1977) Regional blood flow during alcohol withdrawal related to consumption and clinical symptomatology. *Acta. Neurol. Scand.* Suppl. 64, 56, 480–481.

Berild D. and Hasselbach H. (1981) Survival after a blood alcohol of 1127 mg/dl. (Letter). *Lancet* ii, 363.

Besson J. A. O., Glen A. I. M., Foreman E. I. et al. (1981) Nuclear magnetic resonance observations in alcoholic cerebral disorder and the role of vasopressin (1981) *Lancet* (Letter) i, 923–924.

Bleuler E. P. (1916) *Textbook of Psychiatry.* Trans. A. A. Brill, 1924; reprinted 1951. New York, Dover Publications, pp. 326–341.

Carlsson C. and Haggendal J. (1967) Arterial noradrenaline levels after ethanol withdrawal (Letter). *Lancet* ii, 889.

Cicero T. J. (1982) Alcohol-induced deficits in the hypothalamic-pituitary-luteinizing hormone axis in the male. *Alcoholism (NY)* 6, 207–215.

Clare A. W. and Cooney J. G. (1973) Alcoholism and road accidents. *J. Ir. Med. Assoc.* 66, 281–286.

Commentaries (1982) Nomenclature and classification of drug- and alcohol-related problems: a shortened version of a WHO memorandum. *Br. J. Addict.* 77, 3–20.

Davies D. L. (1974) Implications for medical practice of an acceptable concept of alcoholism. In: Kessel N., Hawker A. and Chalke H. (ed.), *Alcoholism: A Medical Profile. Proceedings of the First International Medical Conference on Alcoholism.* London, Edsall, pp. 13–19.

Diethelm O. (1965) Chronic alcoholism of Northern Europe (a historical study). *Akt. Fragen Psychiat. Neurol.* 2, 29–39.

Dornhurst A. and Ouyang A. (1971) Effect of alcohol on glucose tolerance. *Lancet* ii, 957–959.

Edwards G. and Gross M. (1976) Alcohol dependence: provisional description of a clinical syndrome. *Br. Med. J.* 1, 1058–1061.

Edwards G., Gross M. M., Keller M. et al. (1977) *Alcohol-related Disabilities.* WHO Offset Publication No. 32.

Edwards G., Kyle E. and Nicholls P. (1974) Alcoholics admitted to four hospitals in England. I. Social class and the interaction of alcoholics with the treatment system. *Q. J. Stud. Alcohol* 35, 499–527.

Forsander O. A. (1974) Biochemical problems in alcohol studies. *Das Medizinische Prisma.* 3. Ingelheim am Rhein, Boehringer.

Freed E. X. (1973) Drug abuse by alcoholics: a review. *Int. J. Addict.* 8, 451–473.

Giacobini E., Izikowitz S. and Wegmann A. (1960) Urinary epinephrine and norepinephrine excretion in delirium tremens. *Arch. Gen. Psychiatry* 3, 289–296.

Gill G. V., Baylis P. H., Flear C. T. G. et al. (1982) Acute biochemical responses to moderate beer drinking. *Br. Med. J.* 285, 1770–1773.

Glatt M. M. (1964) Alcoholism in 'impaired' and drunken driving. *Lancet* i, 161–163.

Glatt M. M. (1967) The question of moderate drinking despite 'loss of control'. *Br. J. Addict.* 62, 267–274.

Glatt M. M. (1976) Alcoholism disease concept and loss of control revisited. *Br. J. Addict.* 71, 135–1444.

Goldstein D. B. and Chin J. H. (1981) Disordering effect of ethanol at different depths in the bilayer of mouse brain membranes. *Alcoholism (NY)* 5, 256–258.

Greenberg R. and Pearlman C. (1967) Delirium tremens and dreaming. *Am. J. Psychiatry* **124**, 133–142.

Gross M. M., Goodenough D., Tobin M. et al. (1966) Sleep disturbance and hallucinations in the acute alcoholic psychoses. *J. Nerv. Ment. Dis.* **142**, 493–514.

Gross M. M., Rosenblatt S. M., Chartoff S. et al. (1971) Evaluation of acute alcoholic psychoses and related states; the daily clinical course rating scale. *Q. J. Stud. Alc.* **32**, 611–619.

Gross M. M., Rosenblatt S. M., Lewis E. et al. (1972) Acute alcoholic psychoses and related syndromes; psychosocial and clinical characteristics and the implications. *Br. J. Addict.* **67**, 15–31.

Hershon H. I. (1973) Alcoholism, physical dependence and disease; comment on 'The alcohologist's addiction'. *Q. J. Stud. Alcohol* **34**, 506–508.

Heuckenkamp P.-U. and Zöllner N. (1973) Fructose, alcohol and lactacidaemia. (Letters.) *Lancet* **i**, 314.

Hore B. D. (1974) Do we need the term—'Alcoholism'? *J. Alcohol.* **9**, 69.

Jellinek E. M. (1960) *The Disease Concept of Alcoholism*, Section III, 1.2. New Haven, Hillhouse, pp. 35–41.

Jenkins J. S. and Connolly J. (1968) Adrenocortical response to ethanol in man. *Br. Med. J.* **2**, 804–805.

Johnson R. A., Noll E. C. and Rodney W. M. (1982) Survival after a serum ethanol concentration of 1½%. (Letter). *Lancet* **ii**, 1394.

Jones B. M. and Jones M. K. (1976) Alcohol effects in women during the menstrual cycle. *Ann. NY Acad. Sci.* **273**, 567–587.

Keller M. (1960) Definition of alcoholism. *Q. J. Stud. Alcohol* **21**, 125–134.

Keller M. (1972) On the loss of control phenomenon in alcoholism. *Br. J. Addict.* **67**, 153–166.

Keller M. (1977) A lexicon of disablements related to alcohol consumption. In: Edwards G., Gross M. M., Keller M., Moser J. and Room R. (ed.) *Alcohol-related Disabilities.* WHO Offset Publication No. 32, pp. 23–60.

Lieber C. S. (1977) Metabolism of ethanol. In: Lieber C. S. (ed.), *Metabolic Aspects of Alcoholism.* Lancaster, MTP Press, pp. 1–29.

Lieber C. S. (1981) Metabolic effects of ethanol on the liver and other digestive organs. In: Leevy C. M. (ed.), *Clinics in Gastroenterology.* London and Philadelphia, W. B. Saunders, pp. 315–342.

Madden J. S. (1976) On defining alcoholism. *Br. J. Addict.* **71**, 145–148.

Madden J. S. and Jones D. (1972) Bout and continuous drinking in alcoholism. *Br. J. Addict.* **67**, 245–250.

Nelker G. (1975) Prevention of alcohol through control of the total consumption. In: *Proceedings of the 31st International Conference on Alcoholism and Drug Dependence.* Lausanne, International Council on Alcohol and Addictions, pp. 90–97.

Noble E. P., Alkana R. L. and Parker E. S. (1974) Ethanol-induced CNS depression and its reversal: a review. In: Chafetz M. E. (ed.), *Proceedings of the Fourth Annual Alcoholism Conference of the National Institute on Alcohol Abuse and Alcoholism.* Rockville, Maryland, NIAAA, pp. 134–170.

Ogata M., Mendelson J. H., Mello N. K. et al. (1971) Adrenal function and alcoholism. II, Catecholamines. *Psychosom. Med.* **33**, 159–180.

Orford J. and Hawker A. (1974) Note on the ordering of symptoms in alcohol dependence. *Psychol. Med.* **4**, 281–288.

Park P. (1962) Drinking experiences of 806 Finnish alcoholics in comparison with similar experiences of 192 English alcoholics. *Acta Psychiatr. Scand.* **38**, 227–246.

Park P. and Whitehead P. C. (1973) Development, sequence and dimensions of alcoholism. *Q. J. Stud. Alcohol* **34**, 887–904.

Pattison E. M. (1969) Comment on 'The alcoholic game'. *Q. J. Stud. Alcohol* **30**, 953–956.

Peters T. J. (1982) Ethanol metabolism. *Br. Med. Bull.* **38**, 17–20.

van Praag H. M. (1982) Neurotransmitters and CNS disease: depression. *Lancet* **ii,** 1259–1264.

Robinson D. (1972) The alcohologist's addiction; some implications of having lost control over the disease concept of alcoholism. *Q. J. Stud. Alcohol* **33,** 1028–1042.

Robinson D. (1973) Alcoholism as a social fact: notes on the sociologist's viewpoint in relation to a proposed study of referral behaviour. *Br. J. Addict.* **68,** 91–97.

Walker R. (1976) Personal communication.

World Health Organisation (1952) Alcoholism Subcommittee Second Report. *Tech. Rep. Ser.* No. 48.

World Health Organisation Memorandum (1981) Nomenclature and classification of drug- and alcohol-related problems. *Bull. WHO.* **59,** 225–242.

Chapter 3

DISABILITIES AND SOCIAL FEATURES IN ALCOHOL DEPENDENCE

I your glass
Will modestly discover to yourself
That of yourself which you yet know not of. SHAKESPEARE

PHYSICAL DISABILITIES AND ALCOHOL

The physical disabilities which heavy drinkers are prone to develop are not all necessarily the consequences of excess alcohol consumption. The style of living adopted by some problem drinkers contributes to somatic ill-health. Nutritional deficiency and concomitant drug usage are factors that in certain alcoholic subjects impair physical well-being. Tobacco dependence, which is so frequent among alcoholics, explains their high incidence of lung cancer, and contributes substantially to their tendency to develop other respiratory tract diseases and cardiovascular conditions. The conceptual problems are illustrated by the alleged association between alcohol dependence and peptic ulcer (gastric and duodenal). Although the association is disputed, it is feasible that a high level of alcohol intake, dietary habits, or smoking may lead to peptic ulcers in some heavy drinkers; in certain patients the operation of partial gastrectomy has unleashed excess drinking; it is also possible that a link between peptic ulceration and alcohol dependence could arise from shared personality factors or from a common heredity.

An example of the difficulties inherent in the attribution of somatic conditions to the excess consumption of alcohol *per se* is provided by the correlation between alcohol intake and cancer. Doll (1977) has commented on the relationship of alcohol consumption to cancers of the upper respiratory and digestive tracts, to liver cancer (as a complication of cirrhosis), and possibly to some malignant tumours of the pancreas and rectum. One in twenty cases of cancer may be due to alcoholic drinks, yet pure alcohol is not carcinogenic to animals. As part of the explanation Doll suggested that alcohol solubilizes a carcinogenic agent, or that an agent of this nature is another component of fluids containing alcohol. Alcohol intake has also been linked to cancers of the breast and thyroid (Breslow and Enstrom, 1974), although here again an association could be indirect and arise from dietary or other habits that may accompany high alcohol consumption (Rosenberg et al., 1982).

Another problem, in regard to illnesses such as liver cirrhosis that have several causes apart from drinking, lies in the divergences between reports of the proportions of patients who are alcoholic. The proportion identified as chronic excessive drinkers depends not only on the actual contribution of heavy drinking to the disabilities but on the intensity and skill of the diagnostic search for alcohol dependence among the patients.

Persons who chronically consume large amounts of alcohol exhibit a mortality rate that is approximately 2·5 times the expected level. The deaths occur from physical complications, accidents, suicide and from concomitant tobacco dependence (Schmidt and de Lindt, 1972; Klatsky et al., 1981; Petersson et al., 1982). Furthermore, alcohol consumption contributes to morbidity and mortality in subjects who are not necessarily dependent on alcohol. Klatsky and colleagues (1981) linked an intake of only three to five drinks daily to a mortality rate about 50% higher than expected. Alcohol misuse and intoxication lead to injuries and death from accidents on the road, at work and in the home, as well as from fires, particularly domestic fires. The combination induced by alcohol of increased bravado and decreased psychomotor ability can produce drowning, often from falling into water; a study of males who drowned noted that 35% possessed a BAC over 80 mg/dl at autopsy (Plueckhan, 1982).

The organic changes that can develop in the course of chronic excessive alcohol consumption will be considered according to the systems which are impaired.

Nervous system

Damage to cerebral neurons during alcohol dependence produces deficits in mental function. Presumably widespread impairment and death of neurons may arise both as a direct toxic effect of alcohol, and from nutritional deficiency, particularly shortage of thiamine (aneurine) and folate. In some patients dementia, or other syndromes indicating nervous system damage, are left in the wake of delirium tremens or withdrawal fits; in these subjects the marked abstinence features exhausted brain cells already injured in the course of alcoholism.

Generalized cerebral impairment

The techniques of computerized tomography (CT) brain scan and of psychometric testing reveal that over 50% of clinically normal alcoholics possess brain damage (Ron et al., 1982; Wilkinson, 1982; Parsons and Leber, 1981). 'Clinically normal' refers to the usual kind of problem drinker seen in treatment, who at interview does not exhibit features of cerebral impairment. The X-ray changes show considerable widening of cortical sulci, enlarged ventricles and cerebellar shrinkage; the global nature of the disorder is confirmed by psychometric studies, which generally do not point to impairment confined to particular areas of the brain (Parsons and Leber, 1981). The CT and psychological deficits are at least partially reversible after months of abstinence; for this reason the term 'shrinkage' is preferable to 'atrophy' as a description of the organic alterations. The changes are independent of liver damage (Lee et al., 1979).

Patients with cerebral impairment are less likely to cooperate or stay in treatment, or to remain abstinent (Guthrie and Elliott, 1980). Their powers to understand the complexities of counselling are reduced, as are their problem-solving abilities and memory. Their judgement and self-restraint are similarly impaired.

The role of deficiency of thiamine and other nutriments is unclear, but it is likely that alcohol *per se* is an important factor. Experimental animals who were given alcohol together with an adequate diet have developed brain lesions (Freund, 1970; Riley and Walker, 1978). Among social drinkers a correlation has been found between psychometric deficits and level of drinking (Parker and Noble, 1977; MacVane et al., 1982); presumably the nutritional state of the subjects was adequate.

The common occurrence of cerebral impairment in problem drinkers who are seen for treatment, and its improvement with prolonged abstinence, strengthens the grounds for the therapist to advise abstention unless the degree of alcohol dependence is minor.

Korsakov's psychosis

This syndrome was first described in 1887 by the Russian psychiatrist S. S. Korsakov.* The pathological changes are centred in the mamillary bodies, where there are haemorrhages, cell necrosis and a marked glial reaction. Both direct toxicity from alcohol, and deficiency of B vitamins, have been considered to play a role in the aetiology (Gross, 1977). Additionally a genetic vulnerability might be involved. The transketolase enzyme system depends for its activity on the thiamine derivative thiamine pyrophosphate (TPP). The affinity of transketolase for TPP has been reported as lower among alcoholics with severe memory impairment than among controls (Blass and Gibson, 1977). A transketolase anomaly, if confirmed, could constitute an inherited enzyme variant that renders the cerebral metabolism of glucose

---

*Korsakov is unique among psychiatrists in providing the eponym for three designations; his name is included in the titles of a psychosis, a journal and a psychiatric hospital. A short summary of his career and excerpts from his description of the psychosis are accessible in the *Journal of the American Medical Association* **221**, 1700 (1970).

vulnerable to injury, as from alcohol or from thiamine depletion. It is feasible to suggest that memory blackouts for behaviour while intoxicated are a *forme fruste* of Korsakov's psychosis; since an excess quantity of alcohol on one occasion may produce temporary impairment of the neurons subserving memory, then a high level of repeated consumption could lead to neuronal death and prolonged memory disturbance of the kind described by Korsakov.

The most striking clinical feature of the disorder is an impaired memory for recent events which the patient may cover by fabricated stories to fill the gaps in recollection. So an inpatient may try to remind the ward doctor that the two met in a shop the previous day, although the patient had not left the hospital during the last month. The invented material is called a 'confabulation', even though the term really designates a conversation. Strictly speaking, when two physicians are discussing a patient who is making up items to conceal forgetfulness, it is the doctors who are confabulating, not the patient. The misapplication of the term has become acceptable by custom.

Other aspects of Korsakov's psychosis are a lack of drive, and bland euphoria or slight depression. The condition complicates other conditions apart from alcohol dependence, but when it follows excessive drinking it is frequently accompanied by peripheral neuritis. The amnesic and other psychological anomalies of the disorder have been fully reviewed by Butters and Cermak (1980).

Wernicke's encephalopathy

Two of the first 3 patients described by Wernicke in 1881 were alcoholics. The pathological features comprise vacuolar congestion and petechial haemorrhages in the upper part of the brain stem and in the hypothalamus. The lesions have been reproduced in animals by the experimental deprivation of thiamine (vitamin B_1, aneurine). Structures subserving consciousness (the reticular activating system) and memory (the mamillary bodies) are affected, together with the tracts passing in the midbrain to and from the cerebellum, as well as the oculomotor nuclei. A triad of features is therefore observed in the fully developed clinical picture; mental changes taking the form of delirium or dementia, cerebellar dysfunction and ophthalmoplegia. Although in severe cases death may ensue, milder varieties are common and are sometimes missed diagnostically. The mental changes can be slight, cerebellar anomalies may be inapparent on cursory examination, and the strabismus and diplopia are in some instances transitory or absent. Harper (1979) found the lesions of Wernicke's encephalopathy in 51 (1·7%) of 3000 brains examined by autopsy at a general hospital; although 45 of the patients with encephalopathy were alcoholic, only seven were recognized during life to possess the disorder.

General remarks

The distinction is not necessarily clear-cut between Korsakov's psychosis and Wernicke's encephalopathy. Pathologically there is an overlap of the areas damaged in Korsakov's psychosis and Wernicke's encephalopathy. The lack of unclear demarcation between the illnesses was recognized by Victor et al. (1971) when they employed the descriptive term 'Wernicke–Korsakoff syndrome'.

There also exists pathological and clinical overlap between Korsakov's psychosis and the severe dementia that occasionally results from generalized cerebral impairment. Anatomically there are structures additional to the mamillary bodies which play a role in memory function and that can be damaged in the course of alcohol dependence. From the clinical aspect cognitive decrements, memory weakness (with or without confabulation), emotional blunting and volitional deficit occur in either disorder.

In each condition a considerable degree of improvement is possible. Provided alcohol is avoided progress may continue slowly for 2 years. The improvements are presumably due to a return of activity in neurons or axons that were temporarily damaged but not destroyed, or to alternative neural systems taking over the functions of deceased cells; the former explanation appears more likely.

It is not possible to predict the extent of eventual recovery in an individual patient. If drinking is resumed the affected cerebral systems are vulnerable and may quickly show fresh dysfunction, but drinking does not always produce a recrudescence of cerebral damage. Lack of exacerbation of brain disorder despite resumption of drinking is difficult to explain; it could possibly be attributed to a lower level of alcohol intake when drinking is renewed or to a sustained improvement of nutritional status.

Marchiafava's disease

This uncommon condition was first described among Italian males who drink wine. It is characterized at autopsy mainly by acute demyelination of the corpus callosum. Other tracts connecting the cerebral hemispheres, and the cerebral white matter itself, may also be affected by degeneration. Initial delirium or coarsening of personality progress to dementia, dysarthria, paralysis, coma and death.

Cerebellar and pontine degeneration

Destructive lesions in the cerebellar cortex can develop in dependent drinkers. The short-term effects of alcohol on cerebellar function are inadequately understood. The long-term results of chronic excessive alcohol consumption on the cerebellum may be more extensive and frequent than is realized; direct involvement of the cerebellum rather than reduced conduction along the cerebellar tracts in the brainstem could account for the cerebellar ataxia, often temporary, that is not uncommon among alcoholic subjects.

An infrequent sequal of alcoholism is extensive demyelination of the nerve tracts in the pons. The lesions from the neuropathological basis of the condition known as 'pontine degeneration' or 'central pontine myelosis'. Recovery has been reported of a female patient whose treatment consisted of maintenance of respiration, vitamins, and correction of fluid and electrolyte balance (Levitt and Shenker, 1979). Both cerebellar degeneration and pontine myelosis may result from nutritional deficiency rather than from the toxic effects of alcohol (Pearce, 1977).

Subdural haematoma

Intoxicated persons are liable to fall and injure their heads; bleeding inside the skull can ensue. Alcoholics are said to be particularly prone to the development of subdural haematoma. The clinical features of the condition may not develop until a few weeks after an apparently slight head injury; they must not be mistaken for the acute results of alcohol, for abstinence delirium, or for the effects of sedatives.

Peripheral neuritis

Among persons who are dependent on alcohol this disorder may occur alone or in conjunction with damage to the central nervous system. The causative agents of peripheral neuropathy in nonalcoholics include a variety of toxins, and thiamine deficiency. In dependent drinkers also both these kinds of factor are implicated—a toxic substance (alcohol) and malnutrition. The extent of the degeneration of peripheral neurons in alcoholic neuritis reflects the severity and duration of the alcoholism (Mandsley and Mayer, 1965).

The alcoholic patient with peripheral neuritis can be symptomless, or complain of paraesthesiae, pain or lack of sensation in the hands and feet. In the symptomless patient the condition may be detected on physical examination by noting that the tendon reflexes are diminished or absent in the legs and, less commonly, in the arms. More severe cases show impairment of all forms of sensibility in the peripheral segments of the limbs; muscle atrophy, foot drop and wrist drop may supervene. Nerve conduction studies show anomalies of sensory and motor nerves, which take the form of slowing of conduction speed, prolonged latency to peak potential, and reduced amplitude of the action potential (Walsh and McCleod, 1973).

Saturday night palsy

The picturesque title applies to a sequel that may develop if an individual falls asleep, perhaps when drunk, with the arm over the back of a chair. The radial nerve is compressed between the chair and the humerus; on awaking the patient notices wrist drop. Usually the paralysis remits in a few weeks, during which period the hand should be maintained in the cocked position by a splint.

Respiratory tract

Tumours of the upper parts of the air and food passages are associated with alcohol dependence (Schmidt and de Lint, 1972; Sundby, 1974; Adelstein and White, 1976). Lowry (1975) noted that 57% of his patients with supraglotic carcinoma were alcoholics. Although he did not detect an association between drinking and cancer of the vocal cords, nasopharynx or anterior oral cavity most of his subjects with cancer of the tongue, tonsil and oropharynx had severe drinking problems. On the relevance of smoking to the findings Lowry referred to the implications of tobacco and alcohol consumption among Jewish persons, who in the U.S.A. smoke to the same degree as the rest of the population, but who drink less; Jews have a low incidence of cancer of the upper portions of the respiratory and digestive tracts. McMichael (1978) described the upturn of deaths from cancer of the larynx and oesophagus that took place in Britain and Australia subsequent to the 1939–45 war. The rises followed some 15 years after a similar trend in alcohol consumption and were, in McMichael's view, partly attributable to alcohol acting as a carcinogen or as a co-carcinogen.

Carcinoma of the bronchus is more common in alcoholics than in nonalcoholics (Schmidt and de Lint, 1972; Adelstein and White, 1976); the relationship is attributed to the high cigarette consumption of alcoholic subjects. Persons dependent on alcohol are liable to bronchitis and pneumonia, partly from smoking and in part from lowered general resistance to intercurrent infections. Tuberculosis and alcohol dependence are associated (Leading Article, 1970), although the reports of a high incidence of pulmonary tuberculosis among excessive drinkers generally date back to the period of high prevalence of tuberculous disease. Patients with phthisis who are also alcoholic tend not to cooperate with treatment for their lung infection and have a poorer prognosis than nonalcoholic subjects.

Gastrointestinal tract

Carcinoma of the oesophagus has an increased prevalence among alcoholics (Williams and Horm, 1977; Schmidt and Popham, 1981). Gastritis induced by alcohol is a well known feature; it is the usual cause of morning sickness in males. Alcoholic gastritis can lead to severe, even fatal, haematemesis. Some studies have concluded that heavy drinkers have a higher incidence of both gastric and duodenal ulcer (Pell and d'Alonzo, 1968; Schmidt and de Lint, 1972). Possible reasons for an association have been discussed in the first paragraph of this chapter, but later reports have not found a correlation between alcohol intake and peptic ulcer (Friedman et al., 1974; Paffenberger et al., 1974).

Pancreatitis, both acute and chronic, can develop as a consequence of alcoholism. Trapnell and Duncan noted in 1975 that over the previous two decades British studies had detected a rising incidence of alcohol dependence in patients with pancreatitis. James et al. (1973) considered that alcohol was the probable cause in nearly half of their London patients with chronic pancreatitis, and suggested that the high incidence of alcoholic pancreatitis reflects the increased consumption of alcohol in England over the previous 20 years. A multinational study has correlated the personal level of alcohol consumption with the liability to chronic pancreatitis; the investigation did not find a safe drinking level below which alcohol does not induce the condition (Durbec and Sarles, 1978; Sarles et al., 1979).

There are several liver complications associated with dependence on alcohol; they have been reviewed by an international group of researchers (Occasional Survey, 1981). Fatty infiltration of the liver (steatosis) may arise in the course of alcoholism. Several mechanisms have been postulated for the production of alcoholic fatty liver. They include the effects of alcohol metabolism to increase hepatic lipogenesis and to diminish oxidation of fatty acids in the liver. In addition alcohol stimulates the peripheral release of catecholamines; catecholamine-mediated enhancement of lipolysis in adipose tissue increases the free fatty acids in the serum that are available for transport to the liver. Since the consumption of alcohol so induces an immediate triglyceridaemia the repetition of this phenomenon may contribute to fatty liver.

The patient with fatty liver is not usually ill. On examination the liver is moderately enlarged and may be tender; these findings are often incidental. The evidence that fatty liver constitutes a precursor of cirrhosis is equivocal, but Lieber and DeCarli (1977) stressed three points. Firstly, alcoholic hepatitis can undoubtedly lead to cirrhosis, and there are electron microscopic similarities in the appearances of hepatocytes from patients with alcoholic fatty liver and from patients with alcoholic hepatitis. Secondly, the experimental provision of a moderate intake of alcohol to baboons leads to fatty liver, while a higher alcohol consumption induces hepatitis and cirrhosis; this suggests that fatty liver is a precursor of the other two disorders. Thirdly, baboons who are experimentally given alcohol as part of their diet show an increase of liver collagen both during the fatty liver phase and in cirrhosis. Lieber and DeCarli postulated that although fat accumulation in the liver is reversible, and that by itself it may be harmless, fatty deposition results from a severe disturbance of liver metabolism that could progress to produce hepatitis and also cirrhosis.

Acute alcoholic hepatitis is a severe and sometimes fatal complication of heavy drinking. The liver is enlarged and tender; fever, leucocytosis, jaundice and signs of hepatic failure and portal hypertension are present.

Chronic hepatitis in alcoholics possesses the histopathological features of an inflammatory reaction of the liver, with deposits of hyaline (Mallory bodies) in the liver cells, death of hepatocytes and fibrous deposition. Cirrhosis may follow. A minority of patients who become abstinent after alcoholic hepatitis incur further liver damage from chronic aggressive hepatitis.

An immunological component is probable in alcoholic hepatitis. There is a reduction of circulating T lymphocytes, possibly arising from their sequestration in the liver (Bernstein et al., 1974). Normal liver antigen inhibits in laboratory testing the migration of mononuclear cells taken from the blood of patients with alcoholic hepatitis; the inhibition is not noted with mononuclear cells from normal controls or from cirrhotics (Mihas et al., 1975). Cell-mediated immunity to normal or damaged liver tissue may perpetuate alcoholic hepatitis and lead to the eventual development of cirrhosis.

Alcoholic cirrhosis (Laennec's cirrhosis) is shown on light microscopy by an extensive loss of hepatocytes, disorganization of the liver lobules, and linkage of portal tracts by bands of fibrosis. For many years a debate has taken place on the respective roles of alcohol toxicity and of nutritional deficiency in the causation of cirrhosis. The animal experiments of Charles Lieber and his colleagues have thrown some light on the issue. Baboons who were fed alcohol in an amount producing up to 50% of total calory intake developed fatty livers; some displayed alcoholic hepatitis, and a proportion showed cirrhosis; baboons given an isocaloric control diet retained normal livers (Rubin and Lieber, 1974). So alcohol alone has experimentally reproduced the liver lesions of alcoholism: fatty liver, hepatitis and cirrhosis. It remains possible, nevertheless, that unknown nutritional factors could contribute to the hepatotoxicity of alcohol in the production of some cases of human cirrhosis.

Most hazardous drinkers do not develop severe alcoholic liver disease (ALD). The susceptibility of certain subjects to incur this complication could depend on a variety of factors: quantity and pattern of alcohol consumption, nutrition, genetic predisposition, and injurious agents additional to alcohol. Wilkinson et al. (1971), in Australia, considered that female alcoholics are more predisposed than males both to cirrhosis and also to brain damage. Some studies have reported an association between ALD and HLA antigens; a link would point to a genetic vulnerability to ALD among heavy drinkers. The reports were reviewed by Eddleston and Davis (1982), but the uncertain status of an association is illustrated by an extensive British investigation with contrary findings (Faizallah et al., 1982).

The majority of cirrhotics are alcoholic, at least in Westernized countries; the same nations also possess substantial rates of other alcohol disabilities and high levels of *per capita* alcohol consumption. In the U.S.A. the proportion of patients with cirrhosis who are alcoholic is about 80%; for example, Reid et al. (1968) considered that 84% of their cirrhotic subjects in Baltimore had alcoholism. Recent British findings have approached this level. Forshaw (1972) noted in Liverpool that 64% of his patients with cirrhosis were excessive users of alcohol. Two London studies have respectively reported that 65% and 72% of their patients with chronic liver disease were alcoholic (Hodgson and Thompson, 1976; Blendis et al., 1975). Over an 18 year period there was a four-fold increase of cirrhosis incidence among patients of a general hospital in Britain (Saunders et al., 1981a).

Transient anomalies of liver function tests are common among alcoholics, with the test results returning to normal after a few weeks of abstinence. These temporary anomalies are not usually of sinister import, although it should be noted that liver biopsy can demonstrate cirrhosis when liver function tests are normal.

A common finding among heavy drinkers is a rise in the serum level of the enzyme gamma-glutamyltransferase (γ-GT, gamma-glutamyl-transpeptidase). A survey of 169 patients in an alcoholic unit indicated that 103 (61%) had elevated levels of γ-GT (Spencer-Peet et al., 1973). The rise after drinking is produced by induction of the enzyme in the liver and does not in itself indicate liver damage. Raised serum concentrations of γ-GT do occur in most forms of liver disorder, such as acute and chronic hepatitis, cirrhosis and cholestasis; the enzyme is not restricted to the liver, and elevations of the γ-GT level are found in myocardial infarction, lobar pneumonia, pancreatitis and inflammatory bowel disease. But the test is a useful pointer to the level of drinking and can be employed for this purpose (Morgan et al., 1981; Chick et al., 1981).

Primary carcinoma of the liver is a fatal development in patients with alcoholic cirrhosis. A more cheerful point is the finding of many, though not all, studies that alcohol abstinence improves the outlook for cirrhosis in alcoholics, even in patients with oesophageal varices (Dagradi, 1972; Brunt et al., 1974).

Haemochromatosis is a disorder in which large quantities of haemosiderin, a pigment containing iron, are laid down in many parts of the body, including the liver. The disease can complicate alcohol dependence; several factors have been implicated to explain the association between the two conditions. Iron deposition may be promoted by the folic acid deficiency found in alcoholics. Iron absorption is increased in alcoholic cirrhosis. Finally, extensive consumption of alcoholic beverages can unintentionally raise the level of ingestion of iron; some alcohol preparations (notably wine) have a high iron content, while in southern Africa increased intake of the metal can result from the use of iron containers employed for the storage and consumption of alcoholic drinks.

The blood

Abnormalities of the red cells, white cells and platelets can each complicate a high level of alcohol intake (Eichner, 1973).

Anaemia may develop in the course of chronic excess alcohol consumption. Nutritional deficiencies of iron and folic acid play a role (many observers doubt the occurrence of vitamin B_{12} deficiency in alcohol dependence). It should be noted that other mechanisms than inadequacy of diet could induce a low level of serum folate in alcoholics; the alternative processes include malabsorption, a direct anti-folate effect of alcohol, and an enhanced utilization of folate as a cofactor in the liver enzyme activity that is induced by alcohol (Scott, 1974). Megaloblastic changes in the marrow together with macrocytosis have been reported in patients who possess normal serum, red blood cell, and liver folate levels; this pattern of findings suggests that alcohol has a direct toxic action on the development of erythroblasts (Wu et al., 1974). In addition to megaloblastosis the bone marrow cells of excessive drinkers may show vacuolation of normoblasts and abnormal iron accumulation in ring sideroblasts. It has been proposed that the sideroblast development is caused by pyridoxine deficiency, leading to failure of haem synthesis and to accumulation of non-haem iron in the mitochondria of red cells (Lindenbaum, 1977).

Anaemia, and infrequently acanthocytes (spur cells) may ensue in alcoholic cirrhosis, as in cirrhosis from other causes. Several kinds of haemolytic anaemia have been reported in alcoholism. Zieve's syndrome, in the full development of its clinical picture, consists of the combination of jaundice, liver disease, hyperlipaemia and haemolysis (Zieve, 1958). The condition is said to be accompanied occasionally by pancreatitis, and usually to improve with abstinence. The features of Zieve's syndrome occur in variable combination; Eichner (1973) pointed out that there are several mechanisms for haemolysis in alcoholic liver disease and considered that the various aspects of the syndrome do not share a common pathogenic pathway. The validity of grouping the described aspects into a syndrome is therefore in doubt.

Leucopenia and a diminished granulocyte reserve of the marrow have been encountered in dependent drinkers. Thrombocytopenia has also been noted (Chanarin, 1982). A low platelet count in alcoholic subjects is often due to the hypersplenism of cirrhosis, but has developed in non-cirrhotic alcoholics. Folic acid deficiency and a toxic result of alcohol could contribute to the diminished platelet count. Rebound thrombocytosis after withdrawal of alcohol can occur in alcoholic patients, not all of whom show initial thrombocytopenia; the thrombocythaemia may lead to thromboembolic disease in some patients (Haselager and Vreeken, 1977).

Glucose metabolism

Hypoglycaemia is a complication that may prove fatal, particularly when its presence is not suspected as the underlying cause of coma in a person who appears merely to be drunk. Alcohol impairment of gluconeogenesis forms the responsible mechanism. The condition is especially likely to develop in problem drinkers who are malnourished, because of their depleted liver stores of glycogen.

Alcohol can produce the opposite result of a rise in blood sugar (Dornhurst and Ouyang, 1971). The effect can ensue although there is no reduction of insulin secretion from alcohol-mediated pancreatitis; it is not a consequence of the caloric value of alcohol. Putative factors for the impairment of glucose tolerance are decreased peripheral utilization of glucose and adrenergic-mediated glycogenolysis. Alcoholics have an increased mortality from diabetes mellitus (Schmidt and de Lint, 1972). The repeated production by alcohol of lowered glucose tolerance, as well as pancreatic damage, may form a basis for the association between alcohol dependence and diabetes (Hed et al., 1968; Phillips and Safrit, 1971).

Cardiovascular system

The mortality rate from circulatory disorders is increased in alcohol dependence, including death and sudden death from cerebrovascular lesions and from coronary heart disease (Schmidt and de Lint, 1972; Sundby, 1974; Nicholls et al., 1974). Atherosclerosis is a frequent feature underlying the enhanced incidence of circulatory diseases among problem drinkers. In this respect tobacco smoking is an important agent which is prevalent among alcoholic subjects and that must contribute substantially to their proneness to cardiovascular illness. Hypertriglyceridaemia is a risk factor for ischaemic heart disease and peripheral vascular disease. Chait et al. (1972) reported that alcoholism was the responsible agent in 31 out of 211 patients with hypertriglyceridaemia; in their series of subjects alcohol consumption was, after diabetes mellitus, the most frequent cause of secondary hypertriglyceridaemia.

Hypertension offers another method by which alcohol consumption could lead to cardiovascular disease, including atherosclerosis. Both systolic and diastolic blood pressure levels are positively associated with the amount of alcohol intake. There is a three-fold rise of deaths from strokes among heavy drinkers compared with infrequent drinkers (Kozarevic et al., 1980); the enhanced stroke mortality is due to alcohol induced hypertension. But even moderate quantities of alcohol (more than three drinks a day) increase the risk of hypertension (Klatsky et al., 1977). Although associated somatic, psychological and social factors (e.g. 'stress') could play a role in jointly raising the levels of alcohol intake and of blood pressure, it is likely that regular drinking can cause or aggravate hypertension; a possible mechanism exists through alcohol-induced corticosteroid excess (Ramsay, 1977). Abstention often lowers the blood pressure substantially, among alcoholics (Saunders et al., 1981b) and among regular drinkers treated for hypertension (Saunders et al., 1982).

It should be stated that low quantities of alcohol (up to two drinks daily) may protect against atheroma and even promote longevity (Klatsky et al., 1979). A protective result from alcohol might arise from its effect in raising the ratio in the serum of high density lipoprotein relative to low density lipoprotein. Any protection afforded by small amounts of alcohol is slight; its existence has been doubted (Petersson et al., 1982).

An acute effect of alcohol is depression of myocardial activity. Alcoholic heart muscle disease (formerly known as alcoholic cardio-myopathy) is a chronic degenerative heart condition encountered among alcoholics. Light microscopy shows that the heart muscle fibres lack hyaline, are oedematous and contain hydropic vacuoles; patchy areas of fibrosis are present. Clinically cardiomegaly and low-output heart failure are found. Specific changes in the electrocardiogram (ECG) have been claimed, especially in the T wave, which was described by Evans (1959) as spinous, dimpled, cloven or inverted. Transient ECG changes of this nature have been found in alcoholics admitted to a psychiatric unit (Priest et al., 1966), but it is improbable that pathognomonic ECG alterations actually exist (Brigden and Robinson, 1964).

Doubts used to exist concerning the correctness of the view that cardiomyopathy is a product of excessive drinking (*Leading Article,* 1974). Härtell et al. (1969) noted the infrequency of recognition of the condition in alcoholics. The pathological and clinical features that are attributed to alcoholic heart disease do not differ from the features of congestive cardiomyopathy in nondrinkers. But a consensus of opinion would indicate that disease of the heart muscle is a complication, although uncommon, of alcohol dependence. It is generally agreed that patients who have heart muscle disease associated with a high alcohol intake improve their prognosis if they refrain from alcohol. The literature on the subject has been reviewed by Alderman and Coltart (1982) and by Wodak and Richardson (1982).

Other heart conditions have been encountered among heavy drinkers. The first is wet beriberi; in this disorder nutritional deficiency of thiamine (vitamin B_1) leads to a hyperkinetic circulation and high output failure. The illness responds quickly to administration of thiamine. Arrhythmias can arise during bout drinking without overt myocardial disease (Ettinger et al., 1981); they can also follow single large doses of alcohol (Singer and Lundberg, 1972). Abstinence improves the disorder of heart rhythm. The condition has been termed the 'holiday heart syndrome'.

The remaining cardiac disorder is cobalt cardiomyopathy; this is an acute form of heart failure that has occurred in certain regions (e.g. Quebec, Belgium) when cobalt was added to beer to improve the durability and appearance of the foamy 'head'. Polycythaemia and pericardial effusions have been characteristic features of the latter condition, which is unlikely to recur since widespread prohibition of the contamination of beer by cobalt.

Striated muscle

Alcoholic myopathy provides a spectrum of disorders, acute and chronic. Muscle damage may be symptomless, and the presence of muscle disorder is only revealed by biochemical evidence such as an elevated serum level of the enzyme creatine phosphokinase. An acute form of myopathy, with muscle pains and tenderness, can complicate excessive drinking. Another variant, less dramatic though probably more common, consists of chronic wasting and weakness of muscles, (Hanid et al., 1981). Skeletal muscle and myocardium are allied, so it is interesting to note that acute skeletal muscle necrosis (rhabdomyolysis) and acute cardiomyopathy have been described as developing concurrently in alcoholics after periods of intensified drinking (Seneviratne, 1975).

Endocrine system

Acute and chronic alcohol administration lowers the plasma level of testosterone, which is the hormone closely connected with male secondary sexual features and libido. In consequence reduction of libido, impotence and testicular atrophy are frequent clinical features in alcohol dependent males. Several mechanisms are involved. Alcohol exerts a direct toxic effect on the testis to inhibit testosterone production and spermatogenesis; alcohol also impairs the hypothalamic-pituitary axis that is responsible for the release of gonadotrophins; nutritional deficiencies of vitamin A and zinc in heavy drinkers could impair androgen formation (McClain et al., 1979).

Male excessive drinkers can also exhibit an increase of circulating oestrogens (oestrone and oestradiol). Female secondary sexual characteristics develop that take the form of gynaecomastia, redistribution of body fat, a female escutcheon, spider angiomata and liver palms. The high levels of oestrogens further contribute to testicular atrophy, reduced libido and impotence. The increase of oestrogens in the blood is not produced by a fall in the clearance of normally produced oestrogens, but is associated with induction of hepatic aromatase, which is the liver enzyme system that converts androgens to oestrogens (Gordon et al., 1979).

Among female alcoholics oestrogen levels are generally within normal limits, but failure of ovulation has been demonstrated (van Thiel and

Gavaler, 1982). The long-term effects of high alcohol consumption on gonadal function, especially in females, await fuller investigation.

When alcohol is administered acutely there is an increase of adrenocortical activity and a rise of plasma cortisol levels. Animal experiments suggest that there is hypothalamic-pituitary as well as direct adrenal stimulation, but human data point mostly to a straight effect on adrenal glucocorticoid secretion that is exerted by alcohol or its metabolite acetaldehyde (Cobb and van Thiel, 1982). Cushing's syndrome has been reported to accompany the prolonged excessive use of alcohol; most of the cushingoid abnormalities remit in the course of 1–3 weeks of abstention from alcohol (Smals et al., 1976). Paton (1976) has reported on Cushing's syndrome in patients with histological evidence of alcoholic hepatitis or cirrhosis, and advised that enquiry about drinking habits is essential in patients with the syndrome, especially females. Rees et al. (1977) have also described alcoholic patients with corticosteroid hypersecretion; they too have stressed that alcohol intake should receive examination when the diagnosis of Cushing's syndrome is considered. The latter investigators noted that in their patients the alcohol-induced cushingoid syndrome reverted to normal on withdrawal of alcohol.

Chromosomes

A high incidence of chromosome anomalies has been suspected in alcoholics; both the sex and autosomal chromosomes have been implicated. The aberrations, if they occur, might putatively arise either as a hereditary accompaniment or as a result of the drinking or other practices of the subjects.

With respect to sex chromosomes early reports were not confirmed that an extra Y chromosome, constituting the 47, XYY karyotype, is linked with antisocial behaviour and dependence on alcohol. Bartholomew and Sutherland (1969) investigated 164 prisoners and found no alcoholic prisoner with this sex chromosome abnormality. Their study did uncover 1 alcoholic with another sex chromosome anomaly, of the 47, XXY type (Klinefelter's syndrome). But the same investigators referred to a Melbourne study of 170 male alcoholics, none of whom possessed the positive chromatin finding that indicates an extra X chromosome.

An extraordinarily high proportion of dependent drinkers has been reported by de Torok (1972) to possess an abnormal complement of autosomal chromosomes. His examination of the chromosomes present in incubated lymphocytes showed that the percentage of recently drinking alcoholic subjects with the normal diploid karyotype of 46 chromosomes was only 14%, dropping to 4·4% among alcoholics with brain damage; in some cells there were merely 18 chromosomes. By comparison, karyotypes were normal in 47·17% of alcoholics who reported abstinence for 5 or more years and in 91·6% of nonalcoholic controls. The study revealed few duplications or deficiencies of the sex chromosomes among the problem drinkers.

Other investigators have not found an abnormal number of chromosomes in alcoholics (Wahlström et al., 1970; Lilly, 1975). In her study Lilly did uncover a more subtle alteration, in the form of a statistically significant increase in the total of chromatid interchanges among alcoholics compared with controls. The possibility exists, therefore, that in alcoholics there are refined structural alterations of chromosomes that are normal in karyotype complement. Badr and Hussain (1982) have reviewed the conflicting reports and provided data from their own study which revealed an increased number of both numerical and structural aberrations of the chromosomes in their alcoholic subjects.

In view of the disparity of evidence it remains an undecided issue whether there is a raised incidence of microscopically detectable chromosome aberrations in excessive drinkers. If repeated studies point to a high level of anomalies, whether of number or of the refinements of structure, it would be more reasonable to view the abnormalities as acquired rather than inherited: alcoholics do not show the gross developmental disorders that accompany hereditary anomalies of the chromosomes.

Dupuytren's contracture

The frequency of Dupuytren's deformity of the palmar fascia is said to be increased in alcohol dependence and in alcoholic cirrhosis (Su and Patek, 1970; *Editorial, 1972*). The increase of this disorder is alleged to exist among alcoholic subjects who do not have evidence of significant liver disease, although the condition is considered to be especially frequent among alcoholics with cirrhosis (Wolfe et al., 1956).

Since the contracture comprises a type III collagen disorder that is inherited through an autosomal dominant gene (Hueston, 1974) it seems unlikely that the condition is especially common among problem drinkers. If an association were confirmed it might be relevant to the association and to the previous discussion on chromosomes that aberrant chromosome complements have been reported in cells taken from the palmar fascia of patients with Dupuytren's contracture (Bowser-Riley et al., 1975; Madden, 1976a).

Alcohol and the fetus

It has been suspected for centuries that excess alcohol consumption in pregnant women is a cause of developmental anomalies and growth retardation in their infants. The first scientific study emanated towards the end of the nineteenth century from a doctor to Liverpool prison (Sullivan, 1899); the investigator employed two control groups of women who avoided alcohol while pregnant and found that female alcoholics who drank when pregnant were more likely to produce stillbirths or babies who died as infants. In the 1960s French doctors described abnormalities in babies born to heavily drinking mothers; their reports have been reviewed by Kessel (1977). Jones et al. (1973) reported from Seattle a specific syndrome arising in the progeny of alcoholic mothers who drink heavily during pregnancy.

The features that have been described involve physical and mental retardation, with failure to thrive, irritability and childhood hyper-activity, as well as several malformations of the head and face. The cranial and facial abnormalities involve microcephaly, low set or poorly formed ears, short palpebral fissures, small eyes, and epicanthic folds. The centre of the face is broad and flat, with a short upturned nose; the upper lip has a long philtrum (central groove) and a thin vermilion edge. Other reported anomalies are skin capillary haemangiomas, dislocated hips, congenital heart disease, abnormal palmar creases, and minor genital abnormalities (Hanson, 1977).

Some of the affected infants were at first considered to have other conditions, such as Noonan's syndrome, of genetic origin (Hall and Orenstein, 1974). A similar pattern of dysmorphogenesis can follow anticonvulsant medication (Hill, 1976) and is found in phenylketonuria (Lipson et al., 1981). Adverse medicosocial factors among the mothers are present in addition to excessive alcohol intake; the accompanying factors that could contribute to fetal damage take the form of poverty, inadequate nutrition, heavy smoking, drug misuse, and sporadic clinic attendance. But there is an increasing weight of clinical evidence and animal experimental data to implicate alcohol as a potent teratogen (Leading Article, 1976). It is now accepted that alcohol can damage the fetus, although the fully developed fetal alcohol syndrome is less common than minor degrees of developmental retardation. A Belfast study uncovered fetal alcohol effects in 4 per 1000 births, although only 1·7 per 1000 births possessed the distinctive syndrome (Halliday et al., 1982).

Is there a safe level of drinking during pregnancy? The lowest amount of regular consumption that was associated with infant deficits (in the form of low birth weight) averaged two drinks daily (Littler, 1977). Daily consumption, even in moderation, at a level of one to two drinks per day, has been noted to increase the risk of spontaneous abortion during the second trimester (Harlap and Shiono, 1980). Yet while there are no clear data on a possible safe level, there is no firm evidence to proscribe alcohol completely during pregnancy.

Women (whether moderate or heavy drinkers) tend to reduce their alcohol intake during pregnancy, often before they realise that they are pregnant (Little et al., 1976); the feature suggests an innate protective mechanism. Unfortunately not all women reduce their drinking when pregnant. It is necessary to warn pregnant women and those who are likely to conceive that there is a risk to the fetus from more than the infrequent light use of alcohol. The advice should receive routine inclusion in antenatal care, as should ascertainment of the alcohol intake of the patients. Counselling of pregnant women who drink heavily decreases growth retardation among infants born to the subjects who lower their alcohol consumption (Rosett et al., 1980). Pregnant women whose drinking is at a level sufficiently high to show features of alcohol dependence require especially intensive treatment of their dependence.

Other physical disorders

Varsamis et al. (1974) investigated immunoglobulins among psychiatric patients and noted an increase of IgA in alcoholic, compared with control, subjects. They referred to a report that IgA returns to normal when alcoholics become abstinent; in their research alcohol consumption had no effect on levels of IgG or IgM. Immunoglobulin levels are usually increased in alcoholic liver disease; there is probably an alteration of cell-mediated immunity in the liver complications of alcohol dependence so that immunological mechanisms may play a role in the production or continuance of hepatic damage induced by alcohol (Lieber and DeCarli, 1977).

Excessive drinkers can develop general impairment, distinct from local enhancement within the liver, of cell-mediated immune processes. The proportion of T lymphocytes in the circulation is decreased. In addition there is reduction of phagocyte activity, in part derived from the diminished granulocyte reserve in the marrow. Nutritional deficiencies of vitamins and of zinc are probably implicated. The generalized immunodeficiency and decreased phagocyte action contribute to the susceptibility to infections that is displayed by dependent drinkers (Morgan, 1982).

Prostaglandins await investigation in alcoholics. Keller (1972) has sceptically observed that whatever trait is studied, alcoholics are found to differ from a control population. It is probable that anomalies of prostaglandins will be discovered among alcoholic subjects. That the revelation will contribute substantially to an understanding of alcohol dependence and its management is less likely.

The disorders of bone that can develop in excessive drinkers have been described by Saville (1977) and by Parsons and Cundy (1981). Among patients with alcoholic neuritis, bone and joint changes in the feet, accompanied by painless ulcers, may ensue (Charcot's feet). Avascular necrosis of the femoral head can occur in the course of alcohol dependence and lead to osteoarthritis of the hip; a possible mechanism involves obstruction of small vessels in the femoral head by fat globules arising during alcohol-induced hyperlipaemia. Excess alcohol consumption can also lead to osteoporosis, with increased risk of fractures of the femoral neck, the wrist, the upper humerus, and the vertebrae. Osteoporotic changes among alcoholics may be mediated by deficiencies or metabolic disturbance that affect the distribution in the bones of calcium, phosphorus or nitrogen.

Acute renal failure can follow excessive ingestion of beer. The disorder has been attributed to a direct nephrotoxic effect of alcohol, to myoglobinuria from alcohol-induced muscle damage, to cobalt, or to a mycotoxin from barley fungi (Canavese et al., 1981).

Alcohol induces the hepatic enzyme delta-aminolaevulinic acid synthase, which is the initial and rate-controlling enzyme for the manufacture of haem. Among alcoholics, therefore, disturbances of haem synthesis can occur (McColl et al., 1981), but even small amounts of alcohol are able to precipitate attacks of acute porphyria in susceptible subjects. Alcohol also aggravates cutaneous hepatic porphyria. Patients with, and carriers of, acute porphyria should avoid alcohol (Goldberg et al., 1981; Doss et al., 1982).

PSYCHOLOGICAL DISABILITIES IN ALCOHOL DEPENDENCE

Depression

A depressed mood is a common accompaniment of chronic excessive drinking. It is possible to offer several explanations, which tend to be mutually complementary rather than contradictory.

Firstly, a mood of unhappiness can develop as an understandable mental reaction to the consequences imposed on the alcoholic by drinking. Secondly, depression could arise from neurochemical disturbances, not yet understood, that take place during heavy alcohol intake.

Both the above explanations derive from the observation that the level of dysthymia in problem drinkers rises during drinking and wanes during abstinence. McNamee et al. (1968) reported an increase of anxiety and depression in alcoholic subjects after several days of drinking. In a study employing psychological tests the amount of emotional tension among dependent drinkers was raised during drinking sessions (van der Spuy, 1972). With regard to anxiety or tension it is often found in general psychiatric practice that these symptoms are accompanied by depression. It is then sometimes a matter of subjective interpretation (by patient and psychiatrist) whether the dysthymic complaints should receive the label of anxiety or depression. The present fashion is to choose the second title. The biochemical mechanisms by which excessive drinking could induce depression are not elucidated; current views on the general aetiology of depression point to deficient activity of the neuronal systems activated by the monoamine neurotransmitters noradrenaline and serotonin.

A third factor to account for the conjunction of alcohol dependence and depression lies in the personality of some excessive drinkers who possess a basically depressive frame of mind. Unfortunately there are considerable difficulties attached to the assessment of the prealcoholic mental (and physical) status of alcoholic subjects. Only a prospective study is capable of adequately surmounting the difficulties. Such a study would assess the features of a group of subjects and follow them over several years to determine which became dependent on alcohol; the aspects of the future alcoholics as shown at their initial examination can then receive differentiation from the initial characteristics of the nonalcoholics. The prospective study of the McCords (1960) did not notice depression among the young persons who later developed alcohol problems, but the subjects were examined before adolescence at a time of life when depression is minimal and fleeting. Yet although the following proposition has not received scientific validation from prospective studies it is offered for its face value. Clinical observation and common sense lead to the conclusion that some persons take to heavy drinking partly because they have a chronically dysphoric outlook on life and themselves and react in a neurotically depressed manner to psychological stresses.

A fourth reason for the association of depression and excessive drinking lies in the supervention of one or more phases of depression in individuals who have basically robust personalities but who drink heavily to relieve their affective disorder. There has been a perennial debate in psychiatry concerning the classification of depression (Kiloh et al., 1972). One viewpoint proposes two types of depression, neurotic and psychotic; neurotic depression constitutes a reaction to unfavourable circumstance in patients with neurotic temperaments; psychotic depression (sometimes referred to as endogenous depression) represents a development that is presumed to arise mainly from innate biochemical processes in patients who are relatively free from neurotic traits. In contrast, the alternative psychiatric viewpoint postulates a continuum of depressive disorder, whereby depressed subjects differ in the severity, not in the fundamental quality, of their illness. Whichever view the reader may hold it is a matter of practical observation that although the majority of depressed persons do not drink heavily, a minority take alcohol excessively in order to ease their distress. Patients who drink heavily during periods of 'psychotic' or 'severe' depression often moderate their drinking when their mood improves, but a proportion continue the practice of uncontrolled drinking that was acquired during their affective disorder. Similarly, some patients who are subject to mania drink excessively during manic phases because of undue exuberance combined with lessened self-criticism and self-restraint; when their mood reverts to normal they usually, though not always, regain control of their drinking.

Depression can also occur as a hangover symptom; as such it is of brief duration. A depressed mood may additionally develop during the abstinence syndrome, when it endures rather longer, for some days. Depression as a feature of alcohol withdrawal leads in some instances to a resumption of drinking.

There is a final reason why problem drinkers complain of depression: it is a fashionable symptom that readily arouses the interest of the doctor. Alcoholic patients resemble other patients by claiming to feel depressed when not really depressed, because the complaint is respectable and promotes attention. For a more dishonest motive excessive drinkers sometimes report depression in order to obtain a sick note to cover work absenteeism produced by drinking.

Alcohol unleashes attempts at self-harm amongst both alcoholics and nonalcoholics. Kessel (1965) surveyed a group of patients in Edinburgh who committed acts of self-poisoning: 56% of the males and 23% of the females had been drinking immediately prior to their self-poisoning behaviour; 39% of the men and 8% of the females were alcohol dependent, so both alcoholics and nonalcoholics were widely represented among those who were drinking at the time of self-poisoning. Patel et al. (1972) examined self-poisoning subjects in Glasgow and noted that the behaviour was immediately preceded by heavy drinking among 70% of the males and among 40% of the females; the blood alcohol concentrations of the subjects averaged 146 mg/dl on admission to hospital.

The cause of alcohol dependence is commonly punctuated by self-harm and ended by suicide. Ritson and Hassall (1970) noted that 20 out of a sample of 100 problem drinkers gave a history of drug overdoses. Kessell's report on self-poisoning has been noted above; 5 out of the 6 patients who committed suicide in the following year were alcoholic. Another investigation has reported on two groups of dependent drinkers: 131 subjects who had been treated in a psychiatric hospital and followed-up for periods ranging from 1 to 11 years, and 81 others who were surveyed 4–5 years after discharge from an observation ward (Kessell and Grossman, 1961). The suicides in the first group amounted to 8% and in the second sample to 7%; none of the 46 females in the study died by suicide. The authors noted that the suicide rate for the alcoholic men was 75–85 times the expected rate for males of their ages. In the 1972 study of self-poisoning by Patel et al. 59% of the patients possessed an alcohol problem; interestingly, 50% of the married women had a husband who was a problem drinker, and alcohol misuse by a husband or parent was often a major factor determining drug overdose in females. From Toronto Schmidt and de Lint (1972) reported a death rate from suicide in alcoholics that was 6 times higher than the expected rate. An English study of 935 problem drinkers who were followed up for 10–15 years found that 46 subjects incurred deaths recorded as suicidal;

the finding was 24·9 times greater than the expected rate (Nicholls et al., 1974). Sundby (1974) estimated that the rate of suicide among male excessive drinkers who had been treated in Oslo was 5·8 times higher than the expected rate for that capital city, and 8·0 times larger than the expected national rate.

Frankel et al. (1976) have examined the literature on drinking and self-injury; the authors reviewed three explanations for the relationship between alcohol dependence and suicide. Firstly, chronic excessive drinking leads to suicide; secondly, the repeated high consumption of alcohol constitutes a slow form of suicide; thirdly, dependence on alcohol and suicide share a common causation. The first examination appears more applicable; alcoholics with depression bear a closer resemblance to alcoholics without depression than they do to non-alcoholics who are depressed (Woodruff et al., 1973); dependent drinkers who are depressed generally improve in mood with a period of abstinence (Smith et al., 1971; Smith and Layden, 1972). In other words, psychological and biochemical reactions to excessive drinking form the most influential causes of depression and suicidal actions among alcoholic subjects.

Jealousy

Morbid doubts concerning the fidelity of the sexual partner are frequently held by excessive drinkers, both male and female. The jealous ideas range from fleeting suspicions when intoxicated to firm convictions that persist during abstinence. Unfounded accusations of unfaithfulness can arise and are frequently extreme or insulting; the spouse may be accused of incest, of homosexuality, or of prostitution. Violence may accompany the jealous statements.

The reactions of the spouse are often surprisingly light. When the accusations of infidelity only occur while drunk, and are followed in the morning by repentance and by a claim (possibly genuine) of amnesia for the intoxicated behaviour, then the spouse may shrug off the jealousy as not representative of the sober attitude of the drinker. Usually the spouse is correct in adopting a response of relative unconcern. But more permanent delusions of sexual jealousy, held by a male heavy drinker, present a risk to the life of the spouse. Mowatt (1966) interviewed patients with delusions of sexual jealousy who were detained in the security hospital at Broadmoor; he found alcohol dependence had been a feature in 10 of 46 jealous murderers and in 1 of 18 jealous attempted murderers.

Traditionally, morbid jealousy in alcoholics is considered to arise partly from a toxic effect of alcohol, and partly from a psychological reaction to the sexual difficulties of the excessive drinkers.

Impotence is common among males who chronically misuse alcohol (Lemere and Smith, 1973; Akhtar, 1977); the impotence develops both as an immediate temporary effect of alcohol intoxication and as a long term feature. An impotent alcoholic can suspect that the marital partner is seeking intercourse elsewhere. Spouses, whether male or female, of problem drinkers often dislike intercourse with a partner who is drinking heavily and tend to lose interest in the sex act. Instead of attributing the partner's coolness to the drinking an excessive drinker can then project the blame and consider that the spouse's lack of sexual response has arisen because the latter is obtaining sexual satisfaction outside the marriage.

This orthodox explanation for the psychological processes underlying jealousy in problem drinkers has held sway for many decades; it was, for example, outlined in 1916 by Bleuler. The present author has conducted interviews with the spouses of alcoholic patients to determine the relevant sexual problems and frequency of accusations of infidelity that were levelled by the excessive drinkers against their partners. Neither impaired potency in male alcoholics nor reduced libido in spouses (male or female) were associated in a consistent pattern with the subsequent onset of jealous accusations by the heavy drinkers. With some patients one or both of these sexual difficulties, or intoxication, did precipitate morbid jealousy; other patients possessed a preoccupation with jealousy which existed before the heavy drinking and was magnified during the alcohol dependence. Yet by contrast some problem drinkers expressed jealousy when sexual difficulties were absent, while with certain subjects the sexual problems under discussion occurred without jealous accusations. Thus additional factors that are pathogenic of morbid jealousy, but are additional to those of the classic explanation, must exist in the constitutions of jealous alcoholics and in their marriages.

In a series of 125 married alcoholic patients treated by the author, 41·3% of the male and 47·6% of the female subjects had, according to their marital partners, accused the latter of infidelity. The percentages were considerably higher than those obtained by Glatt (1961) from alcoholic patients. In Glatt's investigation the patients answered a questionnaire which asked if they experienced subjective feelings of jealousy relating to spouse or friend of the opposite sex; only 21·8% of the male and 24·6% of the female subjects replied affirmatively. The low proportion of excessive drinkers in the latter research who admitted to jealousy illustrates the mental mechanism of denial, by which individuals can disclaim to themselves and to others that they have developed undesirable ideas, emotions or behaviour. The mechanism is enhanced in dependent drinkers, who have a facility for denying (with varying degrees of awareness) the extent and the consequences of their drinking.

Alcoholic hallucinosis

The syndrome consists of a prolonged state of auditory hallucinations which occur in clear consciousness. The hallucinations take the form of

voices, and are often accompanied by delusions which, in th
thinking, explain the presence of the hallucinated sounds.
voices refer to the patient in the third person, and com
subject's character and activities in a derogatory manner.
other signs, such as thought disorder or affective incongruit
suggest schizophrenia. The patient retains considerable (
reality with respect to the attributed location of the hallucinated voices;
the alcoholic subject cannot see the person or persons who might be
making the sounds, so considers the noises to emanate from sites where
mouth movements cannot be viewed by the subject. For instance, the
voices may only develop in a crowded bar, where the patient could not
simultaneously look at every possible speaker, or they might be
delusionally attributed to people in an imaginary van which is mobile and
therefore unseen.

The psychosis usually remits subsequent to hospital admission and
withdrawal from alcohol. In two groups of subjects the auditory
hallucinations persist: among excessive drinkers with marked features of
dementia, and among patients who are eventually considered to have
schizophrenia (Benedetti, 1952).

The term 'alcoholic hallucinosis' has been employed in quite a
different way, to refer to the hallucinations, visual and auditory, that
occur during both early and advanced stages of delirium tremens. The
ambiguity of use is unfortunate.

RECOGNITION OF ALCOHOL DEPENDENCE

It is increasingly common for problem drinkers to seek advice to curb
their drinking, or for relations to request help because a member of their
family is dependent on alcohol. But alcoholism remains in many
instances a state of denial; the extent of alcohol intake is hidden by heavy
drinkers, concealed by relatives, and kept secret by work associates.
Drinking problems are often not revealed to medical practitioners,
nurses or social workers. An investigation of male alcoholics indicated
that over a 1-year period 74% of the subjects had given a false reason to
their doctor in order to obtain a sick note for absenteeism, when the
absences from work were in reality caused by excess drinking (Edwards
et al., 1967).

Wilkins (1974), in a study of primary health care, has uncovered
many features that lead to the suspicion of a drinking problem. The
aspects which he showed to place the individual at risk of being an
alcoholic and which should evoke the need for appropriate enquiry
included family and interpersonal difficulties, certain physical diseases
or emotional symptoms, some occupations, psychological problems in
the children, accidents, criminal offences, smelling of drink during
interview, and residence in a hostel for the homeless. In Wilkins' study

the indicators of excessive drinking differed in their predictive power. There was a 75% prevalence of alcohol dependence among his patients who smelled of drink during medical consultation; the frequency was 50% among subjects who developed gastritis or peptic ulcer, among those who underwent an accident at work or on the road, and in patients who requested a sick note for reasons that were probably false. The frequency of excessive drinking was 25% amongst subjects who complained of anxiety or depression, who had undergone marital disharmony or divorce, were single males over 40 years, or who worked in the brewery or catering trades.

Wilkins included in his general practice investigation a Spare Time Activities Questionnaire (STAQ) which is capable of administration in 7–8 minutes. The examination is composed of general questions concerning neutral recreational activities like smoking, gambling and television viewing, together with specific questions about drinking and associated problems. False positive results are unlikely, since non-alcoholics do not admit to the symptoms of alcoholism, but when STAQ was repeated a year later 67% of the patients classed as alcoholic on the first occasion were categorized otherwise. The low repeat reliability illustrates the difficulties of case finding among alcohol misusers.

A smaller proportion of false negative results has been claimed for the Michigan Alcoholism Screening test (MAST). This instrument is a 25-item questionnaire that both professionals and nonprofessionals can administer. The scoring of each item is weighted according to its potential as an indicator of alcoholism. In the first full study of its use MAST was given to 5 groups, that ranged in likelihood of alcohol dependence from apparently normal controls, through drunken drivers to alcoholics in hospital (Selzer, 1971); 249 of the 526 subjects were demonstrated as alcohol dependent by the questionnaire. MAST failed to uncover no more than 15 (6·02%) of the problem drinkers; the 15 diagnostic failures were due to concealment by alcoholics of significant aspects of their drinking behaviour.

There have been several reports from the United States to confirm the screening value of MAST. In a general hospital the test identified 10% of medical and surgical inpatients as alcohol dependent; it picked out 90% of the alcoholics when the doctors had only detected 10% of the excessive drinkers (Moore, 1972a); the instrument has also been useful in a psychiatric hospital (Moore, 1972b). Among U.S. Navy subjects MAST indicated alcoholism in 97% of medically diagnosed alcoholics (Favazza and Pires, 1974). A shortened form of the questionnaire, using the 10 questions that proved most discriminatory in previous studies, correlated highly with the full version in the discrimination of dependent drinkers from nonalcoholics (Pokorny et al., 1972). When MAST was applied to drivers convicted of drunken driving the results showed that a higher proportion of repeat offenders than first offenders achieved scores within its alcoholism range (Yoder and Moore, 1973). The MAST screening measure has been successfully employed outside the United States, in Scotland (Quinn and Johnstone, 1976) and in Italy (Benussi et al., 1982).

A medical committee of the National Council on Alcoholism in the United States has drawn up criteria for the diagnosis of alcoholism (Criteria Committee, 1972). The items were weighted for predictive power and placed in two broad categories. The first compartment consists of physiological and clinical aspects, including major alcohol-associated illnesses. The second category is composed of behavioural, psychological and attitudinal features. Items that convey a definite diagnosis of alcoholism include the withdrawal syndrome of physical dependence, high tolerance (shown by a blood alcohol concentration of 150 mg/dl without gross intoxication), and drinking despite resultant job loss or disruption of marriage. Listed by the committee among features that should arouse the suspicion of an injurious level of drinking are several kinds of anaemia, cigarette burns, frequent car accidents, inappropriate telephone calls, and variations in the medical excuses offered for work absenteeism.

The same report pointed out that the following factors reinforce the risk of an alcohol problem: a history of alcoholism or teetotalism in the family of either the subject or spouse, female relatives of more than one generation who develop recurrent depression, the last child of a large family or birth into the last half of the sibship in a large family, a childhood home that was broken or subject to parental discord, ethnic groups in the U.S.A. prone to excessive drinking (e.g. Irish and Scandinavian), and heavy smoking.

Alcohol dependence therefore is protean in its manifestations. Where the condition is not volunteered by the drinker, or by a relative or associate, it may sometimes be suspected from easily made observations, such as the presence of a flushed face with dilated venules, or an aroma of drink from a person keeping an appointment with a professional adviser. Yet often the presenting features are not likely to arouse suspicion because they are common symptoms of many illnesses. The foremost aspects may be psychiatric (anxiety, depression or an attempt at self-harm) or point to vague physical illnesses (often gastrointestinal or respiratory). Dependence on alcohol has replaced syphilis as the 'Great Imitator' of diseases. Alternatively, alcohol dependence can exhibit through behavioural features that affect the family, work, or the law; or dependence may be suspected in subjects from certain backgrounds or occupations where a high level of alcohol intake is common.

It is important to remember the common occurrence of drinking problems. For example, Jarman and Jellet (1979) investigated medical and orthopaedic inpatients and emergency department outpatients of a London teaching hospital; 19·5% were problem drinkers, mostly from diagnostic groups not usually associated with alcohol dependence. Jariwalla and colleagues (1979) concluded, from their own study and from a review of other investigations among general medical inpatients, that alcohol misuse is an important major or contributory cause of many acute admissions to medical wards. Petersson and coworkers (1982) analysed mortality among middle-aged males; they reported that excessive drinking was the most common underlying factor, and formed a feature that was considerably under-represented in official death statistics.

Members of the nonmedical and medical caring professions are well placed to detect high levels of drinking, and to initiate and pursue appropriate counselling. Early recognition and counselling allows heavily drinking subjects whose dependence is minimal to moderate their intake, and can motivate and guide drinkers whose dependence is more pronounced towards abstinence. Pollak (1978) has described the recognition and effective treatment of problem drinkers in general medical practice. Barrison et al. (1982) have recounted the detection of abnormal drinkers among hospital inpatients at a stage when most of the subjects probably did not require abstention. In order to protect the fetus, enquiry and advice about smoking habits form a routine part of antenatal care; for the same purpose comparable measures should be included about drinking during pregnancy.

When excessive drinking is a possibility it is imperative to pursue enquiries with the subject and if necessary with other persons, particularly relatives. Three kinds of investigation can be undertaken: medical tests, questionnaires and a drinking history. The laboratory tests available to doctors include (in decreasing order of sensitivity) serum gamma-glutamyltransferase (Dunbar et al., 1982), mean cell volume of the red blood cells (Chick et al., 1981), serum aspartate transferase (Morgan et al., 1981), serum ferritin (Kristensson), and serum urate (Ramsay, 1979). Elevation of one or more of these features points, in the absence of other causes, to a hazardous level of drinking; a drinking history is then necessary to determine the strength, if any, of dependence on alcohol and whether abstinence or moderation are required.

The blood alcohol concentration is another biochemical test that can be used (Holt et al., 1980), although it must be employed sensitively to avoid the impression of incrimination; alcohol in the blood at an unusual time, or a high level of blood alcohol in a person who is not showing marked intoxication, would indicate undue reliance on alcohol. It has been suggested that fractures, especially multiple fractures, observed on routine chest X-rays also offer a useful indicator of alcohol dependence (Israel et al., 1980; Lindsell et al., 1982).

Questionnaires are sometimes employed in practical work as well as in research. Suitable measures include MAST, in its long or short

version, and CAGE (Ewing and Rouse, 1970); the latter is more brie
but leads to a rather high proportion of false positive inclusions.

A careful drinking history (Table 5) forms the central and unavoidable part of the enquiries. Tactful and kindly yet frank questions should be directed, not merely at drinking practices, but at the effects of drinking on physical and mental well-being, and on interpersonal and occupational adjustment. It is correct to put leading questions to a possible dependent drinker, since nonalcoholics do not admit to the symptoms of alcohol dependence; direct enquiries about alcohol symptomatology should be framed in a way that suggests some degree of positive answers, to avoid brisk but untruthful denials.

Table 5. Drinking history

Timing, frequency, amount of drinking (sometimes helpful to analyse previous seven days).
Withdrawal symptoms: tremor, sweating, quivering sensation in epigastrium.
Drinking to relieve withdrawal symptoms.
Frequent memory blackouts.
Family effects (disharmony, separation, divorce).
Occupational effects (absences from work, trouble with superiors, job loss, re-employment at a lower status).
Legal effects (drinking and driving offences, drunkenness convictions).
Previous help for drinking (medical, Alcoholics Anonymous, alcoholism council, other sources).
Do relatives and friends consider subject is a normal drinker?
Does the subject consider the drinking is normal?

A patient manner of interview, supplemented when necessary by information from other persons, generally suffices to uncover alcohol dependence, even against initial evasions. Awareness of the factors that should alert to the suspicion of a high level of alcohol intake, and readiness to seek further information in appropriate instances, will enhance its detection, and therefore its effective treatment.

It is useful to summarize the necessary viewpoint and approach by the following question, which should always be kept in mind by the therapist: 'Has this person a problem with alcohol, and if so what can I do to help?'

Fortunately, although heavy drinkers may avoid the voluntary disclosure of their high intake, and may initially deny that they possess its features, they often wish that their drinking problem could receive recognition and advice. A sympathetic yet insistent interviewer is frequently able to elicit from an excessive drinker the extent and consequences of the alcohol consumption, with immediate relief of guilt in the subject and with prospects of long-term benefit.

FEMALE PROBLEM DRINKERS

s of female with male excessive drinkers have indicated rences in the drinking histories and other characteristics of ps. There has been an increase in the number of young adult inkers of both sexes, but until recently female subjects showed a later age of onset of excessive drinking (although they appeared for treatment at about the same time of life, between 35–50 years of age). Some studies have found a less favourable outcome in females than in males (Glatt, 1961; Pemberton, 1967). A later review concluded that there is no sex difference in outcome when the prognostic factors are taken into account (Annis and Liban, 1980). Women who drink heavily are more likely than male counterparts to drink alone, to develop dependence on alcohol after a stressful event, to undergo broken marriages and to report depressive symptoms (Sclare, 1970; Beckman, 1978). Relatives of female excessive drinkers have a higher incidence of psychiatric disorder than relatives of male problem drinkers; compared with male alcoholics, females with alcohol dependence are more likely to possess second degree relatives with affective disorder (Winokur and Clayton, 1968). Schuckit et al. (1969) considered that 19 out of 70 female problem drinkers they studied had pre-existing affective disorder; they suggested that there exist in women two types of alcohol dependence, which they labelled 'primary' and 'affective'.

Most of the studies which propose an affective basis for many instances of female alcoholism have been published from one research unit; the reports require confirmation from other centres. Major difficulties of relevance ensue from the uncertainties that are current in psychiatry concerning the classification, aetiology and treatment of depression. Without entering into the disputed territory a practical point for treatment is that the value of physical therapies for depression has not been demonstrated for the majority of problem drinkers of either sex. The treatment of alcoholic women is along the same lines as for males.

During the 1970s there was a recent increase in the number of female alcoholics presenting or referred for treatment. The rise is relatively greater than the corresponding increase for men. In 1964 the proportion of male to female heavy drinkers attending the Merseyside, Lancashire and Cheshire Council on Alcoholism was 8 : 1; by 1975 the ratio had altered to 2½ males to 1 female. A growing number of alcoholic females aged between 20 and 30 are now cared for by treatment centres. The change in sex incidence and age presumably reflects the emancipation of the female drinker, with weakened taboos on drinking by females, including young women.

Sclare (1975) has commented on the augmented number of female problem drinkers that appeared for treatment. He described three forms of alcohol misuse among women:

1. Girls in their teens or early twenties who drink heavily with their boyfriends.
2. Women in early middle life whose children have grown up and who drink socially in a replication of traditional male drinking.
3. Women in early middle age who are unhappy because of loneliness arising from separation, divorce, widowhood, or because of neglect by a husband who is unfaithful or excessively devoted to his work.

Some attention has centred on the part that sex roles play in alcohol use, and on the relationship between drinking and sex-role conflicts in women. The blurring of distinctions between the sexes in respect to permitted behaviour has contributed to the growth of drinking among women and, for a minority, of excessive drinking. It is argued that female problem drinkers undergo internal conflicts of a conscious and unconscious nature between their feminine and masculine tendencies (Wilsnack, 1976). The issues have been reviewed by Leland (1982).

One motivation for drinking heavily that is encountered among alcoholic females lies in the wish to punish the male spouse, through the intoxicated behaviour of the wife. The antagonism between the couple may reach the stage that the husband overtly expresses indifference or malevolence to the welfare of the problem drinker and disbelieves her ability to recover. At this point the desire of the female excessive drinker to distress her husband may paradoxically provide an effective incentive to cease alcohol consumption!

YOUNG PROBLEM DRINKERS

The majority of young people who drink learn to take alcohol in an unharmful way, but a minority develop problems from repeated excessive drinking. As with problem drinkers from other age groups, young problem drinkers possess a wide range of backgrounds and personalities, although compared with older subjects they tend to originate from more disturbed families and to show more pronounced abnormalities of personality. A study in Sydney examined young alcoholics (aged 30 or less) and compared them with a control group of older problem drinkers (Rosenberg, 1969). The young alcoholics differed from the other alcoholic subjects in showing more neurotic tendencies; they were more likely to live alone or take drugs, and less likely to show stability of residence. Most of the youthful heavy drinkers were hostile towards their fathers, whom they felt had treated them unfairly, or with disinterest, or were often away from home. In contradistinction to their attitudes to their fathers the young excessive drinkers felt closer towards their mothers, yet complained that their maternal parents exerted poor discipline. Seventy-eight per cent of younger subjects had convictions for drunkenness, violence, larceny or drunken driving; 48% of them had made at least one suicidal action. Freed (1973) has also noted that young persons with drinking problems are more prone to drug misuse than heavy drinkers from older age groups.

An Edinburgh report on young problem drinkers found that three-quarters of the study group were convicted of offences (Ritson and Hassall, 1970). The subjects frequently showed unsatisfactory childhoods and often contracted unhappy marriages. They commonly complained of anxiety, tension or sleep disturbance, and under-participated in social activities.

Another investigation in Edinburgh demonstrated differences between a group of subjects who were alcoholic by the age of 30 and a sample who became dependent on alcohol after that age (Foulds and Hassall, 1969). The former subjects showed a greater incidence of unhappy relationships with their mothers, possessed a higher number of convictions and prison sentences, made more suicidal attempts and underwent more marital disruption. Eighty per cent of the subjects whose excessive drinking began early were considered to possess personality disorders, compared with only about one-third of those whose alcohol dependence developed after the age of 30.

In summary, the studies confirm the commonsense expectation that young problem drinkers are more aberrant in their families of origin and emotional constitutions than subjects who avoid severe alcohol difficulties until later in life. In regard to outcome not every report shows that young excessive drinkers have a less favourable prognosis than older subjects, but where a difference in outcome is found it is always in favour of the subjects who are more advanced in age. The enhanced extent of drinking in recent years among teenagers and young adults in many countries, including Britain, has resulted in an increased prevalence of drunkenness and drunkenness convictions in these age groups (Smith, 1981). It is the view of many professional workers in alcoholism that there has also resulted a rise in the number of alcoholics who are aged under 30. The growing incidence of young adults who are problem drinkers includes females, many of whom are married and are mothers.

PROBLEM DRINKING AMONG THE ELDERLY

Alcohol difficulties among the aged are more common than is sometimes realized (Zimberg, 1974). Elderly people constitute in many countries a rapidly expanding age group. By the end of the century about 16% of the population of the United States will be aged 65 or over. Many elderly persons suffer from loneliness, anxiety and failing health, with a reduction of meaningful activity and recreational interests. In consequence some senior citizens become unduly reliant on alcohol for solace.

Drinking problems in the elderly are aggravated by the decreased tolerance to alcohol that develops with age.

Furthermore, many elderly problem drinkers add to their difficulties by the consumption of sedatives and minor tranquillizers that are unwisely prescribed by their doctors. Old age is accompanied by an enhanced susceptiblity to drugs, for more than one reason. The brain becomes more affected by psychoactive substances; there is reduced elimination of drugs; the ability to compensate for drug effects is impaired (Castleden et al., 1979).

It is generally agreed that there are two categories of elderly people who drink excessively. Some have been alcohol dependent from an earlier period and continue their abnormal intake into old age; others develop problem drinking when senior citizens (Mishara and Kastenbaum, 1980). Their drinking is commonly hidden, and often abetted, by relatives. Concomitant or resultant ill-health is a frequent feature.

Treatment requires relief of the psychological, social and somatic stresses associated with aging (Peppers and Stover, 1979). Elderly problem drinkers can benefit considerably from the special alcohol treatment services, even though the facilities may be geared to younger age groups. But integration, after initial detoxification, into the general service systems for the aged is frequently the appropriate course to adopt. It is often possible and beneficial to link the two kinds of service (Smith, 1980). Comprehensive after care, with community centre attendance and home visits by staff when necessary, comprise essential and helpful aspects of a therapeutic programme for elderly problem drinkers.

SPOUSES OF PROBLEM DRINKERS

Wives of excessive drinkers have been the subject of many studies. Two contrasting descriptions have been proposed for their personalities and behaviour. The first view postulates that wives of problem drinkers possess character disorders which pre-date the alcohol usage of their husbands, determine their choice of married partner and subtly contribute to the excessive drinking of their spouses. The alternative concept considers that the anomalies shown by wives constitute in most instances stress reactions to the excessive drinking of their husbands.

An early proponent of the first viewpoint was Whalen (1953), who vividly described four types of wives of heavy drinkers. 'Suffering Susan' has a need for punishment, and selects a husband who satisfies this through his drinking. 'Controlling Catherine' chooses an inept husband whom she can dominate. 'Wavering Winifred' possesses a strong desire for affection and selects a weak spouse who loves her keenly; his drinking behaviour rouses sympathy for her plight. 'Punitive Polly' is aggressive and intensely involved in her career.

Futterman (1953) considered that wives unconsciously fostered the drinking of their alcoholic spouses in order to preserve a controlling and motherly attitude to their husbands. Some wives have been reported to decompensate in mental health and develop a neurotic breakdown when the drinking of their husbands decreased (McDonald, 1956). Daughters of problem drinkers are disproportionately liable to marry abnormal drinkers (Nice, 1979).

Jackson (1954) was in the forefront of adherents to the concept of a stress reaction in wives of alcohol misusers. She described coping mechanisms by which wives attempt to deal with the excess drinking of their husbands, and concluded that the behaviour of wives represents understandable reactions to their marital difficulties. Kogen et al. (1963) found that only 19 out of 50 wives of dependent drinkers showed demonstrable personality impairment when administered the Minnesota Multiphasic Personality Inventory (MMPI).

One of the first reviews of the literature on wives of heavy drinkers was conducted by Bailey (1961). She noted that the high proportion of problem drinkers who were married had overthrown the stereotype of the alcoholic as an undersocialized, marginal member of society. In Bailey's view the studies she analysed gave support to the hypothesis that alcohol dependence is a cumulative stress that affects the family in several distinct ways. She pointed to a research necessity (which remains still unfulfilled) for investigation of alcoholic marriages that, without seeking help, remain intact or terminate. A subsequent study by Bailey et al. (1962) of psychophysiological symptoms among wives of chronic alcohol misusers produced important findings; among wives who had separated from their partners 74% had possessed marked symptoms while living with their husbands, compared to 55% subsequent to separation; 82% of wives living with sober husbands recalled the possession of marked discomfort during the time that their husbands were drinking, although only 43% retained strong symptoms after their husbands became abstinent.

The concept of a stress reaction has also received support from James and Goldman (1971). Seventy-two per cent of their group of wives of problem drinkers had married before the commencement of excess drinking, in 6% of instances before their husbands drank at all. Most of the wives were therefore not in a position to predict alcoholism when they chose a partner. During marriage their reaction patterns altered as the alcohol intake of their husbands progressed from a social level to dependent drinking, and finally towards abstinence. 3·1% of the wives with abstinent husbands attributed the cessation of drinking to their leaving or threatening to leave the alcoholic partner.

A subgroup of wives of excessive drinkers was noted by Rae and Forbes (1966); its members scored highly on the psychopathic deviate scale of the MMPI. The wives in this subgroup were masculine in outlook, and in competitive rather than in complementary relationship with their husbands; the latter were confused about their own marital socio-sexual roles (Rae and Drewery, 1972). The husbands carried a poorer prognosis than spouses whose wives were not socially deviant; in the uncommon event of the marital partners of socially deviant wives achieving sobriety the wives frequently became psychiatrically ill (Rae, 1972).

Edwards et al. (1973) concluded from an analysis of the literature that the predominant view of wives of problem drinkers is that they generally possess normal basic personalities. The personality dysfunctions and behaviour patterns of the wives tend to develop as responses to their spouses; the wives show less abnormalities when their husbands become abstinent.

What kinds of response are shown by wives of alcoholics? The patterns vary, but frequent features are anxiety, insecurity, anger, social isolation, and refusal of the sex act. Sometimes there develops an extreme and prolonged denial to others of an alcohol problem in the home. A degree of role transfer is almost inevitable, with the female partner adopting a more dominant part in decisions and responsibilities.

The reactions of the wives of excessive drinkers are of considerable importance in determining the outcome of the drinking. A continuum for their responses has been proposed that ranges from disengagement to engagement (Orford et al., 1975). Features that point to the disengagement of a wife from an alcoholic husband comprise avoidance of the spouse, refusal to sleep together, being too frightened or angry to act effectively when the husband is drunk, or indulging the drinking by giving alcohol or paying bills. These aspects are associated with a continuance of excessive drinking. Responses which indicate that the wife is actively engaged in gaining the sobriety of her husband include pleading with the partner to stop drinking, stressing that drinking makes the husband ill, starting a row because he is drunk, getting herself drunk to deter the partner from drinking excessively, barring alcohol from the house or pouring it away when discovered in the home, belittling the husband's drinking in front of others, and striking the spouse because of his alcohol intake. Measures of this nature taken against excessive drinking were reported by Orford and his colleagues to improve the outcome. The same group of investigators has also noted that marriages which retain cohesiveness and continue to provide mutual satisfaction are more likely to develop an abatement of the drinking of the husband than are partnerships with a low level of affection and respect (Orford et al., 1976).

A fuller understanding of the psychosocial complications within the marriages of problem drinkers could be gained by widening the basis of study to take in more global concepts of marriage (Orford, 1975).

Relevant studies by ethanologists have concentrated too narrowly on drinking. It would be beneficial to set alcoholism-complicated marriages in the wider range of what is generally known and understood about marital partnerships and about problem marriages.

Husbands of problem drinkers

In contrast to the theme of wives of alcohol misusers little has been written concerning husbands of females who drink excessively (Jacob and Seilhamer, 1982). Rimmer (1974) has noted the paucity of publications and presented data on 25 husbands whose alcoholic wives were admitted to a private mental hospital. Fifteen of the husbands had undergone a psychiatric illness, in 4 instances before the onset of the wives' alcoholism. Eight husbands had developed an affective-depressive disorder, 5 were alcoholic, 1 was a sociopath, and no diagnosis was made for the remaining husband with a psychiatric condition; altogether 9 of the 25 husbands were clearly dependent on alcohol or drank heavily. Another study, of 58 husbands with alcoholic wives, reported that 20 had developed past or present high levels of drinking (Altman et al., 1980).

The assortative mating of two alcoholics by a marriage provides considerable difficulties for the therapist. Fortunately most problem drinkers do not marry a partner who already shows or who develops dependence on alcohol.

OFFSPRING OF PROBLEM DRINKERS

Several categories of social and psychological problems are common among the progeny of alcoholic parents. One is alcohol dependence itself, which is more frequently encountered in the adult progeny of dependent drinkers than in the descendents of nonalcoholics. It used to be considered that the findings of Roe (1944) had discounted the theory of a genetic contribution to the higher incidence of problem drinking in the offspring of alcoholics. She reported that a high frequency of excessive drinking was not found in subjects who had been reared apart from their alcoholic parents. But the issue was reopened by more recent studies. The newer studies examined adults who were born of alcoholics but who in childhood were reared by adoptive parents or by nonalcoholic parent figures; the researchers also looked at adults who were progeny of nonalcoholics, but who were raised by alcoholic parent surrogates (Schuckit et al., 1972; Goodwin et al., 1973). The later investigations emphasized genetic rather than environmental factors. Yet in the case of children reared by their alcoholic parent identification with the parent and imitation of parental behaviour can play a role in the subsequent development of excessive drinking by the progeny. The unsettling effects of an alcoholic parent on the personality of the growing child might also determine emotional problems in the latter which later find temporary relief from alcohol.

Children of excessive drinkers are affected in other ways than in an increased liability to develop alcohol problems. A high frequency of paternal alcoholism has been found among adolescent drug misusers (Rosenberg, 1971). Delinquency, trouble in school, temper tantrums, fighting with peers, rebelliousness and withdrawal have been noted in young offspring of alcoholics. Aronson and Gilbert (1963) studied schoolteacher judgements of children and found many differences at a statistically significant level between sons of male problem drinkers and control sons. The progeny of the former were more likely to display inappropriate emotional responses, emotional and material acquisitiveness, hostility and self-dissatisfaction. The researchers considered that these features were typical of the 'passive-aggressive personality' which they believed to occur frequently among established dependent drinkers.

Another investigation reported on Swedish children aged between 4 and 12 whose fathers attended an outpatient clinic for problem drinking; the children were compared with demographically similar children of nonalcoholic fathers (Nylander, 1960). The children of the excessive drinkers were significantly less prone to suffer from prolonged physical illness, or from physical illness which required medical treatment, but were as likely as the controls to visit hospital clinics with complaints of physical symptoms; it was considered that the frequent physical symptoms of the alcoholic offspring were often psychogenic. As part of the investigation teachers were asked to make global assessments of the subjects; 48% of the children of the heavy drinkers and 10% of the controls were assessed as problem children.

Nylander (1960) also studied children and adolescents, aged up to 21, who were admitted to a psychiatric department and whose fathers were alcoholic. Behavioural and antisocial problems were the most common reasons for admission of the young subjects; difficulties of this nature involved truancy, school refusal, pilfering, running away and social instability. Other factors leading to psychiatric admission were neurotic features like restlessness and depression, as well as psychosomatic aspects such as headache, giddiness, abdominal pain, enuresis and encopresis.

Both groups of Nylander's subjects were again assessed 21 years later by Rhydelius (1981). Thirty-five per cent of the boys became registered with the Temperance Board of Sweden as alcoholics, compared with 20% of male controls. Six per cent of the females were notified to the Board as alcoholic, compared with 1% of controls. An excess proportion of male and female probands misused drugs.

Melling (1982) noted that parents in alcoholic households took little account of the emotional health of their children. In her study the majority of problem drinkers considered their children were not harmed emotionally. While the reverse view was held by a slight preponderance of the nonalcoholic spouses, help was not sought by the parents for their children even when the youngsters experienced considerable psychological stress.

Mik (1970) investigated boys who were in a reception centre because of antisocial behaviour and compared among the subjects sons of male problem drinkers with a control group. Both samples showed many resemblances in personality structure, but a sentence completion test and the semantic differential test of Osgood did reveal differences between the groups. According to these measuring instruments the children of alcoholic fathers scored more negative feelings towards an authority figure, and more punitive feelings towards a mother figure.

The case records of children and parents interviewed in a child psychiatry clinic were analysed by Chafetz et al. (1971). The homes of children of alcoholics were more unsatisfactory, in terms of parental relationships, separation or divorce, than were the homes of other children. Unlike the children of nonalcoholics the majority of children of excessive drinkers were living with only one parent. The two groups showed striking similarities in their presenting complaints, but the children of the problem drinkers developed in adolescence more school difficulties and more trouble with the police than other adolescents. Cantwell (1972) undertook a comparison of hyperactive children with matched controls; the overactive sample possessed a higher incidence of alcohol dependence in the parents (and other relatives).

Most of the relevant studies have been conducted on disturbed young persons or on extremely deviant parents or on both kinds of subject. The results tend therefore to convey a misleadingly high impression of the psychological and social maladjustments of the children of alcoholics. Kammeier (1971) surveyed more normal subjects, who were adolescent pupils attending a high school. Among her sample the adolescent offspring of alcoholic parents, compared with their peers, displayed greater incidences of school absenteeism, of parental separation or of divorce, and of fathers who were in lower socio-economic categories. The adjustment of the progeny of alcoholics was nevertheless similar to the controls and considerably better than that revealed by other studies.

A considerable proportion, probably the majority, of the offspring of problem drinkers, reach mature years without gross scars on their personalities and without alcohol problems or overt psychiatric illness. The point is worth stressing, so that they and their parents can receive reassurance.

Two reviews of the literature on children of problem drinkers have referred to heavy drinking and child abuse (Wilson and Orford, 1978; El-Guebaly and Offord, 1979). Definitions of violence and of excessive drinking tend to be imprecise, but it appears that child abuse is reported from families in chronic poverty, disorganization and antisocial milieu. Alcohol intoxication rather than alcohol dependence is the more common feature. El-Guebaly and Offord also speculate that the sources of strength among stable children of alcoholic homes include strict parental supervision, the positive influence of the nonalcoholic parent, a stable relationship with any adult, and a sound school atmosphere.

ALCOHOL, VIOLENCE AND CRIME

There are difficulties in establishing the nature of an association between alcohol, alcohol misuse and antisocial behaviour. The relationship should not be viewed as simply causal, since spurious, noncausal associations exist (Collins, 1982).

For example, drinking can take place in venues or with companions that lead to crime. Offenders who are drunk are more likely to be apprehended than those who are sober. Studies of prison populations survey selected samples of offenders; drinking histories that are taken retrospectively possess doubtful accuracy. Alcohol intake may be accompanied by the consumption of drugs. Drunken comportment can provoke other people to aggression.

Alcohol intake is associated with a wide range of criminal or violent behaviour, including accident, suicide, sexual assault, violence within the family, felony and homicide. But drinking is involved only in a proportion of such crimes, usually in a minority (Evans, 1980). Although the presence of alcohol is accompanied by situational and social determinants of aggression, clinical observation supports the view of Coid (1982). He concluded, from a literature survey, that the link between alcohol and violence largely depends on a subgroup of people whose personalities predispose them to excessive drinking and to violence. Their heavy drinking started at a young age; they possess relatives who are violent when intoxicated; they show little concern for their drinking or their aggression. Their antisocial personalities produce a poor prognosis.

Fortunately most problem drinkers are outside this category. the most common kind of offence committed by socially dysfunctional drinkers involves drinking and driving. The peak age group of persons so convicted lies, in Britain, between 20 to 25 years of age. Many, perhaps the majority, of the offenders from this age range do not possess severe alcohol problems, although heavy drinking before driving is a behaviour to which dependent drinkers are, of course, prone. A conviction for drinking and driving does not distinguish problem drinkers who are sociopathic from those who are socially stable.

THE ALCOHOLIC DOCTOR

Doctors are especially prone to develop alcohol dependence (Murray, 1980; Glatt, 1982). Explanations have included the possible selection of a minority of medical undergraduates who are psychologically vulnerable, and the lengthy apprenticeship of medical students that is associated with a relative lack of responsibility and often with convivial drinking. After graduation, stresses at work, freedom from supervision and a high income present further risk factors. The opportunity for a doctor to misuse drugs can lead to alcohol substitution when the drug intake becomes suspected.

Alcoholism is the most frequent condition for which doctors enter psychiatric treatment, and is the commonest reason for disciplinary troubles among medically qualified persons. The fact that doctors, who have some expert knowledge of alcohol and its effects, can readily develop problems from its consumption forcefully illustrates the self-deception of alcohol dependence. The medical profession resembles other occupations by attempting to conceal and cover the excessive drinking of its members. This, of course, allows the drinking to progress until a crisis, when colleagues tend to react harshly. Edwards (1975) has incisively described the process by which colleagues initially refrain from intervention, and then reject the alcoholic doctor at a crucial moment.

Fortunately doctors are often co-operative patients in alcohol therapy. A report of poor treatment results (Murray, 1976) has been followed by studies that indicated generally favourable responses to therapy with respect to abstinence and ability to practise medicine (Goby et al., 1979; Kliner et al., 1980; Johnson and Connolly, 1981). Some alcoholic doctors who are impressed by the aims and methods of Alcoholics Anonymous feel reluctant to attend meetings with nonmedical members. Therefore an international network exists that is composed of and for medical (and dental) problem drinkers. Its branch in the British Isles is known as the British Doctors and Dentists Group; the section contains more than 400 members from Britain and Ireland.

PROBLEM DRINKING IN INDUSTRY

The industrial problems that excessive drinking poses have become increasingly apparent and acknowledged. Despite the rising number of females and young adults who are dependent drinkers the typical subjects seen for treatment are males aged between 30 and 50, who have many years of experience at work, perhaps after an expensive training. Rehabilitation of these experienced personnel is an exercise of economic value to industry.

The majority of alcoholics are employed or, if temporarily out of a job, are about to obtain another post. Moss and Davies (1976) reported that drinking had affected the work of 52% of their alcoholic male subjects, but had resulted in only 4·2% of them becoming unemployable or prematurely retired. A Scottish company devised a policy on problem drinking; in consequence 14% of its managers were found to be alcoholic and were counselled to the extent that no key executive was dismissed for excess alcohol consumption (Gray, 1969).

Edwards et al. (1967) studied by questionnaire male problem drinkers at three regional alcoholism councils in Scotland and England. The subjects possessed some degree of occupational stability; 67% were in employment, and about half were in their current post for at least 2 years. Yet drinking had markedly affected their work, in many directions (*Tables* 6 and 7).

Table 6. Occupational features in male problem drinkers (After Edwards et al., 1967)

	Per cent
Drinking interfered with promotion	76
Not promoted in previous 5 years	90
Holding lower paid job than immediately prior post	47
Dismissed at least once for drinking	75
Dismissed over 5 times for drinking	12
Carried a bottle to work	62
Carried a bottle to work daily	12
Drank before commencing work	88
Drank at times throughout the working day	91

Table 7. Occupational factors over one year in male alcoholics (After Edwards et al., 1967)

	Per cent
Drinking certainly contributed to an accident at work	11
Drinking possibly contributed to an accident at work	32
Drinking led to loss of time from work	98
Drinking led to Monday morning absenteeism	93

A later survey was conducted in England by Saad and Madden (1976) on medically certificated incapacity and unemployment among male alcoholic patients. During the year before interview the average time recorded as lost from work per person amounted to 86·1 days lost because of certified sickness and 35·6 days lost because of unemployment. The illness absenteeism of the excessive drinkers was considerably higher than national figures. The augmented sickness absence was the result of extra spells of invalidism rather than of longer individual periods of sickness incapacity. Although most of the sickness was directly or indirectly caused by drinking a diagnosis indicating dependence on alcohol was mentioned in only a few instances on the medical certificates of the patients; this latter point illustrates the degree of concealment of alcohol dependence and the difficulties in accurate assessment of its incidence. A Stockholm enquiry into two groups of male problem drinkers revealed respective yearly averages of 44·2 and 47·4 days during which the subjects received sickness benefit, compared with 12·2 days for a control sample (Bjerver, 1972). In the U.S.A. a yearly average sickness absence of 19·4 days was reported in unrecovered alcoholics, while nonalcoholic controls averaged only 5·4 days (Pell and D'Alonzo, 1970).

Several risk factors have been invoked to account for the differences in the rates of alcohol problems (including cirrhosis deaths) between occupations (Plant, 1979). Availability of alcohol and social pressure to drink at work are rather obvious features. Collusion of excessive drinking by colleagues is a common aspect of alcohol dependence. Freedom from supervision, very high or low incomes and stressful or hazardous duties also present an alcohol risk. Selection and self-selection of vulnerable people and inadequate screening of entrants form additional features that are associated with alcohol problems in employment.

Plant (1979) noted that people who became unemployed then tended to drink more heavily. Brenner (1975) has discussed the association of alcohol consumption with the state of the economy and proposed a two-stage relationship. The long-term trend of alcohol consumption and alcohol disabilities is positively correlated with *per capita* personal income, but shorter fluctuations are inversely related to the level of employment. In his view, periods of growing unemployment in the United States have soon been followed by an increase of alcohol consumption (in the form of spirits) and by rises of cirrhosis mortality rates, of alcoholic admissions to mental hospitals and of convictions for driving while intoxicated.

On the other hand, the methods and conclusions of Brenner have been questioned (Gravelle et al., 1981). The growth of unemployment in Britain during 1981 was accompanied by a fall in sales of beer and spirits. In England, Cook et al. (1982) found no significant differences in numbers of heavy drinkers between employed and unemployed persons when age, social class and town of residence were taken into consideration. There are clearly variations in personal reactions to unemployment. Some individuals who fall out of work devote a considerable portion of their extra free time to drinking. Others, probably the majority in Britain, respond to the fall in income by curtailing expenditure on alcohol.

Among the employed or potentially employed the amount lost to production because of alcohol misuse was considered, for England and Wales at the start of the 1980s, to lie between £530 million and £540 million (Holtermann and Burchell, 1981). The losses to production arise from impairment of performance, absenteeism, sickness, unemployment and death.

A growing number of companies now have programmes for the

detection and treatment of their alcoholic employees (Hore, 1981). This applies in West Germany, and especially in the United States where there are over 300 major organizations with alcoholism policies. They include General Motors, Eastman Kodak, the Bell Telephone Company, Consolidated Edison, U.S. Steel, Goodyear Rubber, and the U.S. Navy. Ford and Heinz have banned alcohol from their canteens and dining rooms. Among trade unions in the U.S.A. that focus interest on alcohol are the United Steelworkers, United Transportation Union, the International Brotherhood of Teamsters, and the Oil, Chemical and Atomic Workers International Union.

The largest employer in Britain, the Civil Service, is enlightened and realistic. Alcoholic public servants can receive sick leave for treatment, rehabilitation may subsequently be arranged, or transfer provided to another section of the Service. In the event of treatment failure, retirement with pension on the grounds of ill health is recognized as appropriate (Madden, 1967). The U.K. Government has published a pamphlet which urges employers and trade unions to develop alcohol programmes (Health and Safety Executive, 1981).

In the Liverpool area several companies and government departments operate alcohol policies. Out of 104 persons whom these organizations referred to the local council on alcoholism 60 have remained in their posts or were promoted. Over a 1-year period employers referred 15% of the council's case load of problem drinkers.

An alcohol programme for industry

A constructive industrial policy for excessive drinking involves the following essential features (Follman, 1976; Madden, 1976b). Joint agreement is necessary between management and trade unions for a programme that is clearly understood throughout the firm. Employers need to know that the policy can improve efficiency at all levels from factory floor to boardroom; trade unions require reassurance that personnel are not dismissed unnecessarily and that accidents at work are not produced by untreated problem drinkers. The agreed procedures should centre on work output, and employ terms such as 'alcohol-impaired personnel' and 'recurrent poor job performance due to alcohol'; this kind of terminology avoids semantic disputes about distinctions between heavy social drinking, problem drinking and alcohol dependence. Personnel must understand that repeated work impairment from drinking jeopardizes the continued employment of the individual, and that rejection of suggestions for treatment referral, or the long-term failure of treatment, would entail retirement or dismissal. Yet it is also crucial to guarantee that referral for treatment, not dismissal, will form the initial response of the company. The guarantee is necessary to curtail the concealment of excessive drinking that operates within and between all strata of employment.

Excessive drinking is often concealed and unrecognized at work. In a survey of firms the companies were invited to report the number of problem drinkers they employed; the answers suggested that the firms missed 9 out of 10 of their alcoholic personnel (Hawker et al., 1967). An alcohol policy must therefore include education about problem drinking and its manifestations at work.

Identification of problem drinking in industry

Maxwell (1960) gave to male problem drinkers who were under treatment or who had recovered a list of 44 drinking signs affecting their work, and invited them to report on their frequency of occurrence. The on-the-job items that appeared most frequently comprised hangovers at work, increased nervousness, procrastination, red or bleary eyes, uneven work output, hand tremor, avoidance of boss or associates, sensitivity to statements about personal drinking, alcohol consumption before work or at lunchtime, reduced quantity and quality of work.

The same items were checked in a further study by the immediate supervisors of alcoholic employees who had been diagnosed through the medical department of a company (Trice, 1967). The features which the superiors had most commonly noticed among the subjects included leaving the post temporarily, lunchtime drinking, red or bleary eyes, altered mood after lunch, impaired and uneven work performance, absenteeism for a day or half day, more unusual explanations for absences, vociferous talking, prolonged lunch breaks, trembling hands, hangovers at work, avoidance of associates, flushing of the face and an increase of minor illnesses. It would be helpful to list and discuss these signs as part of the educational component of an alcohol programme.

Conclusion

The results of industrial programmes for excessive drinkers afford the highest recorded rates of recovery in the treatment of alcohol dependence. The recovery rates in American firms lie between 50 and 70 per cent (Wiegand, 1972). The satisfactory results possibly arise because the problem drinkers, being in employment, possess some stability of personality, are in the earlier stages of dependence, and have much to lose if they continue to drink excessively. An alcohol policy enables a company to detect a problem drinker at an early stage and to exercise sympathetic pressure on the individual to have treatment. The consequences are often pleasing to all parties.

REFERENCES

Adelstein A. and White G. (1976) Alcoholism and mortality. In: Population Trends 6. London, HMSO, pp. 7–13.
Akhtar M. J. (1977) Sexual disorders in male alcoholics. In: Madden J. S., Walker R. and Kenyon W. H. (ed.), Alcoholism and Drug Dependence: A Multidisciplinary Approach. New York and London, Plenum Press, pp. 3–13.

Alderman E. L. and Coltart D. J. (1982) Alcohol and the heart. *Br. Med. Bull.* **38,** 77–80.

Altman M., Crocker R. W. and Gaines S. D. (1980) Female alcoholics: the men they marry. *Focus Women* **1,** 33–41.

Annis H. M. and Liban C. B. (1980) Alcoholism in women: treatment modalities and outcomes. In: Kalant O. J. (ed.), *Alcohol and Drug Problems in Women.* New York and London, Plenum Press, pp. 385–422.

Aronson H. and Gilbert A. (1963) Preadolescent sons of male alcoholics; an experimental study of personality patterning. *Arch. Gen. Psychiatry* **8,** 235–241.

Badr F. M. and Hussain F. H. (1982) Chromosomal aberrations in chronic male alcoholics. *Alcoholism (NY)* **6,** 122–129.

Bailey M. B. (1961) Alcoholism and marriage; a review of research and professional literature. *Q. J. Stud. Alcohol* **22,** 81–97.

Bailey M. B., Haberman P. and Alksne, II. (1963) Outcomes of alcoholic marriages: endurance, termination or recovery. *Q. J. Stud. Alcohol* **23,** 610–623.

Barrison I. G., Viola L., Mumford J. et al. (1982) Detecting excessive drinking among admissions to a general hospital. *Health Trends* **14,** 80–83.

Bartholomew A. A. and Sutherland G. (1969) Alcoholism, drug dependency and sex chromosome abnormalities. *Med. J. Aust.* **2,** 440–443.

Beckman L. J. (1978) Psychosocial aspects of alcoholism in women. In: Seixas F. A. (ed.), *Currents in Alcoholism. Vol. 4. Psychiatric, Psychological, Social and Epidemiological Studies,* pp. 367–379.

Benedetti G. (1952) *Die Alkoholhalluzinosen.* Stuttgart, Thieme.

Benussi G., Gallibert L., Zorzut G. et al. (1982) Validation of the Michigan Alcoholism Screening Test (MAST) in an Italian urban population. *Drug Alcohol Depend.* **9,** 257–263.

Bernstein I. M., Webster K. H., Williams R. C. et al. (1974) Reduction in circulating T lymphocytes in alcoholic liver disease. *Lancet* **ii,** 488–490.

Bjerver K. (1972) An evaluation of compulsive treatment for alcoholic patients in Stockholm. *Opuscula Medica,* Suppl. 25. Stockholm. Söderjukhuset.

Blass J. P. and Gibson G. E. (1977) Abnormality of a thiamine-requiring enzyme in patients with Wernicke—Korsakoff syndrome. *N. Engl. J. Med.* **297,** 1367–1370.

Blendis L. M., Leeds A. R. and Jenkinson D. A. J. (1975) Incidence of alcoholic liver disease. (Letter.) *Lancet* **ii,** 499.

Bleuler E. P. (1916) *Textbook of Psychiatry.* Trans. A. A. Brill, 1924; reprinted 1951. New York, Dover Publications, pp. 312–313.

Boeke P. E. (1970) Some remarks about alcohol-dementia in clinically-treated alcoholics. *Br. J. Addict.* **65,** 173–180.

Bowser-Riley S., Bain A. D., Noble J. et al. (1975) Chromosome abnormalities in Dupuytren's disease. *Lancet* **ii,** 1282–1283.

Brenner M. H. (1975) Trends in alcohol consumption and associated illnesses. *Am. J. Publ. Health* **65,** 1279—1292.

Breslow N. E. and Enstrom J. E. (1974) Geographic correlations between mortality rates and alcohol-tobacco consumption in the United States. *J. Natl. Cancer Inst.* **53,** 631–639.

Brigden W. W. and Robinson J. (1964) Alcoholic heart disease. *Br. Med. J.* **2,** 1283–1289.

Brunt P. W., Kew M. C., Schever P. J. et al. (1974) Studies in alcoholic liver disease in Britain. *Gut* **15,** 52–58.

Bull J. (1971) Cerebral atrophy in young cannabis smokers. (Letter.) *Lancet* **ii,** 1420.

Butters N. and Cermak L. S. (1980) *Alcoholic Korsakoff's Syndrome: an Information-Processing Approach to Amnesia.* New York, Academic Press.

Canavese C., Stratta P., Ceruti A. et al. (1981) Beer drinker's kidney: a mycotoxicosis? *Lancet* **ii,** 810–811.

Cantwell D. P. (1972) Psychiatric illness in the families of hyperactive children. *Arch. Gen. Psychiatry* **27**, 414–417.

Castleden C. M., Houston A. and George C. F. (1979) Are hypnotics helpful or harmful to elderly patients? *J. Drug Issues* **9**, 55–61.

Chafetz M. E., Blane H. T. and Hill M. J. (1971) Children of alcoholics; observations in a child guidance clinic. *Q. J. Stud. Alcohol* **32**, 687–698.

Chait A. M., Mancini M., February A. W. et al. (1972) Clinical and metabolic study of alcoholic hyperlipidaemia. *Lancet* **ii**, 62–64.

Chanarin I. (1982) Haemopoiesis and alcohol. *Br. Med. Bull.* **38**, 81–86.

Chick J., Kreitman N. and Plant M. (1981) Mean cell volume and gamma-glutamyl-transpeptidase as markers of drinking in working men. *Lancet* **i**, 1249–1251.

Cobb C. F. and van Thiel D. H. (1982) Mechanism of ethanol-induced adrenal stimulation. *Alcoholism (NY)* **6**, 202–206.

Coid J. (1982) Alcoholism and violence. *Drug Alcohol Depend.* **9**, 1–13.

Collins J. J. Jr., (ed.) (1982) *Drinking and Crime: Perspectives on the Relationship between Alcohol Consumption and Criminal Behaviour.* London and New York, Tavistock Publications.

Cook D. G., Cummins R. O., Bartley M. J. et al. (1982) Health of unemployed middle-aged men in Great Britain. *Lancet* **i**, 1290–1294.

Criteria Committee, National Council on Alcoholism (1972) Criteria for the diagnosis of alcoholism. *Ann. Intern. Med.* **77**, 249–258 and *Am J. Psychiatry* **129**, 127–135.

Dagradi A. E. (1972) The natural history of oesophageal varices in patients with alcoholic liver cirrhosis. An endoscopic and clinical study. *Am. J. Gastroenterol.* **57**, 520–540.

de Torok D. (1972) Chromosomal irregularities in alcoholics. *Ann. NY Acad. Sci.* **197**, 90–100.

Doll R. (1977) The prevention of cancer *J. R. Coll. Physicians Lond.* **ii**, 125–140.

Dornhorst A. and Ouyang A. (1971) Effect of alcohol on glucose tolerance. *Lancet* **ii**, 957–959.

Doss M., Baumann H., Sixel F. (1982) Alcohol in acute porphyria (Letter). *Lancet* **i**, 1307.

Dunbar J. A., Hagart J., Martin B. et al. (1982) Drivers, binge drinking and gamma-glutamyl-transpeptidase. *Br. Med. J.* **285**, 1083.

Durbec J. P. and Sarles H. (1978) Multicenter survey on the etiology of pancreatic diseases. Relationship between the relative risk of developing chronic pancreatitis and alcohol, protein and lipid consumption. *Digestion* **18**, 337–350.

Eddleston A. L. W. F. and Davis M. (1982) Histocompatibility antigens in alcoholic liver disease. In: Sherlock S. (ed.), *Alcohol and Disease.* Edinburgh and London, Churchill Livingstone, pp. 13–16.

Editorial (1972) The puzzle of Dupuytren's contracture. *Lancet* **ii**, 170–171.

Edwards G., Fisher M. K., Hawker A. et al. (1967) Clients of alcoholism information centres. *Br. Med. J.* **2**, 346–349.

Edwards G. (1975) The alcoholic doctor: a case of neglect. *Lancet* **ii**, 1297–1298.

Edwards P., Harvey C. and Whitehead P. C. (1973) Wives of alcoholics; a critical review and analysis. *Q. J. Stud. Alcohol* **34**, 112–132.

Eichner E. R. (1973) The hematologic disorders of alcoholism. *Am. J. Med.* **54**, 621–630.

El-Guebaly N. and Offord D. R. (1979) On being the offspring of an alcoholic: an update. *Alcoholism (NY)* **3**, 148–157.

Ettinger P. O., Wu C. F., de la Cruz C. Jr., Weisee A. B., Ahmed S. S. and Regan T. J. (1981) Arrhythmias and the 'holiday heart': alcohol-associated cardiac rhythm disorders. *Am. Heart J.* **95**, 555–562.

Evans C. M. (1980) Alcohol, violence and aggression. *Br. J. Alc. Alcoholism* **15**, 104–117.

Evans W. (1959) The electrocardiogram of alcoholic cardiomyopathy. *Br. Heart J.* **21**, 445–456.

Ewing J. A. and Rouse B. A. (1970) Paper read at the 29th International Congress on Alcoholism and Drug Dependence, Sydney, Australia, 1970.

Faizallah R., Woodrow J. C., Krasner N. K. et al. (1982) Are HLA antigens important in the development of alcohol-induced liver disease. *Br. Med. J.* **285**, 533–534.

Favazza A. R. and Pires J. (1974) The Michigan Alcoholism Screening Test; application in a general military hospital. *Q. J. Stud. Alcohol* **35**, 925–929.

Follman J. F. (1976) *Alcoholics and Business: Problems, Costs, Solutions.* New York, Amocom. pp. 129–139.

Forshaw J. (1972) Alcoholic cirrhosis of liver. *Br. Med. J.* **4**, 608–609.

Foulds G. A. and Hassall C. (1969) The significance of age of onset of excessive drinking in male alcoholics. *Br. J. Psychiatry* **115**, 1027–1032.

Frankel B. G., Ferrence R. G., Johnson F. G. et al. (1976) Drinking and self-injury: toward untangling the dynamics. *Br. J. Addict.* **71**, 299–306.

Freed E. X. (1973) Drug abuse by alcoholics. *Int. J. Addict.* **8**, 451–473.

Freund G. (1970) Impairment of shock avoidance learning after long-term alcohol ingestion in mice. *Science* **168**, 1599–1601.

Friedman G. D., Siegalaub A. B. and Seltzer C. C. (1974) Cigarettes, alcohol, coffee and peptic ulcer. *N. Engl. J. Med.* **290**, 469–473.

Futterman S. (1953) Personality trends in wives of alcoholics. *Br. J. Psychiat. Soc. Work* **23**, 37–41.

Glatt M. M. (1961) Drinking habits of English (middle class) alcoholics. *Acta Psychiatr. Scand.* **37**, 88–113.

Glatt M. M. (1982) *Alcoholism* Sevenoaks, Kent, Hodder and Stoughton, pp. 232–244.

Goby J., Bradley N. J. and Bespalec D. A. (1979) Physicians treated for alcoholism: a follow-up study. *Alcoholism (NY)* **3**, 121–124.

Goldberg A., McColl K. E. L. and Moore M. R. (1981) Alcohol and porphyria (Letter). *Lancet* **ii**, 925.

Goodwin D. W., Schulsinger F., Hermansen L. et al. (1973) Alcohol problems in adoptees raised apart from alcoholic biological parents. *Arch. Gen. Psychiatry* **28**, 238–243.

Gordon G.G., Southron A. L. and Lieber C. S. (1979) Hypogonadism and feminization in the male: a triple effect of alcohol (1979). *Alcoholism (NY)* **3**, 210–211.

Gravelle H. S. E., Hutchinson G. and Stern J. (1981) Mortality and unemployment: a critique of Brenner's time-series analysis. *Lancet* **ii**, 675–679.

Gray J. (1969) The Scottish experiment. *J. Alcohol.* **4**, 461–466.

Gross M. M. (1977) Psychobiological contributions to the alcohol dependence syndrome: a selective review of recent research. In: Edwards G., Gross M. M., Keller M. et al. (1977) (ed.) *Alcohol-related Disabilities.* WHO Offset Publication No. 32, pp. 107–131.

Guthrie A. and Elliott W. A. (1980) The nature and reversibility of cerebral impairment in alcoholism. *J. Stud. Alc.* **41**, 147–155.

Hall B. D. and Orenstein W. A. (1974) Noonan's phenotype in an offspring of an alcoholic mother. *Lancet* **i**, 680–681.

Halliday H. L., Reid M. McC. and McClure G. (1982) Results of heavy drinking in pregnancy. *Br. J. Obstet. Gynaecol.* **89**, 892–5.

Hanid A., Slavin G., Maw W. et al. (1981) Fibre type changes in striated muscle of alcoholics *J. Clin. Pathol.* **34**, 991–995.

Hanson J. W. (1977) Alcohol and the fetus. *Br. J. Hosp. Med.* **18**, 126–130.

Harlap S. and Shiono P. H. (1980) Alcohol, smoking, and incidence of spontaneous abortions in the first and second trimester. *Lancet* **ii**, 173–176.

Harper C. (1979) Wernicke's encephalopathy: a more common disease than realised. *J. Neurol. Neurosurg. Psychiatry* **42**, 226–231.

Härtell G., Louhija A. and Konttinen A. (1969) Cardiovascular study of 100 chronic alcoholics. *Acta Med. Scand.* **185**, 507–513.

Haselager E. M. and Vreeken J. (1977) Rebound thrombocytosis after alcohol abuse: a possible factor in the pathogenesis of thromboembolic disease. *Lancet* i, 774–775.

Hawker A., Edwards G. and Hensman C. (1967) Problem drinkers on the pay roll: an enquiry in one London Borough *Med. Officer* 117, 313–315.

Health and Safety Executive, The Health Departments, and the Department of Employment (1981) *The Problem Drinker at Work.* London, HMSO.

Hed R., Nygren A. and Sundblad L. (1968) Insulin response in chronic alcoholism. *Lancet* i, 145.

Hill R. M. (1976) Fetal malformations and anti-epileptic drugs. *Am. J. Dis. Child* 130, 923–925.

Hodgson H. J. F. and Thompson R. P. H. (1976) Cirrhosis in south London. *Lancet* ii, 118–121.

Holt S., Stewart I. C., Dixon J. M. J. et al. (1980) Alcohol and the emergency service patient. *Br. Med. J.* 281, 638–640.

Holtermann S. and Burchell A. (1981) *The Costs of Alcohol Misuse* (Government Economic Working Paper no. 37). London, DHSS.

Hore B. D. (1981) Alcohol and alcoholism: their effect on work and the industrial response. In: Hore B. D. and Plant M. A. (eds.) *Alcohol Problems in Employment.* London, Croom Helm, pp. 10–17.

Hueston J. T. (1974) Aetiological questions in Dupuytren's contracture. In: Hueston J. T. and Tubiana R. (ed.). *Dupuytren's Disease.* Edinburgh and London, Churchill Livingstone, pp. 29–36.

Israel Y., Orrego H., Holt S. et al. (1980) Identification of alcohol abuse: thoracic fractures on routine chest X-rays as indicators of alcoholism. *Alcoholism (NY)* 4, 420–422.

Jackson J. K. (1954) The adjustment of the family to the crisis of alcoholism. *Q. J. Stud. Alcohol* 15, 562–586.

Jacob T. and Seilhamer R. A. (1982) The impact on spouses and how they cope. In: Orford J. and Harwin J. (eds.) *Alcohol and the Family.* London and Canberra, Croom Helm, pp. 114–126.

James J. E. and Goldman M. (1971) Behaviour trends of wives of alcoholics. *Q. J. Stud. Alcohol* 32, 373–381.

James D., Agnew J. E. and Bouchier I. A. D. (1973) Chronic pancreatitis in England: a changing picture. *Br. Med. J.* 2, 34–38.

Jariwalla A. G., Adams P. H. and Hore B. D. (1979) Alcohol and acute general medical admissions to hospitals. *Health Trends* 4, 95–97.

Jarman C. M. B. and Kellett J. M. (1972) Alcoholism in the general hospital. *Br. Med. J.* 2, 469–472.

Johnson R. P. and Connolly J. C. (1981) Addicted physicians: a closer look. *JAMA* 245, 253–257.

Jones K. L., Smith D. W., Ulleland C. N. et al. (1973) Pattern of malformation in offspring of chronic alcoholic mothers. *Lancet* i, 1267–1271.

Kammier M. L. (1971) Adolescents from families with and without alcohol problems. *Q. J. Stud. Alcohol* 32, 364–372.

Keller M. (1972) The oddities of alcoholics. *Q. J. Stud. Alcohol* 33, 1147–1148.

Kessel N. (1965) Self-poisoning, I. *Br. Med. J.* 2, 1265–1270.

Kessel N. and Grossman G. (1961) Suicide in alcoholics. *Br. Med. J.* 2, 1671–1672.

Kessel N. (1977) The fetal alcohol syndrome from the public health standpoint. *Health Trends* 9, 86–89.

Kiloh L. G., Andrews G., Neilson M. et al. (1972) The relationship of the syndromes called endogenous and neurotic depression. *Br. J. Psychiatry* 121, 183–196.

Klatsky A. L., Friedman G. D., Siegelaus A. B. et al. (1977) Alcohol consumption and blood pressure. *N. Engl. J. Med.* 296, 1194–2000.

Klatsky A. L., Friedman G. D. and Siegalaub A. B. (1979) Alcohol use, myocardial infarction, sudden cardiac death, and hypertension. *Alcoholism (NY)* 3, 33–39.

Klatsky A. L., Friedman G. D. and Siegalaub A. B. (1981) Alcohol and mortality: a ten-year Kaiser—Permanente experience. *Ann. Intern. Med.* **95**, 139–145.

Kliner D. J., Spicer J. and Barnett P. (1980) Treatment outcomes of alcoholic physicians. *J. Stud. Alc.* **41**, 1217–1220.

Kogan K. L., Fordyce W. E. and Jackson J. K. (1963) Personality disturbances of wives of alcoholics. *Q. J. Stud. Alcohol* **24**, 227–238.

Kozarevic D., McGee D., Vojvodic N. et al. (1980) Frequency of alcohol consumption and morbidity and mortality: the Yugoslavia cardiovascular disease study. *Lancet* **i**, 613–616.

Kristensson H., Fex G. and Trell E. (1981) Serum ferritin, gamma-glutamyl-transferase and alcohol consumption in healthy middle-aged men. *Drug Alcohol Depend.* **8**, 43–50.

Leading Article (1970) Alcohol and tuberculosis. *J. Alcohol.* **5**, 1–3.

Leading Article (1970) Sergei Sergeivich Korsakov (1853–1900): Korsakov's psychosis. *JAMA* **212**, 1700.

Leading Article (1974) Alcoholic cardiomyopathy. *Br. Med. J.* **4**, 731–732.

Leading Article (1976) The fetal alcohol syndrome *Br. Med. J.* **2**, 1404–1405.

Leading Article (1977) Are liver function tests outmoded? *Br. Med. J.* **2**, 75–76.

Lee K., Møller L., Hardt F., Haubek A., Jensen E. (1979) Alcohol-induced brain damage and liver damage in young males. *Lancet* **ii**, 759–761.

Leland J. (1982) Sex roles, family organization and alcohol abuse. In: Orford J. and Harwin J. (eds.) *Alcohol and the Family*. London and Canberra, Croom Helm, pp. 88–113.

Lemere F. and Smith J. W. (1973) Alcohol induced sexual impotence. *Am. J. Psychiatry* **130**, 212–213.

Levitt R. O. and Shenker D. M. (1979) Central pontine myelosis. *Alcoholism (NY)* **3**, 83–85.

Lieber C. S. and Decarli L. M. (1977) Metabolic effects of alcohol on the liver. In: Lieber C. S. (ed.), *Metabolic Aspects of Alcoholism*, Lancaster, MTP Press, pp. 31–79.

Lilly L. J. (1975) Investigations in vitro and in vivo, of the effects of disulfiram (Antabuse) on human lymphocyte chromosomes. *Toxicol. Appl. Pharmacol.* **4**, 331–340.

Lindenbaum J. (1977) Metabolic effects of alcohol on the blood and bone marrow. In: Lieber C. S. (ed.) *Metabolic Aspects of Alcoholism*. Lancaster, MTP Press, pp. 215–247.

Lindsell D. R., Wilson A. G. and Maxwell J. D. (1982) Fractures on the chest radiograph in detection of alcoholic liver disease. *Br. Med. J.* **285**, 597–599.

Lipson A. H., Yu J. S., O'Halloran M. T. et al. (1981) Alcohol and phenylketonuria. (Letter). *Lancet* **i**, 717–718.

Little R. E. (1977) Alcohol consumption during pregnancy and decreased birthweight. *Am. J. Public Health* **67**, 1154–1156.

Little R. E., Schultz F. and Mandell W. (1976) Drinking during pregnancy. *J. Stud. Alc.* **37**, 375–379.

Lowry W. S. (1975) Alcoholism in cancer of the head and neck. *Laryngoscope* **85**, 1275–1280.

MacVane J., Butters N., Montgomery K. et al. (1982) Cognitive functioning in men social drinkers; a replication study. *J. Stud. Alc.* **43**, 81–95.

McClain C. J., van Thiel D. H., Parker S. et al. (1979) Alterations in zinc, vitamin A, and retinol-binding protein in chronic alcoholics: a possible mechanism for night blindness and hypogonadism. *Alcoholism (NY)* **3**, 135–141.

McColl K. E. L., Moore M. R., Thompson G. G. et al. (1981) Abnormal haem biosynthesis in chronic alcoholics. *Eur. J. Clin. Invest.* **11**, 461–468.

McCord W. and McCord J. (1980) *Origins of Alcoholism*. Stanford, Stanford University Press.

McDonald D. E. (1956) Mental disorders in wives of alcoholics. *Q. J. Stud. Alcohol* **17**, 282–287.

McMichael A. J. (1978) Increases in laryngeal cancer in Britain and Australia in relation to alcohol and tobacco consumption trends. *Lancet* **i,** 1244–1247.

McNamee H. B., Mello N. K. and Mendelson J. H. (1968) Experimental analysis of drinking patterns of alcoholics: concurrent psychiatric observations. *Am. J. Psychiatry* **124,** 1063–1069.

Madden J. S. (1967) Alcoholism and drug dependency in the Civil Service. *Br. J. Addict.* **62,** 403.

Madden J. S. (1976a) Chromosome abnormalities in Dupuytren's disease. *Lancet* **i,** 209.

Madden J. S. (1976b) The problem and management of alcoholism in industry. *J. Soc. Occup. Med.* **26,** 61–64.

Mandsley C. and Mayer R. (1965) Nerve conduction in alcoholic polyneuropathy. *Brain* **88,** 335–358.

Maxwell M. A. (1960) Early identification of problem drinkers in industry. *Q. J. Stud. Alcohol* **21,** 655–678.

Melling M. (1982) *Children of Alcoholic Parents: Family Behaviour, Family Relationships and Attitudes of Alcoholic Parents and Their Spouses to Their Children.* Master of Philosophy Thesis, University of Liverpool.

Mendelson J. H. and Mello N. K. (1974) Alcohol, aggression and androgens. In: Frazier S. H. (ed.) *Aggression.* Baltimore, Williams & Wilkins, pp. 225–247.

Mihas A. A., Bull D. M. and Davidson C. S. (1975) Cell-mediated immunity to liver in patients with alcoholic hepatitis. *Lancet* **i,** 951–953.

Mik G. (1970) Sons of alcoholic fathers. *Br. J. Psychiatry* **65,** 305–315.

Mishihara B. L. and Kastenbaum R. (1980) *Alcohol and Drugs* New York, Grune and Stratton.

Moore R. A. (1972a) The prevalence of alcoholism in a community general hospital. *Am. J. Psychiatry* **128,** 638–639.

Moore R. A. (1972b) The diagnosis of alcoholism in a psychiatric hospital; a trial of the Michigan Alcoholism Screening Test (MAST), *Am. J. Psychiatry* **128,** 1565–1569.

Morgan M. Y. (1982) Alcohol and the endocrine system. *Br. Med. Bull.* **38,** 35–42.

Morgan M. Y., Colman J. C. and Sherlock S. (1981) The use of a combination of peripheral markers for diagnosing alcoholism and monitoring for alcohol abuse. *Br. J. Alc. Alcoholism* **16,** 167–177.

Moss M. C. and Davies E. B. (1967) *A Survey of Alcoholism in an English County.* London, Geigy Scientific Publications.

Mowatt R. R. (1966) *Morbid Jealousy and Murder.* London, Tavistock Publications, pp. 105–106.

Murray R. M. (1976) Alcoholism amongst male doctors in Scotland. *Lancet* **ii,** 729–731.

Murray R. M. (1980) An epidemiological and clinical study of alcoholism in the medical profession. In: Madden J. S., Walker R. and Kenyon W. H. (ed.), *Aspects of Alcohol and Drug Dependence.* Tunbridge Wells, Kent, Pitman Medical, pp. 213–219.

Nice J. (1979) Wives of alcoholics as 'repeaters'. *J. Stud. Alc.* **40,** 677–682.

Nicholls P., Edwards G. and Kyle E. (1974) Alcoholics admitted to four hospitals in England. II. General and cause-specific mortality. *Q. J. Stud. Alcohol* **35,** 841–855.

Nylander I. (1960) Children of alcoholic fathers. *Acta Paediatr.* Suppl. 21, 1–134.

Occasional Survey (1981) Alcoholic liver disease: morphological manifestations. Review by an international group. *Lancet* **i,** 708–711.

Orford J. (1975) Alcoholism and marriage: the argument against specialism. *J. Stud. Alcohol* **36,** 1537–1563.

Orford J., Guthrie S., Nicholls P. et al. (1975) Self-reported coping behaviour of wives of alcoholics and its association with outcome. *J. Stud. Alcohol* **36,** 1254–1267.

Orford J., Oppenheimer E., Egert S. et al. (1976) The cohesiveness of alcoholism-complicated marriages and its influence on treatment and outcome. *Br. J. Psychiatry* **128,** 318–339.

Paffenbarger R. S., Wing A. L. and Hyde R. T. (1974) Chronic disease in former college students. 13. Early precursors of peptic ulcer. *Am. J. Epidemiol.* **100**, 307–315.

Parker E. S. and Noble E. P. (1977) Alcohol consumption and cognitive functioning in social drinkers. *J. Stud. Alc.* **38**, 1224–1232.

Parsons V. and Cundy T. (1981) Alcohol and bone disease. *Br. J. Addict.* **76**, 379–382.

Parsons O. A. and Leber W. R. (1981) The relationship between cognitive dysfunction and brain damage in alcoholics: causal, interactive or epiphenomenal? *Alcoholism (NY)* **5**, 326–343.

Patel A. R., Roy M. and Wilson G. M. (1972) Self-poisoning and alcohol. *Lancet* **ii**, 1099–1103.

Paton A. (1976) Alcohol-induced cushingoid syndrome. (Letter.) *Br. Med. J.* **2**, 1054.

Pearce J. M. S. (1977) Neurological aspects of alcoholism. *Hosp. Med.* **18**, 132–142.

Pell S. and D'Alonzo C. A. (1968) The prevalence of chronic diseases among problem drinkers. *Arch. Environ. Health* **16**, 679–684.

Pell S. and D'Alonzo C. A. (1970) Sickness and absenteeism of alcoholics. *J. Occup. Med.* **12**, 198–210.

Pemberton D. A. (1967) A comparison of the outcome of treatment in female and male alcoholics. *Br. J. Psychiatry* **113**, 367–373.

Peppers L. G. and Stover R. G. (1979) The elderly abuser: a challenge for the future. *J. Drug Issues* **9**, 73–83.

Petersson B., Trell E. and Kristensson H. (1982) Alcohol abstention and premature mortality in middle-aged males. *Br. Med. J.* **285**, 1457–1459.

Petersson B., Krantz P., Kristensson H. et al. (1982) Alcohol-related death: a major contributor to mortality in urban middle-aged men. *Lancet* **ii**, 1088–1090.

Phillips G. B. and Safrit H. F. (1971) Alcoholic diabetes. Induction of glucose intolerance with alcohol. *JAMA* **217**, 1513–1519.

Plant N. A. (1979) *Drinking Careers.* London, Tavistock.

Plueckhan V. D. (1982) Alcohol consumption and death by drowning in adults; a 24-year epidemiological analysis. *J. Stud. Alc.* **43**, 445–452.

Pokorny A. D., Miller B. A. and Kaplan H. B. (1972) The brief MAST: a shortened version of the Michigan Alcoholism Screening Test. *Am. J. Psychiatry* **129**, 342–345.

Pollak B. (1978) A two-year study of alcoholics in general practice (1978) *Br. J. Alc. Alcoholism* **13**, 24–35.

Priest R. G., Binns J. K. and Kitchin A. H. (1966) The electrocardiogram in alcoholism and accompanying physical disease. *Br. Med. J.* **1**, 1453–1455.

Quinn M. A. and Johnstone R. V. (1976) Alcohol problems in acute male medical admissions. *Health Bulletin* **34**, 253–256.

Rae J. B. (1972) The influence of the wives on the treatment outcome of alcoholics: a follow-up study at two years. *Br. J. Psychiatry* **120**, 601–613.

Rae J. B. and Forbes A. R. (1966) Clinical and psychometric characteristics of the wives of alcoholics. *Br. J. Psychiatry* **112**, 197–200.

Rae J. B. and Drewery J. (1972) Interpersonal patterns in alcoholic marriages. *Br. J. Psychiatry* **120**, 601–613.

Ramsay L. E. (1977) Liver dysfunction in hypertension. *Lancet* **ii**, 111–114.

Ramsay L. E. (1979) Hyperuricaemia in hypertension: role of alcohol. *Br. Med. J.* **1**, 635–654.

Rees L. H., Besser G. M., Jeffcoate W. J. et al. (1977) Alcohol-induced pseudo-Cushing's syndrome. *Lancet* **i**, 726–728.

Reid N. C. R. W., Brunt P. W., Bias W. B. et al. (1968) Genetic characteristics and cirrhosis: a controlled study of 200 patients. *Br. Med. J.* **2**, 463–465.

Rhydelius P. A. (1981) Children of alcoholic fathers: their social adjustment and their health status over 20 years. *Acta Paediatrica Scand.* Suppl. 286, **70**.

Riley J. N. and Walker D. W. (1978) Morphological alterations in hippocampus after long-term alcohol consumption in mice. *Science* **201**, 646–648.

Rimmer J. (1974) Psychiatric illness in husbands of alcoholics. *Q. J. Stud. Alcohol* **35**, 281–283.

Ritson B. and Hassall C. (1970) *The Management of Alcoholism*. Edinburgh, Livingstone, pp. 71–92, 94.

Roe A. (1944) The adult adjustment of children of alcoholic parents raised in foster-homes. *Q. J. Stud. Alcohol* **5**, 373–393.

Rosenberg C. M. (1969) Young alcoholics. *Br. J. Psychiatry* **115**, 181–188.

Rosenberg C. M. (1971) Sons of alcoholic fathers. *Br. J. Psychiatry* **118**, 469–470.

Rosenberg L., Slone D., Shapiro S. et al. (1982) Breast cancer and alcoholic-beverage consumption. *Lancet* **i**, 267–271.

Roset H. L., Weiner L., Zuckerman B., McKinlay S. and Edelin K. C. (1980) Reduction of alcohol consumption during pregnancy with benefits to the newborn. *Alcoholism (NY)* **4**, 178–184.

Rubin E. and Lieber C. S. (1974) Fatty liver, alcoholic hepatitis and cirrhosis produced by alcohol in primates. *N. Engl. J. Med.* **290**, 129–135.

Saad E. S. M. and Madden J. S. (1976) Certificated incapacity and unemployment in alcoholics. *Br. J. Psychiatry* **128**, 340–345.

Sarles H., Cros R. C., Bidart J. M. and the International Group for the Study of Pancreatic Diseases (1979) A multi-center inquiry into the aetiology of pancreatic diseases. *Digestion* **19**, 110–125.

Saunders J. B., Walter J. R. F., Davies P. and Paton A. (1981a) A 20-year prospective study of cirrhosis. *Br. Med. J.* **282**, 263–266.

Saunders J. B., Beevers D. G. and Paton A. (1981b) Alcohol-induced hypertension. *Lancet* **ii**, 653–656.

Saunders J. B., Bannan L. T., Beevers D. G. et al. (1982) Alcohol and hypertension (Letter). *Lancet* **i**, 401–402.

Saville P. D. (1977) Alcohol and skeletal disease. In: Lieber C. S. (ed.) *Metabolic Aspects of Alcoholism*. Lancaster, MTP Press, pp. 135–147.

Schmidt W. and de Lint J. (1972) Causes of death of alcoholics. *Q. J. Stud. Alcohol* **33**, 171–185.

Schmidt W. and Popham R. E. (1981) The role of drinking and smoking in mortality from cancer and other causes in male alcoholics. *Cancer* **47**, 1031–1041.

Schuckit M. A., Goodwin D. A. and Winokur G. (1972) A study of alcoholism in half siblings. *Am. J. Psychiatry* **128**, 1132–1136.

Schuckit M., Pitts F. N. Jun., Reich T. et al. (1969) Alcoholism: I, Two types of alcoholism in women. *Arch. Gen. Psychiatry* **20**, 301–306.

Sclare A. B. (1970) The female alcoholic. *Br. J. Addict.* **65**, 99–107.

Sclare A. B. (1975) The women alcoholic. *J. Alcohol.* **10**, 134–137.

Scott J. (1974) Macrocytosis of chronic alcoholism. (Letter.) *Lancet* **i**, 1297.

Selzer M. L. (1971) The Michigan Alcoholism Screening Test: the quest for a new diagnostic instrument. *Am. J. Psychiatry* **127**, 1653–1658.

Seneviratne B. I. B. (1975) Acute cardiomyopathy and rhabdomyolysis in chronic alcoholism. *Br. Med. J.* **4**, 328—330.

Singer K. and Lundberg W. B. (1972) Ventricular arrhythmias associated with the ingestion of alcohol. *Ann. Intern. Med.* **77**, 247–248.

Smals A. G., Kloppenborg P. W., Njo K. T. et al. (1976) Alcohol-induced Cushingold syndrome. *Br. Med. J.* **2**, 1298.

Smith J. W. and Layden T. A. (1972) Changes in psychological performance and blood chemistry in alcoholics during and after hospital treatment. *Q. J. Stud. Alcohol* **33**, 379–394.

Smith J. W., Johnson L. C. and Burdick J. A. (1971) Sleep, psychological and clinical changes during alcohol withdrawal in NAD-treated alcoholics. *Q. J. Stud. Alcohol* **32**, 982–984.

Smith M. L. (1980) Issues in planning a treatment programme for the geriatric alcoholic. In: Madden J. S., Walker R. and Kenyon W. H. (eds.) *Aspects of Alcohol and Drug Dependence*. Tunbridge Wells, Kent, Pitman Medical, pp. 305–311.

Smith R. (1981) Alcohol, women, and the young: the same old problem? *Br. Med. J.* **283**, 1170–1172.

Spencer-Peet J., Wood D. C. F. and Glatt M. M. (1973) Screening tests for alcoholism. *Lancet* **ii**, 1089–1090.

Su Chun-Kuang and Patek A. J. (1970) Dupuytren's contracture: its association with alcoholism and cirrhosis. *Arch. Intern. Med.* **126**, 278–281.

Sullivan W. C. (1899) A note on the influence of maternal inebriety on the offspring. *J. Ment. Sci.* **45**, 489–503.

Sundby P. (1974) Prevalence of alcoholism and the size of the socio-medical problems associated with it. In: Kessel N., Hawker A. and Chalke H. (ed.) *Alcoholism: A Medical Profile. Proceedings of the First International Medical Conference on Alcoholism*. London, Edsall, pp. 112–117.

Trapnell J. E. and Duncan E. H. L. (1975) Patterns of incidence in acute pancreatitis. *Br. Med. J.* **2**, 179–183.

Trice H. M. (1967) New light on identifying the alcoholic employee. *Med. Bull.* **2**, 8–15.

van der Spuy H. I. J. (1972) The influence of alcohol on the mood of the alcoholic. *Br. J. Addict.* **67**, 255–265.

van Thiel D. H., Sherins R. J. and Lester R. (1973) Mechanism of hypogonadism in alcohol liver disease. *Gastroenterology* **65**, 574. (Abs. 50).

van Thiel D. H. and Gavaler J. S. (1982) The adverse effects of ethanol upon hypothalamic-pituitary-gonadal function in males and females compared and contrasted. *Alcoholism (NY)* **6**, 179–185.

Varsamis J., Paraskevas F., Averback P. et al. (1974) Heavy drinking and increase in IgA. *Lancet* **i**, 1291–1292.

Victor M., Adams R. and Collins G. (1971) *The Wernicke–Korsakoff Syndrome*. Philadelphia, Davis.

Wahlström J., Forssman H. and Akesson H. O. (1970) Extra Y chromosomes and alcoholism. *Humangenetik* **9**, 105–106.

Walsh J. and McCleod J. (1973) Alcoholic neuropathy: an electrophysiological and histological study. *J. Neurol. Sci.* **10**, 457–469.

Whalen T. (1953) Wives of alcoholics: four types observed in a family service agency. *Q. J. Stud. Alcohol* **14**, 632–641.

Wiegand R. A. (1972) Alcoholism in industry. *Br. J. Addict.* **67**, 181–187.

Wilkins R. H. (1974) *The Hidden Alcoholic in General Practice*. London, Elsek Science.

Wilkinson D. A. (1982) Examination of alcoholics by computed tomography (CT) scans: a critical review. *Alcoholism (NY)* **6**, 31–45.

Wilkinson P., Kornaczewski A., Rankin J. G. et al. (1971) Physical disease in alcoholism. Initial survey of 1,000 patients. *Med. J. Aust.* **1**, 1217–1223.

Williams R. R. and Horm J. W. (1977) Association of cancer sites with tobacco and alcohol consumption and socioeconomic status of patients: interview study from the Third National Cancer Study. *J. Natl. Cancer Inst.* **58**, 525–547.

Wilsnack S. C. (1976) The impact of sex roles and women's alcohol use and abuse. In: Greenblatt M. and Schuckit M. A. (eds.) *Alcoholism Problems in Women and Children*. New York, Grune and Stratton, pp. 37–63.

Wilson C. and Orford J. (1978) Children of alcoholics: report of a preliminary study and comments on the literature. *J. Stud. Alc.* **39**, 121–142.

Winokur G. and Clayton P. (1968) Family case histories. IV. Comparison of male and female alcoholics. *Q. J. Stud. Alcohol* **29**, 885–891.

Wodak A. and Richardson P. J. (1982) Alcohol and the cardiovascular system. *Br. J. Addict.* **77**, 251–258.

Wolfe S. J., Summerskill W. H. J. and Davidson C. S. (1956) Thickening and contraction of the palmar fascia (Dupuytren's contracture) associated with alcoholism and hepatic cirrhosis. *N. Engl. J. Med.* **255**, 559–563.

Woodruff R. A. Jun., Guze J. B., Clayton P. J. et al. (1973) Alcoholism and depression. *Arch. Gen. Psychiatry* **28**, 97–100.

Wu A., Chanarin I. and Levi A. J. (1974) Macrocytosis of chronic alcoholism. *Lancet* **i**, 829–831.

Yoder R. D. and Moore R. A. (1973) Characteristics of convicted drunken drivers. *Q. J. Stud. Alcohol* **34**, 927–936.

Zieve L. (1958) Jaundice, hyperlipemia and hemolytic anaemia: a heretofore unrecognized syndrome associated with alcoholic fatty liver and cirrhosis. *Ann. Intern. Med.* **48**, 471–496.

Zimberg S. (1974) The elderly alcoholic. *Gerontologist* **14**, 221–224.

Chapter 4

TREATMENT OF COMPLICATIONS AND OF WITHDRAWAL FEATURES IN ALCOHOL DEPENDENCE

I must have one at eleven,
It's a duty that ought to be done;
If I don't have one at eleven,
Then I must have eleven at one.

ANON.

Treatment of the person who is in difficulties with alcohol requires a correct attitude of mind in the therapist. A condemnatory viewpoint inhibits effective help; such an approach arises from the prejudice that the excessive drinker is inferior or morally at fault. Although the therapist may attempt to conceal an attitude of this nature the viewpoint is bound to affect a relationship with the client or patient; it interferes with the combination of sympathy and objectivity that is necessary for a constructive appraisal of the subject and of treatment prospects. The issue forms a central theme of publications on therapy (Brill, 1982; Edwards, 1982; Glatt 1982). The proper frame of mind may be promoted by the reflection that predisposition to problem drinking depends on matters that are beyond the control of the individual; given the appropriate loading of socio-economic factors, family background and personal events there is no certainty that any person would not become dependent on alcohol.

The physical and mental complications of alcohol dependence can and should receive treatment in their own right, irrespective of whether the excessive drinker expresses interest in long-term plans for dealing with drinking or other psychosocial problems. Frequently the treatment of complications paves the way for measures aimed at the radical relief of dependence on alcohol.

PHYSICAL COMPLICATIONS

Organic sequelae outside the nervous system

Laryngitis, gastritis, fatty liver or a mild disturbance of liver function tests respond to a period of abstinence. Acute or chronic hepatitis, cirrhosis, pancreatitis, and disorders of skeletal or heart muscle need the advice of a specialist in medicine. Hypoglycaemia is treated by intravenous glucose; 50 ml of 25% solution is given quickly to a comatose patient to prevent death or permanent brain damage; when the patient is able to swallow glucose drinks are administered. Some studies suggest that alcohol, and alcohol dependence, can produce glucose intolerance; if this is suspected in an excessive drinker then antidiabetic measures are needed; the steps to control blood sugar must be kept under review since alcohol abstinence may reduce their necessity. Anaemia from iron or folic acid deficiency requires respectively oral iron, or folic acid 15–20 mg by mouth daily. In an alcoholic subject with anaemia the causes of anaemia in alcoholism must be reviewed; they include an inadequate diet, toxic effects of alcohol on intestinal absorption and bone marrow, and liver cirrhosis (with or without oesophageal varices).

Organic sequelae in the nervous system

Neurological complications of alcoholism include peripheral neuritis, Wernicke's encephalopathy, Korsakoff's psychosis and generalized cerebral impairment. The latter two conditions are here included from the point of view of treatment, although their clinical features are mental rather than physical.

Alcoholic patients with organic neurological sequelae are usually given vitamins, especially the B vitamins and vitamin B_1 (thiamine, aneurine). The emphasis is placed on thiamine but more than one vitamin is provided on the grounds of multiple vitamin deficiency. Animal experiments and human studies provide clear evidence that thiamine shortage produces lesions in the upper part of the brainstem and hypothalamus that are associated with disturbances of mental attention and memory. But it must be conceded that the rationale is poorly established for vitamin administration in some of the neurological complications of excessive drinking. Current thinking has moved towards the concept of a direct toxic effect of alcohol as a major factor in their aetiology. It is imperative to prescribe B vitamins for Wernicke's encephalopathy. It is usual to administer B and C vitamins in other forms· of neurological disorder in alcohol dependence; they can do no harm since the water solubility of these substances ensures their rapid elimination from the body. Folate deficiency can induce dementia, so a depressed level of serum folate in an alcoholic with brain damage requires treatment with folic acid. 'Wet beri-beri', shown by peripheral neuritis and high-output heart failure, is a definite though uncommon indication for thiamine in problem drinkers.

Thiamine, like many nutriments, is normally absorbed through intestinal mucosa by two mechanisms. The first process involves active transport across the lining membrane of the small bowel and is energy dependent; the second route is entirely passive. The former mechanism is impaired during high alcohol intake (Thomson and Majumdar, 1981); the duration of impairment is unknown, but it is likely to last for at least a week after cessation of drinking. Because the usual preparations of thiamine, such as thiamine hydrochloride, require absorption through the active process, they will be ineffective until their absorption is restored. The allithiamine compounds thiamine propyl disulphide and thiamine tetrahydrofurfuryl disulphide are passively absorbed (Thomson et al., 1971; Baker et al., 1975). However, alcoholic patients are often deficient in several nutriments so that the replacement of selected ones could, at least theoretically, prove harmful by stimulation of cerebral metabolism during depletion of other necessary substances (Thomson, 1980). In practice thiamine, accompanied by other vitamins, is often given parenterally for an initial one to two weeks, before proceeding to oral vitamins.

Severe cerebral impairment, with impaired intellectual powers and amnesia, that amounts to clinically obvious dementia, requires if it is pronounced the admission of the drinker to hospital, usually to a psychiatric unit. A stay in hospital spares the brain from further damage by drinking, protects the patient from the consequences of defective judgement and poor grasp of affairs, and affords relief to relatives unable to cope with a severely demented member of the family. Contrary to what is sometimes believed, dementia from injurious drinking always improves with abstention; the degree of improvement cannot be predicted at the time the patient ceases to drink, for instance when entering hospital. Some patients with dementia remain so severely disabled in mental functioning that they become permanent inmates in hospital, especially if they lack families able or willing to care for them elsewhere. In the author's experience the majority improve to the extent that they return to life in the community. In certain instances dependent drinkers who have shown evidence of severe brain damage resume their former occupations, even white collar posts which involve mental and not physical skills. At the height of their dementia problem drinkers with gross impairment generally agree (or at least do not refuse) to enter hospital. In the course of a lengthy period in hospital they can initially be given vitamins, receive detoxification from alcohol, and later be counselled in regard to permanent abstention and to their future residential and occupational requirements and abilities.

PSYCHOLOGICAL COMPLICATIONS

Alcoholic hallucinosis

The term is used as elsewhere in this text to denote a prolonged state of auditory hallucinations without frank delirium. The condition necessitates inpatient care. A period in a psychiatric unit ensures that the brain is no longer influenced by alcohol, that the excessive drinker is given comfort and reassurance for his disturbing experiences, that he does not attempt suicide or wander away in distress, that he does not attack persons whom he imagines are maligning him, and that he receives a major tranquillizer. Abstention from alcohol combined with a tranquillizing drug of the phenothiazine, butyrophenone or thioxanthene class, should produce cessation of the hallucinations within a few weeks. Their persistence for longer than two or three months calls for reconsideration of the diagnosis to establish whether the patient has, in fact, schizophrenia.

Alcoholic jealousy

The management of alcoholic jealousy depends primarily on the risk to the spouse. Fixed delusions by a husband that his wife is unfaithful, particularly if the false beliefs are present while the subject is not drinking, indicate that the couple should part until the jealousy subsides. Usually disengagement can be achieved by admitting the excessive drinker to a psychiatric unit, by legal compulsion if he declines to enter hospital. If the couple remain together in the presence of the delusions the wife must be warned of the risk to her life. Treatment in hospital involves withdrawal from alcohol and the administration of a major tranquillizer.

Alcoholic jealousy does not as a rule warrant such drastic intervention. It is found in a continuum of severity; at the less ominous end are unwarranted accusations of infidelity expressed during intoxication and followed by remorse when the problem drinker is reminded of their occurrence. Although transient sexual jealousy while intoxicated may be associated with violence to the partner, it does not provide a basis for compulsory admission of the alcoholic to hospital. It does, of course, offer a good opportunity for bringing the excessive drinker into therapy without formal compulsion. Recurrent violence from an alcohol misuser who is basically sane and who does not respond to, or co-operate with, a treatment programme offers grounds for legal measures pertinent to marriage. The spouse may feel obliged to seek relief through lawyers rather than from doctors or social workers.

Depression

Depression in an excessive drinker usually responds to a few weeks of abstinence. This is particularly so if the respite from the depressive effects of prolonged excess alcohol consumption is combined with a break from psychological pressures and if the alcoholic patient is able to envisage an abatement, at least temporarily, of his general difficulties. Hospital admission to achieve these measures is frequently, though not necessarily, desirable.

Admission to a psychiatric unit is essential to protect a problem drinker who is so depressed as to be potentially suicidal. The risk of suicide is judged by several factors. They include the depth of sadness and the statements of the subject. An expressed wish to die is often sincere; a death wish can be concealed but may be evinced by indirect expressions of hopelessness or desperation. A suicidal threat or act may be largely manipulative, particularly at the present time in view of the current epidemic of self-poisoning by persons wishing to influence others or gain help. But the motives may be complex; the subject can partly intend a permanent relief to problems from a fatal outcome, while at the same time hoping for a manipulative effect on others if recovery ensues. Studies of suicide and of patients who are depressed (though not necessarily alcoholic) agree that the following features increase the suicidal risk: a family history of suicide, previous attempt at self-injury, male sex, social isolation, old age and physical ill-health.

Occasionally depression in an excessive drinker is of the kind sometimes labelled 'endogenous', arising from a presumed biochemical change in the individual and preceding rather than following the excess drinking. This type of depression, which persists despite abstinence, requires specific physical treatments in the form of an antidepressant drug or a course of electroconvulsive therapy (ECT). But most depressed alcoholics, including those who have made a recent attempt at self-injury or who possess a depressive personality with a persistently dysphoric outlook, improve in mood after a brief spell of abstinence. The majority bounce back to normal cheerfulness within a few weeks of alcohol cessation.

It is important that dependent drinkers are not misdiagnosed as depressives. Too often in the past they were given antidepressant drugs or ECT while in psychiatric units; the physical treatments received the credit for lifting their depression, when the restoration of normal mood was actually due to the stay in hospital and the attendant abstention from alcohol. The most important adverse consequence of unnecessary somatic therapy for depression is that problem drinkers are then viewed primarily as depressed patients; they are discharged from hospital with their underlying alcohol difficulties neither adequately recognized nor treated.

WITHDRAWAL FEATURES

Dependent drinkers are often able to check a phase of drinking, and endure the attendant withdrawal symptoms, without entering a hospital or nursing home. Some achieve this without help from doctors or social workers, through their own determination or with encouragement from relatives or members of Alcoholics Anonymous. Other alcoholic subjects appreciate the prescription from surgery or outpatient clinic of a drug or drugs to counteract the distress of the withdrawal period. Others again need withdrawal from alcohol in hospital because their physical or mental health has required admission, or because they wish to stop drinking at least temporarily but are unable or unwilling to tolerate the withdrawal symptoms while in the community.

Drug treatment during the abstinence syndrome relieves symptoms, and reduces the likelihood of severe withdrawal features in the form of convulsions or delirium tremens. Drug administration also has a placebo effect in reassuring the alcoholic patient that undue suffering will not develop. The placebo result has benefit even in hospital, where the usual procedure for an inpatient is to withdraw the subject at once from alcohol.

Benzodiazepines

Sedatives of the benzodiazepine group are currently the favoured therapy for alcohol withdrawal. They relieve anxiety and promote sleep; in the doses usually given their effect on clarity of consciousness is slight, so benzodiazepines are sometimes described as minor tranquillizers. Although they differ in the periods for which they maintain therapeutic blood levels there are no conclusive data to prove that in comparable dosage some possess clinical advantages over others. They show an anticonvulsive effect, reducing dysrhythmia in the electroencephalogram; this property presumably confers benefit in the prevention of alcohol withdrawal seizures.

The members of the benzodiazepine class of drugs that are perhaps most widely used in the treatment of alcohol withdrawal are diazepam (Valium) and chlordiazepoxide (Librium) Benzodiazepines are considerably less likely to induce misuse or dependence than barbiturates, but when administered to cover the alcohol abstinence syndrome they should only be given for a maximum period of two weeks, and in decreasing dosage during their time of administration.

Diazepam may be employed at an initial level of 10 mg t.d.s. or q.d.s. A dependent drinker in the community should receive the lower dose regime; 10 mg t.d.s. is given for the first two days, then the dosage is reduced in 5 mg stages over a week. At the end of this period the patient is removed from the drug; requests by the problem drinker to continue the medication must be declined. The higher dose regime should be restricted to hospital inpatients, and is not always required with them. When the higher dosage is employed diazepam can be given at the initial level of 10 mg q.d.s. for the first two days, and then withdrawn at a rate of 5 mg daily; after nine days the patient is free from the drug.

Chlordiazepoxide (Librium) can be administered in comparable regimes, at an initial dose of 20 mg t.d.s. or q.d.s. A withdrawal convulsion requires phenytoin (diphenylhydantoin) 100 mg t.d.s. for a week, in addition to the benzodiazepine drug that the patient is receiving.

If a benzodiazepine compound is employed outside hospital, care must be taken to avoid its misuse. The rather long-acting chlordiazepoxide may possess a relatively low misuse potential, and forms the preferred choice for patients in the community.

Other drugs

Chlormethiazole (Heminevrin) has been employed in the treatment of alcohol withdrawal. Although effective as an anticonvulsant sedative, its potential for misuse and dependence is so pronounced that the drug has fallen out of favour.

Drugs which compete with catecholamines for occupation of beta-adrenergic sites, and so block noradrenaline transmission at these sites, have been utilized during alcohol withdrawal. Beta-blockers inhibit the increase of cardiac rate, force and output that is found in the alcohol abstinence syndrome (Carlsson, 1969). Beta-adrenergic blockade also controls the tremor characteristic of hyperadrenergic states such as that of alcohol withdrawal. Beta-blockers are not given to patients with limited cardiac reserve or asthma, as they may induce heart failure or an asthmatic attack respectively (Carlsson and Johansson, 1979). The preparations present the risks of producing heart failure in patients with latent alcoholic heart muscle disease, or of hypoglycaemia in excessive drinkers with diminished reserves of carbohydrate, but these hazards appear more theoretical than real.

Beta-blockers afford some symptomatic relief, but do not obviate the need for sedative and anticonvulsant medication. They are not generally employed for the alcohol abstinence syndrome.

Delirium tremens

The severe abstinence syndrome of delirium tremens requires intensification and prolongation of one of the above drug regimens together with supportive measures to maintain the patient's physical health. Diazepam or chlordiazepoxide may be employed in a daily dose between 100–200 mg for diazepam and 100–400 mg for chlordiazepoxide. Lower doses within these ranges are often sufficient. In severe instances of delirium tremens deficiencies of water, and of the electrolytes sodium, potassium and magnesium, require assessment and correction.

Conclusion

It must be stressed that the alcohol abstinence syndrome is a self-limiting condition which usually leads to full recovery. Yet the majority of alcoholics who withdraw from alcohol without drugs in nonmedical detoxification units do not experience great distress; in one study only 5% of the clients required immediate medical attention (Petersen, 1974). A hospital detoxification centre encountered, during nondrug withdrawal, one example of delirium tremens and a low incidence of other abstinence features (Rossall, 1978). A large survey of 1024 alcoholic patients who were detoxified without drugs noticed one instance of delirium tremens, six subjects who incurred a convulsion, and another six who developed more than one convulsion (Whitfield et al.,

1978); instead of drugs the staff provided reassurance together with sensory input and activity to maintain contact with reality.

When alcohol is withdrawn in hospital it is usual to prescribe drugs briefly in order to relieve symptoms and to prevent the development of delirium tremens or convulsions. Either of these complications may prove fatal; convulsions can be followed by pronounced brain damage (Walsh, 1961). But it is likely that the pharmacological actions of drugs provide a comparatively minor contribution to the relative ease with which most excessive drinkers withdraw from alcohol in hospital. More influential features are the benign course of the abstinence syndrome, and psychological factors such as motivation, the placebo effect of drugs, and reassurance by staff and peers. Since severe forms, including fatalities, of the alcohol abstinence syndrome are less common in recent decades, it is also arguable that the enhancement of nutrition and physical well-being that has occurred among the general population includes many excessive drinkers. Their improved physical status could combine with the growth and popularity of treatment facilities to protect from the development of marked withdrawal features.

REFERENCES

Baker H., Frank O., Zetterman R. K. et al. (1975) Inability of chronic alcoholics with liver disease to use food as a source of folates, thiamine and vitamin B. *Am. J. Clin. Nutr.* **28**, 1377–1380.

Brill L. (1982) *The Clinical Treatment of Substance Abuse.* New York, Free Press.

Carlsson C. (1969) Haemodynamic studies in alcoholics in the withdrawal phase. *Int. J. Clin. Pharmacol.* Suppl. 3, 61–63.

Carlsson C. and Johansson T. (1971) The psychological effects of propranolol in the abstinence phase of chronic alcoholics. *Br. J. Psychiatry* **119**, 605–606.

Drew L. R. H., Moon J. R. and Buchanan F. H. (1973) Inderal (propranolol) in the treatment of alcoholism. *Med. J. Aust.* **2**, 282–285.

Edwards G. (1982) *The Treatment of Drinking Problems: a Guide for the Helping Professions.* London, Grant McIntyre.

Glatt M. M. (1982) *Alcoholism.* Sevenoaks, Kent, Hodder and Stoughton.

Petersen N. W. (1974) Non-hospital detoxication programs. In: *Papers Presented at the 20th International Institute on the Prevention and Treatment of Alcoholism.* Lausanne, International Council on Alcohol and Addictions, pp. 12–16.

Rossall J. C. (1978) Alcohol withdrawal. *Br. J. Psychiatry* **133**, 479–480.

Thomson A. D. (1980) There may yet be time to save your brain (Editorial) *Br. J. Alc. Alcoholism* **15**, 89–92.

Thomson A. D. and Majumdar S. K. (1981) The influence of ethanol on intestinal absorption and utilization of nutrients. *Clin. Gastroenterol.* **10**, 263–293.

Thomson A. D., Frank O., Baker H. et al. (1971) Thiamine propyl disulphide: absorption and utilization. *Ann. Intern. Med.* **74**, 529–534.

Walsh P. J. F. (1961) Korsakov's psychosis precipitated by convulsive seizures in chronic alcoholics. *J. Ment. Sci.* **108**, 560–563.

Whitfield C. L., Thompson G., Lamb A. et al. (1978) Detoxification of 1024 alcoholic patients without psychoactive drugs. *JAMA.* **239**, 1409–1410.

Chapter 5

PSYCHOLOGICAL ASPECTS IN THE TREATMENT OF ALCOHOL DEPENDENCE

Sir, I have no objection to a man's drinking wine, if he can do it in moderation. I found myself apt to excess in it, and therefore, after having been for some time without it, on account of illness, I thought it better not to return to it.

DR SAMUEL JOHNSON

The withdrawal features of physical dependence on alcohol are relatively easily overcome. The long term management of dependence is more complex and prolonged; it requires a radical appraisal by the excessive drinker and therapist of the former's usages and attitudes in respect to alcohol, together with an assessment of the problems and difficulties in the emotions and environment of the subject. Adjustments in these areas, particularly in regard to attitudes to alcohol, are desirable if the client or patient is to curtail drinking and avoid subsequent relapse into excessive alcohol consumption.

MOTIVATION AND TREATMENT GOALS

It is incorrect to assume that nothing can be achieved with an excessive drinker who denies a drinking problem and who rejects the need for abatement of alcohol intake. Because of the serious consequences of high alcohol intake to the drinker and to those in contact with him or her the therapist has a duty to attempt to instil insight and foster a desire for recovery. It is often possible to achieve this result.

It is relevant that some studies have reported that motivation to abstain from alcohol has not been related to outcome (Kendell and Staton, 1966; Aharan et al., 1967; Pattison et al., 1968). Willems and colleagues (1973) noted that the insight of problem drinkers at the time of admission to hospital was unconnected with the results of treatment; in the course of therapy the insight of their patients improved, and its strength when discharged from hospital was correlated with outcome. Gillis and Keet (1969) graded motivation and denial of problem drinking into three categories when their alcoholic patients entered hospital; there was some relationship between these features and response to treatment, but a quarter of their patients, who had strongly denied a drinking problem and who co-operated poorly, improved in respect of drinking.

The outcome of drinking is determined, not by the initial motivation of the subject, but by the capacity of the excessive drinker for a sustained alteration of attitude in the required direction. Maintained motivation depends on many factors, which are not fully understood but which may be summarized under the headings of stability of personality and favourable social circumstances.

An important consideration in the management of alcohol dependence is the point that abstinence is not the only goal of therapy. Although abstention from alcohol does correlate with benefit in other psychosocial spheres of adjustment (Rathod et al., 1966; Malcolm and Madden, 1973) the association is far from invariable. Improvement can occur in many areas of function, including drinking, without permanent abstention (Pattison et al., 1969). In a minority of instances seen in treatment drinking becomes moderate and then stays under the control of the drinker; a frequent outcome for drinking is that it remains abnormal in amount when it occurs, but the relapses into drinking become less frequent and shorter-lived. A useful phrase is 'attenuation of alcohol consumption' (Mottin, 1973). The term favours a therapeutic outlook aimed at reduction of drinking, whether to abstinence, to moderate alcohol intake, or to infrequent, brief recurrences of excessive drinking; the goal is combined with measures to improve the problem drinker's adjustment in other directions.

There is a small proportion of dependent drinkers for whom it is unrealistic to expect a significant permanent reduction of drinking. Problem drinkers in this category often live in unfavourable social circumstances, either alone, or with their peers in decayed urban areas. A few are attracted to, and benefit from, therapy programmes aimed at abstinence, but in general they need different approaches and treatment facilities. Periods of admission to hospital wards may be required to improve, for the time being, their physical status. Socially disintegrated alcoholics are helped by detoxification units, by hostels, and by other measures to ameliorate their material conditions and reduce social alienation. Limited goals are required for most that are not set rigidly and exactingly beyond their capabilities.

LONG-TERM TREATMENT

The long-term and radical treatment of dependence on alcohol is in a considerable measure an educative process. The subject is guided to an awareness of the realities of the drinking and the need for a permanent reduction of alcohol intake. In most instances the reduction requires complete abstention to ensure that drinking does not again escalate inordinately.

Many alcoholics are refreshingly frank about their drinking, but others attempt to conceal its extent and consequences from their therapist, using evasions and subterfuges during interview. In view of the importance that alcohol has held for the excessive drinker, and the deceit and self-deceit that accompany alcoholism, it is understandable that some subjects adopt these measures to cling on to alcohol, and that in deceiving others they deceive themselves. Dependent drinkers desire help and advice for their drinking problem but out of embarrassment are reluctant to reveal its extent until they have tested the outlook and sympathy of the therapist. Annoyance at the deceptions must be avoided; a show of irritation from the therapist can permanently inhibit effective help. At the same time the subject should not be allowed to consider that the therapist has been successfully deceived.

There are several strategems to break down the defence of an excessive drinker who denies a considerable drinking problem. The laboratory tests that have been outlined previously can be employed to detect an injurious level of drinking. It should be remembered that the test results may be affected by nonalcoholic disorders, that they may be normal despite hazardous drinking, and that they do not in themselves indicate more than a consumption level which places the drinker at risk of harm. Neither laboratory investigations nor questionnaires replace the necessity for a drinking history that is taken sympathetically.

Leading questions which expect a positive answer are quite appropriate; a nonalcoholic, no matter how suggestible, will not admit to symptoms of alcohol dependence. A query that requires a straight 'Yes' or 'No' reply may too readily elicit the latter response when the negative answer is incorrect. So, instead of enquiring whether the subject has tremors, or needs to drink from an early part of the day, or misses work through drinking, it is preferable to ask how bad are the shakes, or how much alcohol beverage is required to feel better the morning after copious ingestion, or how often work is missed from drinking. Answers given respectively to these questions such as 'Not bad', 'Not much' and 'Not often' point to physical dependence and impairment of work output by alcohol; the therapist is then on solid ground to enquire further.

In addition to the aspects covered in Table 5 (chapter 3) the excessive drinker can be asked to describe a typical day of drinking, keeping in mind that he or she may try to avoid reference to lunchtime or morning drinking, or to a rise of intake at weekends. The alcoholic patient or client can be given one of the many charts that describe the sequence of events in alcohol dependence, and invited to consider which of its features have been developed by the excessive drinker. Patience may be all that is needed during interview; after probing the reactions and humanity of the therapist, the problem drinker may change over to frankness and contradict what he or she had alleged only ten to twenty minutes previously.

Problem drinkers frequently enter therapy, not because they are in earnest about a curtailment of their drinking, but because they are compelled to do so. In some instances the compulsion is legal; there is direction by the courts following an offence, or without a conviction compulsory treatment for alcoholism is enforced under legal instruments that differ between countries. More commonly the pressure for treatment springs from a relative or employer. Without entering a plea for increased legal provision in the compulsory treatment of problem drinkers (which in any case would first require a sufficiency of treatment facilities) it must be noted that many socially stable alcoholics can be considerably helped even though they may enter treatment reluctantly, almost dishonestly, in the hope of merely sidestepping social consequences of their alcohol intake. As indicated above motivation is only one of the features affecting outcome.

In certain excessive drinkers continued drinking prevents the formation of adequate insight. Alcohol impairment of mental function inhibits clear judgement and self-criticism, while withdrawal symptoms induce a fear of alcohol deprivation. Admission to hospital is then required so that the drinker, once sober and with the abstinence syndrome in the past, can take a more rational view of drinking and other problems.

It has been claimed that emotional symptoms in alcoholics, such as anxiety or depression, must be dealt with first before the excessive drinking can be curtailed. This view stems from the early days of psychoanalysis and from the contention that the drinking arises from a disordered emotional life; according to this concept it is logical and correct to treat first the emotional conflicts and then to expect a subsidence of alcohol intake. The contention is in practice usually unsound; it is futile to hope for a significant improvement in the psychological well-being of an alcoholic while inordinate drinking continues. Psychoanalysis was ineffective for alcohol dependence, as are other forms of psychotherapy that largely pass over the drinking.

A similar view is often held by problem drinkers who request, not psychotherapy or counselling, but chemical help from doctors to suppress emotional distress. In most instances the prescription of drugs while the drinking is ignored merely ensures that the drugs are washed down with copious amounts of alcohol.

There are some exclusions from the rule that the excessive intake of alcohol must lie in the forefront of treatment. A few heavy drinkers have manic or schizophrenic psychoses which preceded and produced their high alcohol consumption; their therapy is aimed primarily at their psychoses. A rather larger number suffer from depression of a character that requires and responds to a course of physical treatment by thymoleptic drugs or electroconvulsive therapy.

Lithium is a mood stabilizing substance employed to reduce the frequency and severity of attacks of recurrent psychotic depression that are either accompanied by one or more episodes of mania (bipolar depression) or that recur without manic phases (unipolar depression). There are reports that lithium reduces drinking and disablement from alcohol in dependent drinkers who are depressed (Kline et al., 1974; Merry et al., 1976). Depression in alcoholism has a variety of causes; the reports therefore require confirmation before lithium can be recommended for widespread use among depressed alcoholics McMillan (1981).

Drugs have only a small role in the treatment of alcohol dependence and should generally be avoided. To this rule there are the exceptions outlined above, as well as the drugs that are briefly given for alcohol withdrawal, and substances like disulfiram that produce an unpleasant reaction if alcohol is also taken. But the indications for the prescription of drugs to problem drinkers are few, while the disadvantages are many. Some of the substances that have been used produce dependence in their own right. An overdose can be deliberately or accidentally taken. The act of taking a drug tends to confirm excessive drinkers in the false impression that the answer to their difficulties is chemical; it psychologically deters them from active self-appraisal while strengthening their confidence in the chemistry of psychotropic agents, including alcohol. Sedatives, tranquillizers and antidepressants have no role in the long-term treatment of alcohol dependence. The reader is invited to peruse again the previous sentence.

DISULFIRAM

This substance bears the proprietary name Antabuse. It is used extensively because its interaction with alcohol in the body can deter alcoholic subjects from drinking. Williams (1937) was the first to suggest that a reaction of this nature could be used therapeutically. He reported that industrial employees working in a vulcanizing process with tetramethylthiuram developed symptoms when they took alcohol. Tetramethylthiuram is the methyl analogue of disulfiram. The clinical use of disulfiram was later developed in Denmark (Hald and Jacobsen, 1948; Martenson-Larsen, 1948).

The features of the disulfiram-ethanol reaction (DER) in a patient primed by disulfiram begin within twenty to thirty minutes of drinking alcohol. There is generalized skin flushing, dyspnoea, palpitations, sweating, nausea, vomiting and headache. An odour in the breath as of stale alcohol beverage is detectable. Pulse rate increases and the blood pressure drops. Severe reactions can progress to cardiovascular shock, cardiac arrhythmias, myocardial infarction, heart failure, convulsions, and death.

The biochemical basis of the DER is debatable. Disulfiram and its metabolites inhibit many enzymes in the body. An important enzyme in the metabolic processes of alcohol degradation is aldehyde dehydrogenase; disulfiram inhibits its activity through competition with nicotinamide adenine dinucleotide for active portions of the aldehyde dehydrogenase molecule. One effect therefore of disulfiram is to block the biotransformation of alcohol at the acetaldehyde stage. During the DER acetaldehyde accumulates; several aspects of the reaction are similar to those produced in experiments when acetaldehyde is given to animals or humans. But not all the elements of the DER can be explained on the basis of excess acetaldehyde. Experimentally administered acetaldehyde produces a rise, not a fall, in blood pressure.

Casier and Merlevede (1961) postulated that disulfiram combines with alcohol to form a quaternary ammonium base responsible for the DER. An alternative explanation relies on the inhibitory effect of disulfiram on the synthesis of noradrenaline (norepinephrine). Disulfiram (or more precisely its metabolite diethyldithiocarbamate) inhibits the enzyme dopamine β-hydroxylase. This is the enzyme that facilitates the transformation of dopamine to noradrenaline; its inhibition leads to accumulation of dopamine and depletion of noradrenaline. Many of the features of the DER are explicable as the combined effect of excess of acetaldehyde and deficiency of noradrenaline on myocardium and arterioles (Morgan and Caplan, 1974; Nakano et al., 1974).

The dose of disulfiram that is adequate in therapy has been lowered over the years; 200 mg to 250 mg taken by mouth once daily are now considered as usually sufficient. To ensure that the alcoholic develops a regular habit of taking the drug, advice is given to consume it in the morning; if the substance produces the side effect of drowsiness it can be ingested on retiring at night. In order to avoid disulfiram reacting with alcohol already in the body the problem drinker is asked not to start the drug until after a day of alcohol abstinence. If an alcoholic who is taking disulfiram drinks, and does not experience a reaction strong enough to deter from further drinking, the dose can be increased to 400 mg daily. A minority of subjects unfortunately do not develop an adequate DER even with high doses of disulfiram.

It is essential to warn the excessive drinker that after the drug has been taken for a few days and accumulated in the body it can be unpleasant or dangerous to drink even a small amount of alcohol. The risk endures for 2–3 days after cessation of a course of disulfiram. The drug is contraindicated in the presence of ischaemic heart disease, cerebrovascular disease, severe liver or brain damage, epilepsy, asthma or diabetes. It should be avoided in persons aged over 60, and in extremely unstable individuals who live alone and are likely to drink in unobserved circumstances.

It is now customary to prescribe disulfiram without testing the strength of the DER by alcohol given under clinical surveillance. If a test with alcohol is administered the following regime is suggested, in which the amount of disulfiram is lower than the quantity formerly considered essential. 600 mg of disulfiram is given daily for 3–5 days prior to the test with alcohol. 800 mg of the drug is administered on the test day, followed after 30–60 minutes by 50 ml of beverage spirits containing 40% of alcohol by volume. The patient is kept under close observation; blood pressure and pulse rate are recorded every 5 minutes. If a moderate reaction does not develop the same quantity of spirits is repeated at 30-minute intervals up to a maximum total of 250 ml. Generalized flushing, severe distress to the patient, or a drop of blood pressure below 90/60 mmHg indicate that sufficient alcohol has been given. Widespread flushing is generally accompanied by sufficient subjective distress to deter the patient from drinking while regularly taking disulfiram.

In the event of a severe DER it is necessary to maintain the circulation with an intravenous infusion. Noradrenaline (Levarterenol) intravenously is of value; sodium ascorbate and an antihistamine have also been suggested by the intravenous route.

Side effects from disulfiram, in the absence of alcohol, include drowsiness, fatigue and mild depression. Perhaps these symptoms arise from depletion of noradrenaline in the brain consequent on inhibition of the enzyme dopamine β-hydroxylase. Other side effects are a metallic taste (presumably caused by sulphur in the drug), anorexia, nausea, headache, acneform and allergic skin rashes.

Peripheral neuropathy, convulsions (Price and Silberfarb, 1976) and psychosis (Liddon and Satran, 1967) are uncommon complications of disulfiram therapy. Administration to normal subjects of the dopamine precursor levodopa combined with fusarine, an inhibitor of dopamine β-hydroxylase, produces mental changes that are reminiscent of, though not specific to, schizophrenia (Hartmann and Keller-Teschke, 1977). This evidence, combined with the hypothesis reviewed by Snyder (1976, 1982), that overactivity of dopamine pathways plays a role in schizophrenia, suggests that the psychotic effects of disulfiram result from inhibition of dopamine β-hydroxylase. In clinical practice disulfiram psychosis is extremely uncommon.

If a persistent side effect such as lethargy or impotence requires cessation of disulfiram, then citrated calcium carbimide (Abstem) can be substituted in a dose of 100 mg once daily. The substitute is less likely to induce unpleasant side effects and can lead to a reaction with alcohol similar to, but perhaps milder than, the reaction produced by disulfiram (Minto and Roberts, 1960).

The psychological aspects of taking disulfiram, and the relationship to motivation that is implied by co-operation with the disulfiram regime, make it difficult to assess the deterrent value of its pharmacological effect. Some problem drinkers do not take disulfiram regularly, but carry its tablets with them to resume if they feel they might drink; others consume the drug daily to placate and reassure their spouses, considering (sometimes correctly) that they could avoid alcohol without it. In certain instances taking disulfiram merely reflects the motivation of alcoholics who for other reasons are not drinking.

There have been two careful comparisons of disulfiram with other treatment schedules. The first compared the drug with aversion therapy and hypnosis (Wallerstein et al., 1957); the second trial involved tranquillizers (Gerard and Saenger, 1966). In both researches the subjects who progressed most favourably were those who received disulfiram. Two further studies analysed the effects of addition of the drug to pre-existing treatment schedules; disulfiram therapy improved the results (Gerrein et al., 1973; Azrin, 1976). The drug has also been found useful with repeated drunkenness offenders who accepted treatment as an alternative to prison (Bourne et al., 1966).

'You can take Antabuse to your patient but you can't make him swallow it.' This aphorism of Pullar-Strecker (1950) vividly describes the main drawback of disulfiram: it requires prolonged compliance from a problem drinker whose desire to abstain may be weak or transient. Implantation of the drug under the skin or between the muscle fibres of the abdominal wall has been employed in the hope that the implant will have a deterrent action of long duration. The concentration of disulfiram in the blood should be over 0.1 mg/dl in order to ensure a reaction to alcohol (Malcolm et al., 1974); regrettably disulfiram implants do not produce this level.

A reaction to implanted disulfiram has been reported that differs from the usual DER in its slowness of development and course; the reaction has been stated to build up over a period of several days of drinking (Wilson et al., 1976, 1978). But it is likely that symptoms developed by subjects who drink after an implant are psychogenic (Madden, 1979). The implanted pellets can be felt though the skin for several months after the operation, so the implant has a talismanic property; patients who have undergone the procedure expect to feel ill if they drink within the ensuing months. Unfortunately it has not been possible to develop a long-lasting injectable form of disulfiram because the quantity of drug that requires administration would entail a volume of injection too large to be practicable. However, disulfiram by the oral route forms a useful adjunct in therapy.

ALCOHOLICS ANONYMOUS

In 1935 two alcoholics generally referred to as 'Bill W. and Doctor Bob', met in Akron, Ohio, to discuss ways in which they could help each other to stay sober. They soon attracted other excessive drinkers and an organization was founded, now well known as 'Alcoholics Anonymous' (A.A.). The movement impressed doctors and other professionals with the determination and ability of many dependent drinkers to cease taking alcohol. Although—or perhaps because—A.A. possesses only a minimum of organized structure it has spread to most parts of the world; the number of A.A. groups continues to expand. A.A. has established itself in many non-English speaking countries; it is the most widely known of several comparable organizations of alcoholics. Among comparable bodies formed by excessive drinkers are Calix (for Roman Catholic alcoholics) and the Link Movement in Sweden. The example of A.A. has also contributed substantially to the development of similar societies of people who rely on mutual help to overcome a shared problem, for example gambling or obesity. Common factors in self-directed groups like A.A. are the absence of professional control and freedom from the restrictions of formal treatment (Yalom, 1975).

Members of A.A. aim to follow a 12-point mental programme. The 'Twelve Steps', as they are called, stress inability to control drinking, reliance on a higher power ('God as we understand him'), a moral self-inventory and aid to other alcoholics. Group meetings centre on the drinking habits of the members and on practical steps to promote their abstention; there is some discussion at a superficial level of other personal and emotional problems. There are no formal rites of initiation or fees, and subjects drift in and out of A.A. as they see fit. An A.A. group may be described as an open psychotherapeutic group, without a trained or official leader, that is composed of self-selected members who have a shared condition. The organization functions best with people who are prepared or able to commit themselves to involvement and change (Robinson, 1979).

Some of the claims made by A.A. for its success rate appear exaggerated, for instance the statement that two-thirds of its members wishing to recover become able to abstain permanently with its help. The literature, scientific and otherwise, on A.A. has been reviewed by Bebbington (1976), who pointed out the difficulties in assessment of the efficacy of the organization. The problems include the anonymous membership with resultant difficulty in counting members and determining their progress, self-selection related to motivational factors affecting outcome, the fluctuating number of members with varying degrees of affiliation and commitment, and the influence of additional treatment from other sources. Bebbington concluded that the characteristics of A.A. make it unlikely that it can be assessed by proper scientific methods.

Reliance has therefore to be placed on impressions, unscientific though they are. The principles and practice of A.A. appear at commonsense level to have much to commend them. Problem drinkers who steadily attend A.A. feel benefit, otherwise they would not continue in regular attendance; some excessive drinkers attend occasionally for many years; others drop off after a period (and do not necessarily resume drinking). A few become over-involved but their intense commitment is preferable to drinking excessively. There are others who dislike the organization, in some instances after a conscientious assessment of what it can offer for their sobriety, in other instances because acceptance of its aims would interfere with drinking. The author advises problem drinkers who show potential for cessation of drinking to contact A. A.; those that are favourably impressed he encourages to re-attend.

CONTROLLED DRINKING

Since Davies (1962) and then Pattison and coworkers (1968) redrew attention to the fact that some alcoholics become able to control their drinking, there has been growing interest in the finding and in the possibility of treatment to promote this outcome. There is no doubt that controlled drinking does develop in a minority of persons who have been alcohol dependent within the most stringent definition of the condition. Pattison et al. (1968), in reviewing the literature noted that the proportion of treated alcoholics who become controlled drinkers varies between 5 and 15%. Experimentally alcohol has been surreptitiously given in small amounts to dependent drinkers who were led to consider that they were receiving a non-alcoholic preparation; neither craving for alcohol nor drinking were provoked (Merry, 1966). Some similar studies have confirmed this finding (Engle and Williams, 1972; Marlatt et al., 1973), though not all have done so (Marconi et al., 1967). The negative instances do not dispel the validity of the phenomenon in some experimental subjects nor refute the case reports of careful follow-up studies on controlled drinking in certain excessive drinkers.

The adoption of normal drinking may help to explain the relative paucity of numbers of elderly problem drinkers seen for therapy. Most heavy drinkers in treatment are middle-aged; their shortened life expectancy is not sufficient to account for their disappearance from treatment facilities as they grow older. The literature that led to acceptance of controlled drinking as a possible outcome was succinctly outlined by Pomerleau et al. (1976), and reviewed at greater length by Heather and Robertson (1981).

There are several reasons why controlled drinking could be preferable to abstinence as a therapy goal.

1. In most countries it is normal to drink occasionally and moderately. Abstention and excess drinking are both in a sense deviant.

2. Abstinent alcoholics are not always psychologically well adjusted (Gerard et al., 1962; Pattison et al., 1968; Gillis and Keet, 1969). On the other hand, significant improvement can develop in drinking and psychosocial functioning without full abstinence (Pattison et al., 1969).

3. Most dependent drinkers, despite therapy, do not become permanently abstinent.
4. Problem drinkers commonly express a desire to drink in a controlled manner, and might be more attracted to enter and remain in a therapy programme if abstinence was not a prerequisite of the treatment.
5. The practice of warning excessive drinkers that they will be unable to maintain moderation if they take alcohol could in some instances determine what happens if they later drink.

Treatment aimed at controlled drinking falls into two categories, which may be combined in the same programme. One approach uses behaviour therapy techniques; the other involves counselling the drinker regarding what appear to be sensible attitudes and usages concerning alcohol.

The relevant behaviour therapies take the form of giving a mild sanction (usually faradic stimulation) for undesirable behaviour, or a reward for desirable activity. One method that has been employed involves training problem drinkers to recognize their blood-alcohol concentrations, using a breathalyser instrument and their own sensations. If their blood-alcohol rises over a predetermined level, such as 60 mg/dl, they can be given a shock of electricity (Lovibond and Caddy, 1970). Covert sensitization has been used with some success to induce controlled drinking; in this technique the undesirable activity or thought is coupled with an unpleasant mental image such as that of nausea (Ashem and Donner, 1968; Hedberg and Campbell, 1975).

The use of reward (positive reinforcement) for moderation in alcohol consumption is a method that has been used for inpatients; the reward involves an improvement in their hospital environment (Bigelow et al., 1972; Cohen et al., 1971). The technique has also been applied to outpatients, with the reward for controlled drinking taking the form of continued investment of time and support by the therapists (Hunt and Azrin, 1973).

Outpatient group discussions have been conducted which centre on the aim of moderate drinking. The alcoholics accept limits on what they should drink, and are encouraged to find more mature solutions to their problems than alcohol ingestion (Cameron and Spence, 1976; Popham and Schmidt, 1976).

It is helpful if problem drinkers who are aiming at moderate drinking keep a diary or notebook to record the occasions on which they take alcohol. They should note the quantities consumed, the emotional and other circumstances behind each incident, and the precautions they adopted or failed to follow in order to restrict alcohol intake. Self-help organizations, for example Drinkwatchers, exist that cater for excessive drinkers who wish to curtail but not cease their alcohol consumption.

The goal of controlled drinking is controversial. It is unattainable for the majority of dependent drinkers yet knowledge of its possibility for a few can induce many to disastrous attempts to reach it. Therapeutic efforts to allow or encourage alcoholics to control their intake have been in some studies unsuccessful (Glatt, 1974) or abandoned (Ewing and Rouse, 1976). Unless the efficacy of controlled drinking programmes is improved, the serious or lethal consequences of excess drinking discourage therapists from the extensive approval of alcohol consumption among their dependent clients or patients.

Although some of the detailed case reports have described the development of controlled drinking in subjects who had been well advanced into alcoholism, it is clear that moderation is more readily attained by persons whose dependence on alcohol is not pronounced. Excessive drinkers with relatively small consumption levels (Popham and Schmidt, 1976), or with few symptoms of dependence (Polich et al., 1980; Finney and Moos, 1981), gain control of their drinking more readily. They tend to be young adults who reject suggestions that they should abstain, and do not possess the serious organic complications that contra-indicate alcohol intake. Improved case finding by the caring professions will uncover a greater number of early problem drinkers within this category.

Abstinence is an essential goal for the majority of subjects whose drinking has brought them into therapy. However, many therapists aim some of their clients towards controlled drinking, after considering the drinking history, the severity of dependence, and the stability and social relationships of the problem drinkers. There is uncertainty regarding a safe level of consumption to recommend to persons whose drinking has led them into difficulties (Robertson and Heather, 1982). Two pints of beer, or the equivalent in other beverages, taken infrequently and only on social occasions, forms an appropriate limit. Rare excursions beyond this level are not advised though they are not necessarily destructive. Essentially the subjects are asked to minimize the role of alcohol in their thought and behaviour.

PSYCHOTHERAPY

A less pretentious term is 'counselling'. It will sometimes be used in this section to ensure that persons who lack for formal training in psychotherapy do not feel excluded on that account from the provision of psychological help to excessive drinkers.

The initial stages of psychotherapy or counselling have been described already. They comprise recognition of problem drinking by the therapist and guidance of the drinker towards insight and motivation. Psychological treatment aims at strengthening the ability of the individual to curb alcohol intake and at a general improvement in mental maturity and psychosocial adjustment. Attenuation of drinking occupies an important part in psychotherapeutic discussions with excessive drinkers; this applies whether the drinking becomes reduced to zero, or to a controlled level, or to a lesser frequency and severity of relapses into inordinate consumption. Heavy drinking during a course of counselling, or drinking immediately prior to a session of individual or group therapy, impair the value of the therapeutic regime.

Individual psychotherapy

The therapeutic influences of counselling in a one-to-one situation are numerous. They include an increase of self-esteem in the problem drinker that is gained from the respect of the therapist, the unburdening of emotionally painful ideas and feelings, relief of guilt, clarification of attitudes and problems through the process of describing them in words, recall of memories that need recollection but have been consciously or unconsciously subdued, and experienced advice from the therapist. The depth of psychological therapy depends on the potentialities of the excessive drinker, on the training and views of the counsellor, and on the goals conjointly set by subject and therapist. At the most superficial level are discussions centred on practical solutions to the drinking, inter-personal, occupational and other difficulties of the client. At the deepest level is prolonged therapy aimed at radical personality realignment; the process requires the alcoholic subject to re-live emotionally and to understand the development from an early age of his or her temperament. At all levels of therapy the counsellor should adopt a relatively passive role, leaving most of the talking and decisions to the subject.

The views and attitudes of the alcoholic client towards the therapist are always subject to a degree of subjective distortion from previous experiences. The bias may be described in general terms as the 'parataxic distortion' of Harry Stack Sullivan, or more specifically in Freudian terminology as transference onto the therapist of ideas and feelings that were derived from early events with persons of significance, particularly parents. In the deeper forms of psychotherapy transference is encouraged and analysed; in the superficial varieties the therapist mentally notes its character without comment. The feelings of the therapist towards the alcoholic subject are significant; the counter-transference reveals something about the therapist but more importantly it conveys information about the client (Balint, 1964). Feelings provoked in the therapist of, for example, an irritable, punitive or protective nature can reveal recurrent patterns of interpersonal behaviour in the excessive drinker; the therapist will guard his own emotions lest they produce a reaction on his part that is against the interests of the subject.

Provided that a significant reduction in drinking is taking place, and that it remains a foremost goal, it is possible that selected problem drinkers can benefit from the kind of intensive, moderately deep psychotherapy described by Davanloo (1978) and Parry (1983) as suitable for some neurotic patients. Those likely to benefit have good motivation, possess intelligence and verbal facility that are rather above average, show sufficient steadiness to attend regularly for therapy, and exhibit a readiness to acknowledge that psychodynamic features underlie feelings, ideas, symptoms and behaviour. Many of these attributes are correlated with a hopeful outcome; therefore as in other alcoholism treatments that are operated on a selective and voluntary basis, the therapist has to live with the doubt whether the successes take place, not because of therapy, but because the subjects who are going to recover are those who are chosen and remain in treatment.

Without decrying the power of psychotherapy to produce emotional insight and adjustment, it must be stated that many dependent drinkers, including those who would co-operate with intensive psychotherapy, obtain considerable improvement by means that avoid self-scrutiny of emotions. The recoveries effected by Alcoholics Anonymous afford obvious illustrations, as do those that occur following an ecstatic or inspirational kind of religious experience. Many recovered alcoholics resemble the majority of mankind in the ability to function adequately while extensively employing unconscious repression and conscious suppression of emotionally painful material.

Group therapy

The curative factors in a therapy group (not conducted specifically for alcohol dependence) have been listed by Yalom (1975). Hope is derived from other group members and from the therapist. Self-esteem is improved by the provision of assistance to others. Feelings, ideas and problems are ventilated in cathartic relief. The group gives advice and information; it offers support, acceptance and approval for its members. Experiences that relate to the primary family group are re-lived correctively; current interpersonal relationships and social skills are examined and improved.

In the case of alcoholic groups several of the above factors appear particularly conducive to improvement. Installation of hope through contact with recovering alcoholics, relief of guilt, opportunities for altruism, and exchange of information about the means to sobriety and the pitfalls involved, are all provided by a therapeutic group. In addition it might be expected that problem drinkers would see through each others' evasions about drinking and could then criticize incisively yet helpfully. In fact the last two points are not always applicable. The therapist may have to rescue an alcoholic group which has been deceived into considering that one of its members does not have serious alcohol difficulties; members can be too indulgent and unconstructive in their comments to each other. Despite these provisos the encouraging example of A.A. has led to the widespread use of group therapy in alcohol treatment programmes.

The kinds of group used in therapy for alcohol dependence (and other conditions) are divided by size into two categories. Large groups are employed as part of milieu therapy for a therapeutic community comprised of a ward or other treatment unit. Large groups range from a dozen up to approximately 60 members, but usually comprise between 15–30 subjects, together with a few staff. The larger the size of the group, then necessarily the more general and less self-revelatory are its discussions. Didactic procedures like films or lectures, followed by an interchange of ideas, are suitable for large groups, as are meetings focused on general topics such as A.A., the problems of social occasions involving alcohol, and employment prospects.

Small groups ideally consist of 8 members and 1 therapist, though the number of members may differ slightly in either direction and a cotherapist or observer may be present. In a residential setting small groups can meet each working day, but outpatient groups usually assemble weekly for a 90-minute session.

Closed groups have a fixed membership, apart perhaps from one or two newcomers to replace defaulters, but practical considerations frequently determine that a group is open, with new members entering as others complete their treatment or drop out prematurely. In a residential surrounding members generally remain in a small group for periods up to three months. If they meet from their homes their stay in a group varies from this duration to a maximum of two years, and the group is more likely to be closed in character.

Duration and depth of group therapy depend on the beliefs and training of the therapist, on the emotional and intellectual assets of the alcoholic members, and on the cultural connotations and acceptability of the therapy. There is an extensive variety of group methodologies that can be employed in counselling problem drinkers. Some groups concentrate on the drinking and on practical routes to sobriety (Madden and Kenyon, 1975); others include a rather deeper analysis of emotions (Rathod et al., 1966). There are groups which aim at emotional reconstruction through exploration of the development from early childhood of the personalities of the members. Certain groups selectively deal with current psychological difficulties, as in transactional analysis, encounter groups or marathon therapy.

As described above the variations of group technique move towards greater transparency of the therapist, that is towards more self-disclosure by the therapist. Marathon therapy has required patients and therapists to confine themselves in one room for 24–48 hours while revealing their feelings. The more weird manifestations of group therapy have tended to arise from Southern California, but it is not chauvinistic to comment that group therapy as a whole, and the innovations towards therapist transparency, are more popular in the U.S.A. than in other countries, where personal reserve and aloofness are, perhaps regrettably, more habitual.

In a hospital ward that is not restricted exclusively to alcoholic patients the alcoholic residents are often constructive and verbal in a large heterogeneous group, but in general problem drinkers should not be placed in a group that includes other patients. In a mixed group the excessive drinking of the alcoholics does not receive the requisite attention and emphasis; high alcohol consumption therefore continues, or recurs, and prevents the excessive drinkers from co-operating or receiving significant benefit. A group run on these lines, with no great advantage to its alcoholic members, has been described at length by Johnson (1963).

Results of psychotherapy

It is notoriously difficult to prove that psychotherapy is beneficial for any condition, so much so that the value of psychotherapy has been questioned for neurotic disorders even though they provide its most extensive field of application. Hill and Blane (1967), in a well-argued review article, considered that most studies of psychotherapy for alcohol dependence have been inadequate in design; they felt that they could not reach a conclusive judgement about its efficacy. One of the few studies that they regarded as adequate did find more marked improvement in alcohol patients who received group psychotherapy compared with controls (Ends and Page, 1957), but there has been a general lack of precise validation of psychotherapeutic techniques in alcoholism treatment. The therapist must perforce rely on the face value of counselling methods, accepting but not inhibited by the knowledge that their worth is, by the highest standards of scientific reasoning, not proved.

FAMILY THERAPY

The title is here employed to denote counselling of interpersonal relationships within the family, rather than just conjoint interviewing of more than one family member. There are two reasons for involving members of the family in addition to the problem drinker; firstly, they often need help in their own right, and secondly the pattern of their reactions to the alcoholic subject may hinder his or her recovery.

Most of the published work on family interactions in alcoholism has centred on excessive drinkers and their marital partners. Some studies have been made of children of alcoholics, but little has been formally established concerning other relatives, for example parents of young alcoholics. The following comments therefore are focused on spouses (wives or husbands), but are in many respects applicable to other family members.

Spouses of actively drinking alcoholics are freqently unhappy, bitter and lonely. Although some connive, with varying degrees of awareness, at continuation of the excessive drinking most spouses desire its cessation. Their emotional disorders usually stem from rather than lead to the alcoholism, although their reactions to the alcohol intake of their partners may come to aggravate the drinking. The spouses can be helped by allowing them to unburden and recognize their feelings, by leading them to the realization that their marital situation is not unique, and by emphasizing the illness aspects of alcohol dependence. It is also beneficial to intimate that professionals and others are able to assist, and to outline the available treatments and treatment agencies. In addition spouses need to understand ways in which they might be working against recovery. When, as in most instances, abstinence is considered the preferable goal rather than an attempt at controlled drinking, the spouses require the simple advice that the alcoholic partner must never be offered a drink. Husbands of female problem drinkers particularly find this injunction unacceptable, perhaps because though their personal alcohol consumption may be moderate, they view the advice as a threat to their own drinking.

Conjoint interviews with both partners and the therapist are useful in establishing a pattern of discussion of problems and conflicts; the therapist is present to keep the peace and to show that difficulties and disputes can be debated without disruptive outbreaks of hostility. A conjoint interview, near the beginning or in the course of therapy, is valuable when the therapist knows that the excess drinker, during individual interviews, is concealing the true nature of the alcohol consumption. After the spouse has revealed in the alcoholic's presence the extent of the drinking the way is open to more fruitful explanation of the necessity and means of its abridgement.

Group therapy may be conducted for spouses of problem drinkers. This can take place in the form of a group composed of spouses alone (Smith, 1969). An alternative arrangement consists of a group membership provided both by the spouses and by their alcoholic partners (Burton and Kaplan, 1968; Cadogan, 1973). In the latter setting each partner in a marriage is given the opportunity to appreciate the difficulties and viewpoints of the spouse, through listening to the spouse and to other members of the group.

The concepts of general systems theory are applicable to understanding and altering the family interactions that are associated with excessive drinking (Steinglass, 1982). The family is regarded as an indivisible network of independent parts. The members interact to achieve homeostasis within the system; problems which arise are not attributable only to one member. Families with an alcoholic member tend to favour short-term stability at the expense of long-term growth, but the theory notes that a radical change in one member can change the system.

Spouses whose alcoholic partners reject the need to curb alcohol intake are in an unenviable position. In the long term much depends on their success in compelling their partners to have treatment. There are many measures open to the spouses that will further this end, or at least make their situation more bearable. Useful means include the acquisition of knowledge about alcohol dependence, avoidance of devices that protect their partners from the social consequences of excess alcohol intake, calm discussion with their partners of the drinking to indicate its unacceptability, and refusal to tolerate violence (Caruana and O'Hagan, 1976).

A problem drinker in process of recovery may present the family with a different set of problems. The relatives may have to cope with a phase of tension in the subject that was formerly suppressed by drinking (a 'dry drunk'), or with an over-enthusiastic approach to therapy and giving personal assistance to other excessive drinkers. The abstinent alcoholic will desire to take over some responsibilities that had been relinquished and which the family may remain reluctant to surrender. In all these circumstances further guidance to the relatives and subject will be appreciated.

The literature on family therapy for alcohol dependence has been reviewed by Harwin (1982), who rightly considered that many important issues remained unresolved. She also took the view that, because of the weaknesses in evaluation studies, the claims on its behalf were not substantiated. Janzen (1977) has also been aware of shortcomings in the research appraisals, but concluded that family therapy is beneficial among families of excessive drinkers.

Al-Anon

Al-Anon is a society composed, on an anonymous basis, of the relatives and friends of excessive drinkers. Many relatives reject the advice to contact the organization, perhaps out of shyness, embarrassment or apathy, or from the opinion that it is not they but the problem drinker who should seek help. But Al-Anon is a fruitful source of assistance; it offers sharing of problems, and advice on coping with an alcoholic who continues to drink excessively or who is in the early stages of recovery.

A prominent feature of Al-Anon thought, based on the experience of its members, advises that relatives of actively drinking alcoholics should distance themselves in emotions and behaviour from the alcohol intake. They should not protect excessive drinkers from the consequences of high alcohol consumption, and should at the same time refrain from efforts to motivate the problem drinker to curtail consumption. The second aspect of the advice is in contradistinction to the report of Orford and colleagues (1975); in their study of male alcoholics Orford and coworkers noted that the subjects possessed an improved prognosis if their wives took active measures against the drinking. The point is forcefully illustrated by the study's finding that male problem drinkers developed a better outcome if they were struck by their wives! The choice between the two courses rests on considerations presented by the respective personalities of the couple and by the responsiveness or intractability of the drinking to pressure from the nonalcoholic spouse. Al-Anon members and researchers would, however, agree that attempts by the spouse to shield the alcohol misuser from the adverse social consequences of excessive drinking merely allow the high alcohol intake to continue.

Alateen

This is a comparable organization for teenage children of problem drinkers. Frequently their view of an alcoholic parent reflects mainly their experiences of the drinking behaviour; attitudes towards the parent may be rejecting, contemptuous or at least indifferent. Alateen can help adolescent sons or daughters towards a greater understanding and sympathy concerning the alcoholic parent, and guide them to a higher degree of maturity and balance in their own reactions and psychological health.

BEHAVIOURAL PSYCHOTHERAPY

Several behavioural techniques have been employed for problem drinking. The first to be used was aversive conditioning; this method involves repeated pairing of drinking, or the thoughts or preparations for drinking, with an unpleasant consequence. It is a common observation that a person, often not alcohol dependent, who has been sick after over-indulgence with an alcoholic beverage may be unable subsequently to drink that beverage because of the nausea it provokes. The nausea can be aroused merely by thoughts of the beverage; sometimes the distaste spreads to other alcoholic drinks; the aversion can last indefinitely. Benjamin Rush, in 1785, proposed this phenomenon in treatment when he suggested that nauseating amounts of drink could be given to alcoholic patients to avert them from further alcohol intake.

In the early twentieth century Pavlov, in the course of his experiments on dogs, showed that the repeated combination of a neutral stimulus with a stimulus that naturally produces a reflex response in the subject leads to the evocation of the response by the neutral stimulus alone. Derivations of his experimental model have been used in aversive conditioning against alcohol.

When aversive conditioning was initially employed the aversive stimulus involved injection of a drug—apomorphine or emetine—to produce nausea or vomiting. After injection of the emetic drug alcohol was given, before the onset of drug-induced nausea or vomiting. The procedure was repeated on each patient several times with the intention of developing a conditioned reflex such that alcohol became linked with the response of nausea.

Although Lemere and Voegtlin (1950) achieved an abstinence rate of 51% in their patients with the use of chemical aversion, this form of conditioning has dropped out of favour for several reasons (Franks, 1963; Eysenck and Rachman, 1965). It is quite unpleasant for the patient and presents risks from inhalation of vomitus and from circulatory collapse. Subjects differ in their sensitivity to emetic drugs, with resultant difficulties in the adjustment of dosage. Theoretically, chemical conditioning is not likely to have a prolonged effect; the conditioned stimulus of alcohol is presented after the unconditioned stimulus of the emetic, and sometimes after the response of nausea; backward conditioning of this nature is generally weak and transient. Furthermore, chemical conditioning does not permit the precise timing of stimuli and response; precision is needed to establish a sound conditioned reflex which is not liable to easy extinction. The results of chemical conditioning have varied widely in different reports, depending on the enthusiasm of the therapists and on the prognostic factors in the subjects.

Faradic stimulation, administered in the form of painful but just bearable electric shocks, came to replace emetic drugs. The alcoholic subject drinks, or makes ready to drink, and then receives a shock; compared with chemical conditioning the procedure is safer, neater, more precise and, on the whole, less unpleasant.

The behavioural technique, whereby undesired behaviour is necessarily followed by an unpleasant stimulus, involves the methodology of classic conditioning. An alternative approach is that of operant conditioning, in which during treatment sessions the subject averts the sanction by avoidance or discontinuance of the drinking behaviour. Operant conditioning may be a more effective means than classic conditioning to extinguish a behavioural pattern. A further refinement is discriminated aversive control; here the problem drinker receives a shock, not for drinking, but for drinking beyond a predetermined amount or speed, or to an extent that raises blood-alcohol concentration over a stated level. The goal of the latter form of aversion therapy is controlled drinking, not abstinence.

The aversive stimulus need not be electrical or chemical. Withdrawal of privileges, such as those available to hospital inpatients, has been employed (Bigelow et al., 1974). Covert sensitization has been utilized, in which the alcoholic repeatedly thinks of an unpleasant effect, like nausea, while drinking or imagining that drinking is taking place (Ashem and Donner, 1968).

Evaluation of aversion therapy

In the assessment of aversion techniques it is difficult to distinguish between their technical efficacy in achieving an alteration of reflex behaviour and the curative benefits of their mental implications.

Aversion therapy provides a form of communication between subject and therapist, during which emotional bonds develop that can induce the excessive drinker to conform with the therapist's expectations of recovery. In addition aversion methods convey to both parties the impression that an active therapy is being conducted that will prove beneficial. The same remarks apply to other forms of alcoholism treatment, except that the duration and intensity of aversion therapy are often in practice considerable, so that a stronger positive relationship ensues between client and therapist. The suffering of the subject during aversion therapy can allay guilt feelings for drinking behaviour and lead the problem drinker to consider that recovery is merited. Studies have been conducted with control groups whose treatment has been similar in other respects to the subjects receiving aversion therapy; the techniques of the conditioning treatment have not always been adequate and therefore may have underestimated its efficacy, but the results of the more adequate studies support the view that aversion therapy to induce abstinence has only a minor role in the treatment of alcohol dependence (Elkins, 1975).

Nonaversive techniques in behavioural modification

Nonaversive methods have in turn largely replaced aversion therapy, although their efficacy also awaits proper validation. They involve the recognition of difficulties and events which precipitated the response of excess drinking, and aim to promote alternative reactions that do not employ alcohol.

For example, instead of imparting in treatment a noxious stimulus for taking alcohol, a reward can be given for behaviour that avoids excessive drinking. The positive reinforcement can take the form of money, or of privileges while in hospital, or of more extensive community support and services to problem drinkers not in hospital (Bigelow et al., 1972; Hunt and Azrin, 1973; Miller, 1975).

Systematic desensitization to emotionally unpleasant stimuli can be employed. Massed exposure to disturbing stimuli ('flooding') is another means of reducing their unpleasantness. The actions of the alcoholic (in drinking or other aspects) can be shaped gradually in a desired direction. As an alternative the alcoholic's behaviour can be modelled after that of another person; in one study (albeit with poor results) aimed at controlled drinking, medical student therapists drank in a moderate manner with the excessive drinkers (Ewing and Rouse, 1976).

The frequent occurrence of phobias among dependent drinkers might suggest the use of behavioural techniques to relieve the pathological fears. In practice, specific phobic therapy is usually not required, because the phobias improve considerably or remit in the course of an adequate period of abstinence. Presumably the phobic features arose, or were aggravated and prolonged, because of the anxiety provoked (as from repeated subclinical withdrawal) during chronic excessive alcohol ingestion. Of course, the persistence of phobias despite abstention forms an indication for behavioural psychotherapy.

Training in social skills and assertiveness is often employed with problem drinkers (Oei and Jackson, 1980; Miller and Eiser, 1977). The assertiveness that is developed comprises the ability to stand for personal rights in a socially acceptable manner; one of the more important rights is the freedom to decline an invitation to drink. Cognitive restructuring is also utilized; the method centres on rational persuasion, imparting of information, and challenging of false assumptions (Oei and Jackson, 1982).

The techniques of behavioural psychotherapy are suitable (with appropriate modifications) whether the client or patient is receiving guidance aimed at abstinence or at controlled drinking. They are often utilized by alcohol treatment units and other centres that specially cater for residential and nonresidential problem drinkers.

ADJUNCTS TO TREATMENT

Videotape self-confrontation

The comportment of excessive drinkers while intoxicated has been recorded on videotape or audiotape and later played back to the subjects (Paredes et al., 1969). Not surprisingly, self-confrontation with drunken behaviour leads to acute distress and increased verbal commitment to change. Unexpectedly, one study noted that feed-back can increase subsequent drinking by some alcoholic subjects (Schaefer et al., 1971). Yet although the efficacy, uselessness or disadvantages of the technique are not adequately explored, self-confrontation of problem drinkers with taped recordings of their intoxicated state could have a small but useful place in therapy.

Apomorphine

Apomorphine was introduced in the treatment of alcohol dependence in 1899; during the early years of its employment the drug was used as a sedative and hypnotic whose actions were particularly applied to delirium tremens. In the 1930s apomorphine was employed as an emetic in aversion therapy by J. Y. Dent, one of the pioneers in Britain of the treatment of excessive drinkers. Subsequently Dr Dent used apomorphine in a different manner: he came to consider that a short course of subemetic doses of apomorphine tablets placed under the tongue relieved craving for alcohol (Dent, 1955). In Denmark

Martensen-Larsen (1974) has employed apomorphine injections, in subemetic or barely emetic dosage, to sober intoxicated patients; the same worker has also administered apomorphine, parenterally or orally, with the aim of relieving alcohol withdrawal features.

Apomorphine produces sedation and drowsiness but is not habit forming. Its effects in the brain may be related to the agonistic action of the drug on dopamine receptors. In the light of current knowledge it is doubtful whether apomorphine has value as a therapy for alcohol dependence. Schlatter and Lal (1972) have summarized the relevant literature, and described their own clinical study of Dent's oral method; their research is the only investigation to utilize a control group. Compared with controls a significant proportion of their patients who were treated with apomorphine developed a decrease of craving for alcohol, yet follow-up 6 months later showed no advantages for apomorphine in the achievement of abstinence.

Although Schlatter and Lal did suggest that a maintenance dose of apomorphine might have some effect in the maintenance of sobriety, neither their report nor the other studies justify confidence in apomorphine as a treatment for alcohol dependence. The usage of apomorphine has been largely conducted by a few enthusiasts who have not to date demonstrated the therapeutic value of the undoubted pharmacological properties of the drug.

ALCOHOLIC UNITS

Special units for the treatment of problem drinking are usually based in a hospital; the services they offer include outpatient clinics, day patient care, and home visits. The most important function of an alcoholic unit is to provide a focus where excessive drinkers enter a long-term network of treatment; the web of support includes voluntary as well as statutory agencies. Special centres for problem drinkers possess experienced staff and provide ample opportunities for the treatment of patients by group techniques.

Blaney et al., (1975) have reported on excessive drinkers who were treated in a special unit by a regime of group psychotherapy, educational techniques, disulfiram, and co-operation with A.A. At follow-up the patients showed a better outcome than controls admitted for shorter periods to a general psychiatric hospital where treatment centred on alcohol withdrawal. In respect of favourable prognostic features that could have influenced the results the patients in the alcoholism centre had a higher proportion who were free of legal troubles from drinking. The feature led to a better outlook but accounted for only a small part of the results. The remaining prognostic features of the two groups were similar in distribution. It is difficult to avoid the inference that the patients in the alcoholic unit gained from the extra investment of therapeutic attention and methods, and from the opportunity to meet recovering and recovered alcoholic subjects.

Alcoholic units are naturally in the forefront of advances in the understanding and treatment of problem drinking. The flexibility of outlook that many exhibit has furnished substantial developments in treatment and in the facilities for treatment, as well as important contributions to the literature. Alcoholic units also serve as centres of professional training and community education. The term 'alcoholism treatment unit' that is sometimes applied conveys a restricted (Glatt, 1982) and rather archaic notion of their activities.

There are, of course, many other important sources of help for problem drinkers. The services include statutory and voluntary agencies that are nonmedical but possess close working relationships with hospitals. Voluntary councils on alcoholism provide an illustration. In Britain the Advisory Committee on Alcoholism (1979) recommended early recognition, and when appropriate, treatment, of excessive drinkers by primary care workers. Given adequate support, community-based personnel whose duties embrace fields additional to alcohol misuse can be guided towards more active intervention with problem drinkers and towards a hopeful outlook that is realistically determined by the results (Shaw et al., 1979). Links between primary care workers and specialized centres for alcohol dependence have strengthened in many countries following the expansion of facilities that cater, both by residential and nonresidential means, specifically for problem drinkers.

Because of the number of alcoholics in the community, the special centres in Britain cannot provide a service, even on an outpatient basis, to all the excessive drinkers in need of attention. General psychiatrists, specialists in medicine and family doctors will continue to treat numerous alcoholic patients. An expanded role inevitably falls on the social services. Fortunately regional councils on alcoholism, that function outside the statutory services, are increasing their case load. One method by which the alcoholism councils amplify their work is through the provision of trained, unpaid volunteers comparable to those provided by marriage guidance councils (Brown, 1980).

DETOXIFICATION CENTRES

Centres exist in several countries where excessive drinkers can be admitted with minimal formality for the purposes of sobering-up and of management of withdrawal symptoms. Detoxification—or detoxication—centres have functioned for many years in Eastern European countries like Poland and Czechoslovakia, in St Louis in the U.S.A. and in Stockholm. Their provision has more recently extended to Britain, though only in a limited manner.

The alternative for problem drinkers who are repeatedly drunk in public is a recurring cycle of drunkenness, fines, imprisonment and drunkenness. Periods in prison have the sole advantage to repeated drunkenness offenders of permitting an improvement of physical health; the alcoholic prisoners are usually discharged at the end of their sentences with no measures for their rehabilitation. The prison doors that revolve for repeated drunkenness offenders merely ensure that the subjects are, in short spells, bodily fit to drink again. Detoxification centres remove public inebriates from the penal area into a system that is logically more appropriate; they are then able to attract a proportion of their clients into long-term supportive arrangements such as halfway houses.

Arrangements for medical cover to detoxification centres are essential; drugs may be required for withdrawal features, while the clients frequently have concurrent physical illness (Hamilton, 1977). But the majority of subjects do not require immediate medical examination or treatment (Petersen, 1974), so the continuous presence of medical staff is unnecessary. The details of practice differ in this respect: some centres are under medical direction; others which are controlled by nonmedical personnel arrange for doctors to visit regularly or enjoy facilities for emergency transfer of clients to hospital.

From Toronto doubts have been expressed about the benefit of detoxification units. The value of the Toronto units has been queried on the grounds that most of their clients chose to remain in them only for a few days during each visit; the longer periods of institutional sojourn required by prison sentences ensure less deterioration of physical health (Smart, 1977). This adverse criticism is important, but hopefully the growing impetus to provide detoxification will lead to more effective means of influencing clients into lengthy treatment programmes. Unless facilities are provided there appears no administrative solution for socially unstable problem drinkers other than the undesirable nexus of drunkenness and repetitive imprisonment.

HALFWAY HOUSES

The term 'half-way house' is used instead of 'hostel' in this section to emphasize the desirable element of rehabilitation. It is also the phrase employed in the United States for a therapeutic residential setting; in the U.S.A. a 'hostel' denotes a shelter for the homeless and vagrant. Excessive drinkers who are alienated from spouses or relatives have considerable difficulty in abstaining after discharge from hospital (Madden, 1967). Halfway houses provide protected environments for problem drinkers admitted to them from hospital, from prison or from the community. They offer mutual support and friendship; the alternative is an isolated existence in lodging houses where companionship and recreation are generally sought only in drinking situations.

The communities that reside in halfway houses vary in composition between the houses. At one pole of a continuum are reasonably integrated alcoholics who lack a domestic environment; at the other extreme are vagrant subjects, often with a prison history. The management of the latter has been discussed at length by Cook (1975). Halfway houses differ in aim and practice depending on their type of resident (Hore, 1976). Some do not utilize a resident warden and have a strict rule against drinking; others furnish more staff supervision and are less rigid about alcohol consumption. Each policy is correct for the appropriate clientèle. Most halfway houses place a time limit on the duration of residence (varying from three months up to two years) although hostels dealing with the more unstable and insecure person-alities tend to provide an indefinite length of stay (Glatt, 1972). There is a requirement for a wide range of accommodation to meet the diverse needs of problem drinkers who do not have family support but who are not necessarily vagrant nor socially disintegrated.

OUTCOME

The outlook for drinking behaviour and psychosocial adjustment in alcohol dependence is largely determined by features in the personality of the subject and by external social circumstances. Both kinds of factor are interrelated: competence of personality helps the individual to obtain and keep a favourable environment despite alcoholism, and helpful social conditions assist the personality to remain intact in the face of excessive drinking. Often the most effective and practical gauge of the personality of a problem drinker is the quality of the social circumstances.

The prognostic features that embrace personality and environment include the network of affective relationships surrounding the excessive drinker, together with steadiness of occupation and residence. Straus and Bacon (1951) have devised a social stability scale for male alcoholics, in which one point is given for each of the following assets:

1. Ever held a steady job for three years.
2. Living in present town for past two years.
3. Living in own home, or that of relatives or friends.
4. Married and living with spouse.

Edwards (1966) has commented on the Straus–Bacon scale, and stressed that social stability is determined conjointly by personality, environment and drinking behaviour.   .

There are several other features appertaining to social stability that have been found in some studies to improve the outcome in alcoholism. Among them are the avoidance of crude spirits or cheap wine, preservation of economic resources, and residence outside a Skid Row district (i.e. away from a decayed neighbourhood replete with inexpensive lodging houses). Another favourable feature is the absence of penal convictions; this extends to convictions for drunkenness but not to drinking and driving offences (Madden and Kenyon, 1975). The latter transgressions are almost an integral part of alcohol dependence; they do not denote socially disintegrated problem drinkers, and do not impair outcome.

McCance and McCance (1969) reported that the following factors were associated with a better response to inpatient treatment of their patients; living with a friend, relative or spouse; if married, a stable marriage; co-operation in hospital; steady job on admission; consumption of culturally accepted drinks and avoidance of cheap wine or barbiturates; no convictions; no history of delirium tremens; first admission for alcoholism; higher social class; residence outside an urban concentration; bout drinking or weekend binges as opposed to the continuous pattern of consumption; and a subculture which does not normally practise heavy drinking.

Additional factors that many researches have noted as prognostically favourable are: motivation, male sex, older age, higher social stratum, and abstinence when first attending for treatment. Associated with a less satisfactory outcome are sociopathic (psychopathic) trends, severe alcoholic brain damage, and an alcoholic marital partner. Patients with alcoholic liver disease frequently respond favourably when impressed by their doctors with the need for abstinence (Katz et al., 1981).

One of the many challenges presented by the alcohol literature is the lack of consensus concerning prognostic factors. The favourable nature of many items has not always been confirmed, or has even been opposed by the evidence of some follow-up reports (Ewing, 1974). Some of the uncertainty is unresolved, but there is agreement that the excessive drinker with the most desirable prognosis has a stable marriage and work record, avoids brushes with the law, accepts the need for change and is frank about the drinking.

A simple test of prognosis is the assessment of the qualities of the spouse. The likelihood of a good outcome is furthered by a wife or husband of mature temperament and poise who feels and expresses love and regard for the problem drinker provided the latter avoids drinking or drinking heavily, and who makes it plain that further excess drinking will not be tolerated. At the other extreme the absence of a spouse implies that the future is considerably less hopeful.

An important study of the spontaneous course of alcohol dependence was published by Lemere in 1953. He enquired from his patients in the U.S.A. about their alcoholic ancestors of the preceding two generations; the drinking of the patients' forerunners had reached its height before there was extensive medical interest in the treatment of excessive drinking, and before A.A. was founded. The methodology has obvious defects in reporting, but affords the most available approach to the natural course of untreated alcoholism in an affluent society. Information was gathered on 500 problem drinkers; 11% became abstinent (all but 4 of them without medical help); 3% came to drink moderately. A further 7% developed increasingly longer periods of sobriety, so that their drinking ceased to be a difficulty. Twenty-nine per cent showed no change throughout their lifetime, 22% stopped drinking in a terminal illness, and 28% died directly from alcohol dependence, nearly half by suicide.

Later studies have combined in their investigations excessive drinkers who were untreated or received varying degrees of help from treatment agencies. Persons who attend for therapy form only a limited sample of problem drinkers (Chick, 1982). A lengthy prospective study of Boston males assessed 110 alcohol misusers at the age of 47 (Vaillant and Milofsky, 1982). Thirty-eight were currently abstinent (21 for at least three years); 18 were asymptomatic social drinkers for at least two years. The findings were in agreement with other community-based reports that spontaneous remission without therapy often develops (Calahan, 1970; Saunders and Kershaw, 1979). The community studies also concur that both spontaneous remission, and its attainment through moderation of intake rather than abstinence, are more likely to take place among young problem drinkers with minimal dependence. The investigations have noted that external factors often contribute critically to remission. Turning points in drinking careers include improvements of interpersonal relationships and of employment, with acquisition of a stable source of hope and self-esteem. The equilibrium can originate from religion, from a nonprofessional mentor, or from Alcoholics Anonymous (Vaillant and Milofsky, 1982). Cessation of problem drinking in response to a favourable change of circumstances resembles the remissions that take place for a similar reason among drug dependent persons.

Follow-up reports of treated alcoholics have presented abstinence rates ranging from 10% in several studies to a report by Moynihan (1964) of nearly 70%. The higher success rates are provided by treatment of selected clients who have advantageous prognoses, and the lowest rates by therapy programmes that do not select their problem drinkers or treat subjects who show poor predictions of outcome. It is therefore difficult to determine how far case selection accounts for the more favourable results and whether treatment improves at all on the spontaneous remission rates among untreated excessive drinkers.

Adverse comments have been offered by Hill and Blane (1967) about the majority of studies of the effects of psychotherapy on problem drinkers; their recommendations for treatment evaluation apply to all forms of alcoholism therapy. Requirements which are desirable for adequate treatment research, and which are often missing or only partially met, include: a comparison group that does not have the therapy under investigation, equal opportunity for assignment of patients to treatment or control groups, clear description of the patient samples and the population from which they were drawn, careful outline of the treatment and of the setting in which it occurred, definition of criteria for recovery, assessment before and after therapy by identical and reliable methods, and lucid presentation of results with statistical tests of differences between patient groups. Common problems in researches on alcohol treatment lie in the fields of improvement criteria (which preferably should embrace psychosocial adjustment as well as drinking outcome) and of sample selection. Perhaps no group of problem drinkers treated in one centre fully resembles a sample treated elsewhere; in order to comprehend the effects of case selection on outcome it is essential to describe the prognostic attributes of the subjects who are studied.

Pokorny and colleagues (1968) have examined treatment reports from several countries, and observed that up to one-third (maximum 37%) of subjects were abstinent at the time of first assessment and approximately a half (maximum 59%) were improved. But several British researches have thrown doubt on the value of treatment, or on some of the accepted modes of treatment. Edwards (1966) reported that neither increased length of inpatient stay nor hypnosis improved the outlook; Edwards and Guthrie (1967) found that inpatient treatment had no advantages over outpatient therapy. Kendall and Staton (1966) compared alcoholics who declined inpatient therapy with similar excessive drinkers who accepted: both groups had the same outcome. Rathod et al. (1966) noted that patients who took their discharge prematurely from an inpatient alcoholic unit fared as well as those who remained for the full course of treatment. Ritson (1968) selected for admission to an alcoholic unit patients who were open about their drinking, accepted the need for abstinence, showed some capacity to use therapeutic community techniques, and were able to attend for weekly follow-up after discharge; subjects who did not meet these requirements were treated only as outpatients yet achieved similar progress.

Another British study revealed no differences in the results between groups of inpatients who were treated either with faradic aversion therapy, group psychotherapy or routine ward milieu; more disturbingly, patients who were subsequently seen at outpatient clinics or at home showed no better progress than those who did not receive after-care (McCance and McCance, 1969). A comparison of short stay (mean 20 days) and long stay (mean 82 days) inpatient treatment of problem drinkers revealed no differences in recovery and improvement rates (Willems et al., 1973). Finally, Edwards and coworkers (1977) compared two comparable groups of alcoholics, who respectively received either one counselling session with their marital partners or several months of treatment, mainly as outpatients; after a year there were no significant differences in outcome between the two groups.

A more positive view of treatment is furnished by the work of Costello (1975a, b; 1977), who collated 58 studies from many countries, including most of the reports referred to above. He applied four criteria of outcome to the alcohol misusers in each study: mortality, problem drinking, no problem drinking (abstinent or drinking with no associated problem), and availability at follow-up. Cluster analysis revealed consistent trends, both for prognostic features in the alcoholics and for successful treatment programmes. Excessive drinkers with a good outlook possessed satisfactory premorbid marital, occupational and social histories, yet even those with poorer prognoses had their outlook improved by a treatment programme that was of high quality. The more effective programmes employed a broad scope of treatment methods. Compared with the less successful programmes the superior regimes were more likely to adopt the following measures: selectivity of client intake, residential treatment, milieu therapy, energetic after-care, counselling of relatives and others collateral to the problem drinker, disulfiram, and behaviour modification. Since group therapy was extensively used among the programmes in the survey it did not differentiate the quality of treatment, except that the programmes with poorer results relied more exclusively on this mode of therapy.

The analysis of Costello goes some way towards the alleviation of doubts about the efficacy of treatment in alcohol dependence. It offers scientific support to the rather obvious if intuitive viewpoint that the more active and wide ranging courses of treatment are likely to prove the most successful.

REFERENCES

Advisory Committee on Alcoholism (1978) *The Pattern and Range of Services for Problem Drinkers.* London, HMSO.

Aharan C. H., Ogilvie R. D. and Partington J. T. (1967) Clinical indications of motivation in alcoholic patients. *Q. J. Stud. Alcohol* **28**, 486–492.

Ashem B. and Donner L. (1968) Covert sensitization with alcoholics: a controlled replication. *Behav. Res. Ther.* **6**, 7–12.

Azrin N. H. (1976) Improvements in the community—reinforcement approach to alcoholism. *Behav. Res. Ther.* **14**, 339–348.

Bailey M. B., Haberman P. and Alksne H. (1962) Outcome of alcoholic marriages: endurance, termination or recovery. *Q. J. Stud. Alcohol* **23**, 610–623.

Balint M. (1964) *The Doctor, his Patient and the Illness,* 2nd ed. London, Baillière Tindall.

Bebbington P. E. (1976) The efficacy of Alcoholics Anonymous: the elusiveness of hard data. *Br. J. Psychiatry* **128**, 572–580.

Bigelow G., Cohen M., Liebson I. A. et al. (1972) Abstinence or moderation; choice by alcoholics. *Behav. Res. Ther.* **10**, 209–214.

Bigelow G., Liebson I. A. and Griffiths R. (1974) Alcoholic drinking; suppression by a brief time-out procedure. *Behav. Res. Ther.* **12**, 107–115.

Blaney R., Radford I. S. and MacKenzie G. (1975) A Belfast study of the prediction of outcome in the treatment of alcoholism. *Br. J. Addict.* **70**, 41–50.

Bourne P. G., Alford J. A. and Bowcock J. Z. (1966) Treatment of skid-row alcoholics with disulfiram. *Q. J. Stud. Alcohol* **27**, 42–48.

Brown R. I. F. (1980) The role, selection and training of voluntary counsellors in alcoholism. In: Madden J. S., Walker R. and Kenyon W. H. (ed.) *Aspects of Alcohol and Drug Dependence.* Tunbridge Wells, Kent, Pitman Medical, pp. 279–289.

Burton G. and Kaplan H. M. (1968) The correlation of excessive drinking behaviour with family pathology and social deterioration. *Br. J. Addict.* **63**, 161–170.

Cadogan D. A. (1973) Marital group therapy in the treatment of alcoholism. *Q. J. Stud. Alc.* **34**, 1187–1194.

Calahan D. (1970) *Problem Drinkers.* San Francisco, Jossey-Bass.

Cameron D. and Spence M. T. (1976) Lessons from an out-patient controlled drinking group. *Br. J. Addict.* **71**, 44–55.

Caruana S. and O'Hagan S. (1976) *Social Aspects of Alcohol and Alcoholism.* London, Edsall, pp. 40–42.

Casier H. and Merlevede E. (1961) Mechanism of the disulfiram-ethanol intoxication symptoms. *Br. J. Addict.* **59**, 105.

Chick J. (1982) Do alcoholics recover? *Br. Med. J.* **285**, 3–4.

Cohen M., Liebson I. A. and Griffiths R. (1971) Moderate drinking by chronic alcoholics. *J. Nerv. Ment. Dis.* **153**, 434–444.

Cook T. (1975) *Vagrant Alcoholics.* London, Routledge & Kegan Paul.

Costello R. M. (1975a) Alcoholism treatment and evaluation: in search of methods. *Int. J. Addict.* **10**, 251–275.

Costello R. M. (1975b) Alcoholism treatment and evaluation: in search of methods. II. *Int. J. Addict.* **10**, 857–867.

Costello R. M. (1977) Programming alcoholism treatment: historical trends. In: Madden J. S., Walker R. and Kenyon W. H. (ed.) *Alcoholism and Drug Dependence: A Multidisciplinary Approach.* New York and London, Plenum, pp. 209–226.

Davanloo H. (1978) *Basic Principles and Techniques in Short-term Dynamic Psychotherapy.* New York, Basic Books.

Davies D. L. (1962) Normal drinking in recovered alcohol addicts. *Q. J. Stud. Alcohol* **23**, 94–104.

Dent J. Y. (1955) *Anxiety and its Treatment; with Special Reference to Alcoholism,* 3rd ed. London, Illingworth.

Edwards G. (1966) Hypnosis in treatment of alcohol addiction: controlled trial, with analysis of factors affecting outcome. *Q. J. Stud. Alcohol* **27**, 221–241.

Edwards G. and Guthrie S. (1967) A controlled trial of inpatient and outpatient treatment of alcohol dependency. *Lancet* **i**, 555–559.

Edwards G., Orford J., Egert S. et al. (1977) Alcoholism: a controlled trial of "treatment" and "outcome". *J. Stud. Alcohol* **38**, 1004–1031.

Elkins R. C. (1975) Aversion therapy for alcoholism: chemical, electrical or verbal imaginary? *Int. J. Addict.* **10**, 157–209.

Ends E. J. and Page C. W. (1957) A study of three types of group psychotherapy with hospitalized male inebriates. *Q. J. Stud. Alcohol* **18**, 263–277.

Engle K. B. and Williams T. K. (1972) Effect of an ounce of vodka on alcoholics' desire for alcohol. *Q. J. Stud. Alcohol* **33**, 1099–1105.

Ewing J. A. (1974) Is there a relationship between type of alcoholism and prognosis? In: Kessel N., Hawker A. and Chalke H. (ed.), *Alcoholism: A Medical Profile. Proceedings of the First International Medical Conference on Alcoholism.* London, Edsall, pp. 152–164.

Ewing J. A. and Rouse B. A (1976) Failure of an experimental treatment program to inculcate controlled drinking in alcoholics. *Br. J. Addict.* **71**, 123–134.

Eysenck H. J. and Rachman S. (1965) *The Causes and Cures of Neurosis: An Introduction to Modern Behaviour Therapy based on Learning Theory and the Principles of Conditioning.* London, Routledge & Kegan Paul, pp. 160–179.

Finney J. W. and Moos R. M. (1981) Characteristics and prognosis of alcoholics who become moderate drinkers and abstainers after treatment. *J. Stud. Alc.* **42**, 94–105.

Franks C. M. (1963) Behaviour therapy, the principles of conditioning and the treatment of the alcoholic. *Q. J. Stud. Alcohol* **24**, 511–529.

Gerard D. L. and Saenger G. (1962) The abstinent alcoholic. *Arch. Gen. Psychiatry* **6**, 83–95.

Gerard D. L. and Saenger G. (1966) *Outpatient Treatment of Alcoholism.* Toronto, University of Toronto Press.

Gerrein J. R., Rosenberg C. M. and Manohar V. (1973) Disulfiram maintenance in outpatient treatment of alcoholism. *Arch. Gen. Psychiatry.* **28**, 798–802.

Gills L. S. and Keet M. (1969) Prognostic factors and treatment results in hospitalized alcoholics. *Q. J. Stud. Alcohol* **30**, 426–437.

Glatt M. M. (1972) *The Alcoholic–and the Help he Needs,* 2nd ed. London, Priory. pp. 148–153.

Glatt M. M. (1974) Loss of control. Extensive interdisciplinary borderland, not a sharp pharmacological borderline. In: Kessel N., Hawker A. and Chalke N. (ed.), *Alcoholism: a Medical Profile. Proceedings of the First International Medical Conference on Alcoholism.* London, Edsall, pp. 121–128.

Glatt M. M. (1982) Treatment of alcohol dependence: long-term treatment of the psychological effects. *Br. Med. Bull.* **38**, 106–108.

Hald J. and Jacobsen E. (1948) A drug sensitising the organism to ethyl alcohol. *Lancet* **ii**, 1001–1004.

Hamilton J. R. (1977) Detoxification—the first step. In: Madden J. S., Walker R. and Kenyon W. H. (ed.) *Alcoholism and Drug Dependence: a Multidisciplinary Approach.* New York and London, Plenum Press, pp. 271–276.

Hartmann E. and Keller-Teschke M. (1977) Biology of schizophrenia: mental effects of dopamine-β-hydroxylase inhibition in normal men. *Lancet* **i**, 37–38.

Harwin J. (1982) The excessive drinker and the family: approaches to treatment. In: Orford J. and Harwin J. (ed.) *Alcohol and the Family.* London, Croom Helm, pp. 201–240.

Heather N. and Robertson I. (1981) *Controlled Drinking.* London and New York, Methuen.

Hedberg A. G. and Campbell L. (1975) A comparison of four behavioural treatments of alcoholism. *J. Behav. Ther.* **5**, 251–256.

Hill M. J. and Blane H. T. (1967) Evaluation of psychotherapy with alcoholics: a critical review. *Q. J. Stud. Alcohol* **28**, 76–104.

Hore B. (1976) *Alcohol Dependence.* London, Butterworths, pp. 120–122.

Hunt G. M. and Azrin N. H. (1973) A community-reinforcement approach to alcoholism. *Behav. Res. Ther.* **11**, 321–325.

Janzen C. (1977) Families in the treatment of alcoholism. *J. Stud. Alc.* **38**, 114–130.

Johnson J. A. (1963) *Group Therapy: a Practical Approach.* New York, McGraw Hill.

Katz A. K., Morgan M. Y. and Sherlock S. (1981) Alcoholism treatment in a medical setting. *J. Stud. Alc.* **42**, 136–143.

Kendall R. E. and Staton M. C. (1966) the fate of untreated alcoholics. *Q. J. Stud. Alcohol* **27**, 30–34.

Kline N. S., Wren J. C., Cooper T. B. et al. (1974) Evaluation of lithium therapy in chronic and periodic alcoholism. *Am. J. Med. Sci.* **268**, 15–22.

Lemere F. (1953) What happens to alcoholics. *Am. J. Psychiatry* **109**, 674–676.

Lemere F. and Voegtlin W. L. (1950) An evaluation of the aversion treatment of alcoholism. *Q. J. Stud. Alcohol* **11**, 199–204.

Liddon S. C. and Satran R. (1967) Disulfiram (Antabuse) psychosis. *Am. J. Psychiatry* **123**, 1284–1289.

Lovibond S. H. and Caddy G. (1970) Discriminated aversive control in the moderation of alcoholics' drinking behaviour. *Behav. Ther.* **1**, 437–444.

McCance C. and McCance P. F. (1969) Alcoholism in North-East Scotland: its treatment and outcome. *Br. J. Psychiatry* **115**, 189–198.

McMillan T. M. (1981) Lithium and the treatment of alcoholism: a critical review. *Br. J. Addict.* **76**, 245–258.

Madden J. S. (1967) Setting up a therapeutic community (Letter.) *Lancet* **i**, 220.

Madden J. S. and Kenyon W. H. (1975) Group counselling of alcoholics by a voluntary agency. *Br. J. Psychiatry* **126**, 289–291.

Madden J. S. (1979) Disulfiram implants. *Br. J. Alc. Alcoholism* **14**, 7–10

Malcolm M. T. and Madden J. S. (1973) The use of disulfiram implantation in alcoholism. *Br. J. Psychiatry* **123**, 41–45.

Malcolm M. T., Madden J. S. and Williams A. E. (1974) Disulfiram implantation critically evaluated. *Br. J. Psychiatry* **125**, 485–489.

Marconi J., Fink K. and Moya L. (1967) Experimental study on alcoholics' desire for alcohol. *Q. J. Stud. Alcohol.* **33**, 1099–1105.

Marlatt G. A., Denning B. and Reid J. B. (1973) Loss of control drinking in alcoholics; an experimental analogue. *J. Abnorm. Psychol.* **81**, 233–241.

Martensen-Larsen O. (1948) Treatment of alcoholism with a sensitising drug. *Lancet* **ii**, 1004–1006.

Martensen-Larsen O. (1974) Apomorphine or disulfiram in the treatment of the alcoholic. In: *Papers presented at the 20th International Institute on the Prevention and Treatment of Alcoholism.* Lausanne, International Council on Alcohol and Addictions, pp. 120–122.

Merry J. (1966) The 'loss of control' myth. *Lancet* **i**, 1257–1258.

Merry J., Reynolds C. M., Bailey J. et al. (1976) Prophylactic treatment of alcoholism by lithium carbonate; a controlled study. *Lancet* **ii**, 481–482.

Miller P. M. and Barlow D. H. (1973) Behavioural approaches to the treatment of alcoholism. *J. Nerv. Ment. Dis.* **157**, 10–20.

Miller P. M. (1975) A behavioural intervention program for chronic public drunkenness offenders. *Arch. Gen. Psychiatry* **32**, 915–918.

Miller P. and Eisler R. (1977) Assertive behaviour of alcoholics; a descriptive analysis. *Behav. Ther.* **8**, 146–149.

Minto A. and Roberts F. J. (1960) 'Temposil': a new drug in the treatment of alcoholism. *J. Ment. Sci.* **106**, 288–295.

Morgan R. and Caplan E. J. (1974) Acute alcohol intoxication, the disulfiram reaction, and methyl alcohol intoxication. In: Kissin B. and Begleiter H. (ed.) *The Biology of Alcoholism. Vol. 3. Clinical Pathology.* New York, Plenum Press, pp. 183–208.

Mottin J. L. (1973) Drug-induced attenuation of alcohol consumption: a review and evaluation of claimed, potential or current therapies. *Q. J. Stud. Alcohol* **29**, 610–633.

Moynihan N. G. (1964) the treatment of alcoholism in general practice. In: *Selected Papers Presented at the 10th European Institute on the Prevention and Treatment of Alcoholism.* Lausanne, International Council on Alcohol and Alcoholism, pp. 71–84.

Nakano J., Gin A. C. and Nakano S. K. (1974) Effects of disulfiram on cardiovascular response to acetaldehyde and ethanol in dogs. *Q. J. Stud. Acohol* **35**, 620–634.

Oei T. P. S. and Jackson P. (1980) Long-term effects of groups and individual social skills training with alcoholics. *Addict. Behav.* **5**, 129–136.

Oei T. P. S. and Jackson P. R. (1982) Social skills and cognitive behavioural approaches to the treatment of problem drinking. *J. Stud. Alc.* **43**, 532–547.

Orford J. (1973) A comparison of alcoholics whose drinking is totally controlled and those whose drinking is mainly controlled. *Behav. Res. Ther.* **11**, 565–576.

Orford J., Guthrie S., Nicholls P. et al. (1975) Self-reported coping behaviour of wives of alcoholics and its association with drinking outcome. *J. Stud. Alcohol.* **36**, 1254–1267.

Paredes A., Ludwig K. D., Hassenfeld I. N. et al. (1969) A clinical study of alcoholics using audiovisual self-image feedback. *J. Nerv. Ment. Dis.* **148**, 449–456.

Parry R. (1983) *Basic Psychotherapy* 2nd ed. Edinburgh, Churchill Livingstone.

Pattison E. M., Headley E. B., Gleser G. C. et al. (1968) Abstinence and normal drinking: an assessment of changes in drinking patterns in alcoholics after treatment. *Q. J. Stud. Alcohol* **29**, 610–633.

Pattison E. M., Coe R. and Rhodes R. J. (1969) Evaluation of alcoholism treatment; a comparison of three facilities. *Arch. Gen. Psychiatry* **29**, 478–488.

Petersen N. W. (1974) Non-hospital detoxication programs. In: *Papers presented at the 20th International Institute on the Prevention and Treatment of Alcoholism.* Lausanne, International Council on Alcohol and Addictions, pp. 12–16.

Pixley J. M. and Stiefel J. R. (1963) Group therapy for wives of alcoholics. *Q. J. Stud. Alcohol* **24**, 304–314.

Pokorny A. D., Miller B. A. and Cleveland S. E. (1968) Response to treatment of alcoholism: a follow-up study. *Q. J. Stud. Alcohol* **29**, 364–381.

Polich J. M., Armor D. J. and Braiker H. B. (1980) *The Course of Alcoholism: Four Years after Treatment.* Santa Monica, Rand Corporation.

Pomerleau O., Pertschuk M. and Stinnett J. (1976) A critical examination of some current assumptions about alcoholism. *J. Stud. Alcohol* **37**, 849–867.

Popham R. E. and Schmidt W. (1976) Some factors affecting the likelihood of moderate drinking by treated alcoholics. *J. Stud. Alcohol* **37**, 868–882.

Price T. R. P. and Silberfarb M. D. (1976) Disulfiram-induced convulsions without challenge by alcohol. *J. Stud. Alcohol* **37**, 908–982.

Pullar-Strecker H. (1950) Discussion on modern technique for the treatment of acute and prolonged alcoholism. *Br. J. Addict.* **47**, 16–20.

Rathod N. H., Gregory E., Blows D. et al. (1966) A two-year follow-up study of alcoholic patients. *Br. J. Psychiatry* **112**, 683–692.

Ritson B. (1968) The prognosis of alcohol addicts treated by a specialised unit. *Br. J. Psychiatry* **114**, 1019–1029.

Robertson I. H. and Heather N. (1982) A survey of controlled drinking in Britain. *Br. J. Alc. Alcoholism.* **17**, 102–105.

Robinson D. (1979) *Talking out of Alcoholism: The Self-Help Process of Alcoholics Anonymous.* London, Croom Helm and Baltimore, University Park Press.

Saunders W. M. and Kershaw P. W. (1979) Spontaneous remission from alcoholism—a community study. *Br. J. Addict.* **74**, 251–256.

Schaefer H. H., Sobell M. B. and Mills K. C. (1971) Some sobering data on the use of self-confrontation with alcoholics. *Behav. Ther.* **2**, 28–39.

Schlatter E. K. E. and Lal S. (1972) Treatment of alcoholism with Dent's oral apomorphine method. *Q. J. Stud. Alcohol* **33**, 430–436.

Shaw S., Cartwright A., Spratley T. et al. (1978) *Responding to Drinking Problems.* London, Croom Helm.

Smart R. G. (1977) The Ontario detoxication system: an evaluation of its effectiveness. In: Madden J. S., Walker R. and Kenyon W. H. (ed.) *Alcoholism and Drug Dependence: a Multidisciplinary Approach.* New York and London, Plenum Press, pp. 321–328.

Smith C. G. (1969) Alcoholics: their treatment and their wives. *Br. J. Psychiatry* **115**, 1039–1042.

Snyder S. H. (1976) The dopamine hypothesis of schizophrenia: focus on the dopamine receptors. *Am. J. Psychiatry* **133**, 197–202.

Snyder S. H. (1982) Neurotransmitters and disease: schizophrenia. *Lancet* **ii**, 970–974.

Steinglass P. (1982) The roles of alcohol in family systems. In: Orford J. and Harwin J. (ed.) *Alcohol and the Family.* London, Croom Helm.

Straus R. and Bacon S. D. (1951) Alcoholism and social stability. A study of occupational integration in 2,023 male clinic patients. *Q. J. Stud. Alcohol* **12**, 231–260.

Vaillant G. E. and Milousky E. S. (1982) Natural history of male alcoholism. IV. Paths to recovery. *Arch. Gen. Psychiatry* **39**, 127–133.

Wallerstein R. S., Chotlos J. W., Friend M. B. et al. (1957) *Hospital Treatment of Alcoholism: a Comparative Experimental Study.* New York, Basic Books.

Willems P. J. A., Letemendia F. J. J. and Arroyave F. (1973) A two-year follow-up study comparing short with long stay in-patient treatment of alcoholics. *Br. J. Psychiatry* **122**, 637–648.

Williams E. C. (1937) Effect of alcohol on workers with carbon disulphide. *JAMA* **109**, 1472–1473.

Wilson A., Davidson W. J. and White J. (1976) Disulfiram implantation: placebo, psychological deterrent, and pharmacological deterrent effects. *Br. J. Psychiatry* **129**, 277–280.

Wilson A., Davidson W. J., Blanchard R. et al. (1978) Disulfiram implantation: a placebo controlled trial with two-year follow-up. *J. Stud. Alc.* **39**, 809–819.

Yalom I. D. (1975) *The Theory and Practice of Group Psychotherapy,* 2nd ed. New York, Basic Books, pp. 3–104, 428–431.

Chapter 6

OPIOIDS AND GENERAL SEDATIVES

Divine, nectareous juice! Which whoso tastes,
Insatiate riots in the sweet repasts,
Nor other home, nor other care intends,
But quits his house, his country and his friends.

THE ODYSSEY (after Alexander Pope's translation).

OPIOIDS

The term 'opioid' applies to drugs which are similar in pharmacological action to morphine. The opioid class of preparations comprises substances naturally occurring in opium, derivatives obtained by chemical manipulation of opium constituents, and synthetic products. In strict observance 'opiate' refers to the alkaloids morphine and codeine that are present in opium, and to their direct derivatives; the word is, however, often used interchangeably with 'opioid'.

Opium is the juice obtained by incision of the unripe capsules of the poppy *Papaver somniferum*. The extruded juice is at first milky in appearance, but soon alters to a dark brown mass that has a characteristic odour and a bitter taste. The medical properties of opium have long been known and used; they were possibly utilized in Sumeria about the 4th millenium B.C. The ancient Egyptians employed the poppy to sedate children; during the 3rd century B.C. opium was described by Theophrastes. Galen prescribed opium, in the medicine theriac, to the Emperor Marcus Aurelius: the Emperor came to rely on the preparation for sleep, and was unable to cope without it (Birley, 1966).

Opium became extensively used by Arab physicians; during the 17th and 18th centuries opium consumption spread from the Middle East to Europe and China. The English commander, Clive of India, and the writers Coleridge and De Quincey, were dependent on opium. Widespread opium dependence in the industrial slums of Manchester was described by Mrs Gaskell in her novel *Mary Barton* (1848). At that time opium was available in Britain without prescription and was only

158

gradually brought under tighter legal control; the restrictions on its sale were accompanied, rightly or wrongly, by a change of view from consideration of its excessive use as an undesirable habit to the concepts of addiction and disease (Berridge and Edwards, 1981). Opium was grown in India under British rule and exported to China; the resultant popularity of the poppy in the regions near the China Sea led to the Opium Wars with China in the early 19th century and to the recent repercussion of large scale smuggling of heroin from the Far East into Europe. During the American Civil War many of the wounded became dependent on opium as a consequence of its medical use to allay pain.

The principal constituents of opium are the alkaloids morphine, codeine, papaverine and thebaine. Morphine is the most well known ingredient; the drug was so named in 1803 after Morpheus, the Greek god of dreams and sleep. The structure of the morphine molecule was not fully appreciated until 1925; its composition was confirmed by synthesis in 1952. The formula is illustrated in *Fig.* 2.

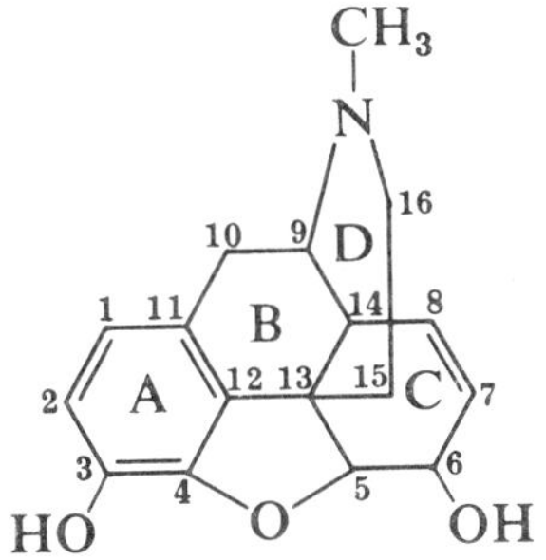

Fig. 2. Morphine.

It is interesting to visualize in the pentacyclic morphine formula the basic structure usually found in opioid analgesics (*Fig.* 3). The essential features of opioid structure are:

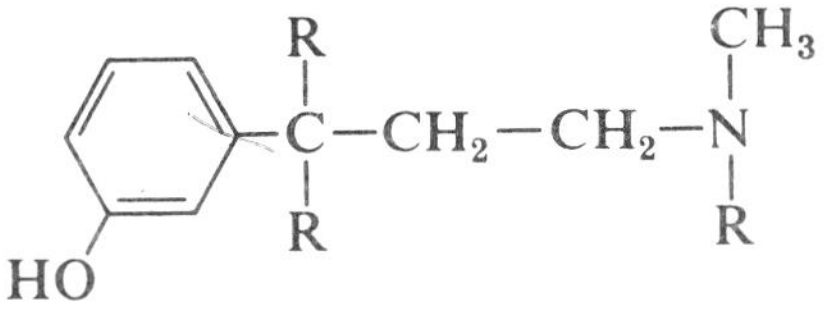

Fig. 3. Basic arrangement usually found in opioid analgesics.

1. An aromatic ring joined to a carbon atom.
2. Linkage of the carbon atom to a tertiary amino group; the link is formed by two saturated carbon atoms.
3. A phenolic hydroxyl group in the meta position, if the tertiary nitrogen is part of a fused piperidine ring.

Certain substitutes for the methyl group attached to the nitrogen atom produce opioid agonists–antagonists, that is drugs which can reverse the effects of morphine-like compounds but which themselves have some analgesic or psychotropic activity.

A review of the structure of opioids has been provided by Jacobson (1972), who noted the lack of refined understanding of the relationship between their physico-chemical features and pharmacological actions. More definitive analysis is needed of partition coefficients, and of steric and electronic factors.

Morphine-like drugs interact with receptors in the central nervous system and in the peripheral autonomic system. The naturally occurring substances (ligands), which act on the same receptors, are the endogenous opioid peptides composed of endorphins and enkephalins. The endogenous opioid peptides are located particularly in areas of the CNS that are associated with the perception of pain, with neuroendocrine functions, and with the central control of autonomic nervous activity. Opioid peptides are also present in peripheral cells, especially those which affect bowel motility. Presumably exogenous opioid drugs and endogenous opioid peptides exert similar actions.

There are at least three opioid receptors in the brain; they receive their titles from Greek letters—delta, kappa, and mu. The mu receptors are particularly responsible for analgesia, respiratory depression, euphoria and dependence.

The clinical effects of morphine are numerous. The drug diminishes hunger and appetite. Through a direct action on the nerve plexuses in the intestinal wall the tone of smooth muscle is increased in the stomach and small and large intestine, peristaltic movements are reduced, and the anal sphincter is contracted; the result is constipation. The involuntary muscle of the biliary tract and sphincter is also contracted; increased tone in the detrusor musculature of the bladder and in the vesical sphincter can lead to urgency or urinary retention.

Hypotension, particularly when adopting the upright posture, may occur; this can induce dizziness and fainting, although the effects of morphine on the circulatory system are considerably less pronounced than on respiration. The pupil is narrowed, but as pupil size normally fluctuates, small miotic pupils are not diagnostic of recent opioid consumption. The blood vessels of the skin are dilated, especially in the face and neck, with a sensation of warmth.

Morphine has a depressant effect on many activities of the brain. In small doses the higher cortical functions that promote self control are impaired first, so that apparent stimulation and elation sometimes occur, but any effect from disinhibition is transient. Slowing of thought and blunting of affect develop; the subject becomes unable to concentrate adequately or to feel strong or unpleasant emotions. The parts of the brain subserving pain and the respiratory centre are especially depressed. The vomiting centre in the medulla is at first stimulated, so that nausea and vomiting may follow on injection of morphine; when the drug effect progresses the vomiting centre is impaired. The nervous arc responsible for the cough relax is also inhibited.

Extremely high doses can lead to convulsions, but more commonly severe cerebral depression develops, with coma and decreased respiration. Death may ensue.

The three other important constituents of opium require a brief discussion. Codeine (methylmorphine) is less potent than morphine in the production of either analgesia or dependence. It is given orally to relieve pain and suppress cough. Papaverine has been employed clinically for its depressant action on involuntary muscle. Thebaine is too toxic for clinical use but has useful transformation products, including the opioid antagonists naloxone and naltrexone.

Simple alteration of the morphine molecule produces heroin (3, 6-diacetylmorphine, diamorphine). After intravenous injection heroin penetrates the blood-brain barrier more quickly than morphine; the rapid penetrance of heroin into the brain may account for its strong dependence-producing quality. Heroin was first formed in 1874 at St. Mary's Hospital, London; thus heroin and penicillin emanate from the same institution. When heroin was introduced into clinical practice in 1898 it was claimed not to produce dependence and was hailed as a cure for opium and morphine dependence. Subsequent disillusion led to its prohibition in most countries; in Britain it is employed for severe pain as it is alleged to have greater analgesic power than morphine and to produce less constipation. In the body heroin is rapidly transformed into morphine and excreted as such in the urine.

There are other drugs, possessing minor chemical modifications to the structure of morphine or codeine, which are sometimes used in therapeutics and which can lead to dependence; they include desmorphine, dihydromorphine (Dilaudid), pholcodine and dihydrocodeine (DF 118).

A range of synthetic opioids has been evolved that shows progressive simplification of the morphine molecule (Fishman and Hahn, 1975). Levorphanol (Dromoran, Levodromoran) lacks the oxygen bridge between rings A and C of the morphine structure. Phenazocine (Narphen, Prinadol) has the additional loss of ring C. Further removal of ring B leads to a class of analgesic of which the original and most familiar member is pethidine (meperidine, Demerol). The structure of pethidine is shown in *Fig.* 4.

Pethidine is unusual because doses of the drug not greatly in excess of the therapeutic range may produce excitation, with tremors, twitching, dilated pupils and convulsions. The stimulant effects can develop in drug misusers who are tolerant to normal quantities and are taking rather larger amounts, for example, 200 mg in an intravenous dose. Excitatory features may result, not from pethidine itself but from its metabolite norpethidine (normeperidine).

Methadone has been described as *ersatz* morphine, as it was first synthesized in Germany during World War II when that country was isolated from supplies of opium. The formula of methadone (presented in *Fig.* 5) illustrates a further modification of morphine, with a break in ring D.

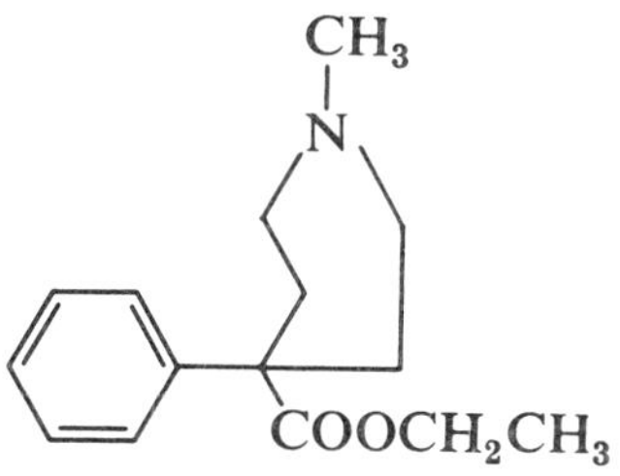

Fig. 4. Pethidine (Meperidine)

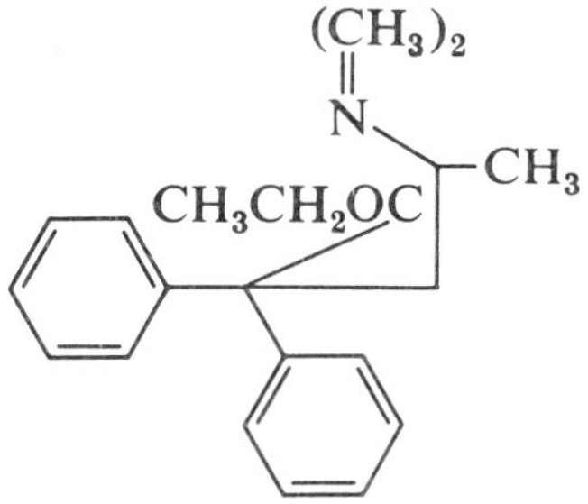

Fig. 5. Methadone.

Methadone is employed in general medicine as an antitussive and spasmolytic agent. Its clinical effects, including the timing of withdrawal features, are more drawn out than those of heroin or morphine. Cessation of methadone after its repeated use produces an abstinence syndrome that is similar in quality but of less intensity than the syndrome induced by cessation of heroin or morphine; the methadone deprivation syndrome takes longer to begin, and has a rather more prolonged course. Given in adequate dosage methadone suppresses the withdrawal symptoms of other opioids. A frequent and humane method of withdrawing an inpatient from heroin or morphine consists of the substitution of oral methadone, which is then reduced progressively to zero over a period of 10–20 days. Methadone is also prescribed in a long term regime, known as methadone maintenance, to outpatients who are dependent on opioids.

Dextromoramide (Palfium) contains a modification of the methadone structure. Dependence occurs to dextromoramide; chronic excessive users of the drug have been shown to develop withdrawal symptoms when placebo is substituted, or when given the opioid antagonist nalorphine (Seymour-Shove and Wilson, 1967).

Dependence also develops to another methadone derivative, dipipanone (Pipadone); its formula is given in *Fig.* 6. Marketed in a combined preparation with the antihistamine cyclizine, the substance has, under

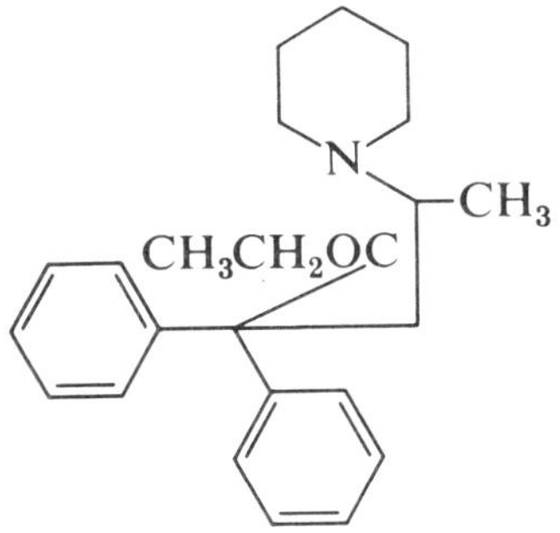

Fig. 6. Dipipanone.

the name of Diconal, acquired a vogue for misuse in Ireland and Britain. During 1975 dipipanone misuse and dependence was so extensive in England and Wales that offences involving the drug outnumbered those from heroin or cocaine (James et al., 1976). Although offences with heroin or cocaine subsequently became more numerous than dipipanone convictions the drug remained widely misused in the British Isles.

Dipipanone provokes an intense, albeit transient, feeling of euphoria when taken intravenously; the effect makes the substance highly attractive to drug users. Furthermore, the drug can produce arterial closure with infarction at sites remote from the vein used for injection;

strokes and bowel gangrene have resulted. For these reasons ampoules or tablets of dipipanone should not be prescribed to drug dependent patients.

Dextropropoxyphene (propoxyphene) is another substance that is structurally related to methadone. In clinical practice the drug is used for the relief of pain; it is available in oral preparations, some of which also contain the nonopioid analgesics aspirin or paracetamol. The most widely employed preparation of the drug in Britain is Distalgesic, which is a mixture of dextropropoxyphene and paracetamol. Large doses of dextropropoxyphene produce convulsions, delusions, hallucinations and clouding of consciousness, as well as respiratory depression and pulmonary oedema. The drug is not intended for injection; its intravenous or subcutaneous administration produces irritant effects around the injection sites.

There have been several reports from the United States of misuse and dependence on dextropropoxyphene (Miller et al., 1970; Tennant, 1973a; Maletzky, 1974). The accounts have described dependence in subjects who were not psychiatrically ill nor considered prone to dependence; the studies have noted that dependence can arise without initial euphoria, and have related the role of doctors in the unwitting production of dextropropoxyphene misuse. The United Kingdom has also provided accounts of dependence on dextropropoxyphene (Harris and Harper, 1979; Whittington, 1979).

Opioid agonists–antagonists

The discovery in 1915 that N-allylnorcodeine antagonized the depressant effect of morphine on respiration was the first observation that some of the actions of opioids could be pharmacologically blocked. Competitive antagonism involves occupancy of the opioid receptor site by a drug that exerts little or no action at the site. Naloxone (Narcan) is the only drug that is believed completely to lack a positive action; that is, naloxone is probably a pure opioid antagonist. The other antagonist compounds each possess a measure of activity at the opioid receptor site; they constitute partial agonists. N-allylnormorphine (nalorphine, Nalline) is another substance that counteracts the depressant effect of morphine and heroin on breathing; it was formerly employed as an intravenous antidote for opioid overdosage. In addition nalorphine blocks the euphoric effects of morphine, and precipitates an abstinence syndrome in subjects who are physically dependent on morphine, heroin or allied drugs. Because of the last effect it has been used diagnostically to detect opioid physical dependence. Nalorphine also possesses agonistic effects; when given alone it depresses respiration, is a sedative and miotic, and produces physical dependence.

Levallorphan (Lorfan) is another antagonist that was employed to counteract respiratory depression from morphine-like drugs. If the depression of breathing is not due to opioid overdose then levallorphan exerts a direct depressant effect on respiration; this can occur, for instance, when barbiturate coma is wrongly attributed to heroin. For this reason naloxone is a preferable antidote to levallorphan or nalorphine as it does not exert an agonistic effect on breathing if the coma is not, in fact, a result of opioid poisoning. Naloxone has also been noted to reverse coma from alcohol (Jeffrys et al., 1980), although it may be premature to employ the drug routinely in suspected alcohol coma (Gallant, 1981). It is claimed that naloxone does not induce physical dependence. When given to subjects who are physically dependent on a morphinoid substance naloxone uncovers the opioid abstinence syndrome; because nalophine has virtually no agonistic action it should be preferred to nalorphine as a diagnostic measure of opioid physical dependence.

Both naloxone and its analogue naltrexone block the euphoric effect of heroin (Wikler; 1975). Naltrexone possesses some mild agonistic effects; sleepiness, talkativeness and racing thoughts have been reported after its administration (Martin et al., 1973).

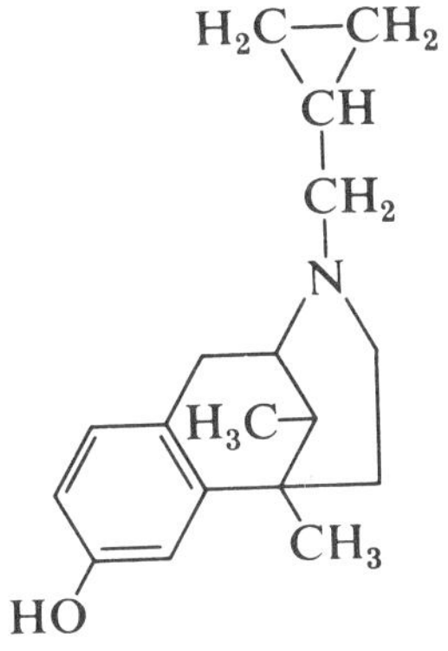

Fig. 7. Cyclazocine.

Cyclazocine (*Fig.* 7) is an opioid antagonist that also possesses agonistic properties. It prevents the euphoric results of heroin and morphine and precipitates abstinence features in patients physically dependent on these substances. When taken by itself cyclazocine can produce sedation or distressing symptoms of visual illusions, auditory hallucinations and difficulty in the control of thinking; tolerance develops to its psychotomimetic features. When cyclazocine is withdrawn after its regular administration an abstinence syndrome appears. Naloxone, naltrexone and cyclaxocine have been employed by some clinicians in the U.S.A. to keep patients in a heroin-free state.

Pentazocine (Fortral, Talwin) is given therapeutically because of its analgesic property. Misuse of and dependence on pentazocine has been documented in the U.S.A. and in Britain (Lewis, 1973a; King and Betts, 1979). In the United States the practice has arisen of intravenously injecting 'T and Blues', which is a mixture of Talwin and pyribenzamine that often contains talc and other ingredients. The practice has led to accidental deaths.

Pentazocine also exerts an antagonistic action: the drug precipitates withdrawal symptoms in subjects who are opioid dependent and should not be given to patients maintained on methadone (U.S. Department of Justice, 1973). Its structural similarity to morphine is shown in *Fig.* 8.

Buprenorphine (Temgesic) is a potent analgesic. It has been claimed that the drug is free from the risk of dependence, and an explanation offered that centres on opioid receptor sites. Withdrawal symptoms and signs are precipitated by the dissociation of an opioid from its attachment to receptor sites; buprenorphine is slow to bind to the mu receptors. Yet while buprenorphine may possess a limited dependence hazard its withdrawal has provoked abstinence features (Jasinski et al., 1978).

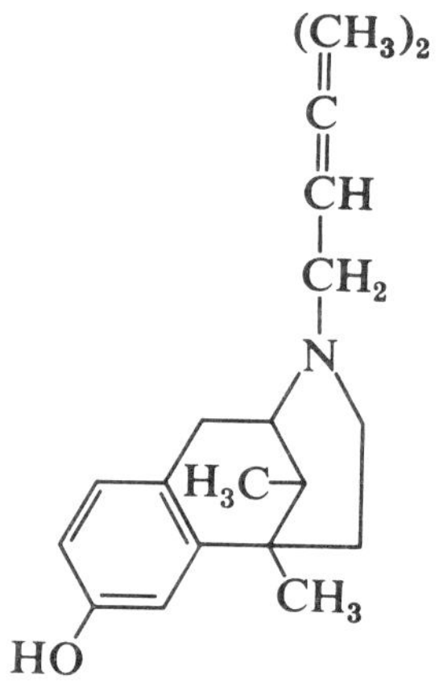

Fig. 8. Pentazocine.

Naloxone is probably a pure opioid antagonist, possessing little or no agonistic properties; the other antagonists described above are also partial agonists. The results of administration of an opioid antagonist that is also a partial agonist depend on whether there is present in the body a morphine-like substance with pure agonistic actions; the results tend towards reversal of the agonistic activity if an agonistic opioid is present.

Opioid absorption, distribution, metabolism and excretion

Morphinoid drugs are readily absorbed from the gastrointestinal tract, through the nasal mucosa (as when heroin powder is sniffed), and from the lungs (as when opium or heroin are smoked). Opioids also pass quickly into the blood following intravenous or intramuscular injection. The effects after injection, particularly intravenous injection, develop more rapidly and more intensely but are briefer than from other routes of administration.

Morphine quickly leaves the blood and temporarily concentrates in the tissues. Its main pathway of detoxification is through conjugation in the liver with glucuronic acid to form morphine-3-monoglucuronide. In man the greater part of injected morphine appears in the urine, mainly in the conjugated form; up to 10% is also excreted in the faeces from bile. Ninety per cent of urinary excretion occurs in the first day, but sensitive tests reveal traces in the urine of several days.

Heroin (diacetylmorphine) quickly crosses the blood-brain barrier. Heroin rapidly undergoes deacetylation to monacetylmorphine and to morphine; it is detected as morphine in the urine. About 10% of codeine (methylmorphine) in the body is demethylated to morphine; the remainder is metabolized in the liver and for the most part excreted in the urine as inactive forms.

Methadone is carried in the plasma extensively bound to plasma proteins; though small amounts are detectable in the urine methadone is mostly transformed in the liver. After repeated administration methadone accumulates in the tissues and is gradually released into the circulation. The plasma half life of a single methadone dose in individuals who are not tolerant of the drug is about 15 hours. Its slower rate of turnover compared to morphine (and heroin) helps to account for its more prolonged action.

Tolerance to opioids

Repeated administration of opioid drugs renders the individual less susceptible to their effects, so that larger doses are needed to obtain the same results. Tolerance does not develop uniformly to all the effects of opioids; in the case of morphine tolerance is marked to the results of the drug on pain, euphoria, level of consciousness and respiration, and least noticeable to the effects of morphine on bowel movements and pupil size.

Tolerance to opioids depends on tissue adaptation to their effects rather than on increased metabolic inactivation of the drugs. Tolerance develops to opioids in a remarkable degree, more so than to general sedatives such as barbiturates or to alcohol. Heroin users are able to consume amounts of the drug that are lethal to nontolerant persons, provided there is access to relatively undiluted preparations. A group of U.S. soldiers in Vietnam who were intravenous users of almost pure heroin reported daily use of 2·5 g or more; two of them described the consumption of over 5 g in a day. In contrast, supplies of illicit heroin in a U.S. city were estimated to provide only 30–35 mg of the active drug for daily administration (Ream et al., 1975).

Tolerance subsides rapidly over the initial few weeks of drug cessation. A consequence of loss of tolerance is that an individual who had developed tolerance, but then lost it during a period of abstinence, cannot in safety resume the former high doses of the drug. Failure to realize this by opioid users who have an abstinent spell in hospital or prison has led after their discharge to accidental overdoses and fatalities (Gardner, 1970).

When tolerance has developed to one drug within the opioid class it is also present to the other opioid substances. This phenomenon is known as cross-tolerance; it allows heroin users to be given in safety moderately large amounts of methadone as a substitute for heroin.

Opioid withdrawal features

The abstinence syndrome that indicates physical dependence to morphine or heroin develops within 4–12 hours of cessation of the drugs. The symptoms and signs reach their peak by the end of the second day and are mostly resolved within 3–4 days, although subtle alterations may last for several weeks. Abrupt withdrawal of methadone produces a syndrome that is slower in onset, is less intense and is longer in duration; the clinical features do not start for 36–48 hours, attain their height around the third day, and may endure for 3–6 weeks.

Prominent symptoms of the opioid abstinence syndrome are fatigue, anxiety, restlessness, irritability, depression and insomnia. Yawning becomes frequent and deep. Increased nasal secretion (rhinorrhoea) develops, with sniffing, itching of the nose, and paroxysms of sneezing. Excess salivation (sialorrhoea) occurs, though not usually to a distressing extent. The eyes produce copious lacrimal fluid; the pupils are dilated. There is enhanced secretion of bronchial fluids and adventitious sounds are heard on auscultation of the chest. Aching pains in the muscles, bones and joints develop. Pains also ensue in the abdomen from overactivity of intestinal musculature; the gut hyperactivity is detectable by auscultation and leads to nausea, severe vomiting and diarrhoea. Anorexia, low food intake and loss of weight are present. Systolic and diastolic blood pressures rise; pulse rate may be lowered, normal or increased; the temperature is slightly elevated.

Fibrillary tremor and twitching of the muscles develop; there is tremor of the tongue. Ejaculation in males, and orgasm in females, spontaneously take place. Subjective sensations of hot or cold occur; the former are less obvious and are accompanied by flushing of the face and neck. Marked feelings of coldness lead to a search for warmth, as by the use of additional blankets. In the skin there is an increase of perspiration;

more notably, the involuntary muscles attached to hairs contract, so that the hairs are erect and the skin around their roots is elevated (pilo-erection). The gooseflesh appearance, combined with the subjective sensation of coldness, has led to the term 'cold turkey' as a slang description for the discomforts of sudden opioid withdrawal.

Subjects who had been experimentally stabilized on morphine have been reported to show lengthy abstinence effects that lasted from 17 to over 30 weeks after withdrawal of the drug. Compared with levels before morphine was given, the subjects developed a prolonged rise in urinary output of adrenaline (norepinephrine) and 17-hydroxycorticosteroid, and a protracted decrease of temperature, pupil size, systolic and diastolic blood pressures, and pulse rate (Ream et al., 1975). REM sleep diminishes while taking heroin; cessation of the drug produces a rebound increase of REM sleep that has been noted to endure for 2 months (Lewis et al., 1970).

It is likely that the processes responsible for physical dependence on opioids begin to operate subclinically in response to a single dose. Patients who are administered therapeutic amounts of morphine on repeated occasions in each day for 7–14 days develop mild withdrawal symptoms, but definite abstinence features have been produced by the opioid antagonist nalorphine after therapeutic doses of morphine, heroin or methadone employed 4 times a day for merely 2–3 days. In former heroin dependent subjects who were given a single dose of methadone followed by the antagonist naloxone withdrawal effects have been induced. Physical dependence to opioids therefore, although it may not be clinically apparent, develops early; presumably it is one factor in the initiation of drug-seeking behaviour.

The speed of onset and duration of physical dependence is assumed to be effected by the quantity and frequency of drug dosage, and by the rate at which the drug and its active metabolites are detoxified and excreted. In regard to dosage there is a peak; daily amounts of morphine in excess of 500 mg do not increase the severity of the abstinence syndrome.

Cross-dependence exists within the opioid class of drugs, though it is not universally distributed between the members. Many, although not all, of the opioids suppress the withdrawal features of morphine and heroin.

The abstinence syndrome is only one factor that determines craving and drug taking behaviour. Some degree of physical dependence develops in patients who receive opioids for more than a few days for medical and surgical conditions; the majority of these patients avoid seeking further supplies when their drugs are stopped. Many of the U.S. soldiers who used heroin regularly in Vietnam ceased to take the drug on returning to their own country (Robins, 1974; Robins et al., 1975; O'Brien et al., 1980). Social factors, such as cultural acceptability and availability of psychotropic drugs, and features within the mental and physical constitutions of individuals, are also important in the production of drug abuse and dependence.

A mechanism for opioid tolerance and withdrawal features

Many of the features of the opioid abstinence syndrome represent over-activity of the physiological functions depressed by opioids; that is, during the early stages of abstinence there is rebound release of body systems from the inhibitory control of the drugs. A more basic appreciation of the related processes of opioid tolerance and physical dependence has emerged from researches into the endogenous opioid peptides, which as explained above are the naturally occurring substances that interact at the same neuronal receptor sites as the exogenous morphine-like drugs.

It is probable that endogenous opioids control various neuronal systems by the inhibition and modulation of neurotransmitter release. Like morphine, the endogenous endorphins and enkephalins inhibit the synaptic pathways subserving pain. Studies employing peripheral neural tissues of animals as experimental models have demonstrated tolerance to morphine and cross-tolerance from the drug to endogenous opioid peptides; when morphine was withdrawn tolerance remained for some time to the naturally occurring substances.

The opioid withdrawal syndrome is explicable as a result of tolerance to the inhibitory action of endogenous opioid peptides on neuro-transmitter release in the central nervous system. During chronic administration of a morphine-like drug the inhibitory control of certain neurotransmitter systems passes from the endogenous compounds to the drug; tolerance develops to both types of substance, so that on withdrawal of the exogenous opioid the endogenous peptides remain for a period unable to resume adequate inhibitory control. Until the drug is cleared from the receptor sites the situation may be exacerbated by possible negative feedback from the receptors to produce a decrease of opioid peptide synthesis. In consequence of defective inhibition of neural activity the abstinence syndrome develops; its abatement is due to gradual resumption of control by the endogenous opioids.

Patterns of opioid misuse and dependence

The forms of opioid misuse and dependence are as diverse as the cultural settings and range of persons who take the substances. It is possibly provocative but instructive to start with the successful business man in South-East Asia who smokes one pipe of opium a night. The opposite extreme is represented by the youngster of African or Puerto Rican ancestry who lives in a single parent household in a Brooklyn ghetto and is a heroin 'street addict'. The middle-aged and middle-class person should be cited who is dependent on pethidine that was prescribed originally for a medical or surgical illness. There is the expatriate member of the Chinese community in Liverpool who drinks a suspension of opium in water. The young consumer of heroin in Britain often prefers to take his drug by smoking the substance, thereby avoiding the medical hazards of injection and the legal risks attached to possession of a syringe containing traces of opioid. For smoking purposes heroin may be mixed with tobacco or placed on the lighted tip of a cigarette, though a more common method involves heating heroin on metal foil and inhaling the sublimate fumes; the latter method spread from Hong Kong and is known as 'chasing the dragon'. Proprietary preparations of opium and its derivatives are in some instances legally available without prescription; they can be misused by persons of any adult or adolescent age.

The illicit intake of opioid does not invariably lead to dependence. The proportion of persons who have misused opioids but have not developed dependence to them is unknown; it is unlikely to be ascertained accurately in view of the illegality of the practice. Some individuals experimentally try an opioid but do not repeat the experience as it was not strikingly attractive or the incident produced nausea and vomiting. Others are able to take opioids occasionally, even intravenous heroin, without the onset of clinically apparent dependence. But the intravenous route of administration provides a rapid and high concentration of drug in the brain and is particularly likely to produce an intractable dependence. An injection of opioid administered intravenously leads to an instantaneous though brief feeling of intense bodily and mental pleasure (the 'flash') that has been likened to an orgasm; the effect is especially strong with heroin. The psychological ramifications of the 'needle' can strengthen the conditioning processes by which some subjects experience withdrawal symptoms and drug craving when faced with situations that have been associated with the practice of injection. Some drug users mistakenly believe that smoking heroin does not induce dependence; a proportion of heroin smokers change to injections while many develop abstinence features and drug seeking behaviour, despite confinement of intake to the smoking route.

Opioid consumption in a young person is sometimes only one feature of a condition of *polydrug misuse*. Drugs are favoured in turn by youngsters, not for their pharmacological idiosyncrasies but for their popularity and ease of access. A phase of injecting a morphine-like drug may be followed by a period of intravenous and oral use of amphetamines or barbiturates. In the course of a few weeks the same individual may inhale a solvent, inject an opioid, smoke cannabis, swallow amylobarbitone, sniff amphetamine and get drunk on alcohol.

Parents of young people taking heroin have reported certain changes associated with drug use by youngsters that could arouse suspicion of developing drug dependence (Rathod et al., 1967). The manifestations in drug users include loss of interest in previous activities, impaired concentration, neglect of personal appearance, periods of dreamy detachment or irritability, aloofness and long spells in the bedroom, poor appetite, a change of acquaintances, unexpected absences from home (to obtain drugs) and heavy cigarette consumption. The above features possess other causes than drug use, but require investigation by caring parents who should keep drug consumption in mind as a possibility. More specific aspects noticed by parents comprise blood spotting on clothes, injection marks, and finding drugs or the equipment required to inject or smoke drugs.

Opioid dependence in young persons is associated with crime. Offences directly involving drugs include illegal possession and distribution of drugs, theft of drugs or prescriptions, forgery and alteration of prescriptions. Crimes may also be committed to obtain money or property that can be exchanged for drugs; heroin misuse is blamed for much of the crime in New York. Some young persons who misuse opioids and other drugs have a history of minor offences predating their drug usage; both their criminality and their drug consumption reflect social deviancy and anti-societal traits.

The problems of drug misuse in industry have been likened on the Eastern seaboard of the United States to the industrial problems of excessive drinking. Both conditions present similar needs to companies for identification, and for education, counselling and treatment. In that region business and industry are tackling the demands presented by the misuse of drugs, including opioids; trade unions have also taken an interest (Carone and Krinsky, 1973).

Physical complications of opioid abuse

Infections

Injections are often administered by drug misusers under conditions contrary to the requirements of hygiene. The substance injected may not be sterile, particularly if diluents like talc, quinine or sugar are added to the active ingredient. Syringes and needles are shared between drug abusers. Attempts at sterilizing the needle may involve heating with a match; the resultant carbon deposits pass under the skin. Users have been known to attempt cleanliness by licking the needle before injection; water used to dissolve or suspend drugs has been collected from lavatory basins. A variety of infections, local and systemic, can therefore develop (Louria et al., 1967; Lewis, 1973b; Richter, 1975). Most of the numerous reports on infections in drug injectors are restricted to opioid misuse, but infections can, of course, follow the unhygienic injection of any psychoactive substance.

At the injection site abscesses can ensue from both the intravenous and subcutaneous methods of administration. In the subcutaneous tissue over veins that have been selected for injection scars develop which are pigmented and often raised; the veins themselves may be infected, thrombosed and visibly thickened; these effects are permanent unless crude tattoos or skilled surgery are employed to hide them. A vein that has active thrombophlebitis will be surrounded by an inflamed area. Infections at the sites of injection may involve local muscles, tendon sheaths and fascial spaces. Obliteration of veins can produce oedema in the limb, that enhances local susceptibility to infection.

Viral hepatitis is a common medical complication. The responsible organism is hepatitis B virus which is conveyed by injection into the drug abuser. In the twelve months to June 1976 there were 1061 reports of acute type B hepatitis from laboratories in England, Wales and Ireland; 227 (21%) of the patients were drug abusers (Notes and News, 1977). Hepatitis B surface antigen (HBsAg) is the serological marker for the presence of hepatitis B virus. The antigen is present in at least 1% of the population, but is found in a considerably higher proportion of persons misusing drugs by injection. Charuvastra and Ehrmann (1975) examined a random sample of 243 opioid dependent patients and uncovered the antigen in 5 (2%) of the subjects. The virus is transmitted in blood, saliva, body excretions and probably in semen.

Drug injectors are symptomless but infectious during the long incubation period (60–160 days) of acute type B hepatitis, or during the carrier state or in quiescent phases of chronic hepatitis. Isolation is not a practical policy for persons who possess HBsAg. The number of carriers in the world is conservately estimated by a WHO scientific group (1983) to number over 200 million. In the U.K. there are probably between 50 000 to 100 000 persons with the virus; the figure for the U.S.A. has been estimated at about 900 000. But the blood and excretions of a drug injector must be handled with respect until the subject is shown to be serologically negative for HBsAg. Unnecessary blood and urine testing should be avoided; staff who collect and analyse blood and urine samples must employ disposable gloves, specially labelled containers and the correct disinfectant. The infectious risk of blood is influenced by the e antigen of the virus (HBeAg). Blood that contains HBeAg is highly infective; blood which does not possess either HBeAg or its antibody is of intermediate infectivity; blood which contains antibody to HBeAg has low infectivity. A person who receives an inoculation accident with HBeAg requires passive immunity with hepatitis B immunoglobulin (Working Party, 1982). An inoculation accident includes a skin prick, contamination of an abrasion or the eye or mouth, or very heavy soiling of intact skin, with blood or other material that is known to contain HBeAg.

A complication of hepatitis B infection is further infection by the delta agent. The agent, which has its own antigen and antibody system, only causes infection when the hepatitis B virus is present; the delta agent, like the virus, is transmitted parenterally. Infection with the delta agent can occur at the same time as hepatitis B infection, or can ensue several years after the onset of the hepatitis B carrier state. The delta agent is itself a cause of acute hepatitis and is possibly a major cause of liver disease among persons who inject drugs. Outbreaks of delta infection in drug misusers have been recorded in several countries, including Italy (Raimondo et al., 1982), Ireland (Shattock et al., 1982), and Sweden (Moestrup et al., 1983).

A major complication of intravenous drug misuse is endocarditis. Compared with other patients who develop endocardial infection intravenous drug users with this condition are less likely to have pre-existing heart disease of a rheumatic or congenital kind. The heart valves most commonly affected are the aortic and mitral; the tricuspid valve is infected in about 10% of cases. The left and right sides of the heart can be infected simultaneously yet the bilateral involvement may not be diagnosed until postmortem. *Staphylococcus aureus, Pseudomonas* and *Candida* are the most frequent organisms, sometimes occurring in combination.

Pulmonary infections are prone to develop in intravenous drug users. Apart from infecting organisms introduced by septic injections the resistance of drug misusers to lung infection is lowered by cigarette smoking, excess alcohol consumption, poor material conditions of living, aspiration into the lungs when consciousness is impaired from drugs, and by the pulmonary oedema that can complicate heroin usage. *Pneumococci, staphylococci* and *streptococci* are the most commonly encountered organisms, but a variety of pathogens may be found, including Gram-negative and anaerobic bacteria. Compared with the general population, subjects dependent on opioids possessed an increased liability to develop tuberculosis when tuberculous infection was generally more common; a comparable susceptibility was found among alcoholics.

Septicaemia is a dangerous sequel of unsterile injections. It is particularly hazardous if the invading organism or organisms are unusual; in this event delay may arise in the recognition of their identity and of their antibiotic sensitivity.

Another serious complication of heroin usage in the United States has been tetanus. The patient can delay seeking medical advice through misinterpretation of the symptoms as abstinence features which simply require more opioids. When a doctor is consulted the initial presentation of the disease may be minimal because recently administered opioid has suppressed the tetanus features of muscle rigidity, spasm and pain. There are therefore clinical difficulties in reaching the diagnosis and in estimating the severity of the illness.

The acquired immunodeficiency syndrome (AIDS) is a form of cellular immunodeficiency that leads to opportunistic infections and tumours; the condition is frequently fatal. Intravenous drug misusers comprise one of the population groups which are prone to develop the condition. The epidemic pattern of AIDS points to an infective agent in its causation.

Pulmonary oedema

The injection or ingestion of an opioid can produce, in a regular user, an acute and often fatal reaction of which the most striking feature is pulmonary oedema. Death can be so sudden after intravenous injection that the deceased is found with the needle, its syringe attached, still in a vein. The fluid secreted into the respiratory tract may be copious enough to exude from the mouth and nose.

The pathogenesis is unclear though several suggestions have been advanced (Harvey, 1981). Accidental overdose leads to a decreased cough reflex, then to coma and central respiratory depression; hypoxia from depression of breathing in turn produces pulmonary oedema. Overdose may accidently occur when illicit supplies of similar appearance but varying strength are taken, or when the user's concentration and judgement are clouded by drugs consumed not many hours previously. But stories (admittedly anecdotal) suggest that the acute heroin reaction with lung oedema can develop after doses that have not previously upset the user. Another suggestion is that opioids or their diluents are directly toxic to alveolocapillary membrane. A final possibility is an allergic reaction; against this hypothesis is the point that if recovery ensues the subject may resume opioid use without recurrence of pulmonary oedema.

Neurological effects

The coma and respiratory depression of opioid overdose are associated with cerebral oedema. The exact mechanism of brain oedema is uncertain, but it is likely that a major role is played by the hypercapnic hypoxia which results from depressed breathing and pulmonary oedema. The raised intracranial pressure can lead to convulsions, which may be generalized, or focal, or take the form of status epilepticus. The seizures cease on recovery from the overdose.

During recovery from coma induced by opioids a delirious state may develop, that lasts from several hours to several days. A long-term sequel of cerebral anoxia (from opioids as from any other cause) is dementia; this is shown by deterioration of intellectual and memory powers, and by blunting of drive and affect. Cerebrovascular accidents (strokes) without demonstrable sources of emboli are a rare complication of opioid overdosage; temporary ischaemia may be the responsible factor. Spongiform degeneration of the white matter of the brain has been described among heroin smokers; the condition, which is sometimes lethal, is considered to be caused by an unknown contaminant in the supplies of drug (Wolters et al., 1982).

Heroin consumption can be complicated by transverse myelitis. There is necrosis of segments of the spinal cord and paraplegia. Here again the mechanism which produces the lesion might involve transient ischaemia.

Impairment of a peripheral nerve can ensue if the nerve has been compressed during coma or sleep induced by opioids. But intravenous injection of a mixture of heroin and adulterants has been followed by disordered function of the brachial or lumbosacral plexus, or of a single nerve, in circumstances when pressure on the affected nerves or injections into them did not occur. In the case of impairment of a single nerve (mononeuropathy) the injection has often been given into another extremity. Injections of illicit heroin have also been followed by polyneuropathy. An immune reaction or direct toxicity of the injectant may be responsible for the non-mechanical effects in peripheral nerves.

Other complications

Perforation of the nasal septum can follow the repeated sniffing of heroin. Cocaine taken through the nose produces the same effect in some instances, but heroin by itself can lead to a nasal perforation.

Opioids may be intentionally injected into sites outside veins ('skin popping') either into the tissues under the skin, or deeper into muscles. The practice of injecting heroin mixtures into muscles risks the production of a form of chronic myopathy. The histological features are inflammation, necrosis of muscle fibre, and the replacement of tissue by fibrous elements. The lesions result from local infection and from a toxic action of the repeated intramuscular injection. The user may have been compelled to resort to 'skin popping' because numerous intravenous injections had thrombosed the available veins.

Acute myopathy is a different complication. In this condition the microscopic appearances of a biopsy specimen reveal a range of abnormalities from structural alterations of intact muscle fibres to extensive necrosis. Clinically there are pains, tenderness and weakness of the muscles. Myoglobinaemia and myoglobinuria are present; acute renal failure can follow.

A separate process that disturbs renal function is the heroin-related nephrotic syndrome. The basic lesion appears to consist of deposits of electron-opaque material on the endothelial (not the epithelial) side of the glomerular basement membrane (Kilcoyne, 1975).

A most comprehensive account of the physical complications of opioids and other drugs of abuse is provided in the text of Sapira and Cherubin (1975).

GENERAL SEDATIVES

Many of the general non-opioid sedatives produce mutually similar states of intoxication and dependence. The similarities justify inclusion of the general sedatives in a single category. Alcohol falls within their province, but by reason of its widespread social and legal acceptability and the extent of its misuse alcohol is often considered separately. The practice of giving special regard to alcohol is followed in the text. Barbiturates, despite their waning clinical use, provide the archetype for general sedatives.

Barbiturates

The first barbiturate to be employed for its sedative-hypnotic effect was barbitone (Veronal); the drug was introduced clinically in 1903. Like its analogues, barbitone is a derivate of the non-sedative barbituric acid. The barbiturates are said to be named after a lady called Barbara, who was a barmaid in a Munich beer hall. Barbiturates have the general formula given in *Fig.* 9.

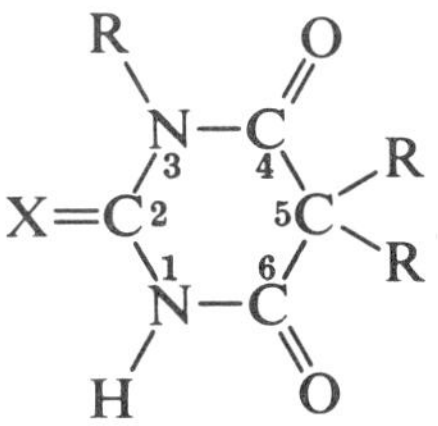

$$
\begin{array}{c}
R \qquad\qquad O \\
\backslash \qquad\qquad \parallel \\
N - C \\
/3 \qquad 4\backslash \quad R \\
X = C \, 2 \qquad 5C \\
\backslash 1 \qquad 6/ \quad R \\
N - C \\
/ \qquad\qquad \backslash\backslash \\
H \qquad\qquad O
\end{array}
$$

Fig. 9. Basic structure of barbiturates.

The individual barbiturates differ in substitutions at the 'R' positions. Oxygen is the usual occupant of the 'X' site; in a few barbiturates it is replaced by sulphur. In Britain the official names of barbiturates end in '-one', in the U.S.A. they terminate in '-al'.

Barbiturates produce widespread depression of neuronal activity throughout the central nervous system, although not all neurons or neuronal systems are depressed equally. Selective depression has been reported of noradrenergic neurons, polysynaptic pathways, the brainstem reticular system and of the cerebral cortex. Reduced activity in the reticular system and hemisphere cortices largely determines the sedative and anticonvulsant results of barbiturates. The depression of activity is produced by a lowered amount of transmission across synapses rather than by decreased conduction in axons.

The mechanisms by which barbiturates reduce synaptic transmission are not fully elucidated. It is thought however that the drugs stabilize nerve membrane so that transfer of ions across the membrane does not easily occur. In this manner the neural action potential is prevented from reaching the level required to initiate or transmit a nerve impulse.

The sedative results of barbiturates begin with mild impairment of attention, of concentration and of the capacities to feel anxious or depressed. As sedation proceeds the individual becomes less able to perform mental and motor tasks; thought and speech are slowed, voice sounds are slurred, emotional responsiveness is diminished. Speed of reaction and co-ordination of muscles are progressively affected together with an impairment of consciousness. Movements become clumsy; walking and standing are increasingly more difficult to accomplish. In low dosage barbiturates facilitate sleep, in large quantity they lead to coma, respiratory depression and a fall in blood pressure. Overdose incurs the risk of a fatal outcome.

Small levels of barbiturate, particularly in children and the elderly, can induce excitement or delirium. Children are vulnerable to this effect because their brains have not reached mature development; the elderly are at risk in this respect because their age is associated with impaired function and death of neurons and with defective cerebral blood supply.

The initial effect of barbiturates on the electroencephalogram is an increase of low voltage fast activity, at first in the frontal cortex and then throughout the hemispheres. Slow waves of large amplitude develop as consciousness is lost.

During barbiturate-induced sleep (as distinct from barbiturate anaesthesia or coma) there is a reduction of the time spent in rapid eye movement (REM) sleep. Repeated nightly administration of a barbiturate is accompanied by a return to the normal quantity of REM sleep—that is, tolerance develops to this effect. Cessation of the regular administration of a barbiturate produces rebound increase of the quantity of REM sleep and of the dreaming associated with this kind of sleep. The rebound effect of REM sleep is a subtle indication of physical dependence; it lasts up to 5 weeks and is produced even by therapeutic doses (Oswald and Priest, 1965). The effect occurs with certain other sedatives, including benzodiazepines, and helps to explain the difficulties encountered by some patients in discontinuing their administration after regular, though not excessive, consumption (Kales et al., 1974).

The immediate results of a single sedative or hypnotic dose of barbiturate may later be followed by lethargy, irritability and impaired concentration. These unwanted symptoms can endure for some hours. They may be caused by residual amounts of barbiturate or of an active metabolite, or might represent a hangover effect from prolonged neurochemical alterations. It is also possible that the sequelae may form early features of the abstinence syndrome which develops in full intensity on cessation of repeated barbiturate consumption.

Barbiturates do not readily dissolve in water, but their sodium salts are water-soluble. Both the pure drugs and the sodium salts are available for oral use; barbiturate preparations for intramuscular or intravenous injection are marketed as the sodium compounds. Those barbiturates that have considerable solubility in lipids exert effects that are quick in onset, are potent while they last, but are short-lived. Thiobarbiturates possess sulphur instead of oxygen in their structure; they have a relatively high degree of lipid solubility. Thiopentone sodium (thiopental sodium, Pentothal) is a sulphur-containing barbiturate which is given intravenously to induce general anaesthesia. It is not misused, since it is not dispensed to the public on prescription and since its effects on consciousness are so rapid and pronounced.

The long-acting barbiturate drug phenobarbitone (phenobarbital, Luminal) is available in oral preparations. The rarity of phenobarbitone misuse is attributable to a number of factors. The euphoric effect of a single dose is slight and is slow to develop; the results on mood of its chronic administration lie in the direction of depression; the slow elimination of phenobarbitone does not favour the rapid, repetitive development of withdrawal features from its repeated consumption. The infrequency of misuse of phenobarbitone is striking in view of the numbers of epileptic patients who take the substance on prescription because of its anticonvulsant property.

Most of the remaining barbiturates that have been employed clinically have also been extensively misused. The popularity of an individual barbiturate in medical practice has often determined its incidence of misuse. Barbiturates that have been widely prescribed and have come to produce problems of misuse and dependence are many. They include amylobarbitone (amobarbital, Amytal) and its sodium derivative; quinalbarbitone (secobarbital, Seconal) and its salt with sodium; barbitone (Soneryl); pentobarbitone sodium (pentobarbital sodium, Nembutal); and the preparation Tuinal which contains the sodium forms of amylobarbitone and quinalbarbitone.

Most of the barbiturate drugs are metabolized in the liver and appear in the urine as the unchanged forms in only small quantities. The transformation of barbiturates into less active metabolites is controlled by the group of enzymes known as the 'microsomal enzyme oxidizing system' (MEOS). Barbiturates competitively interfere with the metabolic inactivation of other substances transformed by MEOS. The competition for MEOS between barbiturates and alcohol, together with the additive depressant effects of the two kinds of substance on the brain, explains why the combination of barbiturates and alcohol is hazardous and sometimes lethal.

General sedatives such as barbiturates stimulate the activity of hepatic microsomal enzymes. Induction of MEOS by sedatives augments the rate of transformation of several substances that are substrates of this enzyme system, including phenytoin, warfarin and steroids. Enzyme induction by general sedatives therefore has importance in many spheres of medicine; it also contributes to the development of tolerance.

Tolerance

A decrease in intensity and duration of response to a given dose of barbiturate is determined, as with tolerance to other drugs, both by an enhanced rate of metabolic transformation and by adaptation of target tissues to the effects of the substance. Tolerance to barbiturates and allied sedatives does not occur to the degree produced by opioids; the lethal dose of a barbiturate in a regular user is little larger than the therapeutic amount. Cross-tolerance and cross-dependence are found between individual members of the barbiturate class, and between them and other general sedatives.

Acute tolerance ensues with a large, single dose of barbiturate; when the blood concentration of the drug is falling the features of intoxication are less prominent than at similar blood levels when the concentration was rising. It is not known whether the mechanisms which underlie acute tolerance are identical to those responsible for the neural adaptation that occurs in the course of long-term drug administration.

Abstinence syndrome of the barbiturate type

The abrupt withdrawal of barbiturates after their prolonged, excessive consumption produces a distinctive abstinence syndrome. Its features are similar to the symptoms and signs that follow withdrawal of alcohol and other general sedatives (Essig, 1966; Ewing and Bakewell, 1967). The syndrome has been noted, for example, with chloral hydrate and paraldehyde, as well as with later sedatives: meprobamate (Equanil, Miltown), methaqualone, ethchlorvynol (Placidyl), and methyprylone (methprylon, Noludar). A withdrawal syndrome of the barbiturate type also follows the cessation of the continuous excess use of glutethimide (Doriden), and of the benzodiazepine group of sedatives (Brandon, 1975).

In the case of cessation of a short-acting barbiturate the abstinence syndrome starts within 24 hours, reaches a peak in 2–3 days, and then subsides. Anxiety and restlessness are prominent features; there is anorexia and less commonly nausea and vomiting. Tremors develop,· and sleep is fitful. When sleep does occur it is accompanied by vivid, frequent dreams; these can progress to hallucinations noticed when falling asleep or waking, and then to visual and auditory hallucinations while fully awake. The hallucinations are accompanied by defective appreciation of surroundings, by illusions, short attention span, impaired reasoning, and by loss of temporal and spatial orientation; in short, the classic picture of delirium is encountered. Pulse and respiration rates are raised, as are the blood pressure and temperature. Convulsions are liable to ensue, singly or in succession; status epilepticus may develop. Cardiovascular collapse can supervene; the abstinence syndrome sometimes has a fatal outcome.

The EEG taken when awake shows an increase of slow waves, together with high voltage paroxysmal discharges. In respect of the sleep EEG record there is a rebound increase of REM sleep that is accompanied by dreaming and that should be viewed as an important withdrawal feature of physical dependence.

The abstinence syndrome from cessation of long-acting barbiturates and of the benzodiazepine drugs has a slower course. The syndrome has been produced experimentally in human volunteers by the administration of barbiturates for periods ranging from 92 to 144 days, followed by their sudden cessation (Isbell et al., 1950). On rare occasions in clinical practice a subacute delirious state persists for weeks after barbiturate withdrawal.

Mothers who are physically dependent on barbiturates at their time of delivery give birth to babies who show withdrawal features. The signs observed in the infants present a clinical picture of increased irritability which is similar to that found in babies born to mothers who are regularly taking opioids.

The abstinence syndrome that should most worry doctors is not that provoked by opioid or alcohol cessation, but by barbiturate withdrawal. The prevention of barbiturate withdrawal convulsions requires a phased and not an abrupt removal of barbiturate if a barbiturate dependent person is admitted to a hospital or other institution.

Patterns of barbiturate misuse and dependence

Misuse and dependence on barbiturates, and on combined preparations of barbiturates and amphetamines, were commonly encountered during the vogue of prescribing barbiturates as a supposedly beneficial form of therapy for neuroses and insomnia. The subjects were generally females, aged over 25, who had been introduced to barbiturates by their medical advisers; the patients did not resort to a black market for drugs, and were law-abiding unless their dependence led them to commit offences involving prescriptions. Doctors and nurses were also susceptible to the development of barbiturate dependence, because of occupational contact and ease of access to the drugs. Since doctors became reluctant to prescribe barbiturates drug-dependent patients of these categories are now infrequently seen in Britain. They have been replaced by young persons who misuse barbiturates that are circulated unofficially.

Illegal or medically unauthorized barbiturate consumption is a problem in many countries. Usually barbiturates, when misused, are taken orally, but it is not uncommon for young people to inject intravenously, as suspensions or solutions in water, barbiturates present in crushed tablets or in the powder content of capsules.

The adolescent or young adult who takes illicit barbiturates is generally a polydrug misuser. Barbiturates may be the preferred choice of substance when they are available, or a drug of the barbiturate class can be taken specifically to counteract the stimulant effect of ampheta-mines. Another motive for barbiturate usage is to suppress the opioid abstinence syndrome and craving when opioids are temporarily unobtainable. Dependence on barbiturates is often concealed by the subject. Withdrawal fits from undiagnosed barbiturate misuse have led to unnecessary neurological investigations such as carotid angiography.

Leakage of injected barbiturate material into perivenous tissues produces strong local irritation. Secondary infection may develop; an abscess or ulcer can ensue. If the subject has selected a vein in a finger then spillage of barbiturate into the subcutaneous tissue can lead to necrosis, gangrene and loss of the finger. Overdoses of barbiturate readily produce a fatal outcome. A delayed consequence, fortunately uncommon, of a high dose of barbiturate is organic cerebral impairment; the intervening processes involve centrally determined respiratory depression and cerebral anoxia.

Conclusion

Barbiturates have fallen out of favour in medical practice, because of several disadvantages: they are liable to induce misuse and dependence; they can lead to paradoxical excitement; they interact unfavourably with several other substances; overdose is hazardous. Intravenous, short-acting barbiturates remain in use for induction of anaesthesia; phenobarbitone is of value for epilepsy; otherwise the clinical employ-ment of barbiturates has declined. Questionnaire surveys of psychiatrists and general practitioners in Britain reported that among the respondents seven-tenths of the psychiatrists and two-thirds of the family doctors indicated that they do not prescribe barbiturates to new patients (Barraclough, 1976; Wilkes, 1976). Barbiturates have been replaced in clinical use by the benzodiazepines, which possess similar drawbacks but to a lesser degree.

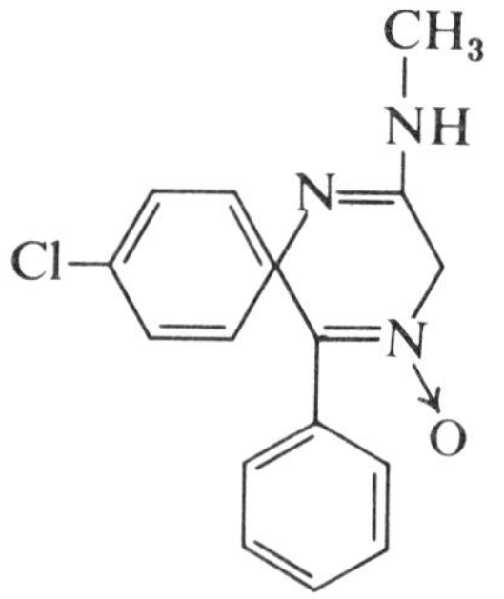

Fig. 10. Chlordiazepoxide.

Benzodiazepines

This group of central nervous system depressants is used in medicine to relieve anxiety and promote sleep. The first benzodiazepine drug in clinical employment was chlordiazepoxide (Librium); its structure is shown in *Fig.* 10. A list, by no means exhaustive of some members of the benzodiazepine group is provided by *Table* 8.

The individual benzodiazepines differ from each other in speed of onset and duration of their action, but it is not clear that dose schedules always take their lengths of activity into proper account. Some of the members of the group share a common active metabolite (oxazepam). The reasons why certain of the benzodiazepine drugs are used as daytime sedatives and others as hypnotics are often arbitrary, though the shorter acting preparations are preferable for night time use, since they exert less effect during the following day.

Table 8. Benzodiazepine drugs.

chlordiazepoxide	(Librium)
diazepam	(Valium)
oxazepam	(Serenid-D, Serenid Forte, Serax)
chlorazepate	(Tranxene)
nitrazepam	(Mogadon)
flurazepam	(Dalmane)
temazepam	(Euhypnos, Normison, Cerepax, Levanxol)
lormetazepam	(Noctamid)
clobazam	(Frisium)

Conventional doses of benzodiazepines produce less impairment of consciousness than therapeutic amounts of barbiturates. In normal dosage the benzodiazepines can precipitate excitement in children and paradoxical aggression in adults. In larger quantities they lead to drowsiness, reduced muscular control, respiratory depression and coma. Overdosage of benzodiazepines is rarely fatal, thereby affording this group of drugs a distinct advantage over the barbiturates.

The mechanism of action of benzodiazepines on the brain is not fully understood, but is associated with the activity of gamma-aminobutyric acid (GABA), which is the principal inhibitory substance within the nervous system. Benzodiazepine receptor sites have been located in the brain (Squires and Braestrup, 1977; Mȯhler and Okada, (1977); the receptors are heterogeneous in molecular (Klepner et al., 1979) and pharmacological (Sieghart and Karobath, 1982) nature. The benzo-diazepine receptors are distinct from the GABA receptors, though activation of the former by benzodiazepines promotes activity at the GABA receptors. Like barbiturates benzodiazepines block the arousal effect on the EEG that is normally produced by stimulation of the reticular activating system. Benzodiazepines raise the seizure threshold of the brain; diazepam, one of their members, is employed intravenously as a valuable anticonvulsant in the treatment of status epilepticus. Benzodiazepines depress REM sleep, and there is a rebound increase of this form of sleep when they are withdrawn.

The liver is the site of metabolism of the benzodiazepines, the microsomal enzyme oxidizing system (MEOS) being responsible for their biotransformation. In common with several other substances that provide substrates for MEOS the benzodiazepines increase the activity of this enzyme system.

Tolerance and withdrawal features can occur with benzodiazepines. The abstinence features are similar to those encountered during barbiturate withdrawal; prominent aspects are anxiety, insomnia, tremors and delirium. Chlordiazepoxide has a long half life in the plasma that lasts from 1 to 2 days. Withdrawal symptoms from this drug therefore reach their peak slowly; seizures, when provoked by chlordiazepoxide withdrawal, may not develop until the seventh or eighth day.

Misusers of benzodiazepines fall into two categories: young people who consume the substances in a subculture of polydrug misuse, and persons who are generally older and have become overattached to the drugs during medical treatment (Mellinger et al., 1971; Ballinger, 1972; Swanson et al., 1973). The lack of a strong and rapid psychotropic effect from benzodiazepines helps to explain the infrequency of the former category of drug misusers and the lower misuse liability of benzodiazepines compared to barbiturates and stimulants. As with barbiturates, the short-acting benzodiazepines appear more likely to promote misuse and dependence than the longer acting forms, presumably because the user is exposed more sharply and more repetitively to drug effects, including withdrawal discomforts. Dependence on benzodiazepines has been reviewed by Allgulander (1978).

There is no doubt that benzodiazepine drugs are over-prescribed. Psychosocial as well as pharmacological determinants contribute to the indiscriminate and unnecessary prescribing practices that exist in respect of benzodiazepines (Shepherd, 1972). Yet emotional symptoms can be treated without tranquillizers, and benzodiazepines have no place in the long-term management of psychological disorders (Learoyd, 1974). Although a prescription may enable the doctor to feel that he or she is active and helpful, there is rarely a need to prescribe benzodiazepines for day-time sedation (Oswald, 1979).

Benzodiazepine drugs are commonly prescribed to people of late middle age and older who complain that sleep is fitful; when a drug is employed as a hypnotic to a person in this age group it is often continued indefinitely. It is not generally realized that from late middle age it is usual for sleep to remain adequate but to be interrupted for more prolonged spells. Longer episodes of wakefulness and drowsiness are normally encountered at night amongst the ageing (Brezinová, 1975). The interrupted sleep requires no treatment from the doctor other than explanation and reassurance.

Several psychosocial features underly the contemporary fashion for minor tranquillizers of the benzodiazepine group. Doctors are influenced to over-value psychotropic drugs by the expectations of patients, and by the sales promotion activities of pharmaceutical manufacturers. There is also an innate tendency among some doctors to place undue reliance on symptomatic chemical therapy for disordered emotions. Finally, both the public and the medical profession are inclined on dubious grounds to view minor emotional discomforts as symptoms of disease.

Bearing in mind the misuse liability of benzodiazepines and the occasional serious sequelae of overdose, it is desirable to reduce the incidence of their prescriptions. If administered at all to a person with emotional distress they should only be employed for a short term. Drugs of the benzodiazepine class are useful in the treatment of alcohol withdrawal, but here again their employment should be brief, for 1–2 weeks, since alcoholics readily become dependent on benzodazepines (Finer, 1970).

The chloral group of sedatives

Chloral is a trichloro derivative of acetaldehyde. The chlorine ions in the chloral molecule render the substance more lipid-soluble than acetaldehyde and therefore more potent in its effects on the central nervous system. Chloral is an unpleasant, unstable oil; a more suitable preparation is achieved by hydrating its molecule with a molecule of water to form chloral hydrate.

For about a century chloral hydrate has been employed as a hypnotic; the drug has been misused for almost as long. The hypnotic dose level of chloral hydrate ranges from 0·5 to 2 g; it is said that soon after its introduction the painter and poet Dante Gabriel Rossetti consumed 12 g nightly. Swinburne was another poet who became an early subject of chloral dependence.

The addition of chloral ('knockout drops') to beverage alcohol has been popularly considered to produce a particularly intoxicating mixture ('Mickey Finn'). Although the two substances have an additive effect it is not proved that their combination is synergistic or especially potent.

Chloral hydrate is quickly transformed in the body to trichlorethanol. Both substances are equipotent in central depressant activity, but in view of the speed of biotransformation of chloral hydrate most of the depressant results of its administration are in fact produced by trichlorethanol. A further metabolite is trichloracetic acid; this compound displaces the anticoagulant drug warfarin from attachment to plasma protein and thus increases the bioavailability of warfarin. Through thi intermediary process chloral hydrate enhances the anticoagulant effec of warfarin.

Triclofos sodium (Tricloryl, Triclos) and chloral betamine (Beta Chlor) are water-soluble halogenated sedatives that are sometimes use clinically; they become converted in the body to yield trichlorethanol a a shared active metabolite. Other chloral derivatives that are occasionall prescribed to produce a central depressant effect are chlorbuto ethchlorvynol (Placidyl) and dichloral phenazone (Welldorm).

Bromides

Preparations containing bromine were first utilized clinically in 1838 they later became extensively prescribed as sedatives, hypnotics an anticonvulsants. The compounds employed have included potassiur bromide, sodium bromide, diluted hydrobromic acid, calcium bromide bromal hydrate and bromoform. Therapeutic doses are near to toxi levels, and prolonged administration has frequently led to a chroni syndrome known as 'bromism', so that bromides are rarely prescribed b doctors at the present time. Bromides remain available in severa countries as proprietary preparations that are legally sold to the publi without the requirement of prescriptions.

Chronic bromine intoxication or bromism has the features o prolonged sedation, delusions, visual and auditory hallucinations (whic are perceived as seen and heard at a distance), and frank delirium. A clinical picture resembling dementia can develop, with memory loss disinhibition, self-neglect, dysarthria, ataxia and extensor planta responses. Tremors, pigmentation, and a skin rash similar to that foun in acne or measles, may ensue. Psychological dependence is a factor with concealment by patients and relatives of the excess bromide consumption.

Carney (1971) described a personal series of patients with bromism in Britain and drew attention to the difficulties of diagnosis. The condition has to be distinguished from neurological illnesses, notably space-occupying lesions and multiple sclerosis; from functional psychoses hysteria, depression of mood and malingering; from rashes of obscure origin and from Addison's disease. Knowledge that the subject may be taking a bromide preparation arouses suspicion; a serum bromine leve over 50 mg/dl confirms the diagnoses. The physical treatment of chronic bromine intoxication consists in promoting the renal excretion o bromine by giving sodium or ammonium chloride together with an appropriate diuretic.

Bromide dependence and bromism are rarely encountered in Britain at present; their infrequency makes the diagnosis more difficult. In West Germany and some other European countries the prevalence of acute bromide intoxication rose in the 1970s (Muller-Derlinghausen et al.,

975); the contribution of bromides to traffic accidents, and chronic romide misuse, also increased (Arnold, 1975). The reason for the mmon occurrence of bromine misuse in some countries has been the citness of many bromine compounds. Most of the preparations btainable without a prescription do not contain the single inorganic alts of bromine (e.g. sodium or potassium bromide). Instead the mpounds possess bromine attached to an organic ureide molecule and re classed as bromoureides.

A pellucid and witty description of the hallucinosis that can follow the rolonged consumption of bromides was provided by Evelyn Waugh 1957) in his autobiographical novel *The Ordeal of Gilbert Pinfold;* the ovelist confirmed that he himself experienced the features described rerein. His medical advisers variously ascribed his illness to the alcohol r bromides that he was consuming; either substance could have caused ie symptomatology, so perhaps both preparations contributed to his xic state.

Jrea group (Ureides)

hese are derivatives of urea or of carbamic acid. Among the members f this group are carbromal, bromisovalum, ethyl carbamate (Urethane) nd carbrital. They are, or ought to be, virtually obsolete sedative-ypnotics. As noted above those that contain bromine (the bromoureides) re prone to misuse, with the development of acute or chronic bromide ntoxication.

Paraldehyde

This substance is administered orally or by intramuscular injection. It as an unpleasant odour, subjectively experienced as an undesirable aste; the smell is apparent to the observer in the breath of patients who ave been given the drug. Paraldehyde has been used in the treatment of status epilepticus and as a powerful sedative for restless patients. When given by injection the dose is 10 ml, divided into 5 ml intramuscularly at wo different sites.

Paraldehyde was formerly employed to sedate patients undergoing abstinence symptoms, particularly the symptoms of withdrawal from alcohol. It was attractive to alcoholics, some of whom developed psychological and physical dependence on the substance. Paraldehyde s now infrequently utilized in medical practice.

Meprobamate

This compound was introduced in the 1950s; it rapidly became a popular drug in medicine as a sedative-hypnotic in a daily dose range of 400–1200 mg. Meprobamate (Equanil, Miltown) soon became misused, and reports emerged of psychological and physical dependence. The drug is distinctly more susceptible to misuse than benzodiazepines (Glatt,

1967; Swanson, 1973). Meprobamate suppresses REM sleep; there is rebound increase in the amount of REM sleep after withdrawal of th drug. In Britain meprobamate is obsolescent.

Methylpentynol

The structure of methylpentynol (Oblivon) is allied to that of alcoho Dependence on methylpentynol has occurred; when taken by abstine alcoholics it has provoked the unwanted resumption of excess drinkin The substance has fallen into disuse.

Glutethimide

This drug (proprietary name Doriden) was introduced in 1954 as hypnotic. The usual dose for this purpose is 500 mg. The acute an chronic effects of glutethimide are similar to the other non-opioi sedatives. Among the results of glutethimide administration are inductio of activity in the microsomal enzyme oxidizing system, suppression o REM sleep, tolerance, and psychological and physical dependence.

Methyprylone (methyprylon)

The formula of methyprylone (Noludar) is similar to that of glutethimide The daily sedative dose ranges from 150 to 400 mg; the hypnotic dos lies between 200 and 400 mg. Tolerance can develop to methyprylone the drug possesses a misuse potential, and both psychological an physical dependence have ensued.

Antihistamines

A slight degree of temporary depression of the central nervous system i a usual effect of a therapeutic dose of an antihistamine. Certain member of the antihistamine group (notably diphenhydramine) are more powerful sedatives than others. Some of the antihistamines have been deliberately prescribed for their sedative effect; they are diphenhydramine (Benadryl), promazine (Phenergan), methapyrilene (Histadyl), hydroxyzine (Atarax, Vistaril), and pyrilamine (Histalon, Neo-Antergan, Neo-Pyramine, Nisaval). The abuse of antihistamines is uncommon, but might not remain so if they were more widely prescribed as sedatives. Diphenhydramine is marketed in conjunction with the sedative methaqualone to form a preparation (Mandrax) that has been extensively misused. The antihistamine drug cyclizine is available in a combination with the synthetic opioid dipipanone; the antihistamine is present to counteract the emetic effect of the opioid, but the preparation (Diconal) has been frequently misused in the British Isles.

Methaqualone

Methaqualone (Quaalude, Sopor) is also marketed as methaqualone hydrochloride (Parest, Somnafac). The sedative dosage is 75 mg 3 or 4 mes a day; for sleep induction the dose is 150–300 mg. The ability of ethaqualone to induce misuse and dependence was first noted in Japan uring the early 1960s (World Health Organisation, 1964; Kato, 1969); ubsequently the misuse of methaqualone was encountered in Europe, ncluding West Germany. Psychological dependence, and later the bstinence syndrome of physical dependence, were successively ported in Britain by Madden (1966) and by Ewart and Priest (1967). he withdrawal features are comparable to those encountered after essation of alcohol or barbiturates. An epidemic of methaqualone misuse in Britain subsided dramatically when the drug laws were altered; ne changed regulations forbid any member of the public to possess the ubstance unless it has been prescribed to that member personally.

Methaqualone has been marketed in a combination (Mandrax) with ne antihistamine sedative diphenhydramine; the use, and misuse, of the reparation spread to North America (Gerald and Schwirian, 1973). eports were also published of methaqualone–diphenhydramine misuse mong U.S. soldiers in West Germany (Tennant, 1973b; Ruck and Moore, 1976). The upsurge of methaqualone misuse in the United tates arose in part because of a popular notion among misusers that the rug possessed aphrodisiac qualities (Harvey, 1980).

REFERENCES

llgulander C. (1978) Dependence on sedative and hypnotic drugs. *Acta Psychiatrica Scand.* Suppl. 270, **57**, 1–120.

rnold W. (1975) Bromureides—real or secondary drugs in the crime and drug scene. In: *Proceedings of the 31st International Congress on Alcoholism and Drug Dependence.* Lausanne, International Council on Alcohol and Addictions, pp. 451–454.

allinger B. R. (1972) Drug dependence in psychiatric admissions. *Br. J. Addict.* **67**, 215–220.

arraclough B. M. (1976) Barbiturate prescribing: psychiatrists' views. *Br. Med. J.* **2**, 927–928.

erridge D. and Edwards G. (1981) *Opium and the People.* London, Allan Lane/St. Martins Press.

irley A. (1966) *Marcus Aurelius.* London, Eyre and Spottiswood, p. 246.

randon S. (1975) The non-barbiturate hypnotics—use and abuse. In: (ed.) Clift A. D. *Sleep Disturbance and Hypnotic Drug Dependence.* Amsterdam, Excerpta Medica, pp. 221–243.

rezinová V. (1975) The number and duration of the episodes of the various EEG stages of sleep in young and older people. *Electroencephalogr. Clin. Neurophysiol.* **39**, 273–278.

arney M. W. P. (1971) Five cases of bromism. *Lancet* **ii**, 523–524.

arone P. A. and Krinsky L. W. (1973) *Drug Abuse in Industry.* Springfield, Charles C. Thomas.

haruvastra V. and Ehrmann M. (1975) Incidence of hepatitis-associated antigen among male narcotic addicts in a drug treatment programme. *Int. J. Addict.* **10**, 1055–1059.

ditorial (1975) Naloxone. *Lancet* **i**, 734.

ssig C. F. (1966) Newer sedative drugs that can cause states of intoxication and dependence of barbiturate type. *JAMA* **196**, 714–717.

Ewart R. B. C. and Priest R. G. (1967) Methaqualone addiction and delirium tremens. *B* *Med. J.* **3**, 92–93.

Ewing J. A. and Bakewell W. E. (1967) Diagnosis and management of depressant dr■ dependence. *Am. J. Psychiatry* **123**, 909–917.

Finer M. J. (1970) Habituation to chlordiazepoxide in an alcoholic population. *JAM*■ **213**, 1342.

Fishman J. and Hahn E. F. (1975) The opiates. In: (ed.) Richter R. W. *Medical Aspects* *Drug Abuse.* Hagerstown, Maryland, Harper & Row, pp. 37–49.

Gallant G. M. (1981) Alcohol, naloxone and the endorphins *Alcoholism (NY)* 469–471.

Gardner R. (1970) Deaths in United Kingdom opioid users 1965–69. *Lancet* 650–653.

Gerald M. C. and Schwirian P. M. (1973) Nonmedical use of methaqualone. *Arch. Ge* *Psychiatry* **28**, 623–631.

Ghodse A. H. (1981) Drug-related problems in London accident and emergenc departments. *Lancet* **ii**, 859–862.

Glatt M. M. (1967) The benzodiazepines. *Br. Med. J.* **2**, 444.

Harris B. and Harper B. (1979) Psychosis after dextropropoxyphene. *Lancet* **ii**, 743.

Harvey S. C. (1980) Hypnotics and Sedatives. In: (ed.) Gilman A. G., Goodman L. S. ar Gilman A. *The Pharmacological Basis of Therapeutics.* (6th edition). New Yor MacMillan, pp. 338–375.

Harvey J. G. (1981) Drug-related mortality in an inner city area. *Drug Alcohol Depend.* ' 239–247.

Isbell H., Altschul S., Kornetsky C. H. et al. (1950) Chronic barbiturate intoxication: ■ experimental study. *Arch. Neurol. Psychiatry* **64**, 1–28.

Jacobson A. E. (1972) Narcotic analgesics and antagonists. In: (ed.) Mulé S. J. and Br■ H. *Chemical and Biological Aspects of Drug Dependence.* Cleveland, CRC Press, p■ 101–118.

James I. P., Morgan H. G. and Gay M. (1976) Addictive abuse of dipipanone (Letter.) *B*■ *Med. J.* **2**, 1448.

Jasinski D. R., Pevnick J. S. and Griffith J. D. (1978) Human pharmacology and abu■ potential of the analgesic buprenorphine. *Arch. Gen. Psychiatry* **35**, 501–516.

Jeffrys D. B., Flanagan R. G. and Volans G. N. (1980) Reversal of ethanol-induced com■ with naloxone. *Lancet* **i**, 308–309.

Kales A., Bixler E. O., Tan T. L. et al. (1974) Chronic hypnotic use; ineffectiveness, dru■ withdrawal insomnia and hypnotic drug dependence. *JAMA* **227**, 513–517.

Kato M. (1969) An epidemiological analysis of the fluctuation of drug dependence ■ Japan. *Int. J. Addict.* **4**, 591–621.

Kilcoyne M. M. (1975) Heroin-related nephrotic syndrome. In: (ed.) Richter R. W■ *Medical Aspects ' of Drug Abuse.* Hagerstown, Maryland, Harper & Ro■ pp. 243–250.

King A. and Betts T. A. (1978) Abuse of pentazocine. *Lancet* **ii**, 21.

Klepner C. A., Lippa S. A., Benson D. I. et al. (1979) Resolution of two biochemically ar■ pharmacologically distinct benzodiazepine receptors. *Pharmacol. Biochem. Beha* **11**, 457–462.

Learoyd B. M. (1974) Psychotropic drugs—are they justified? *Med. J. Aust.* ■ 474–479.

Lewis J. R. (1973a) Use and abuse of pentazocine. *JAMA* **225**, 1530–1531.

Lewis R. J. (1973b) Infections in heroin addicts. *JAMA* **223**, 1036–1037.

Lewis S. A., Oswald I., Evans J. I. et al. (1970) Heroin and human slee■ *Electroencephalogr. Clin. Neurophysiol.* **28**, 374–381.

Louria D. B., Hensle T. and Rose J. (1967) The major medical complications of heroi■ addiction. *Ann. Intern. Med.* **67**, 1–22.

Madden J. S. (1966) Dependency on methaqualone hydrochloride (Melsedin) (Letter *Br. Med. J.* **1**, 676.

Maletzky B. M. (1974) Addiction to propoxyphene (Darvon): a second look. *Int. J. Addict.* **9**, 775–784.

Martin W. R., Jasinski D. R. and Mansky P. A. (1973) Naltrexone, an antagonist for the treatment of heroin dependence. *Arch. Gen. Psychiatry* **28**, 782–791.

Mellinger G. D., Balter M. B. and Manheimer D. I. (1971) Patterns of psychotherapeutic drug use among adults in San Francisco. *Arch. Gen. Psychiatry* **25**, 385–394.

Miller R. R., Feingold A. and Paxinos J. (1970) Propoxyphene hydrochloride: a critical review. *JAMA* **213**, 996–1006.

Moestrup T., Hansson B. G., Widell A. et al. (1983) Clinical aspects of delta infection. *Br. Med. J.* **286**, 87–90.

Möhler H. and Okada T. (1977) Benzodiazepine receptor demonstration in the central nervous system. *Science* **198**, 849–851.

Muller-Derlinghausen B., Poser S. and Poser W. (1975) Chemico-pharmacological investigations in bromism and bromoureide-intoxication. In: *Proceedings of the 31st International Congress on Alcoholism and Drug Dependence.* Lausanne, International Council on Alcohol and Addictions, pp. 521–526.

News and Notes (1977) *Br. Med. J.* **2**, 649.

O'Brien C. P., Nace E. P., Mintz J. et al. (1980) Follow-up of Vietnam veterans. I. Relapse to drug use after Vietnam service. *Drug Alcohol Depend.* **5**, 333–340.

Oswald I. and Priest A. G. (1965) Five weeks to escape the sleeping pill habit. *Br. Med. J.* **2**, 1093–1099.

Oswald I. (1979) The why and how of hypnotic drugs. *Br. Med. J.* **1**, 1167–1168.

Raimondo G., Smedile A., Gallo L. et al. (1982) Multicentre study of prevalence of HBV-associated delta infection and liver disease in drug addicts. *Lancet* **i**, 249–251.

Rathod N. H., de Alarcón R. and Thomson I. G. (1967) Signs of heroin usage detected by drug users and their parents. *Lancet* **ii**, 1411–1414.

Ream N. W., Robinson M. G., Richter R. W. et al. (1975) Opiate dependence and acute abstinence. In: (ed.) Richter R. W. *Medical Aspects of Drug Abuse.* Hagerstown, Maryland, Harper & Row, pp. 81–123.

Richter R. W. (ed.) (1975) *Medical Aspects of Drug Abuse.* Hagerstown, Maryland, Harper & Row, Chapters 15–27, pp. 189–336.

Robins L. N. (1974) *The Vietnam Drug User Returns: Final Report, Sept. 1973.* Washington, U. S. Government Printing Office.

Robins L. N., Helzer J. E. and Davis D. H. (1975) Narcotic use in Southeast Asia and afterward. *Arch. Gen. Psychiatry* **32**, 955–961.

Ruck N. L. and Moore R. J. (1976) Methaqualone (Mandrax) abuse, urine-testing, and identification: clinical correlation between a new mass urinalysis test and a military drug abuse program. *Int. J. Addict.* **11**, 237–244.

Sapira J. D. and Cherubin C. E. (1975) *Drug Abuse. A Guide for the Clinician.* Amsterdam, Excerpta Medica.

Seymour-Shove P. and Wilson C. W. M. (1967) Dependence on dextromoramide. *Br. Med. J.* **1**, 88–90.

Shattock A. G., Kelley M. G., Fielding J. F. et al. (1982) Epidemic hepatitis B with delta antigenaemia among Dublin drug abusers. *J. Irish. Med. Assoc.* **151**, 10.

Shepherd M. (1972) The benzodiazepines. *Prescribers' J.* **12**, 144–147.

Sherlock S. (1976) Predicting progression of acute type-B hepatitis to chronicity. *Lancet* **ii**, 354–356.

Sieghart W. and Karobath M. (1982) Molecular heterogeneity of benzodiazepine receptors. *Nature* **286**, 285–287.

Squires R. F. and Braestrup C. (1977) Benzodiazepine receptors in rat brain. *Nature* **266**, 732–734.

Swanson D. W., Weddige R. L. and Morse R. M. (1973) Abuse of prescription drugs. *Mayo Clin. Proc.* **48**, 359–367.

Tennant F. J., Jun. (1973a) Complications of propoxyphene abuse. *Arch. Intern. Med.* **132**, 191–194.

Tennant F. S., Jun. (1973b) Complications of methaqualone-diphenhydramine (Mandrax R) abuse. *Br. J. Addict.* **68**, 327–330.

U. S. Department of Justice (1973) *Methadone Treatment Manual.* Washington, U. S. Government Printing Office, p. 21.

Waugh E. (1957) *The Ordeal of Gilbert Pinfold.* London, Chapman Hall.

Whittington R. M. (1979) Dextropropoxyphene addiction. *Lancet* **ii**, 743–744.

Wilkes E. (1976) General practitioners and barbiturates (Letter.) *Br. Med. J.* **2**, 939.

Wolters E. Ch., van Wijngaarden G. K., Stam F. C. et al. (1982) Leucoencephalopathy after inhaling 'heroin' pyrolysate. *Lancet* **ii**, 1233–1237.

Working Party (1982) Use of immunoglobulin with high content of antibody to hepatitis B surface antigen (anti-HBs). *Br. Med. J.* **285**, 951–954.

World Health Organisation (1964) *Expert Committee on Addiction-Producing Drugs. Thirteenth Report. Tech. Rep. Ser.* No. 273.

World Health Organisation Scientific Group (1983) Report on a meeting: Prevention of primary liver cancer. *Lancet* **i**, 463–465.

Chapter 7

STIMULANTS AND OTHER DRUGS OF
DEPENDENCE AND MISUSE

The desire for imaginary benefits often involves the loss of present blessings.
Aesop.

STIMULANTS

Central nervous system stimulants exert an alerting effect on the brain that can lead to their repeated self-administration.

Caffeine

The most extensively used stimulant is caffeine, consumed in tea, coffee and cola-flavoured drinks. Some degree of psychological dependence, and tolerance, occur. Caffeine consumption, usually in the form of coffee, has been implicated in a surprising number of diseases. They include cancers of the urinary tract, gastric and colonic carcinoma, peptic ulcer, gout, diabetes, hyperlipoproteinaemia, ischaemic heart disease, cardiac arrhythmias, and stroke. Coffee intake may combine with smoking to raise serum lipoprotein levels, and should be restricted by patients at risk of heart arrhythmias, but there is no clear evidence that coffee drinking is a causal factor in the other disorders (Editorial, 1981). There is an assocation between *per capita* consumption of coffee and pancreatic cancer mortality; yet the relationship may not be directly causal but due to factors, like cigarette smoking, that are common to both conditions (Benarde and Weiss, 1982).

Excessive caffeine intake has been linked with caffeinism, which is a syndrome resembling anxiety neurosis (Greden, 1974). The features take the form of nervousness, irritability, headache and agitation. Other psychological symptoms, such as lethargy and depression, have also been attributed to a high level of caffeine drinking (Finn and Cohen, 1978). Caffeine withdrawal is said to produce headaches and dysphoria (Greden, 1974; White et al., 1980). Caffeinism and a caffeine withdrawal syndrome are uncommon, although the combination of their rarity and of the numerous other causes of their symptoms, means that caffeine can be overlooked as a possible responsible agent. But the practice of taking caffeine beverages is widespread, mildly beneficial and generally without detriment.

Amphetamine-like drugs

Amphetamine and drugs similar to amphetamine in structure and activity form the most widely misused category of stimulant substances. Amphetamine (Benzedrine) was first employed clinically in 1935, as a stimulant compound which could counteract the excessive tendency to fall asleep that is found in the medical condition of narcolepsy. The more extended chemical designation for amphetamine is β-phenylisopropylamine; *Fig.* 11 shows that the drug has similarities to the naturally

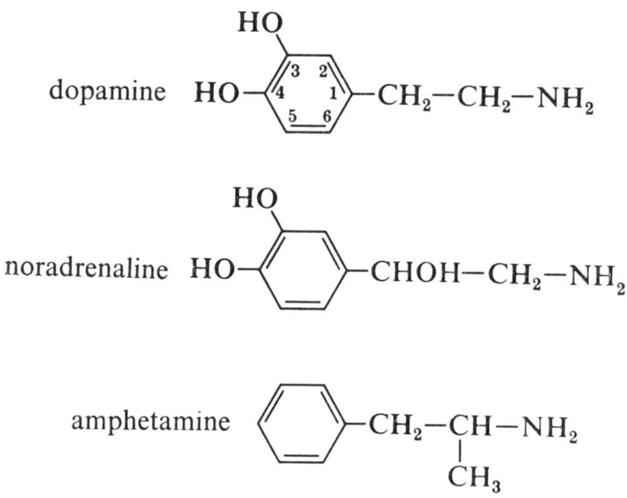

Fig. 11. Dopamine, noradrenaline (norepinephrine) and amphetamine.

occurring neurotransmitter substances dopamine and noradrenaline (norepinephrine).

The mental effects of amphetamine take the form of increased alertness, and a greater sense of well-being and energy. Confidence is enhanced; euphoria develops, together with wakefulness and loss of fatigue. Thought, speech and motor activity become more rapid. There may be increased quantity, though not quality, of output in mental tasks. Appetite is suppressed; patients who began taking amphetamine for its anorectic effect as a treatment for obesity have become dependent on the drug because of its other actions on cerebral processes. When the excitatory effects of a dose of amphetamine subside there can follow some hours of depressed mood and fatigue.

The peripheral effects of amphetamine are similar in many aspects to those produced by excitation of the sympathetic nervous system; that is, amphetamine is a sympathomimetic compound. The drug increases systolic and diastolic blood pressure, and elevates the pulse rate; it produces in therapeutic doses a mild elevation of body temperature.

Amphetamine is believed to stimulate both the cerebral cortex and the reticular activating system of the brain stem. As might be expected with a substance that elevates the level of mental activity, the effects of amphetamine in the waking EEG resemble those of increased psychic alertness: the EEG record is quickened and desynchronized so that there is a preponderance of rapid low voltage waves. Rapid eye movement (REM) sleep is considerably diminished in quantity; when the repeated use of the drug is discontinued there is a rebound increase in the amount of REM sleep. The enhancement of this category of sleep pattern endures up to 2 months and indicates abnormalities of brain function during the withdrawal period (Oswald, 1968).

Amphetamine and its analogues increase the activity of the catecholamines dopamine and noradrenaline at the physiological receptor sites for these two neurotransmitter amines (Carlsson, 1970; Short and Shuster, 1976). Drugs of the amphetamine class augment catecholamine activity by three mechanisms:

1. Release of amines from presynaptic stores in nerve terminals.
2. Prevention of the re-uptake of amines into nerve endings, especially inhibition of dopamine re-uptake; the amine molecules remain in the synaptic cleft where they continue to exert their actions on postsynaptic receptors.
3. Exertion by amphetamines of a direct agonistic activity at the receptor sites for catecholamine transmitters.

There is variation between the compounds of the amphetamine category in respect of the relative importance of each of the above mechanisms. The amphetamines also release 5-hydroxytryptamine (serotonin) from its storage sites in nerve terminals, and may exert an agonist effect on serotonin receptors.

The dextro isomer of amphetamine is dexamphetamine (Dexedrine). Methylamphetamine (methamphetamine, Methedrine, Desoxyn, Fetamin) is also a dextrorotatory substance (*Fig.* 12). Methylamphetamine is considerably soluble in water; its high degree of water solubility has promoted its intravenous use—and misuse.

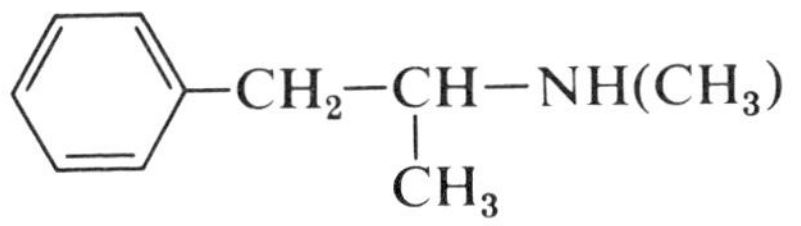

Fig. 12. Methylamphetamine.

All three forms of amphetamine are effective orally. Amphetamine and methylamphetamine are also taken intravenously. Their rapid intake by the intravenous route produces an effect ('rush') on the body and mind which is similar in speed and intensity to that produced by intravenous opioids, but yet recognizable as qualitatively dissimilar.

Tolerance

The degree of tolerance to amphetamines is remarkable. The usual therapeutic dose is in the order of 5–10 mg; the regular user can take several hundred mg daily. This extent of tolerance could not arise from an increased rate of drug metabolism. The responsible neurophysiological mechanism or mechanisms are not understood, though one suggestion has pointed to exhaustion of the stores of noradrenaline in the nerve terminals. Cross-tolerance exists between each of the amphetamines.

Withdrawal features

It was formerly believed that withdrawal effects from amphetamines did not develop, and that the fatigue and depression of mood that ensue on cessation of the drugs were psychogenic reactions to the absence of the 'highs' of stimulation and euphoria. The observation of a rebound increase in amount of REM sleep after amphetamine withdrawal was a firm demonstration of an abstinence feature. The observation led clinicians to realize that the depression and tiredness which occur on ceasing amphetamines, as well as the concomitant symptoms of sleepiness and enhanced appetite, are physically determined aspects of an abstinence syndrome. Patients who are undergoing amphetamine withdrawal require respect for their distress, but they do not need drugs. The amphetamine abstinence syndrome passes its worst intensity within a few days; it is never fatal, and does not call for the initiation or continuance of amphetamines or other medication from physicians.

Other sympathomimetic drugs

There are several drugs possessing both an appetite suppressant and a stimulant effect, that have been prescribed for the former activity but have been misused because of the latter. Substances that fall within this category are allied in structure to amphetamine: they are phenmetrazine (Preludin), phentermine (Duromine, Ionamin, Wilpo) and diethylpropion (Tenuate, Apisate, Tepanil). Methylphenidate (Ritalin) is another drug that has a similar formula to amphetamine; it has been employed clinically for its stimulant effect, and has become a drug of misuse.

Phenylpropanolamine is a synthetic drug that is allied in structure to amphetamine. The preparation has been marketed as a nasal and respiratory decongestant and as a slimming agent. The substance has induced severe hypertensive and psychotic reactions, even in therapeutic doses. Phenylpropanolamine also constitutes a drug of misuse (Editorial, 1982a).

Fenfluramine (Ponderax, Pondimin) is an appetite suppressor that is related in structure to amphetamine, but which commonly induces drowsiness and does not suppress REM sleep. In high quantities fenfluramine produces hallucinations; young persons can take the drug because of its psychotomimetic effects (Levin, 1973). Withdrawal of fenfluramine that had been prescribed in the treatment of obesity has led to a subjective feeling of depression (Steel and Briggs, 1972).

Tranylcypromine (Parnate) is a monoamine oxidase inhibitor (MAOI); that is, it inhibits the specific groups of enzymes responsible for metabolism of the catecholamine neurotransmitters and of serotonin. As an MAOI drug tranylcypromine exerts a gradual effect in promoting the restoration to normal of an abnormally depressed mood, but the substance is unique among the MAOI compounds in two aspects that are presumably related: it has a chemical structure similar to amphetamine (*Fig.* 13) and is prone to misuse (Griffin et al., 1981).

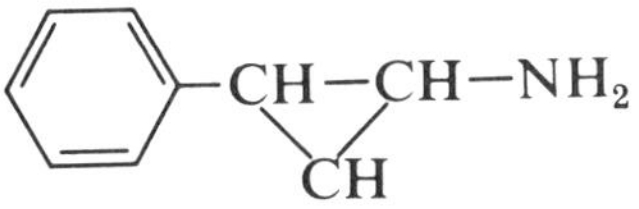

Fig. 13. Tranylcypromine.

Ephedrine is a naturally occurring alkaloid that is found in several plants. Although not classed among the amphetamine-like drugs it has a stimulant effect centrally in the nervous system and promotes peripheral sympathomimetic activity. Under medical supervision it is taken orally or by inhalation as a bronchodilator in the treatment of respiratory disorders. Misuse and dependence to ephedrine can occur, because of its stimulant effect on the mind.

Patterns of misuse and dependence

Therapeutic dependence on amphetamine-like drugs was common in the 1950s and early 1960s among patients who had been prescribed the substances in the hope of reducing appetite or of relieving neurotic depression and fatigue. Doctors became subsequently more chary of prescribing amphetamine and its analogues, so that therapeutic dependence on this class of substance is now infrequent. Its place has been taken by misuse and dependence on amphetamine drugs among adolescents and young adults. The drugs are obtained to a certain extent still from prescriptions, but also from thefts and to a growing degree from illicit manufacture.

Amphetamine-like drugs are consumed orally, by nasal inhalation, and by intravenous injection. Teenagers may start to take them out of curiosity, and continue to consume them at weekends to obtain energy and wakefulness for social events. Recreational use by an individual often ceases with growing maturity and the acceptance of obligations to work and marriage, but can progress as part of a pattern of multiple drug misuse. The person who is increasingly involved with drugs, including amphetamines, may start to inject the latter intravenously. 'Speed', to use an argot term for amphetamines, can be repeatedly administered intravenously for periods ('runs') that endure for several days before terminating in an aftermath of fatigue and prolonged sleep (Hofman, 1975).

As indicated, the consumption of amphetamines may form part of a polydrug misuse pattern, and be intermittently adopted in accordance with their availability. Amphetamines can also be consumed specifically to counteract the depressant effects on the nervous system of general sedatives and opioids. Of course, amphetamines are sometimes the preferred choice of certain drug users, whether the subjects are on the fringe of illicit drug consumption or are deeply implicated in drug usage.

Acute toxicity from heavy amphetamine consumption can develop in a youngster whose consumption has been excessive on a single occasion because of drug naïveté, or may occur with a more experienced drug misuser who has taken a high amount of amphetamine drugs in the course of a few days. The syndrome begins with anxiety, agitation and overactivity. Hallucinatory delirium ensues; hypertension and tachycardia develop. The condition may progress to produce cardiac arrhythmias, convulsions, hyperpyrexia and death. Chlorpromazine or benzodiazepine drugs are given in treatment; forced acid diuresis promotes excretion of amphetamines. Without further therapy restlessness, hallucinations and clouding of consciousness usually subside in a day or two, but severe toxicity requires more energetic measures; rapidly acting hypotensive drugs, anticonvulsants, steps to lower increased body temperature, and artificial respiration may be necessary.

A more prolonged psychosis, not delirious in nature, is elicited by the prolonged excessive consumption of amphetamines (Connell, 1958). One or more weeks of heavy amphetamine intake are required for the development of a classical amphetamine psychosis. Consciousness remains clear but paranoid delusions develop, with auditory, visual and tactile hallucinations. There is often a distinctive form of stereotypic movement of the tongue, lips and mouth; repetitive behaviour of a more complicated kind may also ensue, such as continuous performance of a domestic cleaning task. The theoretical and practical implications of stereotypy have been discussed by Ridley and Baker (1982). Overactivity of speech, thought and action may be present. Tension, irritability, fear and aggressive behaviour are common accompaniments. Formal thought disorder is not a usual feature (Bell, 1965). The psychosis bears several resemblances to schizophrenia (Connell, 1958; Janowsky and Risch, 1979). It is relevant that amphetamine exacerbates the clinical features of schizophrenia; the two conditions of amphetamine psychosis and schizophrenia may have a common neurochemical pathway of stimulation of a catecholamine system or systems in the central nervous system (Snyder, 1972, 1973). Amphetamine psychosis generally has a benign course, with the establishment of significant improvement a few days after cessation of the stimulant substance.

Intravenous injectors of stimulant drugs are liable to develop the infective complication of unsterile injections. Two kinds of non-infective cerebral sequelae are encountered from amphetamines (Sapira and Cherubin, 1975). Firstly, haemorrhage can develop within the skull; the bleeding may be subarachnoid or intracerebral in location, and is presumably a result of the hypertension of sympathetic overactivity. The second neuropathological complication is occlusive vascular disease of the cerebral vessels, with focal neurological signs and an angiographic finding of arterial 'beading'; it has been proposed that the latter syndrome is a form of angiitis.

Cocaine

The drug is naturally present in the leaves of *Erythroxylon coca* and other species of *Erythroxylon* trees growing in the Peruvian and Bolivian Andes. Inhabitants of these regions chew the leaves of coca trees to produce euphoria, subdue anxiety, relieve fatigue and suppress hunger; coca consumption takes place on both an individual and a group basis (Goddard et al., 1969). Payment of manual workers with coca leaves originated with the Spanish conquistadores. Nowadays coca chewing is an understandable reaction to the poverty-stricken existence of the peasants, yet at the same time it affords a substantial contribution towards their inability to better their conditions.

The main effects of cocaine are threefold: stimulation of the CNS, pupil dilatation and local anaesthesia. Pharmacologically the drug is not classed with the sympathomimetic agents; structurally cocaine is related to synthetic local anaesthetics and not to transmitter substances in the nervous system.

Cocaine is effective when taken orally, by sniffing, smoking, and by intravenous injection. The stimulant effects of cocaine on the brain, the hallucinatory delirium of an acute overdose, and the paranoid state induced by its chronic administration resemble the results of amphetamine. Like amphetamine the substance facilitates the release of catecholamines from nerve terminals, and inhibits the re-uptake of noradrenaline into nerve endings. In very large doses 'stimulation' of the CNS by cocaine is followed by convulsions, coma and death.

Regular users of cocaine can take considerable doses; up to 10 g daily has been reported. Yet the drug is so rapidly inactivated in the liver that the safe consumption of high amounts does not imply tolerance. After a period of abstinence cocaine users sometimes revert to the same high dosage that they previously consumed, without serious ill effects. There is some evidence that reverse tolerance occurs, by which the nervous system becomes more sensitive to the effects of the drug (Jaffe, 1980).

It is not clear whether withdrawal features occur, but the possibility exists. After discontinuance of repeated cocaine intake lassitude, fatigue, sleepiness, depression and hunger can ensue (Caldwell, 1979). Users sometimes resort to heavy alcohol consumption to reduce subjective distress when they exhaust their supplies of the drug.

The drug is usually taken by itself, though it may be consumed in intravenous combination with an opioid to offset drowsiness produced by the latter. The most famous fictional user of cocaine has been Conan Doyle's detective character Sherlock Holmes. In real life Sigmund Freud in the 1880s was enthusiastic for cocaine; he wrote: 'I take very small doses of it regularly against depression and against indigestion and with the most brilliant success'. Freud encouraged his wife and friends to take the drug. His biographer Ernest Jones (1953) concluded that from the viewpoint of modern knowledge about cocaine Freud was quickly becoming a public menace. Around that time the well known American surgeon W. H. Halsted, in the course of experiments on himself to elicit the pharmacological properties of cocaine, became dependent on the substance; he freed himself from the drug with considerable difficulty. Halsted was one of the first persons to develop (and recover from) cocaine dependence.

Repeated sniffing of cocaine or heroin can produce infection of the nasal membrane with ulceration and in severe instances perforation of the septum. In the case of cocaine the chain of events is aggravated by the vasoconstriction that the drug produces, and by the reactive hyperaemia that follows the vasoconstrictive phase.

An upsurge of cocaine consumption developed in many countries during the 1970s. The increase involved cocaine powder and cocaine paste; the latter preparation is taken by the smoking route. The use of cocaine paste became more common among the urban youth of Peru, among whom it has induced transitory and prolonged psychotic reactions. Coca paste has also spread to North America, where it is not confined to the young or to low income groups. Cocaine in the form of powder has also become more widely employed in Europe.

Two persons in 1980 were known to the Home Office in England and Wales to be receiving cocaine on prescription. One of them became dependent many years ago on a cocaine spray that was medically prescribed for a nasal condition. That there were only two, and that 409 persons were convicted of cocaine offences in the United Kingdom during the same year, substantiates the impression that subjects recorded as in receipt of drugs on prescription form only a limited sector of the drug misusing population in the U.K.

Khat

Khat (qat) consists of the fresh leaves or buds of *Catha edulis,* an evergreen shrub grown mainly in the Yemen countries and in the nearby parts of Africa. The potency of the leaves quickly subsides after their removal from the plant, so that the price of khat drops progressively in a matter of hours after its collection. The preparation contains over 20 components, several of which are structurally related to amphetamine. The principle constituent is *d. l* cathinone, which was first isolated in 1978; the substance resembles amphetamine in its neurochemical action on dopamine activity and in its effects on behaviour (Wagner et al., 1982). Tannin is also present in khat, and produces gastrointestinal symptoms. When Aden was under British administration the sale of purgatives varied with the level of khat consumption.

Khat is consumed by chewing. Its usage promotes euphoria and lessens the perception of fatigue and hunger. Psychological dependence on khat can develop; some of the effects of the repeated consumption of the preparation are loss of appetite, headaches and constipation; paralytic ileus has been observed (Luquman and Danowski, 1976). Its prolonged usage is also associated with reduced working capacity, malnutrition and lowered resistance to disease. In the Yemen khat is so remunerative to farmers that cultivation of the shrub has been replacing the growth of coffee and other crops.

For many reasons, therefore, the consumption of khat entails socio-economic disadvantages. The Yemen Arab Republic is discouraging the planting, cultivation and usage of khat. The International Arab Association for Social Defence and other organs of the League of Arab States have been engaged in studying the problems produced by the substance.

HALLUCINOGENS

The drugs included under this heading are usually considered together arbitrarily as substances that have intense effects on the mental processes of perception, thought and feeling. Other terms applied to the hallucinogenic drugs are psychotomimetic, psychotogenic and psyche-delic. Their mental results have similarities to the experiences encountered in dreams and in schizophrenia. Arbitrariness of the current classification is shown by the exclusion of many drugs that produce hallucinations; stimulants, opioid antagonists, bromides, atropine-like drugs and anticholinergic compounds can also exert hallucinogenic activity. The hallucinogen mescaline is similar in structure to the amphetamines, which are themselves capable of evoking hallucinations.

Table 9. Hallucinogenic substances

Indolealkylamines:	Lysergic acid diethylamide (LSD)
	Psilocybin
	Psilocin
	Dimethyltryptamine (DMT)
	Diethyltryptamine (DET)
	Dipropyltryptamine (DPT)
	5-Methoxy DMT (MDMT)
	Bufotenin
	Harmalin
Phenylethylamines:	Mescaline
Phenylisopropylamines:	2,5-dimethoxy-4-methylamphetamine (DOM, STP)
	2,5-dimethoxy-4-ethylamphetamine (DOE)
	3-methoxy-4,5-methylenedioxyamphetamine (MMDA)
	Myristicin
	Ditran
	Phencyclidine

A lengthy list of hallucinogens is provided by Sapira and Cherubin (1975). It is possible to subdivide many of the hallucinogen group of drugs by their chemical relationships (Domino, 1975).

LSD

The mental results of LSD are a paradigm for the effects on the mind of the other hallucinogens. LSD is a product of researches into the ergot alkaloids. Ergot is the resting stage of the fungus *Claviceps purpurea.* From mediaeval times there have been recorded outbreaks of ergotism caused by eating rye bread contaminated with the fungus. The manifestations usually take the form of painful gangrene of the fingers, toes and ears due to peripheral vasoconstriction (hence their title 'St Anthony's fire'), but psychotic features have also occurred. Although the nature of the natural hallucinogen is undetermined, lysergic acid is the basic structure in several of the alkaloids found in ergot; lysergic acid diethylamide (LSD-25, LSD) is its derivative. The psychoactive properties of LSD were discovered by Dr Albert Hofmann, who in 1943 during the course of investigations consumed some of the drug and then cycled home under its influence. Although he was accompanied on the journey by an assistant, good fortune contributed to his safe arrival.

LSD is taken orally. Its effects on mental processes develop gradually, reach their height in 2–4 hours, and begin to subside after about 12 hours. Perception is influenced in many ways. Illusions develop: objects may appear larger or smaller than normal, walls or the ceiling recede or grow near, colours and outlines become more vivid and impressive. On closing the eyes after-images are prolonged, or brightly coloured and realistic images may be seen.

Hallucinations are frequent; they are predominantly visual. With open eyes realistic or fantastic visions are perceived, to which strong affects of pleasure or fear are attached. For instance, a frequent user reported that whenever the hallucination appeared of a creature with a human body and the head of a dog then invariably the rest of the LSD experience would prove unpleasant (a 'bad trip'). Synaesthesiae occur; that is, sensations evoked by one sensory modality are transformed into perceptions from another modality. Thus noises may evoke coloured patterns, or colours are experienced as sounds. Appreciation of the body image is distorted; the body as a whole, or a portion such as a limb, appears to enlarge or to shrink.

Affective disturbance is extensive and varied. Elation, depression, mild euphoria or anxiety may be elicited; an evoked mood can rapidly increase in intensity or be transformed into a dissimilar affect. Injuries have occurred to elated persons who overestimated their physical powers; self-harm has been inflicted by subjects suicidally depressed from LSD; users attempting to escape in panic from the psychotomimetic effects of the drug have accidently injured themselves. Through these several routes fatalities have ensued from LSD.

The passage of time is subjectively slowed by the drug. Ideas which simulate profound religious insights occur; the user may consider that under LSD he gains insight into the fundamental concepts of life. Objects seen or heard in the environment can seem to acquire a significant or mystical meaning and importance.

The somatic effects of LSD are mainly sympathomimetic. They include tachycardia, hypertension. increased body temperature, pupil dilatation and tremor. Muscle weakness, nausea and vertigo can also develop.

LSD resembles other psychoactive drugs in respect of the concordance of its mental effects with the drug experience and expectations of the user, with the subject's current mood, and with the social setting in which the drug is taken. The psychic results reported from LSD have altered since the mid-1950s because of changes in the characteristics and expectancy of its users. When patients were given LSD in the 1950s as an adjunct to psychotherapy they experienced events which impressed them (and their therapists) as the recall of psychodynamically important memories. During the ensuing two decades the spread of LSD consumption from sophisticated persons to economically and educationally disadvantaged subjects meant that the drug less frequently evoked intellectual and abstract concepts of a quasi-mystical nature.

The LSD experience is always interesting to the user, and often enjoyable, but in a sizeable proportion of instances it is unpleasant. A distressful experience under LSD represents the most common hazard of the drug; it is unpredictable and can ensue after a series of 'good trips'. The subject of an adverse reaction should be reassured and verbally calmed ('talked down'); a benzodiazepine or phenothiazine drug is helpful. If the person is admitted to hospital discharge is usually feasible within 24 hours (Forrest and Tarala, 1973).

The results of LSD develop, in a person who has not recently taken the drug, with a dose in the nature of 50 micrograms. Tolerance supervenes quickly and markedly. After half a dozen administrations spaced over a few weeks doses up to 800 micrograms or slightly higher may be needed to produce a full reaction.

Fig. 14 shows that part of the LSD molecule resembles the neurotransmitter 5-hydroxytryptamine (5-HT, serotonin). Furthermore, the benzene ring shown at the bottom of the LSD diagram is linked

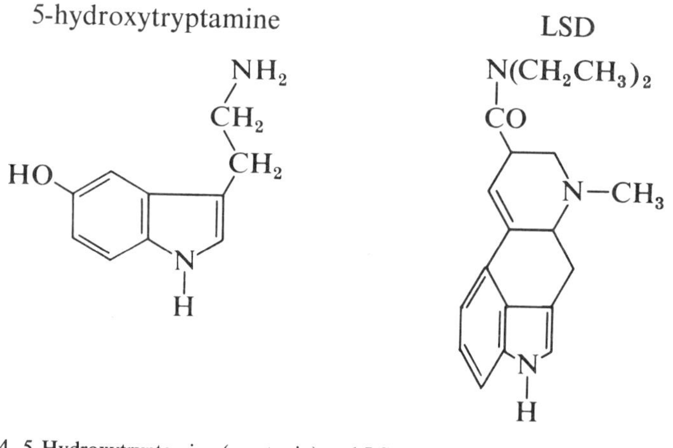

Fig. 14. 5-Hydroxytryptamine (serotonin) and LSD.

by two carbon atoms to a nitrogen atom; this aspect of the molecular configuration of LSD is similar to the structures of the biogenic amines dopamine and noradrenaline (*Fig.* 11). The molecular congruence between LSD and neurotransmitters helps to explain the biological effects of the drug (Johnson et al., 1975). Although LSD affects dopaminergic activity, it is likely that its cerebral effects arise mainly from activation by the drug of serotonin receptors, including those located in the serotoninergic raphe system of the midbrain (Bennett and Snyder, 1976; Freedman, 1981).

Physical dependence to LSD, demonstrated by an abstinence syndrome when the drug is discontinued after regular use, has not been shown. Occasionally users of the substance develop psychological dependence, reaching a phase when they take the drug repeatedly; in some instances consumption takes place three or four times a day on most days of the week. A period of frequent administration does not last indefinitely; it terminates within weeks or months.

Repeated use of LSD can lead to a prolonged psychosis which resembles schizophrenia (Hatrick, 1970; Bowers, 1972). The condition requires admission to a psychiatric unit, and therapy with a major tranquillizer. The psychosis is often at first indistinguishable from schizophrenia, but it usually clears completely and permanently within weeks or months. LSD users who develop temporary schizophreniform illnesses are alleged (on not very sound grounds) to possess an especial predisposition to schizophrenia.

The acute effects of LSD on mental processes can recur suddenly and briefly at intervals of days, weeks or months after taking the drug; their recurrence was first described in 1957 by Cooper. A patient who was known to the present author and who received LSD as treatment for neurosis developed temporary difficulty in crossing roads: as a consequence of the drug, she was hallucinating orange trees in the middle of highways. This type of disconcerting sequel (known as 'flashbacks' or the 'Hyde effect') also occurs with cannabis. A comparable finding is that under the influence of cannabis subjects may re-live experiences previously encountered under LSD.

The frequent use of LSD has been claimed to produce defects in the capacity for abstract thought (McGlothin et al., 1969; Tasker et al., 1972). If this complication does in fact occur, then it could represent a mild schizophreniform impairment of thought processes or result from a minor degree of organic cerebral damage and dementia.

The attribution, on doubtful evidence, of a toxic effect of LSD to human chromosomes illustrates a tendency to exaggerate some of the hazards of unconventional drugs. Chromosomal impairment from any cause can have serious results; the subject is more likely to develop leukaemia, and if the germ cells are affected then progeny subsequently conceived are prone to development defects. Around 1970 statements were issued that authoritatively described chromosomal damage from LSD. In consequence many users discontinued the drug; in the U.S.A. some changed to mescaline, unaware that illicit supplies purporting to be mescaline usually in fact consisted of LSD.

Chromosome harm from LSD is unsubstantiated. It is not established that persons who have taken the drug exhibit a higher proportion of chromosomal irregularities than controls. LSD damages the fetus in more than one species of experimental animal, but it has not been confirmed that children born to LSD users possess an increased incidence of congenital defects.

There are several hallucinogens which, like LSD, bear a structural psilocybin   dimethyltryptamine

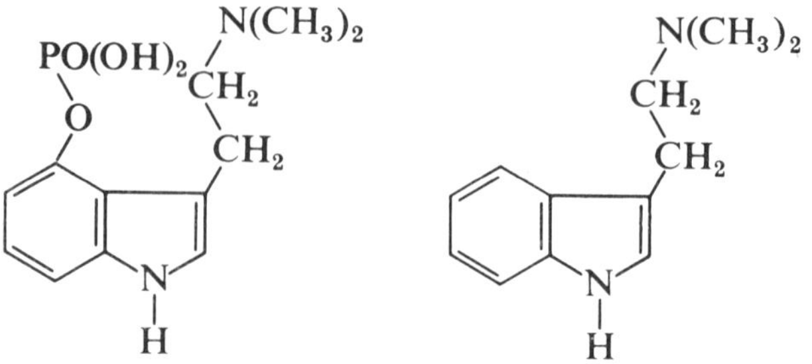

Fig. 15. Psilocybin and dimethyltryptamine (DMT).

similarity to serotonin. Dimethyltryptamine or DMT (*Fig.* 15) is not active by mouth and is taken either as a snuff, or by smoking, or by injection. Psilocybin (*Fig.* 15) and psilocin are the active ingredients of several mushrooms that are consumed for their psychological effects. The first mushroom whose use of this nature has been described was the Mexican plant Psilocybe mexicana. In Britain *Psilocybe semilanceata* (the so-called 'liberty cap' or 'magic mushroom') is taken for its psychotoxic effects, which include visual distortions, visual hallucinations and mild euphoria. During the growing season of the mushrooms (autumn in temperate climates) persons may arrive in hospitals as emergencies because of dysphoric, gastric, sympathomimetic or psychotic reactions (Hyde et al., 1978; Peden and Pringle, 1982). For treatment, it is safest to empty the stomach by lavage or by an emetic, although the reactions tend to resolve within six to twelve hours (Young et al., 1982).

There are, in fact, at least 120 species of hallucinogenic fungi (Schultes and Hofman, 1980). Their heaviest concentration lies in South America though some, such as the psilocybin group, can grow in diverse regions and climates.

Mescaline

Some Indian inhabitants of Mexico and the neighbouring parts of the U.S.A. have the practice of chewing the discs or buttons sliced from the top of the mescal cactus *Lupophora williamsii*. The custom was described in the early sixteenth century, and it is likely that it was employed by the Aztecs before the arrival of Cortes.

In native terminology the psychoactive preparation is called 'peyote' or 'peyotl'. The active ingredient is 3, 4, 5-trimethoxyphenylethylamine, widely known as mescaline. The catecholamine neurotransmitters dopamine and noradrenaline have a structural affinity to mescaline (*Figs.* 11 and 16).

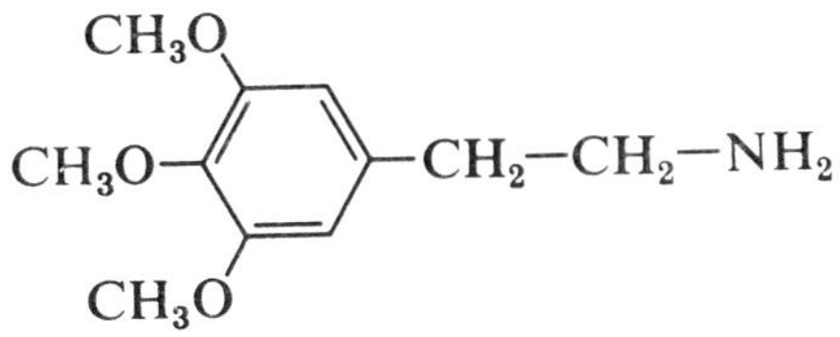

Fig. 16. Mescaline.

Phencyclidine

Phencyclidine (phenylcyclohexyl piperidine, PCP) was employed for a short period as a general anaesthetic, but its clinical use was discontinued as some patients, on emerging from anaesthesia, entered a delirium that endured for several days. Subsequently the drug became widely misused in the United States. Phencyclidine is taken by smoking (with tobacco or other herbal matter in cigarettes), by sniffing, by swallowing and by intravenous injection. The drug is described here for convenience with the hallucinogens, but PCP users report that, although hallucinations and sedation are not uncommon, its major effects are more akin to amphetamine. When the drug is stopped an amphetamine type of abstinence syndrome develops, with craving, depression, desire for sleep and increased appetite (Rawson et al., 1981).

The harm from phencyclidine has been overestimated, but the preparation can produce a psychosis lasting up to a fortnight after single or repeated use. Aggression, convulsions, coma, respiratory depression and death have also been noted (Jacob et al., 1981; Davis, 1982).

Other hallucinogens

2, 5-dimethoxy-4-methylamphetamine (DOM, STP) is a synthetic hallucinogen that is chemically allied to amphetamine. Chlorpromazine is contraindicated in the treatment of a panic state induced by DOM; a benzodiazepine drug such as diazepam should be used instead.

The spices nutmeg and mace contain the psychotomimetic agent myristicin. Grated nutmeg (*Myristica fragrans*), when ingested, produces after a latent period of several hours effects similar to atropine. Excitement, agitation, hallucinations, depersonalization, flushed face, tachycardia, dry mouth and thirst may develop. The product has been consumed by drug misusers to achieve temporary psychotropic effects.

The glycolate esters are synthetic derivatives of atropine. Like their parent drug they can produce a delirious state in which excitement and hallucinations are prominent. Ditron, a member of the group, has undergone a vogue as a drug of misuse.

CANNABIS

Preparations of cannabis are obtained from the *Cannabis sativa* plant (also known as *Cannabis indica* or 'Indian Hemp'). Psychoactive substances are present in all parts of the plant, but are found in highest concentration in the flowering and fruiting tops.

Throughout the world there are considerably over a hundred names for preparations of cannabis. Marihuana is the term often used to refer to the herbal product used in North and Central America, which resembles commercial tobacco in appearance. Hashish commonly denotes the stronger product, in form of a dark brown resin, that is employed in the Indian subcontinent, in the Middle East and parts of Africa, and that is smuggled into Europe. Concentrated extracts ('hash oil') are also prepared; they contain about 60% of the active principles compared with levels up to 8% in herbal preparations, and up to 15% in resin. Other names are khish, bhang, ganja, charas, dagga, and a plethora of slang terms like 'pot', 'smoke', 'draw', 'weed', 'grass', and 'Mary Jane'. As in other varieties of argot a word can drop out of vogue; this has occurred with the once fashionable term 'reefer'.

Cannabis contains over sixty substances, known as 'cannabinoids', which are distinctive to the plant. The foremost active ingredient is chemically classed as either a pyran or monoterpene compound (Mechaulam, 1970); the first alternative is usually chosen, in which case the substance is referred to as the laevo isomer of Δ^9-tetrahydro-cannabinol (Δ^9-THC; *Fig.* 17). When experimentally administered to

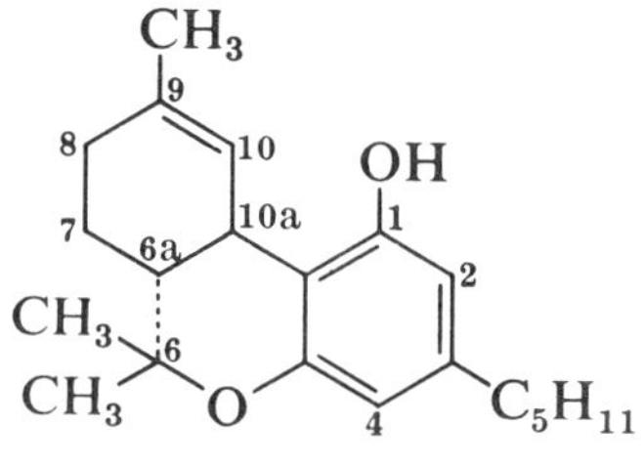

Fig. 17. Δ^9-Tetrahydrocannobinol (Δ^9-THC).

human subjects Δ^9-THC reproduces the effects of unrefined preparations of cannabis (Isbell et al., 1967). It is likely that Δ^9-THC is less psychoactive than its metabolites since the psychological effects of administration of Δ^9-THC are correlated with plasma levels of metabolites rather than with levels of Δ^9-THC itself (Lemberger et al., 1972).

There is a lengthy history attached to cannabis. The substance has been known in China for millenia, and has long been used in India and the Middle East. The Greek historian Herodotus referred in the fifth century B.C. to cannabis inhalation among the Scythians, who lived in the region that now comprises Southern Russia. Its psychic effects were extensively described by the French psychiatrist Moreau in 1845, around the time of a temporary fashion for the substance among intellectuals in France, notably the poet Baudelaire. The results of cannabis on the mind are extremely variable. They depend not merely on the dose level but on the user's expectations and mood, on previous experience with the drug, and on the social setting at the time of consumption. Characteristically, euphoria and a feeling of relaxation develop. If companions are present then vivacity, talkativeness and cheerfulness may prevail; topics not usually considered amusing may give rise to inordinate amusement and giggling, particularly in more immature consumers. At a later stage, or when the subject is alone, contented indifference or sleepiness ensue.

Short-term memory and concentration are impaired with difficulty in carrying out to a definite goal the successive stages of mental problems (temporal disintegration). Conversation is circumstantial, lacking in end point, and interrupted by brief gaps in the stream of thought. Small doses leave relatively intact the ability for simple motor tasks, but diminish performance in complex skills, such as those involved in driving. There is the subjective impression that time is passing slowly.

Sensations appear enhanced to the user in all the external modalities of sight, hearing, touch, taste and smell. Under the influence of the drug music and painting may be more keenly enjoyed. The user may have an unpleasant apprehension of unreality and strangeness relating to the self (depersonalization) or to the environment (derealization). A large dose can transiently provoke anxiety, hallucinations and paranoid delusions.

The waking EEG is slowed because of depression of the reticular activating system. When Δ^9-THC is given experimentally to volunteers the soundness of the first half of sleep is improved, while the second half is more restless. REM sleep is reduced in quantity; cessation of frequent consumption of the drug produces a rebound increase of REM sleep (Feinberg et al., 1975; 1976).

Somatic effects of cannabis include redness of the conjunctivae and dryness of the mouth. Tachycardia ensues; it is prevented by a beta-adrenergic blocking drug. Hypertension occurs while under the influence of cannabis. The drug can also produce postural hypotension. Tremors and, rarely, coma can follow large doses. Cannabis has been thought to lower the level of blood sugar, but biochemical investigation has failed to confirm this effect. Although there is variability between users, some feel hungry after the consumption of cannabis. In the Middle

East cannabis is often taken in a sweet drink, or with sugar or sweets; this is said to have formed the original purpose of Turkish Delight sweetmeats.

Persons who have taken cannabis may subsequently experience its acute effects although they have not recently consumed the drug. This experience of 'flashback' has been termed the 'Hyde effect', after the protagonist in Stephenson's novel *Dr Jekyll and Mr Hyde* who kept turning into another personality although ceasing to take a mind-altering substance. In addition subjects can, as an acute effect of cannabis, experience the results previously induced by LSD. Psychological mechanisms such as association of stimuli must play a role in these related phenomena.

Absorption, distribution, metabolism and excretion

Absorption of Δ^9-THC is almost total after cannabis products are ingested, but the effects of cannabis are more intense and more rapid when cannabis preparations are smoked. Subsequent to ingestion the effects develop after about 30 minutes, and last from 3 to 5 hours. When cannabis is smoked the effects are felt in a few minutes, are at their peak in 10–30 minutes, and terminate after 2–3 hours.

The amount of Δ^9-THC in cannabis products varies considerably, from 0–4% in American herbal preparations to between 5–15% in Asian resinous material. Not more than half of the Δ^9-THC in a cannabis cigarette is absorbed from the lungs, so a 500 mg cigarette possessing 1% of this ingredient would provide at the most in the body 2·5 mg of Δ^9-THC. In the liver Δ^9-THC is quickly hydrolysed into a more active metabolite, 11-hydroxy-Δ^9-THC; the latter is in turn hydrolysed to a less active compound, 8,11-dihydroxy-Δ^9-THC, which is excreted in bile and urine accompanied by only small amounts of its predecessors. Δ^9-THC and its active metabolite pass rapidly into tissues rich in lipid (including the brain); their plasma levels therefore fall sharply within minutes. But the active substances remain detectable in the plasma for several days after a single dose because they are stored in fatty tissues and slowly released into the circulation. Cannabis products may remain in the fatty tissue for over 30 days (Hum and Jones, 1980).

Animal experiments have not fully elucidated the mode of action of Δ^9-THC and its analogues on neurons, but probably multiple mechanisms exist. There is an inhibition of synthesis of RNA and protein that could impair the neurochemical basis of memory storage. Neurotransmitter turnover is altered. The strong lipophilic quality of Δ^9-THC ensures its incorporation into neuronal membranes, with a resultant change in membrane equilibrium.

The long-term effects that arise from storage of cannabis ingredients in the body require further exploration. The shortage of adequate studies is an important reason for keeping the substance illegal. Unrestricted access to cannabis would increase the extent of its consumption and of exposure to possible, though still undetermined, adverse results of its storage and accumulation in body tissues.

Tolerance

Tolerance has been experimentally demonstrated in animals and in man (Nahas, 1975; Hollister, 1979); tissue adaption rather than an increase of metabolism appears to be the more important process for the development of tolerance. Some users report a drop in tolerance; the condition is known as 'reversed tolerance' and enables subjects to obtain the results they desire from a smaller dose. Reversed tolerance may depend on several factors: a more sophisticated and effective technique of administration, greater awareness and mental sensitivity to psychic effects, conditioned responses to the processes of consumption, and induction of the enzyme which converts Δ^9-THC into the more potent metabolite 11-hydroxy-Δ^9-THC. If the user continues to take cannabis over a period then the psychoactive compounds become more rapidly transformed and reversed tolerance disappears.

Dependence

Dependence occurs in a minority of users; it has been reported from several countries (Nahas, 1975); they include Israel, Egypt, England and the U.S.A. The subjects are unable, or unwilling, to cease the frequent use of cannabis although it is adversely affecting their occupational and interpersonal adjustment and involves recurrent legal risks (Madden, 1969). Dependence can lead persons to become traffickers in cannabis in order to ensure their supplies of the substance.

Withdrawal features are rare when the majority of persons who have taken cannabis are considered, but abstinence symptoms and signs can develop. The rebound increase of REM sleep that follows the cessation of a chronic high level of consumption must be viewed as a withdrawal sign. The removal of cannabis from volunteers who were taking the drug in research experiments has provoked numerous abstinence symptoms; they include irritability, restlessness, insomnia, tremor, sweating, vomiting, diarrhoea, anorexia and sudden weight loss (Jones et al., 1976; Greenberg et al., 1976).

Cannabis can therefore produce several aspects of dependence; they comprise tolerance, withdrawal features, craving and a salience given to drug taking over other activities. Other aspects of dependence remain unexplored. It is not known whether heavy users relieve withdrawal symptoms by further drug intake, possess a stereotyped and narrow pattern of consumption, or rapidly reinstate dependence after a period of abstinence (Edwards, 1982).

Acute toxicity

The psychological responses to a single dose of cannabis may be severe. Subjectively unpleasant developments involve anxiety amounting to panic, depressed mood, a sense of unreality appertaining to the self or to the surroundings, illusions, paranoid ideas, hallucinations and delirium. The affective disturbances can arise not so much from the substance itself but from the apprehensiveness of a novice user. These adverse mental reactions to cannabis are self-limiting and endure for a few hours only; they respond to reassurance that is combined, if necessary, with a tranquillizer.

A large dose of cannabis can produce a condition of shock, with lowered blood pressure, fast pulse and cold extremities; coma has ensued. Death has probably, though not certainly, been produced by cannabis overdosage (Graham, 1976).

Chronic toxicity

Repeated smoking of cannabis preparations causes damage to the mucosa of the respiratory tract. An acute effect of cannabis is bronchodilation, but the repeated use of the drug has a constrictive result on air passages. Pulmonary complaints and bronchial tissue changes have been noted after brief phases of cannabis smoking (Henderson et al., 1972).

Multiple drug use is associated with breakage of chromosomes; cannabis does not appear to produce this result, although the evidence conflicts. Cannabis may alter chromosome segregation during cell division, leading to abnormal chromosomal numbers in daughter cells (Report, 1982). Teratogenic properties have been demonstrated in animals, but there is no clear evidence of teratogenicity in humans (McNicol, 1982).

Sperm number and motility are reduced during chronic intake at high doses (Hembree et al., 1979); it is not known whether the sperm effects impair fertility. There are contradictory data on testosterone levels in males. The results of cannabis on female sex hormones and reproduction are not ascertained (Marijuana and Health, 1980).

It is possible that cannabis exerts a mild immunosuppressive activity. The effect could be dangerous if the drug is employed as an antiemetic during cancer chemotherapy.

Prolonged deficits of higher cerebral functions have been described in subjects who have regularly consumed large amounts of cannabis (Tennant and Groesbeck, 1972). The abnormalities of memory, concentration and calculation have been likened to the features of early dementia. Cerebral atrophy, apparent on air encephalography, was reported in each of 10 consecutive young males who were prolonged heavy cannabis smokers (Campbell et al., 1971). The findings were later discounted by computed tomography studies which did not demonstrate cerebral atrophy (Kuehnle et al., 1977; Co et al., 1977).

Amotivational syndrome

It is alleged that prolonged extensive cannabis consumption can produce a state of chronic lethargy, with lack of drive, labile emotions, impaired concentration, and indifference to conventional social values. The amotivational syndrome carries resemblances both to the immediate effects of cannabis, and to the 'drop-out' way of life adopted as a matter of deliberate choice by some regular cannabis users. This life style is not unique to modern Western society; after the Mongol devastation of Persia there appeared in that country groups of people who wore unconventionally long hair, roamed without regular work or abode, advocated love instead of war, and smoked hashish.

The case for a chronic state of diminished motivation and social disruption that is induced by cannabis is difficult to prove since the subjects may without the substance have opted to behave in this manner. Epidemiological and experimental studies have provided conflicting evidence, yet the positive reports justify further enquiries.

Prolonged psychosis

There are many reports that cannabis produces a schizophreniform illness that persists after the drug is withdrawn. It is not easy to substantiate fully the claims. Data are required concerning the prevalence and dosage of cannabis consumption among the mentally well in the same cultures as the patients. Dose levels are difficult to ascertain; epidemiological studies tend to mention approximate amounts; laboratory studies which involve cannabis smoking specify the amount of Δ^9-THC in the material smoked but generally do not give details of inhalation patterns that could affect the results (Petersen, 1979). Subjects could resort to cannabis in attempts to alleviate their psychotic distress, so that their drug usage was a result, not a cause, of their illness. But the evidence is accumulating from many sources.

From their own and other studies Thacore and Shukla (1976) noted the frequency of the following features among cannabis users who have prolonged psychoses: panic, violence, rapidity of thought, persecutory and religious delusions, auditory and visual hallucinations, clear consciousness, insight, favourable outcome, but relapse if cannabis is resumed. The authors suggested that prolonged cannabis consumption leads to tolerance until a saturation point is reached; cerebral decompensation then occurs and psychosis develops.

A study of 2,000 patients attending a psychiatric clinic in Bombay elicited a history of cannabis consumption among 169 (8·5%) of the subjects (Bagadia et al., 1975). The research workers considered that there was a high association between cannabis usage and psychological ill health and proposed three explanations:

1. Cannabis produced or aggravated mental illness among the patients.
2. Cannabis was used to relieve psychic distress.
3. Mental illness led to disinhibited use of cannabis.

The researchers concluded that long term consumption of cannabis can release a latent schizophrenic psychosis and aggravate existing psychological disorder.

Further evidence that cannabis may exert a harmful effect on schizophrenia was provided by Treffert (1979), who described four schizophrenic patients whose condition had been satisfactorily controlled by medication. The patients underwent relapses after cannabis use, while their symptoms remitted when cannabis was discontinued.

There are important reports that cannabis produces a psychotic reaction that is distinguishable from schizophrenia by its clear cut temporal relationship to consumption of the substance. A typical account was provided by Rottanburg and colleagues (1982), who employed laboratory techniques to detect cannabis usage among psychotic patients admitted to hospital. The cannabis users showed schizophreniform and hypomanic features, but differed from the nonusers by their speed of recovery, which took place within a week of initial assessment.

Progression from cannabis to opioids

Cannabis has been asserted to evoke among its users the desire to intensify their chemical euphoria, so that they are led to the consumption of the more potent and more harmful opioid drugs. A substantial number of heroin-dependent persons began their illicit drug use with cannabis, but the opposite does not apply; most people who take cannabis do not escalate drug use to include opioids. Subjects who are extensive cannabis consumers are often members of circles of polydrug misusers; at different periods amphetamines, barbiturates, opioids or hallucinogens may be taken in addition to or in replacement of cannabis, depending on substance availability and group influences.

Cannabis does not possess a specific pharmacological property that would induce opioid consumption. The illogicality of claims for a progression from one substance to another has been demonstrated by Duncan (1975) who pointed out that most heroin takers drank milk prior to their initial use of heroin. Similarly, Malcolm (1976) has drawn attention to an attribution made in all seriousness at the beginning of the century, of tea and coffee drinking as a predisposing cause of opium, alcohol and chloral misuse (McBride, 1910).

Prevalence and correlates of cannabis use

British studies of the prevalence of cannabis use have been reviewed by Kosviner (1976); the findings ranged from 3 to 10% for teenage school attenders and up to 50% for social science students. A survey commissioned during 1973 by BBC television in Britain suggested that over 3 million Britons have taken cannabis at least once. The Le Dain Commission concluded in 1972 that about 1·5 million Canadians have consumed cannabis. The 1974 Report to Congress on Marihuana and Security indicated that 20–25 million citizens of the United States had taken cannabis and that between 1 and 2 million were regular users. A survey conducted on an anonymous basis among U.S. military personnel reported that 35% had taken cannabis in the previous year (Burt et al., 1980). When confronted with figures of these levels it is reasonable to deduce that most of the persons reported as taking cannabis have not been harmed by the substance or progressed to opioids.

Many individuals who consume cannabis do so experimentally on only a few occasions; others pass through a temporary phase of consuming the drug, perhaps at weekly intervals. As with alcohol, it is likely that the frequency of cannabis consumption among users has a unimodal distribution, with most consumers taking the substance infrequently and with the stages into more regular usage progressively involving smaller numbers of persons.

Since the use of cannabis on at least one occasion is so common it follows that many of the individuals who have taken the drug show no statistically abnormal variation of personality from the population as a whole. However, cannabis use is correlated with attitudinal, behavioural and psychological attributes.

Compared with controls cannabis users are less conventional in outlook and less accepting of social norms and religious beliefs (Brill et al., 1971; Kosviner et al., 1974); their use of alcohol and other psychoactive substances is more extensive, and they tend to be more extraverted, more neurotic, and more liable to mild depression and feelings of hopelessness (Smart and Fejer, 1973). In the United States over 60% of high school seniors have taken cannabis at least occasionally, yet investigations show that users perform more poorly in school, are less religious, consume more illicit drugs, are more prone to traffic accidents and demonstrate high scores for deviance and low scores for achievement motivation (Report, 1982). Adults who are heavy cannabis users have been compared with matched controls on psychological tests; the cannabis users reacted more slowly, were poorer in concentration and time estimation, and possessed greater degrees of perceptuo-motor disturbance and neuroticism (Mendhiratta et al., 1978).

Cannabis and the law

Official reports from several countries concurred in stating that the dangers of cannabis had been exaggerated (Home Office, 1968; National Commission 1972, 1973; Government of Canada, 1973). As a result of their suggestions the legal penalties were reduced for possession of a small amount of cannabis for personal use. Sale and distribution of the drug continue to incur more severe sanctions.

The repeal of the former draconian measures is humane and in accordance with our present knowledge, but it would be unwise to free cannabis completely from legal restraints. Personal cannabis consumption in North America is often casual and, even when regular, involves smaller dose levels of the active ingredients than in the Middle and Far East. It is Eastern countries which have most experience of the regular use of potent cannabis preparations and which are the most insistent that the substance should remain illegal. Its recognized hazards, including psychological dependence and adverse effects on driving, are sufficient to make it unwise to legislate to free the drug.

The gaps in knowledge about the consequences of cannabis also justify the retention of its illicit status. Lewis (1968) summarized the literature up to 1965; he noted that much of it was anecdotal and weakened by loose reasoning and contradictory viewpoints.

Since the late 1960s more scientific studies have emerged; two surveys of the later literature have been published in the United States and in Britain (Report, 1982; Advisory Council, 1982). Yet assessment of the possible harmful effects of cannabis is a complex and lengthy task. Aspects that require special consideration are numerous. They embrace the necessity for more animal studies, and for elucidation of the effects in animals and humans of lipid storage of cannabis. The preparations employed illicitly require specification in regard to their frequency and manner of use and to the quantities of their active ingredients which are absorbed into the body. Pre-existing physical and mental features of cannabis users should be outlined, and their health and social adjustment compared with controls. There is a need to clarify the factors that determine cannabis consumption and to delimit the natural history and clinical picture of its usage.

Legislation to permit the use of cannabis would entail that more persons take the drug and that more persons take it extensively. The complications, known and as yet unknown, would become more common. The history of alcohol and tobacco indicates that if there is widespread consumption within the law of a psychoactive drug it becomes impossible to prohibit the substance. It is likely therefore that complete liberalization of cannabis would prove an irreversible step that could not be undone if the desirability of subsequently illegalizing the drug became patent and pressing.

There remains the issue of therapeutic advantages from cannabis or from allied preparations. Under medical prescription, cannabis may be useful for chronic wide-angle glaucoma, for asthma and (with a reservation concerning further immunosuppression) for the nausea and vomiting of cancer chemotherapy. Possibly the drug also has a therapeutic potential in epilepsy and in the relief of spasticity. Although the psychotropic and cardiovascular effects of cannabis limit its usefulness in therapy, such effects may be less troublesome with synthetic cannabinoids such as nabilone.

ATROPINE-LIKE DRUGS

The atropine alkaloids are the active ingredients of *Atropa, Hyoscyamus* and *Datura* plants of the botanical order of Solanaceae. The natural alkaloids are atropine and hyoscine (scopolamine); atropine is an optically inactive blend of equal parts of dextro- and laevo-hyoscyamine. Atropine and to some extent hyoscine are present in the belladonna powders and extracts that are prepared from the leaves and roots of *Atropa belladonna* ('deadly nightshade') and *Atropa lutescens;* atropine is also found in *Datura stramonium* ('Jimson weed'). Hyoscine is mainly obtained from the shrub *Hyoscyamus niger* ('henbane').

Toxic doses of atropine have an effect on the brain which in the initial stages is apparently excitatory; in large amounts the drug produces cerebral depression. Prominent features are talkativeness, excitement, restlessness, and augmented muscular movements which may become purposeless and incoordinated. Auditory and visual hallucinations develop; active delirium ensues. Increasing dosage produces a greater impairment of consciousness and coma follows. The respiratory centre and breathing are at first stimulated and later depressed by atropine.

The central effects of atropine depend on the antagonistic action of the drug towards the neurotransmitter substance acetylcholine. Atropine alkaloids inhibit the muscarinic actions of acetylcholine; they are therefore known as antimuscarinic agents.

The peripheral effects of atropine reflect its anticholinergic action and are a striking part of the clinical picture that the drug produces. The pupils are widened; solanaceous preparations have been applied to the eye to achieve this cosmetic effect, hence the term 'Belladonna'. Superficial blood vessels, especially in the face and neck, are dilated with flushing of the skin; inhibition of the parasympathetic activity of the vagus nerve leads to an augmented rate and force of myocardial contraction. Sweat, saliva, bronchial and gastrointestinal secretions are diminished.

Because of its central effects atropine has been termed a 'deliriant narcotic'. Hyoscine is less likely to produce delirium and excitement.

The latter drug formerly occupied a role in therapy as a sedative and hypnotic.

Solanaceous compounds are occasionally employed by persons who are seeking alteration of consciousness, mental stimulation and hallucinations. The compounds are reputed to have been used in the practice of witchcraft, for which purpose they were taken by the oral route or absorbed from external application. A more recent subcultural device consists in the use of stramonium herbal cigarettes; they are marketed as an asthma remedy but are made into infusions and drunk by drug misusers, with resultant clouding of consciousness and hallucinations (Harrison and Morgan, 1976; Bethel, 1978). Datura plant leaves are also employed; the leaves are eaten or taken as infusions (Belton and Gibbons, 1979).

Atropinic alkaloids have been employed in the treatment of parkinsonism. Synthetic anticholinergic drugs are clinically of value in the same condition, but are also liable to produce delirium and hallucinations particularly in the elderly. Drugs of this category, such as benzhexol, (trihexyphenidyl, Artane, Pipanol) are occasionally taken in excess dosage by young people for their hallucinogenic effect.

INHALANTS AND VOLATILE SOLVENTS

Inhalation of certain gases or of the vapour of some volatile fluids produces depression of the central nervous system. Transient states of intoxication occur; these can be deliberately induced because the user enjoys or is intrigued by the associated psychic effects such as euphoria or hallucinations. The anaesthetic gas nitrous oxide ('laughing gas') has been misused for its disinhibiting effect, but most of the inhaled substances exist at normal temperatures as fluids that are easily vaporized.

Prior to the first medical use of ether (diethyl ether) as a general anaesthetic it was sniffed by medical students in the United States for its euphoriant results. Towards the end of the nineteenth century ether drinking was prevalent in the Ulster province of Ireland; the substance was purchased openly from pharmacists (Connell, 1965). The influence of the clergy brought an end to this epidemic of drug misuse. At the turn of the last century alcohol spirit beverages became subject to high taxation in Austria, Hungary and in East Prussia; the custom then arose of sniffing ether or mixing it with drinks. After World War I there was a vogue in Europe for ether parties.

Chloroform and trichloroethylene (trilene) are other volatile anaesthetics that can be misused. Anaesthetists have been liable to the misuse of anaesthetics, by reasons of the occupational hazard of working with these preparations. Trichlorethylene is also an industrial solvent that has been employed in industry and for cleaning clothes; workers, including the staff of clothes-cleaning establishments, whose operations brought them into contact with trichloroethylene, developed psychological dependence to the substance (Alapin, 1973). Certain other solvents which are inhaled have been incorporated into manufactured goods to enable a resin or wax (for example in glue or shoe cleaner) to remain fluid until the articles are used or form the propellants in aerosol products.

Table 10. Some inhaled volatile preparations and their constituents

Preparations

General anaesthetics	Nail polish
Industrial solvents	Nail polish removers
Glues	Shoe polish
Paint thinners	Aerosol propellants
Paint removers	Antifreeze
Lacquer removers	Petrol (gasoline)

Constituents

Chloroform	Cryofluorane
Trichlorethylene (trilene)	Methyl alcohol
Perchlorethylene	Benzene
Carbon tetrachloride	Toluene (toluol)
Trichlorophane	Naphtha
Trichlorofluoromethane	Acetone
Dichlorodifluoromethane	Ethyl acetate

There is an extensive range of preparations with hydrocarbon chemical constituents that have been inhaled for psychotropic effects; some of the more common misused ones are listed in Table 10. The inhalers are usually teenagers or young adults and are predominantly, though not exclusively, males. From time to time a fashion for sniffing glues develops among adolescents in a school or neighbourhood. Hydrocarbon inhalation is usually a group activity (Stybel et al., 1976), though many clinicians and social workers would confirm the findings of a report from Japan that the more abnormal subjects progress from group to solitary sniffing (Higuchi, 1973). The most common method that is employed involves inhalation of vapour from a paper or plastic bag; the technique induces hypoxia, which adds to the impairment of consciousness and to the dangers. A plastic bag is hazardous in itself when applied to the face because electrostatic forces can attach it firmly to the skin; fatal asphyxiation can then ensue. Hydrocarbon sniffing from a bag is a refinement of the relatively harmless practice among youngsters of producing hypoxia, hypotension and impaired consciousness by the Valsalva technique of attempting to breath out while nostrils and lips are firmly closed.

Liver damage can ensue from hydrocarbon inhalation, particularly if constituents are employed that possess chlorine in their molecular structure. Tremors, depression of mood, respiratory failure and ventricular fibrillation are other sequelae. Several neurological complications have been observed; toluene has been the principal chemical implicated in their causation. The nervous system disorders include acute encephalopathy (King et al., 1981), prolonged cerebellar dysfunction (Boor and Hurtig, 1977), peripheral neuropathy (Korobkin et al., 1975) and status epilepticus (Allister et al., 1981). Reversible renal damage has been noticed (Will and McLaren, 1981).

The acquired immunodeficiency syndrome (AIDS) is a disorder which was initially reported among homosexual males who inhaled amyl or butyl nitrite as sexual stimulants. The suppression of cellular immunity that is central to the condition leads to repeated opportunist infections and to rapidly progressive malignant disease. Although nitrites may alter T lymphocytes (Goedert et al., 1982) and are potentially mutagenic (Jørgenson, 1982) their role is doubtful. The original findings among homosexual drug inhalers can be attributed to the risk of developing AIDS that is known to arise from homosexual promiscuity, and perhaps to concomitant intravenous drug usage.

Bass (1970) collected reports from the United States in the 1960s of 110 sudden deaths from hydrocarbon inhalation. Many of the incidents did not involve plastic bags; several deaths followed stress or exertion. Eighty-one of the dead victims came from middle-income suburban homes. In the half dozen years after 1970 hydrocarbon sniffing led to at least 12 deaths in Scotland and 40 in Great Britain (Oliver and Watson, 1977). During 1981 there were at least 39 deaths in the United Kingdom from the inhalation of solvents and adhesives (Anderson et al., 1982). The deaths are attributable to a direct toxic effect such as cardiac arrhythmia, to asphyxia, trauma and inhalation of vomitus.

Although most youngsters who sniff glues or other preparations do so as a temporary phase which they outgrow without harm, their youthfulness makes the deaths and physical complications appear especially tragic. Young people who are chronically involved in the activity require counselling. The counselling process aims at the development of new activities and friendships, and at the relief of the disturbed family relationships that contribute to and are aggravated by the inhalation practice.

SIMPLE ANALGESICS

The term refers to nonopioid drugs that have a central effect on the relief of pain, and that usually possess an additional result to reduce inflammation. Members of this class of drugs are dissimilar to morphine in activity and structure, although proprietary analgesic preparations often contain the opioid codeine. The principal painkillers in contemporary use are acetylsalicylic acid (aspirin) and paracetamol (acetaminophen, Panadol); amidopyrine is still available in some countries despite its side effect of agranulocytosis. There are numerous other non-steroidal anti-inflammatory drugs that relieve pain.

The nonopioid analgesics were introduced to medical practice towards the end of the nineteenth century. Reports of misuse and chronic intoxication appeared from Germany as early as 1888. In 1948 Gross and Greenberg listed the few published reports of dependence on salicylates, including aspirin. Analgesic misuse later became more widely recognized because of the attendant complications of renal disease.

Aspirin and paracetamol possess a mild sedative action on the central nervous system. The sedative effect, which may be interpreted by users as stimulation, leads some individuals to take analgesics regularly. Tolerance can develop; high dose levels lead to delirium and hallucinations. Certain subjects deliberately seek a considerable degree of intoxication because they enjoy the experience (Madden and Wilson, 1966). Toxic effects (such as dizziness and deafness from the salicylics induced by aspirin) are not readily recognized as such by the subjects; analgesic tablets or powders can then continue to be taken in the belief that they will ease the symptoms they had themselves produced. Doctors do not always detect the cause of the toxic symptoms; patients temporarily deaf from undiagnosed salicylism have been fitted with hearing aids. Psychological dependence occurs, though not physical dependence; subjects who are consuming excess amounts of analgesics quickly feel better once they cease the drug intake.

A frequent sequel of aspirin consumption, even in therapeutic amounts, is bleeding into the stomach. The blood loss may be acute and immediately vomited, but chronic unrecognized loss of extruded blood through the faeces is more usual. The resultant anaemia produces fatigue; the symptoms associated with fatigue form another determinant of continued analgesic use in patients with little comprehension of the purposes and powers of analgesic products.

Prolonged consumption of analgesics has led to the serious renal complication of analgesic nephropathy. There is papillary necrosis, with progressive tubular dysfunction, decrease in glomerular filtration rate, uraemia and death. Typically, patients with the condition show polyuria, polydipsia and sterile pyuria. When analgesic consumption is suspected as the cause of renal disease patients must be specifically asked about the practice; general enquiries about drug taking may lead to denial, because the subjects often consider analgesics as harmless products not worthy of mention. It is important to diagnose correctly analgesic nephrotoxicity (even in severe renal failure), because kidney function improves, remains static, or declines only slowly if analgesic intake ceases (Bell et al., 1969).

Phenacetin was formerly the predominant drug noted in reports of analgesic nephropathy. Paracetamol, which is a metabolite of phenacetin, has been incriminated in isolated cases of renal papillary necrosis (Prescott, 1966). Aspirin, whether alone or in combination with analgesic partners, is capable of producing papillary necrosis; so also can many other non-steroidal anti-inflammatory agents (Editorial, 1982b). It should, however, be noted that the other anti-inflammatory analgesics have not been reported to produce dependence.

There is a considerable extent of public misapprehension about analgesics. Encouraged by advertisements people have taken them for sedation, for energy, for sleep and for relief of emotionally determined headaches (Prescott, 1966; Murray et al., 1970). There have been fatalities in Switzerland and Sweden in consequence of popular myths about the aphrodisiac attributes of analgesics (Seevers, 1962). The custom of regularly consuming painkillers is often learned from relatives or friends. A national opinion poll in Britain indicated that 250 000 inhabitants were taking 5 or more analgesic tablets daily without informing their doctors ('World in Action', 1971). The availability of pain-relieving drugs in general stores and supermarkets conveys a false impression of their safety; the sale of analgesics should be restricted to pharmacy outlets.

Females are more prone than males to the use and misuse of nonopioid analgesics. Neurotic depression, immaturity, anxiety and dependent personality are predisposing factors (Gault et al., 1968; Murray, 1971). Low social class, poor education, unhappy childhoods, family history of analgesic misuse or alcohol dependence, and marriage to drunken husbands have also been noted in the backgrounds of analgesic misusers (Murray, 1973). A comment from Australia may have relevance, that drug dependence is a female equivalent of alcoholism (Whitlock and Lowry, 1967).

The benefits of aspirin and paracetamol in the relief of pain justify their availability without prescriptions, but only from chemists' shops and in small samples. The general public requires more information about the hazards of analgesics and about the inadvisability of the regular consumption of such drugs in the absence of a doctor's consent. Dependence on simple analgesics does not receive the attention its victims deserve, partly because of its legality and partly because of the undramatic and quietly resigned comportment of the subjects.

REFERENCES

Advisory Council on the Misuse of Drugs (1982) *Report of the Expert Group on the Effects of Cannabis Use.* London, Home Office.

Alapin B. (1973) Trichlorethylene addiction and its effects. *Br. J. Addict.* **68,** 331–335.

Allister C., Lush M., Oliver J. S. et al. (1981) Status epilepticus caused by solvent abuse. *Br. Med. J.* **283,** 1156.

Anderson H. R., Dick B., Macnair R. S. et al. (1982) An investigation of 140 deaths associated with volatile substance abuse in the United Kingdom (1971–1981). *Human Toxicol.* **1**, 207–221.

Bagadia V. N., Gopalani J., Natarajan V. et al. (1975) Association of cannabis with mental illness in Bombay–India. In: *Proceedings of the 31st International Conference on Alcoholism and Drug Dependence,* Lausanne, International Council on Alcohol and Addictions, pp. 454–461.

Bass M. (1970) Sudden sniffing death. *JAMA.* **212**, 2075–2079.

Bell D. S. (1965) Comparison of amphetamine psychosis and schizophrenia. *Br. J. Psychiatry* **111**, 701–707.

Bell D., Kerr D. N. S., Swinney J. et al. (1969) Analgesic nephropathy. *Br. Med. J.* **3**, 378–382.

Belton P. A. and Gibbons D. O. (1979) Datura intoxication in West Cornwall. *Br. Med. J.* **1**, 585–586.

Benarde M. and Weiss W. (1982) Coffee consumption and pancreatic cancer: temporal and spatial correlation. *Br. Med. J.* **284**, 400–402.

Bennett J. P. Jr. and Snyder S. H. (1976) Serotinin receptor binding in rat brain membranes. *Mol. Pharmacol.* **12**, 373–389.

Bethel R. G. H. (1978) Abuse of asthma cigarettes. *Br. Med. J.* **2**, 959.

Boor J. W. and Hurtig H. I. (1979) Persistent cerebellar ataxia after exposure to toluene. *Ann. Neurol.* **2**, 440–442.

Bowers M. B., jun. (1972) Acute psychosis induced by psychotomimetic drug abuse. I. Clinical findings. II. Neurochemical findings. *Arch. Gen. Psychiatry* **27**, 437–442.

Brill N. Q., Crumpton E. and Grayson H. M. (1971) Personality factors in marihuana use. *Arch. Gen. Psychiatry* **24**, 163–165.

Burt M. R., Biegal M. M., Carnes Y. et al. (1980) *Worldwide Survey of Nonmedical Drug Use and Alcohol Use Among Military Personnel.* Bethesda, Maryland, Burt Associates Inc.

Caldwell J. (1976) Physiological aspects of cocaine usage. In: Mulé S. J. (ed.) *Cocaine: Chemical, Biological, Clinical, Social and Treatment Aspects.* Cleveland, CRC Press, pp. 187–199.

Campbell A. M. G., Evans M., Thomson J. L. G. et al. (1971) Cerebral atrophy in young cannabis smokers. *Lancet* **ii**, 1219–1224.

Carlsson A. (1970) Amphetamine and brain catecholamines. In: (ed.) Costa E. and Garrattini S. *International Symposium on Amphetamines and Related Compounds.* New York, Raven, pp. 289–300.

Co B. T., Goodwin D. W., Gado M. et al. (1977) Absence of cerebral atrophy in chronic cannabis users. *JAMA.* **237**, 1229–1230.

Connell K. H. (1965) Ether drinking in Ulster. *Q. J. Stud. Alcohol* **26**, 629–653.

Connell P. H. (1958) *Amphetamine Psychosis.* Maudsley Monograph No. 5. London, Oxford University Press.

Cooper H. A. (1955) Hallucinogenic drugs. *Lancet* **268**, 1078.

Davis B. L. (1982) The PCP epidemic: a critical review. *Int. J. Addict.* **17**, 1137–1155.

Domino E. F. (1975) The hallucinogens. In: (ed.) Richter R. W. *Medical Aspects of Drug Abuse.* Hagerstown, Maryland, Harper & Row, pp. 3–15.

Duncan D. F. (1975) Marijuana and heroin: a study of initiation of drug use by heroin addicts. *Br. J. Addict.* **70**, 192–197.

Editorial (1981) Coffee: should we stop drinking it? *Lancet* **i**, 256.

Editorial (1982a) Phenylpropanolamine over the counter. *Lancet* **i**, 839.

Editorial (1982b) Renal papillary necrosis. *Lancet* **ii**, 588–590.

Edwards T. G. (1982) Cannabis and the question of dependence. In: Advisory Council on the Misuse of Drugs. *Report of the Expert Group on the Effects of Cannabis Use.* London, Home Office.

Feinberg I., Jones R., Walker J. M. et al. (1975) Effects of high dosage delta-9-tetrahydrocannabinol on sleep patterns in man. *Clin. Pharmacol. Ther.* **17**, 458–466.

Feinberg I., Jones R., Walker J. M. et al. (1976) Effects of marijuana tetrahydrocannabinol on electroencephalographic sleep patterns. *Clin. Pharmacol. Ther.* **19**, 782–794.

Finn R. and Cohen N. (1978) 'Food allergy': fact or fiction? *Lancet* **i**, 426–428.

Forrest J. A. H. and Tarala R. A. (1973) 60 hospital admissions due to reactions to lysergide (LSD). *Lancet* **ii**, 1310–1313.

Freedman D. X. (1981) Mode of action of hallucinogenic drugs. In: van Praag H. M., Lader M. H., Rafaelsen O. J. and Sachar E. J. (ed.) *Handbook of Biological Psychiatry. Part IV. Brain Mechanisms and Abnormal Behaviour.* New York, Marcel Dekker, pp. 858–884.

Gault M. H., Rudwal T. C., Engles W. et al. (1968) Syndrome associated with the abuse of analgesics. *Ann. Intern. Med.* **68**, 906–923.

Goddard D. and Goddard S. N. and Whitehead P. C. (1969) Social factors associated with coca use in the Andean region. *Int. J. Addict.* **4**, 577–590.

Goedert J. J., Neuland C. Y., Wallen W. C. et al. (1982) Amyl nitrite may alter T lymphocytes in homosexual men. *Lancet* **i**, 412–415.

Government of Canada (1973) *Final Report of the Commission of Inquiry into the Non-medical Use of Drugs.* Ottawa, Information Canada.

Graham J. D. P. (1976) Cannabis and health. In: (ed.) Graham J. D. P. *Cannabis and Health.* London, Academic, pp. 271–320.

Greden J. (1974) Anxiety or caffeinism: a diagnostic dilemma. *Am. J. Psychiatry* **131**, 1089–1092.

Greenberg I., Kuehnle J., Mendelson J. H. et al. (1976) Effects of marihuana use on body weight and caloric intake in humans. *Psychopharmacology* **49**, 79–84.

Griffin N., Draper R. J. and Webb M. G. T. (1981) Addiction to tranylcypromine. *Br. Med. J.* **283**, 346.

Gross M. and Greenberg L. A. (1948) *The Salicylates: A Critical Bibliographical Review.* New Haven, Hillhouse, pp. 191–193.

Harrison E. A. and Morgan D. H. (1976) Abuse of herbal cigarettes containing stramonium (Letter.) *Br. Med. J.* **2**, 1195.

Hatrick J. K. (1970) Delayed psychosis due to LSD. *Lancet* **ii**, 742–744.

Hembree W. C., Nahas G. G., Zeidenberg P. et al. (1979) Changes in human spermatozoa associated with high dose marihuana smoking. In: Nahas G. G. and Paton W. D. M. (ed.) *Marihuana: Biological Effects.* Oxford, Pergamon Press, pp. 429–440.

Henderson A. R., Tennant F. S. and Guerry R. (1972) Respiratory manifestations of hashish smoking. *Arch. Otolaryngol.* **95**, 248–251.

Higuchi K. (1973) Experience of amphetamine and other drug abuse in Japan. In: Broström H., Larsson T. and Ljungstedt N. (ed.). *Drug Dependence—Treatment and Treatment Evaluation.* Stockholm, Almqvist and Wiksell, pp. 28–39.

Hofman F. G. (1975) *A Handbook on Drug and Alcohol Abuse: The Biochemical Aspects.* New York, Oxford University Press, pp. 224–240.

Hollister L. E. (1979) Cannabis and the development of tolerance. In: Nahas G. G. and Paton W. D. M. (ed.) *Marihuana: Biological Effects* Oxford, Pergamon Press, pp. 585–590.

Home Office (1968) *Cannabis: Report by the Advisory Committee on Drug Dependence.* London, HMSO.

Hunt A. and Jones R. T. (1980) Tolerance and disposition of tetrahydrocannabinol in man. *J. Pharmacol. Exp. Ther.* **215**, 35–44.

Hyde C., Glancy G., Omerod P. et al. (1978) Abuse of indigenous psilocybin mushrooms: a new fashion and some psychiatric complications. *Br. J. Psychiatry* **132**, 602–604.

Isbell H., Gorodetzsky C. W., Jasinski D. et al. (1967) Effects of Δ^9-trans-tetrahydro-cannabinol in man. *Psychopharmacologia* **11**, 184–188.

Jacob M., Carlen P. L., Marshman J. A. et al. (1981) Phencyclidine ingestion: drug abuse and psychosis. *Int. J. Addict.* **16**, 749–758.

Jaffe J. H. (1980) Drug addiction and drug abuse. In: Gilman A. G., Goodman L. S. and Gilman A. (ed.) *The Pharmacological Basis of Therapeutics*. 6th edition. New York, MacMillan, pp. 533–584.

Janowsky D. S. and Risch C. (1979) Amphetamine psychosis and psychotic symptoms. *Psychopharmacology* **65**, 73–77.

Johnson C. L., Kang S. and Green J. P. (1975) Stereoelectronic characteristics of LSD and related hallucinogens. In: Sankar D. V. S. (ed.) *LSD—a Total Study*. Westbury, N.Y., PJD Publications, pp. 197–244.

Jones E. (1953) *Sigmund Freud, Life and Work. Volume One: The Young Freud 1856–1900* 3rd impression 1972. London, Hogarth, pp. 86–108.

Jones R. T., Benowitz N. and Rackman J. (1976) Clinical studies of cannabis tolerance and dependence. *Ann. NY Acad. Sci.* **282**, 221–239.

Jørgenson K. A. (1982) Kaposi's sarcoma in homosexual men. *N. Engl. J. Med.* **307**, 893–894.

King M. D., Day R. E., Oliver J. S. et al. (1981) Solvent encephalopathy. *Br. Med. J.* **283**, 663–665.

Korobkin R., Asbury A. K., Sumner A. J. et al. (1975) Glue-sniffing neuropathy. *Arch. Neurol.* **32**, 158–162.

Kosviner A. (1976) Social science and cannabis use. In: (ed.) Graham J. D. P. *Cannabis and Health*. London, Academic, pp. 343–378.

Kosviner A., Hawks D. and Webb M. G. T. (1974) Cannabis use among British university students. *Br. J. Addict.* **69**, 35–60.

Lawson A. A. H. (1976) Intensive therapy of acute poisoning. *Br. J. Hosp. Med.* **16**, 333–348.

Le Dain G. (1972) *'Cannabis': a Report of the Commission of Inquiry into the Non-medical Use of Drugs*. Ottawa, Information Canada.

Lemberger L., Weiss J. L., Watanabe A. M. et al. (1972) Delta-9-tetrahydrocannabinol. Temporal correlation of the psychological effects and blood levels after various routes of administration. *N. Engl. J. Med.* **286**, 685–688.

Levin A. (1973) Abuse of fenfluramine (Letter.) *Br. Med. J.* **2**, 49.

Lewis A. (1968) Cannabis—a review of the international clinical literature. In: *Cannabis: Report by the Advisory Committee on Drug Dependence*. Home Office, London, H.M.S.O., pp. 40–63.

Luquman W. and Danowski T. S. (1976) the use of khat (Catha Edulis) in Yemen: social and medical observations. *Ann. Intern. Med.* **85**, 246–249.

McBride C. A. (1910) *The Modern Treatment of Alcoholism and Drug Narcotism*. London, Rebman, pp. 327–331.

McGlothlin W. H., Arnold D. O. and Freedman D. X. (1969) Organicity measures following repeated LSD ingestion. *Arch. Gen. Psychiatry* **21**, 704–709.

McNicol G. P. (1982) Effects of cannabis derivatives on cell division, growth and development, immune mechanisms, the endocrine system and reproduction. In: Advisory Council on the Misuse of Drugs, *Report of the Expert Group on the Effects of Cannabis*. London, Home Office, pp. 17–26.

Madden J. S. (1969) Dependence on cannabis (Letter.) *The Times*, 14 January.

Madden J. S. and Wilson C. W. M. (1966) Deliberate aspirin intoxication. *Br. Med. J.* **1**, 1090.

Malcolm M. T. (1976) Marijuana and heroin. *Br. J. Addict.* **71**, 196.

Marijuana and Health (1980) *Eighth Annual Report to the U.S. Congress from the Secretary of Health, Education and Welfare*. Washington, U.S. Government Printing Office.

Mechaulam R. (1970) Marihuana chemistry. *Science* **168**, 1159–1166.

Mendhiratta S. S., Wig N. N. and Verma S. K. (1978) Some psychological correlates of long-term heavy cannabis users. *Br. J. Psychiatry* **132**, 482–486.

Moreau J. J. (1945) *Du Hachisch et de l'Aliénation Mentale: Etudes Psychologiques*. Paris, Librarie de Fortin (English edition, 1973, New York, Raven Press).

Murray R. M. (1971) Persistent analgesic abuse in analgesic nephropathy. *J. Psychosom. Res.* **16**, 57–62.

Murray R. M. (1973) The origins of analgesic nephropathy. *Br. J. Psychiatry* **123**, 99–106.

Murray R. M., Timbury G. C. and Linton A. L. (1970) Analgesic abuse in psychiatric patients. *Lancet* **i**, 1303–1305.

Murray R. M., Greene J. G. and Adams J. H. (1971) Analgesic abuse and dementia. *Lancet* **ii**, 242–245.

Nahas G. G. (1975) Marihuana: toxicity and tolerance. In: (ed.) Richter R. W. *Medical Aspects of Drug Abuse*. Hagerstown, Maryland, Harper & Row, pp. 16–37.

National Commission on Marihuana and Drug Abuse (1972) *First Report on Marihuana: a Signal of Misunderstanding*. Washington, U.S. Government Printing Office.

National Commission on Marihuana and Drug Abuse (1973) *Second Report: Drug Use in America: Problem in Perspective*. Washington, U.S. Government Printing Office.

Oliver J. S. and Watson J. M. (1977) Abuse of solvents for 'kicks'. A review of 50 cases. *Lancet* **i**, 84–86.

Oswald I. (1968) Drugs and sleep. *Pharmacol. Rev.* **20**, 273–303.

Peden N. R. and Pringle S. D. (1982) Hallucinogenic fungi. *Lancet* **i**, 396–397.

Petersen R. C. (1979) Importance of inhalation patterns in altering effects of marihuana use. *Lancet* **i**, 727–728.

Prescott L. F. (1966) Analgesic abuse and renal disease in North-East Scotland. *Lancet* **ii**, 1143–1145.

Rawson R. A., Tennant F. S. Jr. and McCann M. (1981) Characteristics of 68 chronic phencyclidine abusers who sought treatment. *Drug Alcohol Depend.* **8**, 223–227.

Report of a Study by a Committee of the Institute of Medicine (1982) *Marijuana and Health*. Washington, National Academy Press.

Ridley R. M. and Baker H. F. (1982) Stereotypy in monkeys and humans. *Psychol. Med.* **12**, 61–72.

Sapira J. D. and Cherubin C. E. (1975) *Drug Abuse. A Guide to the Clinician*. Amsterdam, Excerpta Medica, pp. 216–218, 365–383.

Schultes R. E. and Hofmann A. (1980) *The Botany and Chemistry of Hallucinogens*. Springfield, Illinois, Charles C. Thomas.

Seevers M. H. (1962) Medical perspectives on habituation and addiction. *JAMA* **181**, 92–98.

Short P. H. and Shuster L. (1976) Changes in brain norepinephrine associated with sensitization to *d*-amphetamine. *Psychopharmacology* (Berlin) **48**, 59–67.

Smart R. G. and Fejer D. (1973) Marihuana use among adults in Toronto. *Br. J. Addict.* **68**, 117–128.

Snyder S. H. (1972) Catecholamines in the brain as mediators of amphetamine psychosis. *Arch. Gen. Psychiatry* **27**, 167–179.

Snyder S. H. (1973) Amphetamine psychosis: a 'model' schizophrenia mediated by catecholamines. *Am. J. Psychiatry* **130**, 61–67.

Steel J. M. and Briggs M. (1972) Withdrawal depression in obese patients after fenfluramine treatment. *Br. Med. J.* **3**, 26–27.

Stybel L. J., Allen P. and Lewis F. (1976) Deliberate hydrocarbon inhalation among low-socioeconomic adolescents, not necessarily apprehended by the police. *Int. J. Addict.* **11**, 345–361.

Tennant F. S. Jun. and Groesbeck C. J. (1972) Psychiatric effects of hashish. *Arch. Gen. Psychiatry* **27**, 133–136.

Thacore V. R. and Shukla S. R. P. (1976) Cannabis psychosis and paranoid schizophrenia. *Arch. Gen. Psychiatry* **33**, 383–386.

Tucker G. J., Quinlan D. and Harrow M. (1972) Chronic hallucinogenic drug use and thought disturbance. *Arch. Gen. Psychiatry* **27**, 443–447.

Wagner G. C., Preston K., Ricaurte G. A. et al. (1982) Neurochemical correlates between d,l cathinone and d-amphetamine. *Drug Alcohol Depend.* **9**, 279–281.

White B. C., Lincoln C. A., Pearce N. W. et al. (1980) Anxiety and muscle tension as a consequence of caffeine withdrawal. *Science* **209**, 1547–1548.
Whitlock F. A. and Lowry J. A. (1967) Drug dependence in psychiatric patients. *Med. J. Aust.* **I**, 1157–1166.
Will A. M. and McLaren E. H. (1981) Reversible renal damage due to glue sniffing. *Br. Med. J.* **283**, 525–526.
'World in Action' (1971) Granada Television, 15 December.
Young R. E., Milroy R., Hutchison S. et al. (1982) The rising price of mushrooms. *Lancet* **i**, 213–215.

Chapter 8

TREATMENT OF DRUG MISUSE AND DEPENDENCE

All cases are unique, and very similar to others.
T. S. Eliot, *The Cocktail Party.*

METHODS OF MANAGEMENT AND COUNSELLING OF DRUG USERS

In the management of a drug user it is desirable to present to the patient or client short-term treatment goals that are acceptable to both the subject and therapist, and to offer a choice of long-term goals in a way that will not impair the therapeutic relationship if they are at first rejected by the drug taker. Counselling always forms the keystone of therapy, but there is no single treatment approach suitable for all persons who consume psychoactive drugs (Brill and Jaffe, 1967). In regard to immediate management the patient and therapist might, for example, jointly consider that hospital admission is urgently required for an acute psychotic reaction to a drug, or for drug withdrawal. Another possibility may lie in their agreement to arrange admission of the subject to a therapeutic community sited in a halfway house or hostel. If the drug user is chronically dependent on opioids arrangements might be mutually agreed for inpatient or outpatient detoxification, using oral methadone, or for longer term treatment with a methadone maintenance regime or with an oral opioid antagonist. When the drug taker proposes to continue the intravenous use of amphetamines or barbiturates then the therapist will have to dissent from this aim but may be able to persuade the patient to reattend for further discussions.

The long-term goal of total drug abstention is feasible in many instances, but should represent only one of the ends of a treatment programme aimed at general improvement of the patient's well-being. In some cases permanent abstinence from drugs is unattainable, but it may still be possible to achieve recurrent periods of abstention, or a reduction in level of continued drug consumption, together with distinct improvements to psychosocial adjustment and physical health.

In short, a hierarchy of treatment goals is required, that culminates in total abstinence from drugs but that is always aimed at social rehabilitation.

The following case summaries illustrate the range of approaches and aims.

Case 1. A 32-year-old married woman with a child was living apart from her husband; he was a frequent consumer of cannabis. The wife was receiving on prescription large amounts of methadone in ampoules for injection, as well as antidepressants and rising quantities of oral benzodiazepines. She was persuaded by a clergyman to enter hospital with a view to cutting down her drug consumption. In hospital antidepressants were stopped at once, benzodiazepines were gradually discontinued over 2 weeks, and methadone (in the form of a linctus for oral ingestion) was tapered off over 3 weeks. She was then counselled towards drug abstention; the patient concurred with this goal, except she proposed to take cannabis occasionally. Prospects for the marriage did not seem hopeful, but the patient spent weekend leaves with her husband, and on discharge from hospital returned to him with her child. Subsequently she avoided drugs, except for infrequent cannabis; she has remained with her husband, and is working.

Case 2. A male, aged 28, who possessed an I.Q. of 130, was dependent on opioids and had not worked for several years. Numerous hospital admissions did not check drug consumption; along with a group of companions he had been repeatedly in prison for breaking into chemists' shops and stealing drugs. He was initiated onto outpatient prescriptions of methadone linctus, with the hope that the licit supply would prevent further offences and keep him out of prison. The limited aim was attained; the patient spends much of his time in his parents' home, moodily sipping linctus, and is unemployable; but he is free from further legal convictions.

Case 3. A more unstable and criminal opioid user who was in his middle twenties had received several prison sentences, including two for illegally entering pharmacies to steal drugs. He was offered methadone linctus, with the intention that he would avoid further police trouble produced by drugs. He accepted the treatment, yet the medication did not assist him; his illicit drug consumption continued, and was now supplemented by prescribed opioid. He was arrested for driving under the influence of drugs.

Case 4. A woman in her late sixties had begun morphine on prescription 35 years previously because of a painful back condition. The orthopaedic disability remitted, but she remained dependent on small quantities of morphine, taking by injection 15 mg daily of prescribed drug. She was beginning to press the doctor for an increased supply, so her dependence was discussed with her and she reluctantly agreed to a phased withdrawal of morphine. The withdrawal attempt was not pursued for long, as it provoked strong complaints of depression and lethargy. Patient and doctor then decided to continue morphine at its original level, and alterations of dosage in either direction were avoided.

Case 5. A 28-year-old male, married with children, had not worked for a year. During this time his polydrug use escalated; there were phases when he took LSD and cannabis on repeated occasions every day. Eventually he developed a schizophreniform reaction, with thought disorder and religious delusions. Voluntary admission to hospital followed, because of the drug-induced psychosis. Initially treatment took the form of avoidance of illicit drugs, and the administration of major tranquillizers. The psychotic features took 2 months to clear fully, but as they subsided it became apparent that there were positive features in the patient's personality and marriage which justified the goal of permanent drug abstention. Tranquillizers were discontinued and the patient took an active part in an inpatient therapy group composed of alcoholics and drug users. He went back to his family, found employment, and kept off drugs. The psychosis did not return.

Motivation for treatment fluctuates in drug users. Although it is capable of improvement by counselling, motivation is only one of the many factors which determine outcome. In these respects the incentive of persons who misuse drugs resembles that of alcoholics. At times the subjects can be so disenchanted with the difficulties produced by their drug consumption, or so fearful of consequences not yet experienced, that they desire therapy aimed at abstention. At other periods the same subjects may be reluctant to renounce the attractions of drug taking, unduly fearful of withdrawal symptoms, proud of their drug behaviour and of their skill at obtaining drugs, or just pessimistically unconvinced of the prospects of recovery. A choice of therapies and treatment agencies is available; if they are all rejected by the drug taker than at least he or she should be invited to return when more desirous or hopeful of therapy.

Drug users have been described as hedonistic, impulsive, and unready to accept anxiety or frustration. These terms should be avoided as they are condemnatory rather than informative. People who misuse or are dependent on drugs have been subject to cultural and constitutional factors that are largely beyond their control. They are sometimes troubled by feelings of inadequacy, anxiety, alienation and guilt; the unpleasant emotions contribute to, and are in turn aggravated by, their drug usage. The therapist must be non-moralistic, non-judgemental, be prepared to work with defective, varying motivation and be ready to encounter relapses.

Counselling aims at strengthening the incentive to curtail drug consumption, at developing positive attributes that exist in the personality and social circumstances of the drug user, and at counteracting unhealthy emotional features. The counsellor does not overlook advice of a practical nature, such as the need for the motivated subject to avoid consorting with drug taking acquaintances.

Compulsory care as a condition of probation in hospital, halfway house or hostel, or long-term legally enforced supervision in the community, are of value for selected drug misusers who have been convicted of an offence and who show some potential for co-operation. Indiscriminate admission, even on a voluntary basis, of groups of drug takers to hospital or hostel is not appropriate. The subjects tend to discuss the attractive rather than the unattractive facets of drug consumption; smuggling of drugs into the institution, or drunkenness, are frequent accompaniments. But selected clients, who have latent capabilities and the ability to reflect constructively about themselves, can co-operate and benefit in a group setting. In regard to group therapy in hospital Mayer (1972) has described how drug-dependent patients whose ego strength is preserved may progress in a hospital therapeutic community; the therapy involved frequent meetings of patients and staff to discuss drug consumption, and to consider current rather than past emotions.

Drug withdrawal

Whether initially or at a later phase in therapy, the stage is often reached where the drug user is prepared as a practical step to undergo drug cessation. At this point, if physical dependence is present, it is necessary to overcome withdrawal symptoms and signs before dealing with adverse emotional and social factors.

Hallucinogens and volatile inhalants do not produce physical dependence and withdrawal symptoms; neither do simple analgesics unless the preparations also contain the opioids codeine or dextropropoxyphene. Stimulant drugs produce a degree of physical dependence that is mild, so despite some genuine withdrawal distress on their cessation, there is no need for their prescription. In the case of opioids and general sedatives it is desirable, if the patient is in hospital, for the doctor to prescribe an appropriate member from whichever of these sedative classes the subject was consuming; the selected drug is given in decreasing doses so that the withdrawal symptoms are at no time excessive.

Withdrawal of a nonopioid, general sedative should not be attempted with an outpatient if it entails the physician starting a supply of prescribed drug. In the probable event of the patient's failure to cease licit or illicit drug consumption the doctor may feel obliged to continue prescriptions indefinitely. Problems would then be increased for the patient, for other persons who might illegally accept some of the prescribed substance, and for the doctor.

The withdrawal of general sedatives and opioids is more likely to succeed if the patient is first admitted to hospital. In a hospital setting it is possible to control drug intake, while the subject receives support from staff in an environment unassociated with previous drug usage.

Inpatient medical treatment of the opioid abstinence syndrome

Persons who are physically dependent on opioids may come to undergo sudden deprivation of the drug in a number of ways. For example, they might be involuntarily admitted to a penal institution that does not administer opioids, or voluntarily enter a drug-free therapeutic community such as a hostel, or undergo enforced withdrawal while in society at large because of an abridgement of illegal drug supplies. The intensity of distress of the opioid abstinence syndrome has been likened to that encountered in a bout of influenza; the subjects and their medical advisers often take an exaggerated view of the severity of the symptoms and signs. But in order to spare patients from discomfort it is not the custom to withdraw opioids abruptly from subjects admitted to hospital. It is also possible that sudden withdrawal of opioids from the elderly or physically ill could prove hazardous.

Opioid users who have been taking a preparation that produces relatively mild physical dependence, such as codeine, dextropro-poxyphene, or cough medicine containing a morphine-like drug, can be given the same preparation after admission in decreasing quantity and frequency of dosage; over a period of 7–10 days the product is gradually and fully withdrawn.

Methadone is the drug of choice for inpatient withdrawal of persons who are likely to possess marked physical dependence; they may, for instance, have been regular consumers of heroin, morphine or methadone itself. On admission the patient is given oral methadone in a dose sufficient to suppress all or the greater part of the abstinence syndrome; no other medication is required. The effects of oral methadone endure longer than 24 hours, but it is customary during inpatient detoxification to give the drug initially on 2 or 3 occasions in the day. Usually 40–50 mg a day are adequate, but the dosage varies from a considerably lower level to as high as 90 mg daily, in accordance with the extent of withdrawal features. During ensuing days the level and frequency of administration are both progressively lowered until the drug is completely stopped. It is feasible to complete methadone withdrawal over a 10-day period; the symptoms developed on such a regime are not severe, but in a voluntary setting subjects may take their discharge after methadone is withdrawn over this time interval. They give various excuses for leaving but in fact they depart to obtain opioids. More gradual reduction during a period of 2 to 3 weeks ensures that the patient is likely to remain in hospital. The slower pace of withdrawal allows drug craving to subside and permits time for development of a positive relationship between subject and staff; the relationship is the necessary basis for a constructive mutual examination of the drug intake and emotional and social problems of the patient. The withdrawal phase should not be prolonged unduly; periods of withdrawal that are longer than 3 weeks unnecessarily lengthen the abstinence discomfitures.

Subjects who have been taking opioids (or other drugs) by the oral or nasal routes should never receive prescribed drugs by injection. Administration by injection strengthens physical and psychological dependence, because of more rapid and complete drug absorption and because of the mental associations which are attached to the use of the 'needle'.

Opioid withdrawal is generally a safe procedure but the following three fatalities that occured in different English cities are instructive:

Case 6. A patient treated in hospital for heroin dependence was not prescribed an opioid; continuous narcosis by general sedatives was employed instead. He died in coma, not from opioid withdrawal, but from the treatment administered for the abstinence syndrome. The hospital ceased to employ narcosis for this purpose.

Case 7. An offender known to be dependent on heroin was sent by the court to prison where he was not given drugs. Death occurred during a withdrawal convulsion that resulted from unrecognized physical dependence on barbiturates. Persons who take a morphine-like drug commonly exaggerate their level of intake in the hope of obtaining from doctors generous amounts of opioid; in contrast barbiturate dependence is often concealed or minimized.

Case 8. An inpatient who had completed opioid withdrawal in hospital was found dead in the ward from a self-administered injection of heroin; the drug was passed in to the patient through a window and he had misjudged the amount he could take in safety. A drug-free therapeutic environment is not always easy to maintain; patients withdrawn from opioids should be informed that they have lost their tolerance and are not able with impunity to resume the drugs at the levels taken before withdrawal.

Outpatient opioid withdrawal

It is possible to conduct a planned course of opioid withdrawal on an outpatient basis. The traditional substance employed is methadone, in one of its liquid forms that cannot be injected. The drug user commences methadone at a level sufficient to prevent severe abstinence symptoms, and is expected to avoid completely illicit opioids during the withdrawal regime. Methadone is then gradually reduced in amount until the drug is finally withdrawn. A starting dose of 35–50 mg daily is often a convenient level that prevents marked abstinence features yet does not exceed this requirement. The drug is issued in daily quantities, in order to prevent the recipient consuming a supply prematurely or claiming to do so.

The length of the withdrawal regime varies widely between practitioners. Some employ a 3 weeks course, others take 3 to 4 months to remove the patient from methadone. If the shorter detoxification regime is utilized the dose is reduced by about 2½ mg every day. This quantity is mentioned because it is possible to provide methadone mixture in a preparation that contains 5 mg of the drug in 5 ml of diluent; a plastic spoon that holds 5 ml can also be issued. Reduction of dose by 2½ mg (found in 2½ ml) is equivalent to the easily understood measure of half the capacity of the spoon.

A longer withdrawal regime might allow the drug user more time to develop a therapeutic relationship with professional staff, and permit the recipient to distance himself for a more prolonged period from acquaintances and activities involved with illicit consumption. On the other hand, the more lengthy regime gives a drug user greater opportunity to supplement an official supply of opioid from illegal sources, or to divert prescribed opioid to the illicit market. The longer regimes require extra investment of staff time. The relative superiority of any specific length of outpatient withdrawal regime has not been established.

Treatment of opioid poisoning

Overdosage of an opioid leads to coma and respiratory depression. It is necessary to restore quickly adequate ventilation. Airway obstruction from the tongue falling backward is counteracted by holding the patient's jaw forward while extending the head. The semiprone position avoids inhalation of vomit. If available an airway tube is inserted and oxygen given through an inflation bag. Prolonged respiratory depression requires an endotracheal tube, with the cuff inflated to prevent aspiration of vomit and a mechanical respirator. In the absence of equipment a first-aid method of artificial respiration may be needed. Employment of gastric lavage for swallowed drugs is debatable in view of the dangers of tracheo-bronchial aspiration and of interference with artificial ventilation. Lavage is most likely to be of value within the first hour of ingestion; it is therefore more effective after accidental poisoning since this is reported more quickly than deliberate drug misuse. Lavage of the stomach of a drowsy or comatose patient should only be employed after a cuffed tube has been inserted into the trachea. Emesis of a conscious patient may be effective; vomiting can be induced in an adult or child by ipecacuanha (ipecac) or, in a child, by pharyngeal stimulation.

The opioid antagonist naloxone (Narcan) is the preferable antidote; 400 micrograms are given intravenously every 2 to 3 minutes until the patient is aroused and is breathing satisfactorily. Usually no more than 1·2 mg (3 ml) are needed to produce initial arousal but the patient must thereafter remain under close observation. Narcotic antagonists exert their antidotal effect for only 2 to 3 hours, yet the depressant activity of opioids is more prolonged; methadone can exert a depressant effect for as long as 48 hours. Returning signs of coma or respiratory depression require further doses of naloxone, by intramuscular or intravenous injection.

Lack of significant response after two or three doses of antidote puts in doubt the diagnosis of opioid overdose; other conditions such as barbiturate intoxication or head injury may have produced the coma. Fortunately naloxone does not have a depressant effect on respiration if opioid agonists are absent from the body. This advantage gives naloxone a superiority over the opioid antagonists nalorphine (Nalline) and levallorphan (Lorfan) as a treatment for suspected opioid poisoning. When opioids are not in fact present in the system the two latter substances have an agonistic action that aggravates coma and respiratory depression; they are therefore no longer employed for possible opioid poisoning.

Opioids, the fetus and neonatal opioid withdrawal

The regular consumption of opioids produces a suppressant effect on ovulation and on libido. Yet female opioid misusers do conceive and give birth; the likelihood of pregnancy is enhanced if they enter a methadone maintenance programme. The babies do not have an increased incidence of congenital defects, except that their birth weights are as a group below average (Glass et al., 1975). The retarded intrauterine development of the infants could result from a direct consequence of opioids, or be due to poor maternal diet or to the tobacco, alcohol, or other drug consumption of the mothers. If pregnant women are maintained on a methadone regime it is common practice to keep the drug dosage low, at a daily level around 30–50 mg of methadone.

Opioid administration during pregnancy can induce physical dependence in the fetus since morphine-like drugs readily cross the placenta. Signs of intrauterine fetal distress have been observed when opioids are suddenly withdrawn from the mother. After birth the baby is cut off from opioid circulating in the maternal bloodstream, and can then develop an abstinence syndrome.

Many of the signs of neonatal opioid withdrawal are nonspecific, so the diagnosis partly depends on awareness by the doctor and nurse of the mother's drug dependence. The clinical features include irritability, a coarse and flopping tremor, muscle rigidity, tachypnoea, vomiting and diarrhoea, a shrill cry, sneezing, yawning and lacrimation. The course of the condition is usually towards recovery; specific treatment should be minimal and confined to medication given for neonatal irritability. Drugs that may be employed are phenobarbitone, chlorpromazine or paregoric (camphorated tincture of opium, 3–5 drops before each feed). Methadone is not required. Supportive therapy is utilized to maintain fluid, electrolyte and calorie balance, intercurrent infection is treated by antibiotics, and associated metabolic anomalies are corrected, particularly hypoglycaemia and hypocalcaemia (Glass et al., 1975; Fraser, 1976). If it is suspected that an opioid-dependent mother has been maintaining her drug supply by prostitution then the baby requires examination for gonorrhoea and syphilis.

Fraser (1976) has reviewed the literature on drug dependence in pregnancy. In the light of other studies, and of personal experience in an obstetric department, he warned of several hazards in the way of a fully satisfactory outcome to pregnancy in mothers who are drug-dependent. The subjects attend only spasmodically for antenatal care; drug withdrawal during pregnancy is associated with fetal death; spontaneous abortion and pre-eclamptic toxaemia are more common. The main problem is increased perinatal mortality connected with uncertain dates of start of pregnancy and with low birth weight. Despite these complications the view of Blinick et al. (1973) is acceptable, that the outcome of pregnancy for a patient maintained on methadone is usually favourable for both mother and baby.

Because of the possibility of fetal distress and intrauterine death Fraser (1976) advised against complete withdrawal of opioids during pregnancy. In contrast Liu (1976) and his colleagues have recommended that pregnant women who are dependent on opioids should be identified and weaned off drugs in order to prevent neonatal withdrawal symptoms; this group of workers have cautioned that, in the interests of the fetus, drug withdrawal should take place slowly. The greater opportunity for prenatal care that accompanies methadone maintenance treatment in the United States is considered to reduce fetal distress and mortality.

Withdrawal of general sedatives

Subjects who are physically dependent on barbiturates or other nonopioid depressants should be withdrawn from drugs in hospital by means of a phased reduction of drug intake. Abrupt withdrawal produces distressing and dangerous consequences. Convulsions, for example, are a hazardous feature of the abstinence syndrome of the barbiturate and general sedative type.

In regard to choice of prescribed medication the safest method is to employ in oral form the drug that the patient has been using, or a very similar drug; the amount given is decreased each day or on alternate days until after 10–14 days the medication has been fully withdrawn. Oral pentobarbitone (pentobarbital, Nembutal) can be substituted for any barbiturate; an initial dose of 200–400 mg every 6 hours usually suffices to suppress withdrawal symptoms, although some patients need at first a daily total up to 2·5 g. The administration of an oral anticonvulsant may be beneficial and can do no harm, even though the efficiency of the procedure in the prevention of withdrawal fits is uncertain; phenytoin (diphenylhydantoin) is appropriate in a dose of 100 mg 3 times a day. Withdrawal fits or delirium necessitate a brief increase in the quantity of prescribed sedative and postponement for a day or two of further decrements to its dosage. Repeated convulsions require diazepam by slow intravenous injection if facilities for reversing respiratory depression are available; a slower acting alternative is phenobarbitone (phenobarbital), 200 mg by intramuscular injection.

Therapeutic communities

Although individual or group counselling of co-operative drug patients is provided in psychiatric units the drug rehabilitative agencies known as 'therapeutic communities' are sited outside hospitals. Some communities function under the direction of staff; others are controlled by the residents themselves. The original community controlled by residents was Synanon in the United States. Synanon was founded and directed by heroin users who wished to abstain; they adopted a critical and aggressive style of group discussions. Later therapeutic communities are numerous; Daytop in New York is perhaps the most widely known community organization but therapeutic hostels exist in Britain, such as Phoenix House, Alpha House, and the Ley Community. The usual arrangement is to employ a proportion of staff who have never been dependent on drugs, but former drug-dependent persons also play an important role. Some centres expect their clients to withdraw from drugs before admission. Daytop requires new residents to cease drugs abruptly on arrival. The opioid abstinence syndrome is made more tolerable by reassurance and psychological comfort from other members who have undergone 'cold turkey', but its prospect must deter some drug takers from admission. Others, even after the withdrawal stage, prematurely terminate their rehabilitation. Daytop has developed a scheme of phased re-entry into the community for former drug users; its lengthy rehabilitative programme lasts about 15–20 months (Devlin, 1975).

A follow-up study of former Daytop residents contacted 64% of the subjects who had completed rehabilitation and 39% of those who had dropped out at some stage after the initial 6 months of treatment (Collier and Hijazi, 1974). Eighty four per cent of the contacted Daytop graduates were no longer taking drugs or misusing alcohol, were not again arrested, and were either employed or engaged in furthering their education. Using the same criteria 46% of the drop-outs who were contacted had a satisfactory outcome. In a study of a comparable community Romond and her co-workers (1975) found statistically significant differences in follow-up between the graduates and those who left prematurely; the former were more likely to remain non-dependent on drugs, to be free from new convictions, to continue at employment or in school, and to attend drug therapy programmes as clients or as staff; the researchers did not claim a causal relationship between the length of time in treatment and the outcome. De Leon and colleagues (1982) examined recovery and improvement rates 5 years after treatment in therapeutic communities; clients who had completed treatment were less likely to take drugs or commit crime during the follow-up period than subjects who departed early.

A review of the other follow-up reports of therapeutic communities in the U.S.A. and Britain has been undertaken by Smart (1976), who noted deficiencies in many of the studies. Among the defects was a paucity of control groups consisting of comparable subjects who did not receive a rehabilitative regime. It was also unfortunate that, although communities differed ir the proportion of residents who were polydrug users or who were not dependent on opioids, yet the possible resultant variations in prognosis were not considered. In the reports subjects who had completed rehabilitation tended to be relatively few, often representing less than 15% of the admissions; the recovery rates of these subjects varied from 33% to 92%, compared with 22—50% among drop-outs, but it was not possible to determine which programme characteristics were related to favourable progress. Smart considered that therapeutic communities return too few residents to employment in working roles other than in drug treatment or social service activities. Another criticism that has sometimes been levelled against certain rehabilitative communities for heroin takers in the United States is that their residents consist of a disproportionately high number of middle class or White clientèle which are unrepresentative of the majority of heroin-dependent persons in the U.S.A.

Therapeutic communities or halfway houses outside hospitals are not confined to English-speaking countries. A hospital-based drug dependence unit in Gothenburg has possessed an after-care centre located in the countryside; former drug users and their families have spent lengthy periods in the centre with staff; outpatients from the city have stayed for weekends and summer holidays (Sjöberg, 1973). The system has operated in reverse in Norway; the patients have been initially treated in a clinic placed in rural surroundings, and progressed to a halfway house in Oslo (Teigen, 1973).

Conclusions on general management and counselling

Whatever the location, or the tenets and techniques of the therapist, counselling on drug misuse and dependence requires guidance of the drug user towards a way of living that is less drug orientated. Maturation of attitudes and reactions is promoted; the individual is helped to develop his or her mental and environmental assets and is sympathetically encouraged to counteract problems of personality and of social circumstances. The family is led to realize the drug user's difficulties and is tactfully made aware of its possible contribution to the vicissitudes of the subject. In the interests of the drug misuser every effort must be made to mobilise constructive family pressures and support.

Deeper psychotherapy, aimed at uncovering the origins of emotional problems, is not usually feasible, or essential. A survey of reports on the effect of psychotherapy, particularly of psychodynamically orientated psychotherapy, in drug dependence concluded that the lasting results were generally poor (Harding, 1973). Two studies have reported favourable effects in the long term from psychotherapy; the subjects were drug-dependent physicians and private patients respectively (Modlin and Montes, 1964; Pearson and Little, 1965), and were therefore from special groups not representative of the young persons who currently form the majority of drug users.

Older drug users tend to be more stable; often they are professional persons who became dependent while working with drugs, or individuals whose dependence arose in the course of treatment with medically prescribed substances. In many ways professional and therapeutic drug misusers resemble alcoholics; they are generally over 30 years of age, with few or no criminal convictions, and conform in outlook, appearance and life style with the conventions of society. Professional (Dalton and Duncan, 1975) and therapeutic (Glatt, 1970) drug dependents are readily treated together with problem drinkers in therapeutic groups and in special units for chemical dependence.

Negative attitudes are not uncommon at the present time towards persons who are chemically dependent. The subjects are sometimes considered as untreatable, unco-operative, or just plain unlikeable; whether or not these views are fully realized or voiced by those who hold them the result is exclusion of persons from treatment (Chappel, 1977). Self-awareness by professionals, and appropriate educative courses that involve contact with treatment programmes and subjects, promote positive attitudes that increase the concern and care provided for drug users.

ARRANGEMENTS IN BRITAIN FOR MANAGEMENT OF OPIOID MISUSE

In 1961 an official report noted that the drug misuse problem in Britain was small; the report took the view that alterations were not required in the regulations for drug control, which allowed doctors to prescribe to drug-dependent patients (Report of the Interdepartmental Commitee, 1961). The number of persons dependent on 'narcotics' (opioids and cocaine) was a little over 400; they were mostly middle-aged, with a preponderance of females and of users who had become dependent during treatment or in the course of their medical or paramedical professional work with drugs (*Table* 11); morphine was the substance most usually involved. By 1965 the situation had deteriorated in respect of many drugs, including opioids; a further report in that year recommended the provision of special clinics and restriction of the prescribing powers of doctors (Second Report of the Interdepartmental Committee, 1965). The number of drug misusers had increased considerably; many were now taking heroin intravenously, and were young people who had been introduced illicitly to drugs. The Dangerous Drugs Act of 1967 was implemented the following year; by its provisions it became compulsory for doctors to notify patients dependent on certain drugs to the Chief Medical Officer of the Home Office; the legal right to prescribe heroin or cocaine to persons dependent on these two drugs was restricted to doctors officially licensed for the purpose. Many of the features of the Act, and of other legislation, were subsequently incorporated into the Misuse of Drugs Act 1971. But in view of a common misunderstanding among doctors it should be emphasized that the restrictions on prescribing apply at present only to heroin, cocaine and dipipanone. Around 1968 clinics for the treatment of opioid users were established; the clinics were mostly in London where opioid usage was concentrated.

The clinics supplied opioids on prescription, taking precautions to minimize diversion of prescribed drugs to the black market. A frequent practice, for instance, consisted in sending the prescriptions by post to a selected chemist who issued the prescribed drug in only daily quantities. An even more preferable arrangement involved the patient attending the

Table 11. Yearly totals of narcotic-dependent persons known to the Home Office.

Year	Total	Therapeutic origin	Professional classes (medical or allied)
1960	437	309	63
1961	470	293	61
1962	532	312	57
1963	635	355	56
1964	753	368	58
1965	927	344	45
1966	1349	351	54
1967	1729	313	56
1968	2782	306	43
1969	2881	289	43
1970	2677	295	38
1971	2762	265	44
1972	2936	244	33
1973	3023	207	29
1974	3252	246	19
1975	3425	249	25
1976	3474	241	18
1977	3605	214	14
1978	4116	197	18
1979	4787	206	14
1980	5107	185	7
1981	6157	171	10
1982	7962	179	6

Note: The narcotic drugs listed by the Home Office are mainly morphine, heroin, methadone, pethidine, dextromoramide, dipipanone and cocaine (although the last named is pharmacologically not a narcotic).

Clinic daily, where the drug was issued and seen to be consumed in front of the staff. A remnant of subjects ensued to whom heroin continued to be prescribed but most patients were gradually moved by the clinics away from prescriptions of heroin to issues of methadone. At the end of the first month of the clinics' operation (31 May, 1968) 950 patients were receiving heroin; by the end of 1969 the number was almost halved, to 499.

Bewley (1973) has assessed the sequelae of the measures introduced in 1968; he concluded that the rate of appearance of new cases of opioid dependence declined, that the rise in deaths among opioid users became less pronounced, that some patients were guided into abstention from drugs while others were enabled to lead more stable lives, and that expertise and data on drug usage became more readily obtainable. Yet unfortunately the supplies of methadone from clinics were accompanied by a considerable increase in deaths from overdose of methadone between 1965 and 1969; the majority of deaths were accidental, rather

Table 12. Narcotic dependent persons known to the Home Office as receiving notifiable drugs on prescription at 31 December.

Year	Male	Female	Total	Therapeutic origin	Professional classes (medical or allied)
1969	1067	399	1466	247	26
1970	1051	375	1426	231	26
1971	1133	416	1549	218	22
1972	1209	408	1617	180	23
1973	1370	446	1816	177	14
1974	1458	509	1967	205	11
1975	1438	511	1949	206	8
1976	1387	487	1874	196	8
1977	1466	550	2016	180	10
1978	1703	699	2402	163	9
1979	1892	774	2666	168	5
1980	2009	837	2846	154	5
1981	2732	1112	3844	141	4
1982	3124	1247	4371	127	5

Note: From 1969 new recording procedures made it possible to give details of persons known on a specific date (the last day) of each year.

than suicidal; many were associated with loss of tolerance developed by the subjects during periods of abstention (Gardner, 1970). Although the number of new opioid users notified to the Home Office in the 1970s expanded slightly each year (to 926 in 1975), the total number known to official records remained almost static, at just under 2000 (*Table* 12). The proportion known to be in receipt of heroin, with or without methadone, dropped to 18% by the end of 1974. The alarming rate of rise in opioid misuse during the middle 1960s was therefore checked for the time being, though several features other than the work of special clinics contributed to the amelioration. Restrictive measures like the newfound legal inability of all but a few doctors to prescribe heroin to persons dependent on the drug, vigorous police and customs activity, and the flexible provisions of the 1971 Misuse of Drugs Act were all factors of crucial importance. Explanations of temporal alterations in the incidence of drug misuse must also consider changing fashions and attitudes concerning drug usage.

The advent of the 1980s saw a further upsurge of opioid consumption in many countries, including the United Kingdom. The rise took the form of an increase of illicit heroin imported from Asia. The practice of prescribing opioids had failed in one of its aims, which was to provide a prophylactic alternative to an illicit drug market. The Advisory Council on the Misuse of Drugs published a report on treatment and rehabilitation which drew attention to the deteriorating situation and made many recommendations (Advisory Council, 1982). The proposals included multidisciplinary therapeutic teams, counselling services that might be combined with day centres, increased provision of voluntary services and hostels, the development of training arrangements, and further research into treatment techniques.

The official statistics in Britain were favourably outlined by Johnson (1975). In contrast, Smart and Ogbourne (1974) found that 46·3% of patients attending an opioid clinic in London were not notified to the Home Office, while Bishop et al. (1976) reported that 64% of intravenous drug misusers whom they studied in Bristol were unnotified. The data under-report the number of persons who consume opioids and cocaine, and provide little information (other than police convictions) about the extent of misuse and dependence on other substances. It is significant that a survey of 62 casualty departments in Greater London uncovered as many as 1706 patients in one month with drug problems (Ghodse, 1976). Sixteen per cent of the subjects were definitely dependent on drugs and 12% were probably dependent; barbiturate dependence was common among the patients although this condition is not notifiable. The Department of Health and the Home Office recognize the incomplete nature of the official figures. It is fair to point out that the data, despite their acknowledged imperfections, provide a useful means of monitoring trends that is not available in many countries.

Although the Home Office keeps a list of known narcotic users there is no official 'register'. Contrary to a frequent misconception the category of 'registered addict', which is believed to give a patient an entitlement to drugs, does not exist. Information is quickly supplied in confidence by the Home Office to doctors about individuals, in order to assist in clinical decisions about treatment. But it should be realized that doctors who take a special interest in drug dependence are free to treat as they see fit. Appropriate treatment often includes the refusal to prescribe to an outpatient.

METHADONE MAINTENANCE

Long-term chemotherapy with the synthetic opioid methadone was introduced for the treatment of heroin dependence in the middle 1960s (Dole and Nyswander, 1965; Dole et al., 1966). Methadone main-- tenance is claimed to possess several advantages over a policy of avoiding prescriptions of opioids to outpatients.

1. Methadone in adequate dosage suppresses withdrawal symptoms from deprivation of other opioids. A legal supply of methadone reduces the reliance on illicit drugs of the opioid-dependent persons; the supply checks criminal behaviour required to obtain drugs or to obtain the money or valuables to purchase drugs.
2. Methadone withdrawal symptoms do not appear until 24 hours after consumption of the drug; by contrast heroin withdrawal

features begin within 3–4 hours of taking heroin. In distinction from heroin the drug user who receives methadone does not need to take the drug several times a day, and his state of well-being is on a more level equilibrium.

3. Again unlike heroin, methadone is effective when orally consumed. The patient does not need injections, which possess an intense euphoric effect, other psychological attractions and physical risks.

4. In high dosage (80–120 mg daily) methadone blocks the euphoric effect of heroin so that there is no advantage to the subject if the latter substance is also taken.

5. Patients who are maintained on the methadone may evolve a more stable life style and develop no fresh physical complications. It is claimed that they incur less convictions, improve their morale, and form better marital and occupational adjustments (U.S. Department of Justice, 1973).

6. It was hoped that methadone programmes would curb the drug market, reduce the number of new recruits to illegal drug usage, check crime and reduce welfare costs (U.S. Department of Justice, 1973).

A doctor who is contemplating the treatment of a patient by methadone maintenance should not start until it is clear that the subject's dependence on opioids is well established. Otherwise dependence will be aggravated or initiated in some persons whose opioid usage has been brief and sporadic (Gardner and Connell, 1970), and the risk is increased of diversion of prescribed methadone to the illicit market. Assessment of the chronicity of opioid usage is checked by several methods. The patient's story is appraised; information is gathered from other sources such as hospital records or a central list of drug users (in Britain the Home Office supplies information to treatment clinics from a national list); the patient is examined for injection track marks, recent needle marks, and for withdrawal features; urine tests are performed for morphine, which is a metabolite of heroin. The clinician will bear in mind that needle marks can be simulated by pins, withdrawal symptoms may be feigned, and opioids purposefully taken before urine sampling by an individual who does not consume them regularly.

A diagnostic test that has been employed in the United States involves the administration of an opioid antagonist; in the presence of physical dependence on opioid the test precipitates withdrawal features. The most suitable antagonistic drug is naloxone (Blachley, 1973). Before naloxone is given notes are made of pupil size and of pilo-erection on the chest, of sweating, rhinorrhoea, lacrimation and yawning. A dose of 160 micrograms (0·4 ml) of naloxone hydrochloride is given intramuscularly. If pilo-erection does not develop within 20–30 minutes the drug is repeated, this time intravenously in a dose of 240 micrograms

(0·6 ml); withdrawal signs are then sought 15 minutes later. The combination of pilo-erection, papillary dilatation and sweating is especially indicative of the abstinence syndrome from opioid dependence. In the process of giving the injections the diagnostician should take precautions against infection with hepatitis B virus from the patient's blood. The safety measures include wearing plastic or rubber gloves, application of a fresh solution of an effectual disinfectant to traces of spilt blood, and collection in a bag for later incineration of the needles, syringes and swabs that were employed.

If it is decided to proceed with methadone supplies the drug is dispensed in a liquid form that renders injection difficult or impossible. It is difficult to justify the prescription of ampoules intended for injection; tablets should not be given for oral use as they can be crushed and injected in water.

Opioid-tolerant persons are able to take larger amounts of methadone than the dosages employed in the treatment of pain or cough. A daily dosage of 35–60 mg is usually sufficient to control withdrawal symptoms and is generally adequate. The dose can be raised as high as 120 mg in a day if there are genuine abstinence features or if it is thought desirable to ensure that the drug blocks the euphoric effect of heroin experimentation by the patient. At first methadone is taken daily in a clinic or dispensed each day at a pharmacy; for the weekends arrangements are made for the issue of 2 days' supply on Saturday and none on Sunday. The issue of methadone to cover longer periods than the above runs the risk of the patient rapidly consuming (or distributing) the supply and returning early to request more. However, when the subject is stabilized on a methadone regime and has established mutual rapport and trust with the staff it may be feasible to extend each issue to cover 3 or more days.

Urine surveillance forms part of the programme. The urine is tested for methadone (to ensure that the patient is consuming the drug), and for morphine (to assess whether the subject is taking this substance or heroin, which is rapidly metabolized to morphine and excreted as such). Urine is also examined for other drugs of misuse, particularly barbiturates and amphetamines.

Pentazocine (Fortral, Talwin) is an opioid with both agonistic and antagonistic properties. Although this drug is itself dependence-producing it can precipitate withdrawal features in a person physically dependent on opioids. Pentazocine therefore should not be administered for a medical or surgical condition if the patient is on a methadone regime. If the subject is misusing alcohol, it is safe to combine methadone with disulfiram when the latter drug is indicated as a deterrent against drinking (Charuvastra et al., 1976; Tong et al., 1980).

Some patients continue methadone therapy indefinitely, but those who have been stabilized for several months should receive consideration as candidates for withdrawal of the substance with a view to leading a drug-free life. The goal is discussed and agreed with the patient. Hospital administration may then be arranged for a phased reduction of methadone. Alternatively, more gradual detoxification can take place on an outpatient basis over a period that lasts several weeks or months.

If a supply of methadone is undertaken it should form only one aspect of a therapy programme that develops rapport between patients and staff. It is important to foster reciprocal respect and loyalty; the clients can then receive counselling on relevant psychosocial problems and are encouraged to lead a more settled mode of existence. Some methadone treatment programmes—especially those caring for ethnic minorities— are staffed in the U.S.A. by persons who adopt and favour a life style at variance with conventional norms, but usually staff guide their clients towards employment, enduring family ties and further education.

Objections to methadone maintenance

The treatment is controversial and subject to several adverse criticisms:

1. Some prescribed methadone is distributed illegally.
2. Many patients on legal methadone complement their approved issues by taking illicit drugs.
3. A purpose of methadone maintenance is the abatement of large scale illegal distribution of heroin. Anticriminal activity is not a professional duty of doctors and allied staff, and is not a traditional reason for placing a patient on 'treatment'.
4. Methadone maintenance programmes have failed to reduce the illicit circulation of heroin.
5. As indicated below the efficacy of methadone programmes in achieving other goals is uncertain.
6. Doctors, nurses and other professionals entered their occupations to cure or alleviate the disorders they encounter; methadone maintenance continues the condition it is supposed to treat.
7. Many of the arguments put forward in favour of prescribing an opioid drug apply also to barbiturates, amphetamines and hallucinogens, yet it is generally and correctly considered unwise to issue these kinds of drug to persons who have been taking them illicitly.

Evaluation

Items for consideration in estimating the success of a methadone programme include the proportion of patients who remain in treatment, their continuance of illicit drug use, further criminal convictions, marital adjustment, personality functioning, employment, morbidity and mortality rates. There has been a multiplicity of studies that report an improvement in psychosocial adjustment among their subjects after the commencement of maintenance therapy. Many of the studies lack proper control groups and are therefore inadequate; they have been reviewed by Gossop (1978). A controlled investigation from Hong Kong compared heroin users who were randomly assigned to methadone or placebo (Newman and Whitehall, 1979); those who received methadone were more likely to remain in treatment and reduce their criminal conviction rate than the placebo controls, but the investigators were unable to compare the effects on family stability, working capacity and physical and mental health. A large United States study found that persons who had been taking heroin at least once daily achieved better than expected adjustment from methadone maintenance; they also gained similar benefit from treatment in drug-free therapeutic communities (Sells and Simpson, 1980). On the other hand, another U.S. investigation revealed no advantages in regard to social adjustment, employment status, or self-esteem, and reported that 44% of the subjects who were given methadone later received convictions for criminal offences (Anderson and Nutter, 1975). Wiepert and colleagues (1979) described their own and other British studies which revealed an increase of drug offences among subjects who were prescribed opioids. Paxton and coworkers (1978) in Scotland did not find that methadone was necessary to keep patients in treatment. A review of the various forms of treatment has considered that the differences in client characteristics precluded comparison of results, but noted a trend in the United States away from methadone maintenance towards drug-free therapies (Singh et al., 1982). The author approves this trend as a move towards a wider and more constructive range of treatments, and hopes it will continue in those countries that have chosen to employ maintenance therapy.

Conclusions on methadone maintenance

Many doctors lack either the conviction or the facilities to include methadone maintenance in their armamentarium of therapies; they are sceptical of its value or aware that if they utilize the treatment they will attract numbers of manipulating and untruthful individuals in search of the clinic that is most generous with prescriptions. Other therapists take the view that the careful use of the treatment promotes a constructive therapeutic relationship; they consider (although it has not been systematically proved) that in fully staffed centres methadone therapy augments the spontaneous improvement rate among subjects beyond the improvement level that occurs with age and with duration of opioid dependence. The viewpoints are antithetic; their proponents are not personally antipathetic.

It can be agreed that maintenance treatment should not be employed in an attempt to provide a legal supply of drugs that would reduce illicit drug circulation. Competitive prescribing of this nature favours the general good of society against the needs of individual patients who are led by the method to persist with drug use; the Utilitarian philosophy formulated by Bentham and Mill of 'promoting the greatest good of the greatest number' has been discountenanced as inhumane. Furthermore, the practice simply has not worked. It is important that therapists who prescribe on a long term basis to drug users should allow their decisions to be influenced solely by clinical judgements on their patients and not at all by the claims of public policy (Edwards, 1978; 1979).

Levo-alpha-acetymethadol

Methadone maintenance programmes usually require the patient to attend a clinic or pharmacist daily to consume or collect the drug. The alternative of allowing the subject to take away more than one day's supply has several risks: it favours the diversion of opioid to the black market; it enhances the possibility of accidental overdoses; and it encourages a premature return of the patient with the claim that the supply has been rapidly consumed or lost and that additional amounts are needed to relieve withdrawal symptoms. When patients have received daily methadone for a period the relationship they develop with the staff of the clinic often suffices to prevent such disadvantages. But an alternative would lie in the use of an opioid that has a more prolonged duration of action.

l-alpha-acetylmethadol (acetylmethadol, LAAM) is a long-acting methadone analogue that has been employed in the United States for oral use in a maintenance schedule. The preparation can be dispensed every 72 hours (Lehmann, 1975); the drug has also been issued 3 times a week as a phase in a sequential system of prescribed drugs that began with daily methadone and progressed through acetylmethadol to narcotic antagonists (Goldstein, 1976). A comparison of thrice weekly acetylmethadol with daily methadone reported that the heroin users who were given acetylmethadol developed significantly less illicit drug consumption and remained longer in treatment than those who were given methadone (Freedman and Czertko, 1981). The efficacy of acetylmethadol awaits full evaluation, but the drug offers advantages of convenience to patients and staff from its low frequency of dispensing.

ADJUNCTS IN TREATMENT

Opioid antagonists

The euphoric effects of heroin or morphine are almost completely inapparent if the drug user is taking an opioid antagonist. The antagonists naloxone, naltrexone and cyclazocine have been employed in the United States as prolonged therapy to prevent relapses among opioid-dependent persons who have undergone detoxification.

Naloxone might be considered the most advantageous antagonist as it lacks concomitant agonistic effects and since its withdrawal is unaccompanied by abstinence features. But the required dose is large (2–3 g daily by mouth) and the duration of action of the drug is too brief for practical purposes.

Cyclazocine has received more extensive employment. Withdrawal of cyclazocine produces minor abstinence symptoms, but physical dependence on the drug has not led to its misuse (World Health Organisation, 1975). During the early stages of administration of cyclazocine unpleasant effects can develop, consisting of slowing of thought, motor inco-ordination, irritability, or hallucinations; the undesirable clinical features can be minimized by slow induction onto the drug. After ensuring that the patient is not physically dependent on opioids, oral cyclazocine is started at a level of 250 micrograms twice daily; the dosage is raised by 250 micrograms daily up to 4 mg in a day. When the daily dosage passes 1·0–1·5 mg a single dose in the day can be employed. The patient is warned not to give the drug to opioid-using friends in case it precipitates serious abstinence features in them.

Naltrexone is longer acting. Although its daily use is feasible, Goldstein (1976) recommends its administration in an oral dose of 120 mg three times a week. Naltrexone possesses slight opioid agonistic features; yawning, stretching and a stimulant effect on thought and speech have also been noted (Martin et al., 1973). But naltrexone produces troublesome side effects less frequently than cyclazocine, and is the drug that offers the greater expectations for development in clinical practice.

Long-term therapy by opioid antagonists is not utilized in Britain. In the U.S.A. the treatment is less popular with opioid users than methadone maintenance, though volunteers for therapy by an opioid antagonist do not commonly challenge its blocking effect by taking heroin. As currently employed, treatment with opioid antagonists is expensive. Further studies are required which would compare the results of opioid antagonists and other therapies in regard to illicit drug use, criminal behaviour, and general psychological and social adjustment. Naltrexone is the most promising agent (National Research Council, 1978). Studies have taken place on the development of a clinically useful sustained-release preparation that would consist of a depot injection or implant of naltrexone (Willette and Barnet, 1981).

Abstinence syndrome suppressants without dependence liability

Alpha$_2$-adrenergic blocking drugs have been employed to counteract withdrawal features; they are not subject to the risk of dependence. Drugs of this category interact with presynaptic receptors for noradrenaline and thus, by a negative feedback process, reduce noradrenergic activity. Gold and coworkers (1978, 1979) have hypothesized that repeated opioid administration replicates and thereby decreases endogenous opioid activity, including inhibition by endogenous opioids of the central noradrenergic activity that arises mainly from the locus coeruleus of the brain stem. According to the hypothesis, abrupt cessation of chronic intake of an opioid drug, in the presence of a lowered level of endogenous opioid action, releases rebound hyperactivity of noradrenergic function within the central nervous system. Clonidine and lofexidine are alpha$_2$-adrenergic blocking drugs that are capable of suppressing noradrenergic overactivity during opioid withdrawal. Gold and his team have employed clonidine for this purpose.

Cardiovascular patients who were given clonidine to relieve hypertension have undergone hypertensive crises when the drug was withdrawn (Hunyor et al., 1973; Yudkin, 1977); this dangerous effect may not ensue in the treatment of drug dependence. During administration of the drug, hypotension can occur that may limit its usefulness, but the drug offers a useful alternative to methadone. Recommended amounts range from 200–800 micrograms daily in divided doses; after 5–10 days, the drug is gradually discontinued.

It is likely that further developments will take place in the evolution of pharmacological treatments that relieve withdrawal symptoms yet do not themselves promote dependence.

Acupuncture

The use of acupuncture in the treatment of disease is a traditional Chinese technique. It is based on the outmoded philosophical concept that the cosmos contains two opposing forces which are in equal balance; the Chinese derived from the concept a pathophysiology that considered illness to arise from imbalance of the two forces in the body. The insertion and rapid rotation of needles at particular points through the skin was believed to restore equilibrium between the forces; each point was viewed as specific for a symptom or group of symptoms.

The theory that lay behind acupuncture is of course unacceptable, but there is no doubt that the procedure inhibits the perception of pain to a remarkable degree. With the help of acupuncture it is possible to undergo childbirth and major surgery painlessly and without other means of analgesia or anaesthesia. Although the physiological and psychological effects on the nervous system have not been elucidated, the technique is arousing a growing interest in Western medicine. Recent refinements consist of the insertion of a surgical staple which can be left in the skin for as long as 3 months, and in the replacement of rotation by a mild electric current passed through the acupuncture needle or the staple.

It is perhaps not surprising that the therapy was first employed for heroin dependence in Hong Kong, which is a city that has a severe heroin problem and is situated at the crossroads of influences from mainland China and the Occident. In 1972 Dr H. L. Wen, a Hong Kong neurosurgeon, noted that acupuncture relieved the pains and other symptoms of heroin withdrawal. The point selected for insertion of the needle lies in the concha of the ear. He also considered that acupuncture counteracts the desire to resume heroin; subjects who have been withdrawn are therefore invited to return to an outpatient clinic for further acupuncture treatment.

The therapy has since spread to some drug-dependence centres in other countries. It has been used, though not extensively, in Thailand, Laos, Mauritius, the United States and England. Bourne (1975) described the work of the centres which practice acupuncture; he judged that the procedure does have value in the relief of opioid withdrawal symptoms, but that its efficacy in the prevention of relapse into opioid consumption is not established.

Both classic acupuncture and the related technique of low-frequency electrical stimulation by surface electrodes increase the pain threshold. The analgesia produced by these procedures is counteracted by the opioid antagonist naloxone. Clement-Jones and colleagues (1979) recorded low levels of met-enkephalin in the cerebrospinal fluid of heroin users, and the relief of withdrawal symptoms by electro-acupuncture. Sjölund and Eriksson (1976) have suggested that the analgesia is mediated by inhibitory neural mechanisms which release endogenous morphine-like substances; they noted that the analgesia produced by hypnosis is not influenced by naloxone. It is therefore possible that acupuncture has a physical effect in the central nervous system, although some doctors hold that its results are wholly psychological and arise from the beliefs and expectations of patients and therapists.

When acupuncture is employed to treat intravenous drug injectors precautions should be taken against the spread of hepatitis-B virus. In particular, if a needle or staple is used each should be reserved for exclusive use with one patient.

Transcendental meditation

The practice of transcendental meditation (TM) evolved within the spiritual disciplines of India. In recent years it has spread to other countries where it is employed, not necessarily for spiritual insight, but in the hope of gaining a tranquil outlook on life. Variations of technique are found, though in general TM involves the following procedures: (1) the silent repetition of a word or sound known as a 'Mantra'; (2) concentration on the Mantra to the exclusion of distracting thoughts; (3) muscular relaxation, adopted by sitting in a relaxed position. In the U.S.A. followers of TM are encouraged to practise the technique for 15–20 minutes twice a day.

Because traditional treatments of drug misuse are not as successful as might be desired, and because TM offers for occidental cultures a novel routine to internal calm, the search for tension-relieving alternatives to drug consumption has led to the advocacy of TM. Shafi and colleagues (1974) found that a significantly higher proportion of meditators decreased or discontinued marihuana consumption compared with subjects in a control group who did not practise meditation. There are other comparable reports of diminished drug use by meditators, and of the employment of TM as treatment for drug dependence (Bourne, 1975). The technique has also been adopted for the treatment of alcohol dependence.

In regard to drug consumption the readiness of the subjects to decrease or renounce drug intake must contribute to the results. Persons in the community who wish to attend a training course on TM are often required to abstain from non-prescribed drugs for a fortnight before initiation; presumably those who are unwilling or unable to meet this requirement are less likely to attend. The same proviso applies to drug-dependent subjects in treatment: they would not undertake a practice which is intended to lower their drug usage unless they had some desire to attain this end. Of course, the difficulties that motivation for recovery presents in the assessment of the therapeutic value of transcendental meditation apply to the other therapies that are employed for drug misuse and dependence.

Self-help groups

Organizations exist that are composed of recovering drug users or of families of drug users. Narcotics Anonymous can be likened to Alcoholics Anonymous; similarly Families Anonymous may be compared with Al-Anon. Families Anonymous caters for relatives who are confronted with a wide range of difficulties: drug experimentation, drug dependence, under-achievement, juvenile delinquency and associated behavioural problems.

Self-help organizations for drug users and for relatives provide a potential source of advice and support which therapists can employ for their clients. Voluntary organizations of this nature have been founded in many countries, albeit their presence is not always well known. It is hoped that they will expand their activities and memberships.

OUTCOME OF DRUG MISUSE AND DEPENDENCE

There are many criteria utilized in the assessment of outcome. They include substance use: of drugs, of excess alcohol, or of heroin in subjects receiving methadone maintenance. Urinalysis for drugs is a feature of certain follow-up studies. Convictions and hospital admissions provide information on progress that is obtainable from official records. Several researches have scored success more highly if the clients remain in a long-term programme of care. Working capacity is relevant; so also, (though they are harder to gauge) are interpersonal adjustment and psychological wellbeing. Most studies have employed abstinence from all drugs as one criterion of progress, but several reports of methadone maintenance programmes have rated success if the subject remains in the programme, taking methadone but abstinent from heroin.

The majority of people who experimentally try an illicit drug or drugs are not harmed by the procedure. Those who become repeated drug misusers do not necessarily develop dependence, and if they do the dependence may be temporary, recurrent or prolonged. But since the greater number of reports on the outcome of drug misuse and dependence have concentrated on opioid dependence it is appropriate to consider first several of the more important studies of this condition.

Robins et al. (1975) investigated opioid consumption that took place amongst U.S. soldiers during and after the sojourn of the subjects in Vietnam. Among a general sample of 898 army personnel 43% had consumed opioids in Vietnam; one-third of those who had taken an opioid tried heroin, one-third used opium, and one-third took both preparations. The preferred method for each substance was smoking, though the incidence of heroin injection rose with prolonged use. Forty-six per cent of the subjects who took opioids became dependent; that is, 21% of the soldiers developed opioid dependence during their operational tour. After return, opioid usage essentially decreased to pre-Vietnam levels. Eleven per cent had taken opioids before Vietnam, compared with 10% after return; 1% of the soldiers showed symptoms of dependence after returning from Vietnam. In a subgroup of soldiers who were dependent at the time of leaving Vietnam only 14% remained dependent when interviewed 8 to 12 months later. Continued opioid intake was related to the injection of heroin and to opioid usage in Vietnam for more than 6 months. A further study of Vietnam veterans has been completed by O'Brien and colleagues (1980); the investigation encountered similar results in respect of the frequency and transience of opioid consumption among the military personnel.

The Vietnam findings are unique in the wide extent and short duration of opioid usage and dependence; environment factors played a strong role in determining opioid consumption in Vietnam and its discontinuance on return. Many of the soldiers were essentially stable; the studies illustrate how the drug usage of normal individuals can be affected by the availability of drugs and by social pressures to develop or discontinue their consumption.

In Britain the progress of all heroin dependent persons who were known to the Home Office between 1955 and 1964 was evaluated in the latter year (Bewley, 1965). Fifty-seven subjects were recognized in 1954 and 450 new cases were added in the following 10 years; 327 continued to take heroin throughout the surveyed period; 42 had died. A comparable study was conducted of 1272 heroin dependents who became known to the Home Office between 1947 and 1966 (Bewley et al., 1968); 35 had become dependent during medical treatment. Sixty-nine of the 1237 non-therapeutic subjects had died;

their mortality rate of 27 per 1000 per annum was 28 times the normal demographic rate. The mortality amounted to 1 death per year for every 37 subjects; the U.S.A. rate for death among heroin users was 10 per 1000 per annum, and so was considerably lower than the mortality revealed at that time by the British study.

A follow-up report has been issued on 86 injectors of drugs (mostly opioids) in a provincial town in England (Rathod, 1975); as a policy no opioids were prescribed except to cover withdrawal for inpatients. Five patients died; 11 ceased to use any illicit drug; 17 stopped injecting; the remainder continued to inject, sporadically or more continuously. During the follow-up period 10 subjects consumed alcohol in a way which caused harm. None of the 33 drug injectors who moved away from the town and received opioid maintenance prescriptions elsewhere showed an improvement. Favourable factors were a short duration to the practice of injection, marriage during the follow-up term to a non-injector, and a low index of social deviancy.

The outcome of 66 opioid-dependent females in Britain was assessed after 4 years by d'Orbán (1974). Ten (15%) had died; 21 (32%) were receiving opioids at clinics; 24 (36%) became abstinent from opioids; the course of the remainder was uncertain. Abstinence was inversely related to the number of previous convictions, but bore no association with the other variables that were studied.

British and United States studies lead to the conclusion that abstinence rates for opioid users known to be alive after 5 years lie approximately between 20 and 30% (Chappel et al., 1972; O'Donnell, 1969). A 5-year follow-up report of 1359 heroin users discharged from the Lexington Federal Hospital to New York City revealed that 36% of those aged over 30 were voluntarily abstaining outside institutions; the percentage of voluntary abstainers dropped to 21% among subjects aged under 30 (Duvall et al., 1963).

Length of dependence and the concomitant factor of age are important variables for outcome. Subjects who enter curative (not methadone maintenance) programmes within a few months of the onset of dependence have reasonable prospects of recovery. Those with a longer period of opioid consumption are less likely to become abstinent, but a proportion 'burn out' from active opioid use after a number of years. The concept of spontaneous maturation from opioid dependence was first proposed by Winick (1962) in the United States; he found that subjects who were over 30 years of age or who were using heroin for more than 10 years relapsed less frequently than younger drugtakers with a less prolonged duration of heroin consumption. The finding is similar to the natural diminution of sociopathic trends and of immature EEG rhythms that occurs in persons of antisocial disposition, and is reminiscent of the ability of many criminal recidivists to remain out of prison after the approach of middle age.

The inference that many opioid-dependent persons mature out of their dependence has been a point of dispute. Vaillant (1973) considered that the concept of maturation has been over-optimistic, and was derived in the United States only from data available to the Federal Bureau of Narcotics. In his lengthy study many subjects were actively dependent on heroin for 5 or more years without being reported to the Bureau. Vaillant followed up for 20 years 100 New York heroin-dependent subjects; 35–45% achieved stable abstinence from illicit opioids; 25% remained actively dependent on illicit opioids; 20% had an uncertain drug status, and 23% were dead. About half of the deaths were directly from opioid usage. The stages at which stable abstinence began attained peaks after 5–6 years of dependence and at ages 26–28, but abstinence was noted among the subjects at any duration of heroin usage and at any age. Good outcome was associated with regular employment before first hospital admission, and with stable human relationships. Admission to hospital, or imprisonment without later supervision, were both ineffective; prison followed by parole was of value in the production of abstinence. Methadone maintenance was also helpful in keeping subjects away from illicit opioids, particularly when it accompanied compulsory supervision on parole or licence.

On the other hand, lengthy follow-up studies have been published which demonstrate that a considerable proportion of opioid users become drug free. The observation has been encountered in the U.S.A. (Stephens and Cottrell, 1972), in Hong Kong (Singer, 1975), and in Britain. There are two British studies that assessed drug-taking subjects after 10 years. The first of the reports from Britain traced most of its clients; 15% were dead (equivalent to a rate of 14·8 deaths per 1000 heroin users yearly); 41% remained dependent on opioids; 38% were out of hospital or prison and were either known to be drug free or did not generate information to suggest relapse (Stimson and Oppenheimer, 1982). The study found that abstinence was often initiated by an improvement in social circumstances, such as a stable relationship with a person of the opposite sex; initially abstinence might be accompanied by a phase of high alcohol or cannabis consumption, but the period of alternative substance misuse was transitory. The other 10 year follow-up study from Britain traced all its subjects; although 18·3% had died, during the final 5 years of the period only 20% took drugs while 61·7% abstained (Gordon, 1983). The latter report encountered perhaps an unusually high proportion of recoveries. The investigations would not claim that favourable outcomes among their drug users arose because of therapy.

A survey from Britain of drug-dependent doctors and nurses who had been treated in hospital provides a suitable bridge to the consideration of outcome in a fuller range of psychoactive drugs. There were 65 subjects. Fifteen could not be traced. Of the remainder only 4 of the 38 who had been continuously taking opioids abstained after leaving, while 10 of the

22 persons who were dependent on other substances avoided drugs after discharge (Clark, 1962).

Haastrup (1973) has reviewed several Scandinavian follow-up studies; the investigations are especially worthy of attention because they embraced a wide variety of misused drugs. One of the reports assessed the progress of intravenous amphetamine users who had been hospitalized in Sweden for serum hepatitis; none received psychiatric treatment while in hospital. At the end of 3 years 35% were abstinent; the abstinent rate rose to 45% after 5 years. The figures give an indication of the spontaneous course of intravenous amphetamine usage in Sweden. A Norwegian report that was reviewed by Haastrup examined patients who had become drug-dependent in the course of medical treatment. The investigation found that the following features were positively correlated with a favourable outcome to therapy for drug usage: stability of personality and of social adjustment, satisfactory childhood environment, age under 30 years, absence of an alcohol problem, short period of drug usage, and an adequate stay in hospital for treatment of drug dependence. In the study from Norway outcome was unrelated to education, marital status, or desire to enter hospital.

In Denmark an assessment has been conducted of young drug-taking patients 3 years after hospital treatment (Haastrup, 1973). The study allowed grouping of unfavourable prognostic factors among the subjects into categories:

1. **Childhood circumstances.**
   Broken home.
   Childhood home of social class V (unskilled labour).
   More than 3 months' stay in an institution.
   Siblings with social difficulties.
2. **Personal features before onset of therapy.**
   Started tobacco when aged under 13.
   Left school before age of 15.
   Less than 1½ years' occupation during the previous 3 years.
   Mostly out of work during the previous 2 months.
   Living with other drug misusers for more than 1 week.
3. **Nature of drug usage.**
   More than 100 injections (a number of the patients injected amphetamines only, and had never taken opioids).
   Opioid consumption for more than 1 week.
4. **Aspects of admission and discharge.**
   Not motivated for help at time of admission.
   No expectations from inpatient treatment.
   Discharged without employment.

Summary of outcome in drug misuse and dependence

Despite some contradictions the reports on outcome permit the following conclusions:

1. Drug dependence, especially on opioids, lowers life expectancy, yet most drug-dependent persons are alive after lengthy periods of follow-up.
2. Abstinence can ensue at any time, but more readily develops among those who have been using drugs for only a short phase.
3. Non-injectors of drugs are more likely to improve than drug injectors.
4. Improvement is positively correlated with the degree of social integration that the drug user has established and preserved. A satisfactory outcome is favoured by sustained contact with relatives and with acquaintances who do not use drugs, by minimal convictions and by possession of a job.
5. The development of abstinence from drugs is generally associated with improvement in other psychosocial spheres of adjustment.
6. But the association between abstinence and improvement in other areas of function is not invariable. Some abstinent subjects remain unemployed, or psychologically distressed, or have difficulties with interpersonal relationships. A brief or lengthy period of alcohol misuse is not uncommon after drug cessation.
7. There is a tendency for opioid-dependent persons to mature out of drug usage; approximately 40% of opioid users are abstinent by the end of 10 years. The proportion of recoveries is sufficient to counteract the pessimism that sometimes pervades professionals and drug users.
8. Neither indiscriminate admission to psychiatric units, nor prison sentences, have proved therapeutic value. There is more likelihood of benefit from the provision of care to outpatients and to co-operative inpatients, from compulsory supervision, and from residence in therapeutic communities.
9. There is a paucity of adequate studies on the results of treatment. The central issue is the task of matching modes of intervention to drug users, of ascertaining which therapies induce benefits in particular circumstances to specific categories of patient or client (Ogbourne, 1980).

It is arguable that a lack of commitment by the statutory health and social agencies has impaired the results of therapy. More knowledge and experience would convince professional persons that substantial numbers of drug users can respond to help. Positive attitudes reduce unease and perplexity when encountering drug takers and favour the ready and effective provision of counselling and other forms of care.

REFERENCES

Advisory Council on the Misuse of Drugs (1982) *Treatment and Rehabilitation.* London, H.M.S.O.

Anderson G. S. and Nutter R. W. (1975) Clients and outcomes of a methadone treatment program. *Int. J. Addict.* **10**, 937–948.

Bewley T. (1965) Heroin addiction in the United Kingdom (1954–1964). *Br. Med. J.* **2**, 1284–1286.

Bewley T. H. (1973) Evaluation of addiction treatment in England. In: Boström H., Larsson T. and Ljungstedt N. (ed.) *Drug Dependence—Treatment and Treatment Evaluation.* Stockholm, Almqvist and Wiksell, p. 275–286.

Bewley T. H., Ben-Arie D. and James I. P. (1968) Morbidity and mortality from heroin dependence. 1. Survey of heroin addicts known to the Home Office, *Br. Med. J.* **1**, 725–726.

Bishop B. P., Cave G. C., Gay M. J. et al. (1976) A city looks at its problem of drug abuse by injection. *Br. J. Psychiatry* **129**, 465–471.

Blachley P. H. (1973) Naloxone for diagnosis in methadone programs. *JAMA* **224**, 334–335.

Blinick G., Jerez E. and Wallach R. O. (1973) Methadone maintenance, pregnancy and progeny. *JAMA* **225**, 477–479.

Bourne P. G. (1975) New and innovative techniques in the treatment of drug abuse. In: *Proceedings of the 31st International Congress on Alcoholism and Drug Dependence.* Lausanne, International Council on Alcohol and Addictions, pp. 40–51.

Brill L. and Jaffe J. H. (1967) The relevancy of some newer American treatment approaches for England. *Br. J. Addict.* **62**, 375–386.

Chappel J. N. (1977) Physician attitudes: effect on the treatment of chemically dependent patients. *JAMA* **237**, 2318–2319.

Chapple P. A. L., Someckh D. E. and Taylor M. E. (1972) Follow-up of cases of opiate addiction. 1. General findings and a suggested method of staging. *Br. J. Addict.* **67**, 33–38.

Charuvastra C. V., Panell J., Hopper M. et al. (1976) The medical safety of the combined usage of disulfiram and methadone. *Arch. Gen. Psychiatry* **33**, 391–393.

Clark J. A. (1962) The prognosis in drug addiction. *J. Ment Sci.* **108**, 411–418.

Clement-Jones V., McLoughlin L., Lowry P. J. et al. (1979) Acupuncture in heroin addicts: changes in met-enkephalin and β-endorphin in blood and cerebrospinal fluid. *Lancet* **ii**, 380–382.

Collier W. V. and Hijazi Y. A. (1974) A follow-up study of former residents of a therapeutic community. *Int. J. Addict.* **9**, 805–826.

Dalton M. S. and Duncan D. W. (1975) Drug dependent doctors. In: *Proceedings of the 31st International Congress on Alcoholism and Drug Dependence.* Lausanne, International Council on Alcohol and Addictions, pp. 292–293.

De Leon G., Wexler H. K. and Jainchill N. (1982) The therapeutic community; success and improvement rates after 5 years of treatment. *Int. J. Addict.* **17**, 403–407.

Dole V. P. and Nyswander M. E. (1965) A medical treatment for diacetylmorphine (heroin) addiction. *JAMA* **193** 646–650.

Dole V. P., Nyswander M. E. and Kreek M. J. (1966) Narcotic blockade: a medical technique for stopping heroin use by addicts. *Arch. Intern. Med.* **118**, 304–309.

d'Orbán P. T. (1974) A follow-up study of female narcotic addicts: variables related to outcome. *Br. J. Addict.* **124**, 28–33.

Duvall H. J., Locke B. Z. and Brill L. (1963) Follow-up study of narcotic drug addicts five years after hospitalization. *Public Health Rep.* **78**, 185–193.

Edwards G. (1978) Some years on. Evolutions in the 'British System'. In: West D. J. (ed.). *Problems of Drug Abuse in Britain.* Cambridge, Institute of Criminology, pp. 1–45.

Edwards G. (1979) British policies on opiate addiction: ten years working of the revised response, and options for the future. *Br. J. Psychiatry* **134**, 1–13.

Fraser A. C. (1976) Drug addiction in pregnancy. *Lancet* **ii**, 896–899.

Freedman R. R. and Czertko G. (1981) A comparison of thrice weekly LAAM and daily methadone in employed heroin addicts. *Drug Alcohol Depend* **8**, 215–222.

Gardner R. (1970) Death in United Kingdom opioid users 1965–1969. *Lancet* **ii**, 650–653.

Gardner R. and Connell P. H. (1970) One year's experience in a drug dependence clinic. *Lancet* **ii**, 455–458.

Ghodse A. H. (1976) Drug problems dealt with by 62 London casualty departments. A preliminary report. *Br. J. Prev. Soc. Med.* **30**, 251–256.

Glass L., Evans H. E. and Rajegowda B. K. (1975) Neonatal narcotic withdrawal. In: Richter R. W. (ed.) *Medical Aspects of Drug Abuse,* Hagerstown, Maryland, Harper and Row, pp. 124–133.

Glatt M. M. (1970) Psychotherapy of drug dependence: some theoretical considerations. *Br. J. Addict.* **65**, 51–62.

Gold M. S., Redmond E. Jr. and Kleber H. D. (1978) Clonidine blocks acute opiate-withdrawal symptoms. *Lancet* **ii**, 599–602.

Gold M. S., Redmond E. Jr. and Kleber H. D. (1979) Noradrenergic hyperactivity in opiate withdrawal supported by clonidine reversal of opiate withdrawal. *Am. J. Psychiatry* **136**, 100–101.

Goldstein A. (1976) Heroin addiction: sequential treatment employing pharmacological supports. *Arch. Gen. Psychiatry* **33**, 353–358.

Gordon A. M. (1983) Drugs and delinquency: a ten year follow-up of drug clinic patients. *Br. J. Psychiatry* **142**, 169–173.

Gossop M. (1978) A review of the evidence for methadone maintenance as a treatment for narcotic addiction. *Lancet* **i**, 812–815.

Haastrup S. (1973) The traditional follow-up technique in addiction treatment. In: Boström H., Larsson T. and Ljungstedt N. (ed.) *Drug Dependence—Treatment and Treatment Evaluation.* Stockholm, Almqvist and Wiksell, pp. 237–256.

Harding G. T. (1973) Psychotherapy in the treatment of drug abuse. In: Boström H., Larsson T. and Ljungstedt N. (ed.) *Drug Dependence—Treatment and Treatment Evaluation,* Stockholm, Almqvist and Wiksell, pp. 59–78.

Hunyor S., Hansson L., Harrison T. S. et al. (1973) Effects of clonidine withdrawal: possible mechanisms and suggestions for management. *Br. Med. J.* **2**, 209–211.

Jaffe J. H. (1980) Drug addiction and drug abuse. In: Gilman A. G., Goodman L. S. and Gilman A. (ed.). *The Pharmacological Basis of Therapeutics,* 6th edition. New York, MacMillan, pp. 535–584.

Johnson B. D. (1975) Interpreting official British studies on addiction. *Int. J. Addict.* **10**, 225–230.

Lehmann W. X. (1975) the use of L-alpha-acetylmethadol (LAAM) as compared to methadone in the maintenance and treatment of young heroin addicts. In: *Proceedings of the 31st International Congress on Alcoholism and Drug Dependence.* Lausanne, International Council on Alcohol and Addictions, pp. 799–801.

Liu D. T., Tylden E. and Tukel S. H. (1976) Fetal response to drug withdrawal (Letter.) *Lancet* **ii**, 588.

Martin W. R., Jasinski D. R. and Mansky P. A. (1973) Naltrexone, an antagonist for the treatment of heroin dependence. *Arch. Gen. Psychiatry* **28**, 784–791.

Mayer J. (1972) Treatment of drug addiction: past myths and present problems. *Br. J. Addict.* **67**, 137–142.

Modlin H. C. and Montes A. (1964) Narcotics addiction in physicians. *Am. J. Psychiatry* **121**, 358–365.

National Research Council on Clinical Evaluation of Narcotic Antagonists (1978) Clinical evaluation of naltrexone treatment of opiate-dependent individuals. *Arch. Gen. Psychiatry* **35**, 335–340.

Newman R. G. and Whitehall W. B. (1979) Double-blind comparisons of methadone and placebo maintenance treatments of narcotic addicts in Hong Kong. *Lancet* **ii**, 485–488.

O'Brien W. (1973) The Daytop model for addiction treatment. In: Boström H., Larsson T. and Ljungstedt N. (ed.) *Drug Dependence—Treatment and Treatment Evaluation.* Stockholm, Almqvist and Wiksell, pp. 308–312.

O'Brien C. P., Nace E. P., Mintz J. et al. (1980) Follow-up of Vietnam veterans. I. Relapse to drug use after Vietnam service. *Drug Alcohol Depend.* 5, 333–340.

O'Donnell J. A. (1969) *Narcotic Addicts in Kentucky.* Washington, U.S. Government Printing Office.

Ogbourne A. L. (1980) Controlled evaluative studies of treatment for alcohol and drug abuse. *Acta Psychiatric Scand.* Suppl. 284, 62, 66–76.

Paxton R., Mullin P. and Beattie J. (1978) The effects of methadone maintenance with opioid takers: a review and some findings from one British city. *Br. J. Psychiatry* 132, 473–481.

Pearson M. M. and Little R. B. (1965) The treatment of drug addiction: private experience with 84 addicts. *Am. J. Psychiatry* 122, 164–169.

Rathod N. H. (1975) *Follow Up Study of Narcotic Injectors in a New Town.* London, South West Thames Regional Health Authority.

Report of the Interdepartmental Committee on Drug Addiction (1961) London, H.M.S.O.

Robins L. N., Helzer J. E. and Davis D. H. (1975) Narcotic use in Southeast Asia and afterward: an intensive study of 898 Vietnam returnees. *Arch. Gen. Psychiatry* 32, 955–961.

Romond A. M., Forrest C. K. and Kleber H. D. (1975) Follow-up of participants in a drug dependence therapeutic community. *Arch. Gen. Psychiatry* 32, 369–374.

Second Report of the Interdepartmental Committee on Drug Addiction (1965) London, H.M.S.O.

Sells S. B. and Simpson D. D. (1980) The case for drug abuse effectiveness, based on the DARP research program. *Br. J. Addict.* 75, 117–131.

Shafi M., Lavely R. and Jaffe R. (1974) Meditation and Marijuana. *Am. J. Psychiatry* 131, 60–63.

Singer K. (1975) *The Prognosis of Narcotic Addiction.* London, Butterworths.

Singh B. K., Jue G. W., Lehman W. et al. (1982) A descriptive overview of treatment modalities in federally funded abuse treatment programs. *Int. J. Addict.* 17, 977–1000.

Sjöberg C. (1973) Experiences of certain treatment facilities for addicts in Gothenburg. In: Boström H., Larsson T. and Ljungstedt N. (ed.) *Drug Dependence—Treatment and Treatment Evaluation.* Stockholm, Almqvist and Wiksell, pp. 106–115.

Sjölund B. and Eriksson M. (1976) Electro-acupuncture and endogenous morphines (Letter.) *Lancet* ii, 1085.

Smart R. G. (1976) Outcome studies of therapeutic community and halfway house treatment for addicts. *Int. J. Addict.* 11, 143–159.

Smart R. G. and Ogbourne A. (1974) Losses to the addiction notification system. *Br. J. Addict.* 69, 225–230.

Stephens R. and Cottrell E. (1972) A follow-up study of 200 narcotic addicts committed for treatment under the Narcotic Addict Rehabilitation Act (NARA). *Br. J. Addict.* 67, 45–63.

Stimson G. V. and Oppenheimer E. (1982) *Heroin Addiction: Treatment and Control in Britain.* Edinburgh, Churchill Livingstone.

Teigen A. (1973) The Hov treatment unit and the Oslo Halfway House. In: Boström H., Larsson T. and Ljungstedt N. (ed.) *Drug Dependence—Treatment and Treatment Evaluation.* Stockholm, Almqvist and Wiksell, pp. 116–126.

Tong T. G., Benowitz N. L. and Kreek M. J. (1980) Methadone disulfiram interaction during methadone maintenance. *J. Clin. Pharmacol.* 20, 506–513.

U.S. Department of Justice (1973) *Methadone Treatment Manual.* Washington, U.S. Government Printing Office, pp. 1–6.

Vaillant G. E. (1973) A 20-year follow-up of New York narcotic addicts. *Arch. Gen. Psychiatry* 29, 237–241.

Wiepert G. D., d'Orbán P. T. and Bewley T. H. (1979) Delinquency by opiate addicts treated at two London Clinics. *Br. J. Psychiatry* **134**, 14–23.

Winick C. (1962) Maturing out of narcotic addiction. *Bull. Nar.* **14**, 1–7.

Willette R. E. and Barnet G. (ed.) (1981) *Narcotic Antagonists. Naltrexone, Pharmaco-chemistry and Sustained-Release Preparations.* Rockville, Maryland, National Institute on Drug Abuse.

World Health Organisation (1975) *Evaluation of Dependence Liability and Dependence Potential of Drugs. Report of a WHO Scientific Group.* Tech. Rep. Ser. No. 577, p.25.

Yudkin J. S. (1977) Withdrawal of clonidine. *Lancet* **i**, 546.

Chapter 9

PREVENTION

The health of the people is really the foundation upon which all their happiness and all their powers as a State depend. DISRAELI

There is an undoubted need for preventive measures directed against the problems presented by alcohol and drugs. A virtually world-wide rise of alcohol consumption has developed since 1945 which has led to an augmented incidence of alcohol problems. Among the more prominent hazards that alcohol now presents are traffic accidents; road accidents and injuries can follow drinking by pedestrians as well as by drivers (Irwin et al., 1983). The increase of illicit drug consumption that has taken place in many countries during this century, and particularly since the early 1960s, has also focused attention on the necessity for energetic prophylactic controls.

Measures to curtail the extent of excessive drinking have not been so vigorously pursued as controls against drugs, presumably because the production, distribution and consumption of alcoholic beverages form an innate cluster of features in many cultures. But methods to forestall both alcohol and drug-induced problems should form an important topic of debate and concern. Persons who look after alcohol and drug casualties can be likened to individuals who tend victims that have fallen over a cliff, while new casualties are incessantly arriving. Fencing off the vulnerable points by prevention is more sensible than the mere improvement of treatment services.

Prevention should centre, not just on the potentially harmful forms of alcohol and drug consumption, but on lowering the magnitude and severity of the problems presented by the misuse of these substances (World Health Organisation, 1974; 1980). In this way a wider strategy of goals and methods is provided. The problems associated with substance consumption are diverse. They include acute intoxication, dependence, behaviours arising from intoxication or dependence, physical and mental disabilities induced by harmful usage, injurious consequences to other persons, financial costs of substance misuse and dependence, and the social economic results of diversion of capital and labour to the production and distribution of drugs and alcohol.

261

In broad terms, the preventive curbs or checks on alcohol and drug problems are grouped as fiscal, legal and social. Fiscal measures involve taxes on licit sales, imposed to reduce levels of consumption. Legal devices are composed of laws and law enforcement agencies; they are intended to curb illegal consumption, and to restrain legal intake and antisocial behaviour from alcohol or drug use as far as possible within statutory bounds. Social methods consist of well-informed public attitudes that work to prevent the injurious consumption of alcohol and drugs and that promote understanding, detection and treatment of the attendant problems.

FISCAL MEASURES

Allusions to health safety are employed by lawgivers in Britain to justify increased taxes on tobacco, but most countries (including the United Kingdom) do not usually avail themselves of the opportunity to restrain alcohol consumption by fiscal control. In regard to other psychoactive substances governments necessarily rely on laws, which do not involve taxation, to limit their use. This section concentrates on the feasibility of restricting by taxes the problems arising from licit alcohol usage.

A relationship has become increasingly apparent between the price of alcohol beverages, consumption levels of alcohol, and the incidence of alcohol disabilities. In 1956 Dr Ledermann in France proposed a mathematical equation which provided a frequency curve for the variations of individual alcohol consumption in a drinking population. The Ledermann equation has been described for English readers by de Lint (1974). The equation furnished a log normal wave, in which the alcohol consumption of most individuals, expressed as a daily average, falls within small amounts, but there are high quantities which are ingested only by a minority of persons. The exactness of the equation as a description of the dispersal of drinking levels within populations is no longer accepted, but the hypothesis of Ledermann drew attention to a crucial issue. The significant point is that a rise in the national *per capita* level of consumption is accompanied by a rise in the number of individuals who drink amounts known to be associated with alcoholic disabilities. A fall in the total consumption of a population decreases the proportion of subjects with drinking difficulties.

National consumption levels and alcohol problems are strongly correlated (Advisory Committee on Alcohol, 1977; Smith, 1982; Davies, 1982). Consumption is in turn radically affected by the price of beverage alcohol relative to personal disposable income (Royal College of Psychiatrists, 1979). There is, for example, a notable association in many countries between the relative cost of alcohol beverages and mortality from cirrhosis of the liver (de Lint and Schmidt, 1971). The correlations between consumption, alcohol damage and price are apparently not related to the preferred beverage (beer, wine or spirits) of a community that drinks alcohol (Popham et al., 1975).

The cost of alcoholic drinks is amenable to government guidance through taxation. Fiscal measures have been successfully used in Britain on two occasions in recent centuries with the deliberate aim of lowering a high level of alcohol consumption and of reducing the attendant social and medical consequences. On the first instance an epidemic of gin drinking had arisen in London around 1690 and reached its height in the 1740s. The high intake of gin in the metropolis led to widespread degradation, poverty, crime, and to considerable adult and infant mortality; the consequences were vividly drawn by the artist Hogarth and described in writing by the magistrate Fielding. Progressively severe taxation subdued the incidence of excessive gin consumption and gave benefit, in particular, to the poorer inhabitants (Trevelyan, 1945; Glatt, 1958).

During the Industrial Revolution intemperate drinking again became prevalent, in response to the appalling social conditions of the workers and to the decay of rural traditions; at that period it was said, for instance, that gin afforded 'the quickest way out of Manchester'. There was some improvement towards the end of the nineteenth century, but during the Great War the extent of drinking was still so high that offical measures were necessary to reduce alcohol intake and render Britain more effective for wartime purposes. The strategies included increases in beer duty, and dilution of beer and spirits; the dilution of alcoholic beverages in effect raised the duty paid on the alcohol in both kinds of commodity. The fiscal action was accompanied by several other factors; the latter included legal restrictions on the production and hours of sale of alcoholic drinks, as well as popular support for the legislative checks. It is therefore not possible to disentangle the effects of fiscal changes from other features that could have simultaneously contributed to the fall in alcohol consumption; but in view of data from other countries on the association between cost, consumption and alcohol problems it is likely that the increased duties on alcohol contributed substantially to the marked improvement that took place. The considerable decrease in alcohol intake was accompanied by a reduction in the problems produced by excessive drinking, for example in deaths from liver cirrhosis and in convictions for drunkenness (*Tables* 13 and 14.)

Fiscal control of alcohol consumption is a measure easily available to governments; the strategem falls short of prohibition. Unfortunately, during the second half of the century, the real price of beverage alcohol (its cost relative to personal disposable income) has decreased in many countries. The price in nominal terms has increased with inflation, but has lagged behind the rises in wages and salaries that have resulted from enhanced economic output and from inflationary pressures. The cheaper relative price of alcohol in several parts of the world has enlarged on a

Table 13. Liquor consumption in the United Kingdom, 1913–22, in gallons per head (proof gallons for spirits)

Year	Beer	Spirits	Wine
1913	27·8	0·70	0·25
1914	26·7	0·69	0·23
1915	22·8	0·76	0·22
1916	20·8	0·61	0·22
1917	12·6	0·41	0·15
1918	10·0	0·33	0·25
1919	17·5	0·49	0·43
1920	20·8	0·47	0·32
1921	18·6	0·39	0·24
1922	15·9	0·36	0·26

The data in *Tables* 13 and 14 are taken from Wilson G. B. (1939)

Table 14. Cirrhosis death rates and drunkenness convictions for England and Wales, 1913–22.

Year	Cirrhosis death rate per million	Drunkenness convictions
1913	97	196215
1914	99	194384
1915	93	144335
1916	79	87536
1917	63	48473
1918	46	30225
1919	37	59829
1920	42	96415
1921	51	79609
1922	50	78799

multinational scale its availability, overall consumption and prevalence of excessive use (de Lint, 1974, 1977).

An improvement could be effected by an increase in liquor taxes. The political feasibility of a fiscal rise, imposed not primarily for revenue but for health and social reasons, depends on the readiness of legislators and national populations to accept the device. Acceptance would become easy if alcohol problems continued to grow, but it is hoped that governmental and public attitudes will become more enlightened and sensitive to the current level of alcohol problems, before the deteriorating situation makes obvious the need for tight and strict protective laws.

Bruun et al. (1975) have provided an extensive literature survey of the relationship between the national levels of alcohol consumption and the incidence of public health problems associated with alcohol. The authors also reviewed data which show the powerful effects of price and availability of alcohol on overall consumption.

LEGAL MEASURES

Government controls of the legal availability of alcohol and drugs are of considerable importance. The restrictions interfere with freedom, but the dictum of John Stuart Mill is too idealistic, that 'the liberty of the individual must thus far be limited; he must not make himself a nuisance to other people'. Human nature is such that an uninhibited access to psychoactive substances would prove disastrous. It could indeed be argued that the relevant statutory controls render persons more free to choose ways of living that do not involve the hardships and restraints that would be imposed on themselves and others by the unwise use of alcohol or drugs.

Legislation takes the form of limits on production and sale. Law making and enforcement requires the consent and co-operation of the population, although the consent may be only tacit or given with some reluctance. With respect to alcohol, prohibition is a measure that finds support in Muslim countries, but is not an instrument that meets with public approval in most regions. Restrictions on the production of alcoholic beverages are little practised at present; they would entail understandable opposition from the many financial interests that would be threatened. But since it is thought worthwhile and reasonable to encourage financially opium growing farmers to substitute other crops for the poppy, it could be feasible to employ economic and legal devices to deploy agriculture, industry and commerce away in part from the resources of land, capital and labour that are currently concentrated on alcohol production. There is an early precedent: in the year 81 A.D. the Emperor Domitian enacted the closure of many vineyards throughout the Roman Empire.

Licensing of premises for the sale of alcohol beverages and restrictions of the hours in which drinks can be sold are traditional measures. It is said that in Britain there is more legislation appertaining to alcohol than to any other feature covered by the law. Some of the British legislation on drink is rightly devoted to ensuring that customers encounter honest practices, but a substantial proportion of the drink regulations consists of curbs on the numbers of alcohol outlets, of guarantees of the moral and social soundness of licensees and of limitations on the permitted hours of sale. It is here appropriate to note that there are also self-imposed restraints by advertisers, for instance on advertisements that equate alcohol with youth and sexual prowess; these advertising restraints have forestalled a possible necessity for Government intervention. The success of the licensing restrictions of 1915–16 in Britain, combined with increasing taxation on drink, has already been mentioned; the restrictions and their results have been analysed in detail by Smart (1974).

Two official committees in the United Kingdom have recommended relaxation of the licensing laws for Scotland, and for England and Wales respectively. The recommendations for Scotland were set out in the Report of the Departmental Committee on Scottish Licensing Laws (Clayson Report) in 1973; they were based on the assumption that Scottish traditions of drinking, the unattractive nature of Scottish licensed premises, and the narrow range of licensing hours had combined to produce high rates of alcohol misuse and dependence in Scotland. The high rates of alcohol problems that Scotland possesses especially contrast with England where the total consumption of alcohol is little lower than in Scotland. The Clayson Report proposed that licensing hours should be relaxed, that steps be taken to foster on licensed premises activities other than drinking (e.g. sale of snacks, tea, coffee and soft drinks), that advertising be more cautious, and that liquor be taxed according to its alcohol content. Few people would have disagreed that Scottish pubs needed to become less orientated towards heavy and rapid drinking; the modest extensions of licensing hours that were introduced after the Clayson report did not precipitate an increase of alcohol problems.

The comparable Report for England and Wales, known as the Erroll Report, also recommended more liberal licensing laws (Report of the Departmental Committee on Liquor Licensing, 1972). While the alcoholism problem in England and Wales is not small, it is less severe than in several countries on the European mainland where licensing legislation is distinctly more liberal. It has indeed been suggested that the 'civilised' drinking laws of many Continental nations could advantageously give way to the more rigid controls that operate in Britain (Glatt, 1974a). The Erroll proposals encountered effective opposition from many quarters, including the medical profession and the licensed trade. Its proposals were not adopted.

The tightness or laxity of alcohol controls in Europe is by and large reflected in consumption levels and cirrhosis death rates. Countries like the United Kingdom which possess relatively tight controls show less alcohol intake *per capita* and lower cirrhosis mortality than states with loose restraints (Davies and Walsh, 1983).

In Finland, Sweden and Norway there exist, as preventive devices, state monopolies of the production and sale of most forms of alcohol beverages. The attempt to reduce alcohol problems by elimination of the private profit motive appears logical at face value, but has not prevented a considerable degree of alcohol dependence and other alcohol problems in those countries. (In Finland the adverse consequences derive rather from the social effects of severe acute intoxication than from dependence.) A small proportion of the state profits from alcohol is devoted in

Scandinavia to the prevention and treatment of alcohol dependence; keeping in mind the contribution of alcoholics to national revenues it is hoped that a fair and reasonable return is offered in preventive and remedial services. A similar comment applies to countries where private enterprise conducts the manufacture and distribution of alcoholic drinks. Governments, breweries and distilleries can make substantial contributions to prevention and treatment from the taxes and profits that accrue from alcohol sales.

International control on drugs

The improved means of transport for people and drugs that have developed in the twentieth century have favoured the illicit conveyance of drugs between countries. The expanded methods of travel have contributed to the growth of international associations organized for illegal drug running. The professional smuggling of drugs has been increased in several countries by the presence in them of immigrant communities from regions where opium, heroin or cannabis are grown or manufactured. The promotion of heroin manufacture from opium that took place in or near the areas where opium is grown has allowed the transport of opioids in a form that is compact and highly profitable. Increased ease of travel has also fostered drug smuggling on a more amateur level by young persons.

An international system of drug control is therefore essential. There are several international bodies concerned with drug misuse and dependence. The work of the League of Nations and other organizations in the earlier part of the century has been described by Glatt (1974b); their responsibilities have to a large extent been taken over at the highest level by the Commission on Narcotic Drugs of the United Nations Economic and Social Council. The Commission includes representatives from countries which have major problems of drug dependence or which substantially contribute to the production of the relevant drugs. The Commission makes policy recommendations to the UN Economic and Social Council and to governments; it also assists the Council in the supervision of international agreements. The Commission is in turn advised by the World Health Organization, in particular by the WHO Expert Committee on Drug Dependence. Countries which are not members of the United Nations can receive election to the Commission.

Supervision of the control measures agreed between nations, as distinct from policy recommendations, is the central function of the International Narcotics Control Board. The Board, which is often referred to as the 'INCB', offers in addition, at the request of governments, consultations and field missions to limit the abuse of drugs.

The United Nations Fund for Drug Abuse Control (UNFDAC) provides financial resources for multinational and national programmes.

The activities it finances are aimed at reducing the demand for illicit drugs by the promotion of preventive and rehabilitative measures. The Fund assists governments in the agricultural replacement of illicit crops by new licit crops, and by advice on national legislation. UNFDAC also contributes to the financial support of medical, pharmacological and sociological research, and provides aid to educative courses conducted for drug control enforcement officers. The Fund supports the United Nations Narcotics Laboratory which in turn gives technical information to national narcotics laboratories; the Laboratory also offers fellowships and training to scientists from developing countries.

The United Nations Fund for Drug Abuse Control additionally provides assistance to the United Nations Division of Narcotic Drugs; the aims and activities of the latter organization are broadly the same as those of UNFDAC. Recent years have seen an expansion of the procedures that the Division of Narcotic Drugs sponsors or initiates.

There are other UN agencies, which cover a wider sphere than alcohol or drug problems, but which take an interest in substance misuse and dependence. Among their number are the UN Division of Social Affairs and the UN Economic and Social Council. The United Nations Educational, Scientific and Cultural Organisations (UNESCO) has convened meetings to debate ways of preventing and counteracting illicit drug use. UNESCO is concerned about the use of drugs by young persons in the more developed and industrial countries; the helpful role of educational means, including the mass media, in counteracting drug misuse has been a particular interest of UNESCO.

The principal international agreement to control psychoactive drugs is the Single Convention on Narcotic Drugs. The Convention was confirmed in 1961 and came into force during 1964. The Convention covers morphine-like drugs, cocaine and cannabis (pharmacologically cocaine and cannabis are, of course, not narcotics); the agreement now also refers to the plants from which these drugs may be obained (the opium poppy, coca bush, and cannabis shrub). The contracting nations to the agreement have bound themselves to prohibit the use for nonmedical purposes of the substances specified by the Convention, and to restrict the production, manufacture, export, import and distribution of the drugs. The Convention was amended in 1972 by a Protocol, which gave the International Narcotics Control Board more authority to ensure compliance among member states; the Protocol adopted a modern attitude towards drug misusers, whom it considered no longer merely as criminals but also as sick persons who required treatment and social reintegration. The 1961 Convention did not cover amphetamines, barbiturates nor hallucinogens. Later attempts to restrict these compounds led to the 1974 Convention on Psychotropic Substances. The latter Convention has gained the adherence or notification of many countries, though a few important states have not so far participated.

A fresh direction has been provided by the foundation in 1977 of the WHO Division of Mental Health, which is concerned with programmes in psychiatry, in the behavioural sciences and in the psychosocial aspects of health care, including projects for alcohol and drug dependence. The Division elicits governmental co-operation in the prevention and rehabilitation of psychiatric and psychosocial disorders. Highly relevant to its aims is the consideration of the World Health Organization that in some countries, particularly in the more developed nations, dependence on drugs and alcohol should receive priority among health and social problems. The strategies of the Division of Mental Health include integration of the relevant services into general health facilities and their extension into rural and other under-served areas; research stimulated by the Division is mainly centred on collaboration and on the exchange of information between countries. There are of course many features, apart from the psychiatric aspects, which appertain to alcohol and drug dependence; it is therefore encouraging to note that the WHO Division of Mental Health favours community participation and the development of appropriate skills in professional persons additional to mental health specialists.

Drug legislation in Britain

The principal legal measure currently in force is the Misuse of Drugs Act 1971. A brief account of the circumstances leading up to this Act, and of the legislation it replaced, can afford interest to the reader, particularly in regard to the interplay between changing patterns of illicit drug use and the legal code.

In 1926 a Departmental Committee on Morphine and Heroin Addiction (the 'Rolleston Committee') reported to the Government on the situation at that time relating to drug dependence; the Committee was especially concerned with morphine and heroin. The Rolleston Report noted that drug dependence was numerically a small problem in the United Kingdom; it was considered that it was legitimate to administer morphine or heroin to persons dependent on these substances when, *'after every effort has been made for the cure of addiction'* (Report's italics) complete withdrawal would produce either serious symptoms or incapacity from a useful and fairly normal life that the patient would lead while taking a non-progressive and usually small quantity of drug. As a result of the Rolleston Report legal permission was continued for doctors to prescribe morphine and heroin to persons dependent on these substances.

A quarter of a century later a similar Committee was officially constituted to review and make recommendations on the contemporary situation. The Interdepartmental Committee on Drug Addiction (known after its chairman as the 'Brain Committee') issued its conclusions in 1961. The Brain Committee took account of drugs other than morphine and heroin, including the newer opioids, anaesthetic gases, stimulants, barbiturates and cannabis; it noted that the incidence of drug dependence remained small and proposed that certain substances affecting the nervous system should become subject to tighter controls; but in general the Committee advised that the current legal arrangements required little alteration. The Committee referred to the mistaken impression that drug-dependent persons are entitled to receive prescriptions for drugs (a misapprehension that is still prevalent at the present time).

Subsequent to the Brain Report of 1961 the incidence of drug misuse and dependence rose considerably. The reasons for the deterioration included the global increase in illicit drug use, and the influx of about a hundred heroin users from Canada (where heroin was, and is, completely banned) to Britain where the drug could be obtained legally, often without expense; another cogent factor was the excess prescribing of heroin by a handful of London doctors. The increase of drug misuse embraced substances other than opioids, but governmental concern and legislation fastened on morphine-like drugs. The Dangerous Drugs Act of 1967 withdrew the legal ability of doctors in general to prescribe heroin and cocaine to persons dependent on drugs, and confined the prescription of these two compounds, as a form of management of drug dependence, to specially licensed doctors. Treatment centres, mainly in London, were established for drug users; in practice, the centres dealt for the most part with patients whose drug consumption included opioids. Doctors became obliged by the Act to notify to the Chief Medical Officer of the Home Office persons whom they suspected to be dependent on a wide range of specified morphine-like drugs and cocaine.

The rise of opioid usage was slowed in Britain during the late 1960s. As already noted several factors which developed around that time can be adduced. Drug consumption became less fashionable among young persons; excess prescribing was reduced when prescriptions for opioids were brought more under the direction of experts in drug dependence; police and customs activities were strengthened. The so-called 'British system' is not a system; it does not offer a comprehensive arrangement for the control and treatment of drug dependence, and the rationale and practice of prescribing opioids are not generally accepted. But credit must be given to the officials at the Home Office, to the staff of the special clinics, and to the police drug squads for their zeal and for the success of their combined efforts in preventing for over a decade further rapid escalation of drug consumption. Regrettably their efforts could not resist the results of a vast increase in the international distribution of heroin that commenced in the early 1980s.

The several drug Acts that had been enacted over the years came to require codification into a single and flexible Act. The measure, which annulled much of the previous drug legislation, passed through Parliament as the Misuse of Drugs Act 1971. This Act lays down three categories of controlled drugs in order of harmfulness and legal penalties. Class A comprises raw and prepared opium, many specific opioid drugs, coca leaf and cocaine, hallucinogens, cannabinol (except where contained in cannabis or cannabis resin) and cannabinol derivatives. Codeine, cannabis and cannabis resin, together with several stimulant drugs, are placed in Class B. Methaqualone is a member of Class C. In order to promote research on cannabis the Act permits the use of this substance, and its derivatives, under specified conditions for scientific investigation.

The Misuse of Drugs Act and its Regulations now provide, in place of previous legislation, the statutory prohibition to medical practitioners to forbid the prescription of heroin, dipipanone (Diconal) or cocaine to drug-dependent persons (who are legally referred to as 'addicts'). For the purpose of the law a person is regarded as addicted 'if, as a result of the repeated administration of a drug, he has become so dependent upon it that he has an overpowering desire for its administration to be continued'. The Home Secretary is empowered to provide licences to certain doctors for the prescription of these drugs to addicts; licences can be granted to doctors in National Health Service hospitals that treat addicts and to doctors in equivalent private institutions. Licences to prescribe the preparations cannot be issued for the treatment of drug dependence in general practice. A licence is not required for the administration of

Table 15. Misuse of Drugs Act 1971 and the Misuse of Drugs (Notification of and Supply to Addicts) Regulations 1973.

These legal measures oblige a medical practitioner to notify the Chief Medical Officer of the Home Office of any person whom the doctor considers, or has reasonable grounds to suspect, is addicted to certain controlled drugs, namely: the following substances together with (in general) any stereoisomeric forms, esters or other products which contain them.

cocaine	hydromorphone	oxycodone
dextromoramide	levorphanol	pethidine
diamorphine (heroin)	methadone	phenazocine
dipipanone	morphine	piritramide
hydrocodone	opium	

heroin, dipipanone or cocaine if the drug is needed for the purpose of treating organic disease or injury. The Act and its regulations also currently furnish the legal compulsion on doctors to notify to the Chief Medical Officer of the Home Office persons whom they suspect are, or might be, addicted to the drugs specified in *Table* 15.

The Misuse of Drugs Act provides the Home Secretary with the powers to make Regulations. This allows speedy alteration of the legal control of a drug, in order to adapt to changing circumstances of its misuse, without the delays that would be imposed by waiting for

Parliamentary consent. The rapidity and flexibility so achieved afford important innovatory advantages to the Act.

The Misuse of Drugs Act procured the establishment of the Advisory Council on the Misuse of Drugs. The Council advises on the problems presented by drug misuse and dependence and offers recommendations concerning education, treatment, rehabilitation and research.

SOCIAL MEASURES

Community measures comprise attitudes and customs that militate against the harmful use of alcohol and drugs, public awareness of the dangers that may arise from these substances, and social concern for the effective preventive, diagnostic and treatment programmes. There is also a need for the provision by society of meaningful alternatives to substance consumption for the reduction of environmental and emotional stress.

Education is often viewed as an important instrument to lower the extent of alcohol and drug problems. In fact, educational programmes have not been demonstrated to possess great efficiency. Education should alter three aspects in its recipients: their knowledge, attitudes and behaviour. Of these aspects knowledge is the least important and the easiest to measure; behaviour is the most significant and the hardest to evaluate. Assessment of an alcohol and drug education programme is preferably performed by workers other than those occupied in the teaching activities; the assessment process should ascertain and compare the attributes of recipients before education with their subsequent attributes in the short and especially in the long term. Studies of educative programmes on substance misuse have tended to show only minor and often transitory changes in the knowledge and attitudes of recipients; important alterations in behaviour are rarely demonstrated.

A characteristic result of a drug education course has been described by Bruhn et al. (1975), who studied the effects of a 10-day programme held for several occupational groups; most recipients changed their priorities at the end of the course, by coming to attach higher significance to the concepts of self-awareness and sensitivity to other persons; yet their opinions about drugs did not alter. Smart and Fejer (1974) have outlined some of the problems of drug education, pointing for example, to inadequate definitions of goals by programme planners and to competition from persuasive influences in the mass media; they stressed the need to formulate programmes in the light of studies on communication and on persuasion.

Some positive results have been reported for alcohol education. A review of 21 alcoholism prevention projects in the United States experienced difficulty in obtaining suitable data for assessment; only seven programmes could be evaluated. Positive effects were, however, noted from five out of the seven programmes that were suitable for evaluation; two of the programmes led to beneficial results on behaviour (Staulcup et al., 1979). Urban campaigns in the Soviet Union that combine public education with improved recreational facilities have been shown to lower alcohol consumption and to reduce crime and industrial absenteeism (Viktorov, 1982; Ryan, 1983).

With regard to educational tactics that might be avoided or employed, the uselessness of shock or scare tactics has been noted for alcohol information strategies by Haaranen (1975), and for drug usage by Dorn and Thompson (1974). Edwards (1975) has provided a helpful account of preventive measures for alcohol problems, which could be incorporated into educational programmes; Einstein (1975) and Jayasuriya (1975) have outlined suggestions for training on drug misuse and on its prevention.

Despite the failure to demonstrate scientifically the value of much of the educational efforts that have been deployed there is a need for the provision of information and responsible attitudes about alcohol and drugs. There is some consensus among the published studies about the items which the organizers of relevant educational courses could usefully consider and incorporate:

1. There is a variety of target groups and their needs. Recipients include community leaders and policy makers, professionals in the spheres of treatment and law enforcement, the general public and high risk groups.
2. Persons who are especially at risk of developing problems from alcohol or drug consumption are found in circumstances of diminished family and social control (as in certain occupations or in conditions of migration, war or rapid cultural change). They are also encountered among the socially disadvantaged, in the emotionally unstable, in children of chronically excessive drinkers, and in those who show truancy, indiscipline, or failure to fulfil their educational or career potentials. There exists an occupational hazard in some walks of life, especially amongst people whose duties involve access to drugs or alcohol. Because most communities disapprove of illicit drugs but accept alcohol, persons who become drug misusers may tend to reject conventions, while many alcoholics are basically orthodox and normal people who came to drink excessively as a consequence of culturally determined alcohol usage.
3. Economic and social factors are crucial in determining the availability and acceptance of alcohol and drugs. Many points are relevant to this cardinal theme: the price of alcohol beverages; the cost of street drugs as a stimulus to illicit drug production and distribution; the allotment of agricultural and other financial resources to the manufacture of alcoholic beverages, and in some

regions to the production of drugs; the influence of social class, age, sex, affluence, poverty, leisure and religion; mores and myths regarding alcohol and drugs; the quality of the environment. The complexity of the issues should be noted. For instance, there are practical difficulties in altering a peasant economy that subsists on the growth of the poppy; or there is the paradox between the nineteenth century view in industrial nations that excessive drinking was a practice associated with collective and personal indigence, and the contemporary notion that alcoholism is provoked by opulence.

4. Pharmacological facts require some elucidation. But like all other points in an educational programme information about the effects of alcohol and drugs on the body and mind should be tempered to the needs and interests of the audience. It is often inexpedient to convey knowledge about rarely employed drugs of misuse to lay persons in case curiosity and experimentation are thereby provoked. But the data which are presented must be factual and honest; if the nature and frequency of the hazards of substance consumption are exaggerated the educator forfeits credibility and loses the trust of the audience. In view of legislation on drinking and driving young persons are often keen to learn about the physical and mental effects of alcohol; their willingness to listen can be employed to impart additional information about hazardous alcohol consumption.

5. Methods and facilities for prevention, recognition and treatment require explanation. The aims here would include public acceptance of preventive measures, facilitation of case finding (including self-recognition of early personal or drug problems), and support for improvements in therapeutic resources. A useful feature to discuss is the need to monitor preventive and treatment policies, including the education programmes themselves. Attention can also be drawn to the necessity for better epidemiological research to underpin preventive strategies (Edwards et al., 1976; Edwards, 1979).

6. Programme planners must accept that people selectively desire and respond to instruction on topics and viewpoints that confirm their prejudices concerning substances liable to misuse (Dembo and Miran, 1976). Discussions, rather than formal lectures, are therefore the method of choice. Content should focus on problems of people, not on alcohol or drugs *per se* (de Haes and Schuurman, 1975), and should extend to cover mental health, maturity and interpersonal relationships. Encouraging people in this way to discuss and think for themselves can promote the informed decision-making skills that are necessary to reduce the likelihood of personal alcohol or drug problems.

7. The issue is often raised of a safe level of drinking. It is convenient here to think in terms of units of alcohol; a 'unit' is the equivalent of 10 grams or 1 cl of ethyl alcohol. A quantity which approximates to this amount is found in a half pint (280 ml) of beer, a single measure of spirits, in a glass of table wine, or in a glass of sherry or other fortified wine. The Royal College of Psychiatrists (1979) advised a level which, expressed as a daily average, consists of 8 units or 80 grams; the College added that it is unwise to drink regularly at this level and that females should take considerably less. The risk of cirrhosis is minimal with an average daily drinking level below 6 units (60 grams) in males and 2 units (20 grams) in females; above these limits the danger of cirrhosis increases, and does so particularly sharply among females (Pequignot et al., 1974).

When a comprehensive viewpoint is adopted that looks at historical as well as current trends, it is apparent that powerful social and economic considerations determine the substance consumption patterns of populations. The more widespread influences are, of course, modulated by temporal and regional factors; Shaw (1982) has described the local features that promoted a rise of alcohol intake in Britain during recent decades. At the present time there are strong economic and political arguments and pressures which oppose efforts to reduce national alcohol consumption levels (Mosher, 1982); there are also forces, open and secret, that hinder the efforts of programmes aimed at forestalling the misuse of drugs. A prudent policy of prevention must, therefore, take into account the opposition it will encounter among certain sections of the community.

In the basic analysis, prevention depends on political decisions that are determined by public attitudes (Kendell, 1979). The World Health Organisation (1982) has emphasized the important role that education and open discussion can exert to create a social awareness which will in turn stimulate the will of legislators.

The extent of the difficulties presented by alcohol and drugs has over the centuries shown recurrent cycles of recruitment and decline. The increased prevalence of alcohol and drug disabilities and dependence that has developed in the past three decades may perforce need to progress further before it subsides. But the author is optimistic that pressures are strengthening in many countries which will lead to a degree of regression in alcohol and drug problems during the not too distant future.

The longer term is naturally more uncertain. It is clear that some people will always exist who find solace and relief in unwise or excessive consumption of some substance or other. Hopefully, fuller knowledge and discussion at public level will mould the attitudes of society in such a way that the problems produced by alcohol and drug consumption will become confined to a minimal level. It is the responsibility of informed persons to guide public opinion towards this end.

REFERENCES

Advisory Committee on Alcoholism (1977) *Report on Prevention*, London, D.H.S.S.

Bruhn J. G., Philips B. U. and Gouin H. D. (1975) The effects of drug education courses on attitudinal change in adult participants. *Int. J. Addict.* **10**, 69–96.

Bruun K., Edwards G., Lumio M. et al. (1975) *Alcohol Control Policies in Public Health Perspective.* Helsinki, Finnish Foundation for Alcohol Studies, and New Brunswick, Rutgers University Center of Alcohol Studies.

Davies P. (1982) Some empirical grounds for controlling alcohol consumption. *Br. J. Alc. Alcoholism* **17**, 109–116.

Davies P. and Walsh D. (1983) *Alcohol Problems and Alcohol Control in Europe.* London, Croom Helm. New York, Gardner Press.

de Haes W. and Schuurman J. (1975) Results of an evaluation study of three drug education methods. *Int. J. Hlth Educ.* **18**, issue 4 Suppl., 1–16.

de Lint J. (1977) Alcohol control policy as a strategy of prevention: a critical examination of the evidence. In: Madden J. S., Walker R. and Kenyon W. H. (ed.) *Alcoholism and Drug Dependence: a Multidisciplinary Approach.* New York, Plenum Press, pp. 425–450.

de Lint J. and Schmidt W. (1971) The epidemiology of alcoholism. In: Israel Y. and Mardones J. (ed.) *Biological Basis of Alcoholism.* New York, Wiley, pp. 423–442.

Dembo R. and Miran M. (1976) Evaluation of drug prevention programs by youths in a middle-class community. *Int. J. Addict.* **11**, 881–903.

Dorn N. and Thompson A. (1974) *Planning Teaching about Drugs, Alcohol and Cigarettes.* London, Institute for the Study of Drug Dependence.

Edwards G. (1975) Alternative strategies for minimizing alcohol problems. *J. Alcohol.* **10**, 45–46.

Edwards G., Russell M. A. H., Hawks D. et al. (1976) *Drugs and Drug Dependence.* London, Saxon House, pp. 90–91.

Edwards G. (1979) Drinking problems: putting the Third World on the map. *Lancet* **ii**, 402–404.

Einstein S. (1974) Drug abuse training and education: the physician. *Int. J. Addict.* **9**, 81–99.

Glatt M. M. (1958) The English drink problem: its rise and decline through the ages. *Br. J. Addict.* **55**, 51–67.

Glatt M. M. (1974a) Public health implications of the Erroll and Clayson Licensing Reports. *Br. J. Addict.* **69**, 105–108.

Glatt M. M. (1974b) *A Guide to Addiction and its Treatment.* Lancaster, MTP Press, pp. 288–290.

Haaranen A. (1975) Popular alcohol information in Finland. In: *Proceedings of the 31st International Congress on Alcoholism and Drug Dependence.* Lausanne, International Council on Alcohol and Addictions, pp. 596–598.

Irwin S. T., Patterson C. C. and Rutherford W. H. (1983) Association between alcohol consumption and adult pedestrians who sustain injuries in road traffic accidents. *Br. Med. J.* **286**, 521.

Jayasuriya D. C. (1975) Strategies for introducing drug abuse preventive education in developing countries. In: *Proceedings of the 31st International Congress on Alcoholism and Drug Dependence.* Lausanne, International Council on Alcohol and Addictions, pp. 611–616.

Kendell R. E. (1979) Alcoholism: a medical or a political problem? *Br. Med. J.* **1**, 367–371.

Mosher J. F. (1982) International trends in alcohol consumption, alcohol-related problems and alcohol control policies. In: Armyr G., Elmer Å. and Herz V. (ed.). *Alcohol in the World of the 80s.* Stockholm, Sober Förlags A. B. Lausanne, International Council on Alcohol and Addictions, pp. 201–218.

Pequignot G., Chabert C., Eydoux H. et al. (1974) Augmentation du risque de cirrhose en fonction de la ration d'alcool. *Revue de l'Alcoolisme* **20**, 191–202.

Popham R. E., Schmidt W. and de Lint J. (1975) The prevention of alcoholism: epidemiological studies of the effects of Government control measures. *Br. J. Addict.* **70**, 125–144.

Report of the Departmental Committee on Morphine and Heroin Addiction (Rolleston Committee) (1926) London, H.M.S.O.

Report of the Interdepartmental Committee on Drug Addiction (Brain Committee) (1961) London, H.M.S.O.

Report of the Departmental Committee on Liquor Licensing (Erroll Committee) (1972) London, H.M.S.O.

Report of the Department Committee on Scottish Licensing Law (Clayson Committee) (1973) Edinburgh, H.M.S.O.

Royal College of Psychiatrists (1979) *Alcohol and Alcoholism. The Report of a Special Committee of the Royal College of Psychiatrists* London, Tavistock Publications.

Ryan M. (1983) Campaign for sobriety. *Br. Med. J.* **286**, 537–538.

Shaw S. (1982) Social influences on the use of alcohol in the family. In: Orford J. and Harwin J. (ed.). *Alcohol and the Family.* London, Croom Helm, pp. 56–72.

Smart R. G. (1974) The effect of licensing restrictions during 1914–1918 on drunkenness and liver cirrhosis deaths in Britain. *Br. J. Addict.* **69**, 109–121.

Smart R. G. and Fejer D. (1974) *Drug Education: Current Issues, Future Directions* (Addiction Research Foundation Program Report Series No. 3). Toronto, Addiction Research Foundation of Ontario.

Smith R. (1982) *Alcohol Problems.* London, The Publishers, British Medical Journal.

Staulcup H., Kenward K. and Frigo D. (1979) A review of federal primary alcoholism prevention projects. *J. Stud. Alc.* **40**, 943–968.

Trevelyan G. M. (1945) *History of England.* London, Longmans Green, p. 525.

Viktorov D. (1982) Na trezvuyu goluvu. *Literaturnaya Gazeta* 4 August, **31**, 12.

Wilson G. (1940) *Alcohol and the Nation.* London, Nicholson and Watson, Appendix F.

World Health Organisation (1974) *Problems and Programmes related to Alcohol and Drug Dependence in 33 countries.* WHO Offset Publications No. 6.

World Health Organisation (1980) Problems Related to Alcohol Consumption. Report of a WHO Expert Committee. *WHO Tech. Rep. Ser. No. 650* Geneva, WHO.

World Health Organisation (1982) *Alcohol Consumption and Alcohol Related Problems: Development of National Policies and Programmes. Report on Technical Discussions of 35th World Health Assembly.* Geneva, WHO.

INDEX